Mother of Capital

'As some are pointing at rent to claim that we are moving out of capitalism and into "techno-feudalism", it seems urgent to rethink the relation between capital and rent. In this inventive book, Costa takes us back into the womb of history to show that it was a transmutation of rent that gave birth to capital, and that the two never parted ways since then.'

—Xavier Lafrance, Professor of Politics,
Université du Québec à Montréal

'Sorting out, as Marx put it, this "shitty rent business", has been a long and winding road. It is fantastic to see Matthew Costa's book on the topic of rent theory, which will vivify new rounds of debate.'

—Adam David Morton, Professor in Political Economy,
University of Sydney

Mother of Capital

How Rent Gave Birth to Modernity

Matthew Costa

PLUTO PRESS

First published 2026 by Pluto Press
New Wing, Somerset House, Strand, London WC2R 1LA
and Pluto Press, Inc.
1930 Village Center Circle, 3-834, Las Vegas, NV 89134

www.plutobooks.com

British Library Cataloguing in Publication Data
A catalogue record for this book is available from the British Library

ISBN 978 0 7453 5054 7 Paperback
ISBN 978 0 7453 5056 1 PDF
ISBN 978 0 7453 5055 4 EPUB

This book is printed on paper suitable for recycling and made from fully managed and sustained forest sources. Logging, pulping and manufacturing processes are expected to conform to the environmental standards of the country of origin.

Typeset by Stanford DTP Services, Northampton, England

Simultaneously printed in the United Kingdom and United States of America

EU GPSR Authorised Representative
LOGOS EUROPE, 9 rue Nicolas Poussin, 17000, LA ROCHELLE, France
Email: Contact@logoseurope.eu

Contents

Acknowledgements vi

Introduction 1
1 Capitalism and the engine of history 11
2 The tributary rent relation 34
3 Tributary tendencies and contradictions 46
4 Tributary ideology, resistance, and critique 61
5 From tributary to capitalist rent 73
6 Resistance and critique in transition 93
7 The political economy of capitalist rent 107
8 Resistance to rent under capitalism 125
9 The critical social theorists 135
10 The critique of differential rent 150
11 Capitalist rent as proletarianisation 159
12 Rent and capitalist domination 169
13 The ideology of capitalist rent 179
14 Proletarian imaginaries 189
15 Deproletarianisation 200

Conclusion: Capital, mother of what? 215

Notes 233
Index 306

Acknowledgements

Thanks to my family for their ceaseless love and support, and thanks especially to my mother for her incredible generosity. Thanks to my father for challenging me, since my childhood, to develop myself intellectually. Thanks to my brilliant friends for precious insight, laughter, and companionship on the journey.

I am intellectually indebted to friends and colleagues both in the University of Sydney's Department of Political Economy and outside it for exposing me to whole fields of new ideas and scholarship during the years of my research. My deepest thanks to Martijn Konings and Mike Beggs for many hours spent reading and responding to my writing, but also to Adam Morton, Frank Stillwell, Bill Dunn, Damien Cahill, and the Department's wider community of academics and students. I also thank my anonymous readers for the gift of their time and insight.

While I am grateful for the assistance I received from an extraordinary intellectual community, any errors in this work are my own.

Likewise, my views are mine alone and not attributable to any employer.

Introduction

For most of us, 'rent' is what we pay to keep a roof over our heads. But in economics, the word has a special meaning. In economics, a rent is a surplus. An economic rent is anything someone receives beyond what they have truly earned, or beyond what is thought necessary. There are many kinds of economic rent. Paretian rent, for example, is when the owner of a productive resource, like labour or capital, is paid more than is needed to get them to supply it.[1] It is a core concept of microeconomics. Another core concept is the consumer surplus or rent, which arises when consumers can purchase goods or services for less than what they are willing to pay.[2] Economists regard some rents, like consumer rent, as good. But many are seen as suspect.

Since the 1970s, an economic literature has flourished calling attention to 'rent-seeking': private interests seeking special privileges from the state, or seeking income by political means rather than through productive effort.[3] Meanwhile, contemporary followers of the nineteenth-century political economist Henry George argue that rents derived from land and natural resources represent an 'unearned increment' that should be taxed away by the state.[4] More recently, an alarm has been raised over network monopoly rents extracted by owners of giant cloud-based software platforms in the digital economy.[5]

The arsenal of rent theory, it seems, primes economists of all stripes to see a society replete with rents. Progressive economists tend to highlight rents in high-profit sectors like finance, insurance, technology, and real estate. Conservatives, meanwhile, tend to emphasise rents attained by labour unions and the beneficiaries of regulations or 'red tape'.

Strangely, while economists see problematic rents everywhere, they generally insist these are not really part of capitalism. Economists, left and right, refer to 'rentier' or 'crony' capitalism, contrasting the disappointment of capitalism as it is, with a better, purer, rent-free capitalism – capitalism as it should be.[6]

Lately, theorists across the ideological spectrum have taken this logic further, arguing capitalism is now so ridden with rents that it is no longer worthy of the name. In *The Coming of Neo-Feudalism*, conservative observer Joel Kotkin argues that powerful centrifugal forces are eroding social mobility and the middle class, dividing wealth and power between a rent extracting neo-feudal elite and masses of rent-paying serfs.[7] Critics of capitalism make parallel claims, but without nostalgia. For these theorists, feudalism is the polestar for theorising the present era. Just as a 'neoliberal' epoch emerged from the breakdown of the post-war order in the 1970s, a new era of rent extraction marks the displacement of neoliberal capitalism with something 'even worse'.[8] Theorists of neo- or techno-feudalism now debate whether rent's resurgence represents a grim new capitalist epoch, or the end of capitalism itself.[9]

I will return to these debates. What is interesting, though, is that all these deployments of rent theory embed the same paradox. Rent theorists, across the ideological spectrum, are united in treating rent as ubiquitous under capitalism, yet insisting or implying it is alien.

As theorists increasingly lean on rent theory to understand our present and future, it is high time for a deeper look at its origins and contradictions. As this book will show, economic theory, stretching back to classical political economy, is unified by a common purpose: analysing society to help states govern it. Rent theory, I argue, is no exception. Economists identify new forms of rent to help states decide what to do with them. Economists deem some rents necessary and earmark them for state protection, but they stigmatise other rents and mark them for excision. These 'bad' rents generally receive the most attention.

As we will see, the economic theory of rent, as with all economic theory, developed as a managerial tool for the state – whether that state was progressive or conservative. Indeed, conservative and progressive economists are largely united in their concern about rents or unearned income. They differ only on which rents they think the state should target, and whether the state should eliminate rents with regulations, redistribution, competition or *laissez faire* policies. When rent theory is viewed from this perspective, it becomes clear that despite its highly 'critical' tone, it is not a tool for critiquing capitalism but for managing, protecting, and refining it. And this should sound a note of caution to radical critics of capitalism who draw on rent theory to theorise contemporary capitalism and even to predict its demise.

That said, this book will show there is another tradition of thought that conceives rent in a completely different way – one that steps entirely outside the 'state's-eye view' of economics. This tradition understands the history and theory of rent in terms of what are called 'social-property relations'. Working in this other tradition, this book will recast rent, not as a conceptual aid to state policy, but as the fundamental social dynamic that set capitalism and modernity itself in motion. This tradition sees rent not as a blight on capitalism, but as its mother. Rent, this tradition insists, is in capitalism's DNA.

Chapter 1 will lay the groundwork for this book's argument by tackling two central problems of social theory: what capitalism is, and what drives historical change. Nobody can claim to know how capitalism works today or where it is headed without offering their solution to these two problems. Yanis Varoufakis, for example, runs headlong into these problems when he claims something called 'techno-feudalism' has 'killed capitalism'.[10] Jodi Dean does too, when she (somewhat more cautiously) posits that capitalism is 'undergoing systemic transformation and transitioning into a different mode of production'.[11] But these two problems are as much of a challenge to those who claim capitalism is robust and eternal as to those who claim it is dying or dead. Indeed, the question of capitalism's birth – the focus of this book – is perennial exactly because it demands we test claimed solutions to these problems against the historical record.

Joining a tradition as old as capitalism itself, I define capitalism as a form of 'social-property relations' – as a certain way of organising society to produce what it needs to survive. Drawing on this tradition, I argue that historical change happens because social-property relations are transformed by the process that reproduces them. I call this 'endogenous transformation'. In Chapter 1, I explain and defend the idea of endogenous transformation, and

I critique three more common ways of explaining historical and social change. I call these three other approaches 'non-transformation', 'exogenous transformation', and 'agent–structure dualism'. As we will see, most efforts to explain the origins of capitalism (not to mention its future) follow one of these three approaches. And all three of them fail, I argue, because they cannot distinguish capitalism from other systems, or they cannot coherently explain why societies change over time.

Having outlined the endogenous transformation model and distinguished it from other approaches within and outside the social-property relations tradition, the rest of this book applies the approach to reinterpret the history and world-historical significance of rent. It will sketch how, through the process of endogenous transformation, rent gave birth to capital. I will trace how rent began as a peculiar variety of tributary social-property relations, and how it endogenously transformed into a competitive, *proletarianising* relation that uprooted tributary social-property relations altogether, and finally became a constitutive element of capitalist social-property relations. The history of rent and its critique, I argue, reveals *proletarianisation*, not commercialisation, as the central transformative process and indicium of capitalist transition.

As much of this book concerns events that happened in England, it is important to emphasise that what I am focused on is the endogenous transformation of social-property relations, not of English society *per se*. Theorists of Uneven and Combined Development have charged social-property relations theorists with 'internalism' and 'Eurocentrism' because they generally explain the transition to capitalism by reference to events occurring largely in England and Europe.[12] As Inayatullah and Blaney note, however, this accusation confuses a 'categorical' focus on social-property relations, with a 'spatial' focus on England and Europe.[13] I focus primarily on events in England, but by no means exclusively. My argument is not that England gave birth to capital but that the tributary rent relation did, albeit in England.

And while I insist the capitalism we know today was *born* in England, I do not claim it was generated exclusively by English social-property relations. As I show in Chapters 2 and 3, the transformation of the English rent relation into a capitalist relation was influenced not only by its own unfolding dynamics, but also by those of surrounding tributary social-property relations – those in Viking Scandinavia, Feudal Normandy, and even those in the Eastern tributary societies of the Silk Road, including Imperial China. Historical change is not endogenous to a particular place or places, but to social-property relations that are reproduced, that interact and mutate, *across* space and time.

In Chapter 2, I will explain the general structure of the tributary rent relation, a variety of tributary social-property relations, and their unique rules of reproduction. I will show that England's rent relation developed a peculiar 'federalised' form as it adapted to local conditions, and this, I argue, was fateful for both English and global society. Chapters 3 and 4 trace how the tributary rent relation unfolded in England and Europe from the eleventh to the fourteenth century. In Chapter 5, I present the crux of my argument that rent is the *mother of capital*, showing how, through an interplay of structure and agency, England's unique federalised rent relation endogenously transformed into a competitive relation, and manifested a fundamentally new social logic. This new, competitive English rent relation would show an unprecedented *proletarianising* tendency. Its dynamics would systematically uproot peasant subsistence agriculture in England and shift the mainstay of agricultural production into new relations of capitalist wage labour. I show how the expansion of this new capitalist rent relation generated the modern English state, England's Protestant Reformation and finally the English Revolution.

In Chapter 7, I will show how the capitalist rent relation was integral to the development of classical British capitalism after the Restoration of 1660. In doing so, it became a permanent and constitutive element of capitalist social-property relations. The capitalist rent relation, I argue, encouraged the landed class to assume a new double identity as landlords and aristocrats, promoting capitalist development across both its economic and political spheres.

Readers familiar with the celebrated 'Brenner debate' will note my account closely tracks Brenner's thesis on the agrarian roots of English capitalism.[14] I am indebted both to Brenner and to later historians who have defended and extended his thesis.[15] The question arises: is my account a systematisation of Brenner's or is it ultimately a break? In my view, this book integrates, systematises, and extends Brenner's insights by placing social-property relations – namely the rent relation – at the very centre of the narrative. The precedent for this move is not Brenner but Marx, who centred capital to explain its internal dynamics. Brenner's focus on social-property relations, though different, likewise takes its lead from an aspect of Marx's method.[16] So if my conclusions do depart from Brenner's, they share a similar trajectory.

At a time of renewed interest in the dynamics of rent, this book not only uncovers rent's neglected world-historical significance but also an extensive and neglected body of critical rent theory. This forgotten body of work is centuries older than economics, or even its predecessor, political economy. And whereas economics emerges from the state, this older tradition emerges from subalterns: first, the medieval peasantry, and later the working class or proletariat. As we will see, wherever this critical tradition expressed itself, its subaltern orientation led it to theorise society and rent in terms of social-property relations. And thus it could track, over centuries, the endogenous transformation of social-property relations that gave birth to modernity.

As subaltern rent theory sank into obscurity, I argue, later critical social theory and the social-property relations approach lost contact with its own history. This book recovers that history. It reconstructs subaltern theories of rent that were marginal even in their own time. It treats these as serious contributions to the social-property relations tradition. And it recasts these writings, for the first time, in light of the social transformations they were trying to decipher. This book is, in equal measure, a history of rent and of its critique. As we will see, the lost critique of rent entails lost perspectives on the nature of human society, its history, and its possible futures.

It must be asked, however, why have historical theories of rent, and critical theories in particular, fallen into obscurity? The apathy of contemporary economics for its history is well documented.[17] More puzzling, however, is that contemporary critical social theorists, who take pride in their historicism, give little attention to their pre-Marxian forbears.

The reason, I think, is that Marx reorganised critical social theory so radically that its previous paradigm became unintelligible. In Volume I of *Das Kapital*, the only volume published in his lifetime, Marx boldly and famously centred the logic of capital. And to do this he largely abstracted rent away. The move was so fruitful, it seems, that earlier interest in rent seemed obsolete. Like those fighting yesterday's war, earlier critics who focused on rent seemed hung up on a dying feudalism and a waning aristocracy that capitalism had long since eclipsed.

Yet, as I will show, this rendering obscures the world-historical significance of rent. Only once rent is recognised as capital's mother can pre-Marxian critiques of rent be seen in their proper light, as analyses of social-property relations. For critics before Marx, rent theory was not some intellectual blind alley. Rent was the key that unlocked the nature of capital and a path beyond it.

As Chapter 9 will show, working in Marx's shadow, later intellectual historians have missed and obscured the richness of earlier critical social theory. Their work is largely a procession of efforts to lump early critics under Marxological labels like 'utopian', 'Ricardian', or 'proto-Marxian'. But, as we will see, these labels do not survive contact with the work they are supposed to describe.

To recover the tradition of critical social theory, I argue, we must abandon Marxological labels and start applying his method. We must take a materialist approach to intellectual history. In *The German Ideology*, Marx and Engels argued that ideas should be investigated in relation to 'the individuals and world conditions which are the source of the ideas'.[18] They saw ideas as intellectual products, to be examined in relation to their 'producers' and 'conditions of production'.[19] A materialist approach examines the relationship between material conditions and ideas empirically. As Neal Wood argues, this requires close attention to the 'interplay' between the development of ideas and their 'concrete historical context'.[20] The aim is to 'penetrate and reveal this interaction and to explain the nature of the relationship'.[21]

Materialist approaches to intellectual history treat ideas as fully part of the material world. Ideas are only ever expressed in sensuous forms – in the language and social practices of individuals, classes, and institutions. Because ideas and language are part of human sociality, social-property relations are partly constituted by ideas. Materialist approaches to the history of thought can be contrasted with idealist approaches. Idealist approaches conceive ideas as occupying a separate, immaterial sphere. Instead of seeing ideas as an aspect of society, they see them as evolving in their own sphere, divorced from material conditions.[22]

A materialist approach to the history of thought, in my view, must examine at least three layers of social relations that shape the production of ideas: first there is the individual thinker's life and their immediate social context, including their class location;[23] second, there is the thinker's network of intellectual relationships, their community of inquiry; and third there is the thinker's broader historical and social context, including the prevailing social-property relations. A materialist approach considers how all three layers interact and influence the production of ideas. In other words, a materialist approach demands that social and intellectual history be studied together, as two integrated dimensions of the social and material world.

This principle is reflected in the book's structure. Its chapters alternate between the history of rent and the history of rent theory – between the ideas and the conditions that produced them. Critical theories of rent, we will see, always emerged from subaltern movements that resisted rent or from intellectuals who sympathised with these movements. The history of critique is inseparable from the history of resistance. They speak to and reinforce each other.

Rent's history and this book stretch across three broad epochs: tributary, transitional, and capitalist. As I will argue, in each epoch rent took a different form, corresponding to distinct forms of resistance and critique. In Chapter 2, I will show how localised resistance to the tributary rent relation was inscribed in its structure. In Chapter 3, we will see how an endogenous crisis of the tributary rent relation generated the conditions for *generalised* political resistance to rent, culminating in a peasants' revolt. And we will see how these resistance movements generated both theological and folk critiques of rent and of tributary social-property relations.

In Chapter 6, I explore resistance and critique during the English transition to capitalism. I will show how the logic of capitalist rent undermined traditional strategies of peasant resistance and explain the strategies and fate of two key movements that challenged rent amid the transition: the urban Levellers and the rural Diggers. The Diggers, I argue, though less numerous and organised, were the first truly *proletarian* social movement, and developed the first truly proletarian critique of rent.

Chapters 9 to 15 explore resistance to and critique of rent in the capitalist epoch. I will show how following the Glorious Revolution, the proletarianising logic of capitalist rent entrenched capitalist social-property relations more fully in England, and resistance to rent took on new forms. Resistance shifted from struggles over land and enclosure, fought by a dwindling peasantry, to a two-front struggle waged by a landless working class. On the political stage, the working class struggled against the aristocratic state, which advanced the political preconditions of capital social-property relations. In the workplace, workers struggled against industrial capital. I argue that working-class interest in rent and aristocracy was not a distraction from its struggles against capital but an integral part of them.

As I chronicle these early working-class struggles, I show how a tradition of critical social theory grew from them. I argue that applying doctrinal labels like 'Utopian Socialism' to this body of thought is no longer defensible. I redefine modern Critical Social Theory in materialist terms, as a distinctive social and historical process. As I will show, modern critical social theorists coalesced into a loose scientific community that critiqued political economy from a subaltern perspective. Whereas political economy did social science for the capitalist state, Critical Social Theory did it to advance proletarian interests.

In Chapters 10 to 15, I reconstruct Critical Social Theory's rich and varied contribution to the critique of rent and the analysis of social-property relations. As I will argue, though critical social theorists engaged more with political economy than with each other, their shared scientific and proletarian orientation led them to converge. They critiqued political economy's approach to rent (Chapter 10) and instead theorised capitalist rent as a *proletar-*

ianising relation (Chapter 11). Rent theory, I will show, was the cornerstone of their broader social analysis. It not only unlocked theories of capitalist domination (Chapter 12), but also theories of ideology (Chapter 13), post-capitalist society (Chapter 14), and proletarian self-emancipation (Chapter 15). Remarkably, proletarian self-emancipation, they argued, would emerge from the logic of capital itself. This conclusion will no doubt give readers of Marx a sense of *déjà vu*. But having recognised rent as the mother of capital, it was only logical for Critical Social Theory to posit that capital too might be pregnant with its own successor.

This book largely refrains from comparing Critical Social Theory to Marx and his theories of rent. This is a worthy enterprise, but recovering the 800 years of history and thought before Marx is quite enough for one book to attempt. And there is value in separating the two projects. Critical Social Theory has hitherto been greatly distorted by an overeagerness to read it against Marx. My task has been to present it in the light of its historical context, not the work of a later thinker. And only by casting off Marx's shadow does a true comparison with Marx become possible. I leave this latter task to others.

In the book's conclusion, I will explain its upshot for present discussions of capitalism, its future, and rent. The social-property relations tradition, I argue, converges on proletarianisation as the key marker of capitalism and capitalist transition. Once rent proletarianised England, I claim, capitalist, tributary and kin-ordered social-property relations began interacting in complex ways, resulting in proletarianisation on a global scale. And if proletarianisation is the measure, then the global transition to capitalism is not over but ongoing. The social-property relations tradition, I argue, challenges both those who see capitalism as eternal and those who now argue it is dying. Among these are theorists like Varoufakis, Dean, and Durand who argue that capital is giving way to a new rent-dominated techno-feudalism. Such theorists, I argue, must reckon more fully with ongoing global proletarianisation and with rent as a genuinely capitalist phenomenon.

1

Capitalism and the engine of history

How was capitalism born? This question has been debated fiercely by academics like Maurice Dobb, Paul Sweezy, Immanuel Wallerstein, Robert Brenner, and many more – for nearly a century.[1] Before them, it was tackled by generations of political economists from Adam Smith to Karl Marx. And as we will see later, in Chapter 6, the question is as old as capitalism itself.

The question is perennial because it is bound up with two deep problems of social theory, each of which bears on both the present and future. First, explaining how capitalism was born means getting specific about what capitalism is. It means defining the unchanging essence of a system of unmatched changeability. It means coherently distinguishing capitalism from other systems, real or imagined – like hunter-gatherer societies, feudalism, or communism. Defining capitalism clearly is a precondition for claiming to know how it works and where it is going. Second, capitalism's birth was a profound moment of change. Explaining it forces us to state (or at least betray) our views on what fundamental social change is, and what drives it. In other words, it forces us to offer our theory of history. And theories of history speak not only to the past but to the present and future, which are history in the making. And while some think capitalism's origin is of mere historical interest, this historical dimension is the crux of its enduring importance. The question raises enduring problems of social theory, but in a context where we can use historical evidence to solve them. It invites evidence, not speculation.

Whereas this book tackles the perennial question, this chapter tackles the two deep theoretical problems it raises: what capitalism is, and what drives history. My answer, we will see, is that capitalism is a form of 'social-property relations' and that the 'endogenous transformation' of social-property relations drives history. As I explain what this means, I will critique three alternative views, which I call 'non-transformation', 'exogenous transformation', and 'agent–structure dualism'. Most efforts to explain the origin of capitalism have followed one of these three approaches. All of them fail, I argue, because they cannot distinguish capitalism from other systems, or they cannot explain why societies change.

WHAT ARE SOCIAL-PROPERTY RELATIONS?

The social-property relations approach is a materialist method of social and historical analysis. It makes the bold claim that if we understand how a society produces what it needs to survive, we can explain almost everything important about that society. The approach tries to explain history, and how societies work, by focusing on 'the specific ways in which human beings establish social relations among themselves and with nature in order to produce their material conditions of existence'.[2] Many famous theorists, both mainstream and radical, have used the social-property relations approach. But its most famous advocate is undoubtedly the nineteenth-century radical German intellectual Karl Marx. The 'relationship of the owners of the conditions of production to the immediate producers …', he wrote, reveals 'the innermost secret, the hidden basis of the entire social edifice'.[3] The social-property relations approach holds that social-property relations are central and 'shape other sets of social, political and cultural relations'.[4] The approach is less a doctrine than a methodology. It is a way of explaining society and history. The real test of its strength is how convincingly it explains society and history compared to other approaches.

The American economic historian Robert Brenner coined the term 'social-property relations'. He defined it to include 'the relations among direct producers, relations among exploiters, and relations between exploiters and direct producers that, taken together, make possible/specify the regular access of individuals and families to the means of production (land, labour, tools) and/or the social product per se'.[5] I will use Brenner's term 'social-property relations' in favour of Marx's preferred term 'relations of production'. They mean the same thing, but the term 'social-property relations' reminds us we are talking about something broader than the nuts and bolts of producing what we need to survive – the art of hunting, farming, or manufacturing.[6]

Today, the social-property relations approach is often associated narrowly with the work of Robert Brenner, Ellen Meiksins Wood, and a group of theorists known as 'Political Marxists'. But I use the term in an ecumenical sense, to include all social and historical theorists to the extent they focus on social-property relations, regardless of how they describe themselves. I include in the tradition not only contemporary social-property relations theorists, but also earlier critical theorists whose ideas this book will recover. Marx and Engels, whose thought is largely beyond this book's scope, are key figures in the social-property relations tradition. But there are Marxists who reject or depart from the social-property relations approach.[7] And not all social-property relations theorists are Marxists. Adam Smith, lauded as the father of classical political economy, and as capitalism's most famous celebrant, left us a splendid analysis of social-property relations in his early *Lectures on Jurisprudence*.[8] Political economy and economics have always analysed social-property relations to some extent, so their thought has often served as a springboard or foil for more radical traditions.

But the social-property relations tradition is far older than Karl Marx or Adam Smith. As we will see, there was a strong focus on social-property relations in the pre-Marxian tradition of Critical Social Theory, roughly contemporaneous with classical political economy. As Chapter 6 will show, even in early modern England, as capitalist social-property relations were first spreading across the English countryside, a group called the Diggers were already theorising and critiquing them. In medieval times too, a distinct analysis of feudal social-property relations can be detected in the critiques of England's rebellious peasants and dissident priests, as we will see in Chapter 4.

The social-property relations approach distinguishes historical modes of production by their peculiar social-property relations.[9] It focuses on how production is organised and how one class extracts surplus from another – whether as tribute, profit or otherwise. There are many ways to classify modes of production and the social-property relations that define them. I use Eric Wolf's typology, which includes 'kin-ordered', 'tributary', and 'capitalist' social-property relations.[10]

As we will see, this book constantly distinguishes between tributary and capitalist social-property relations. Under tributary social-property relations, the producers are peasants who have direct access to means of production – land, stock, and tools – and a tribute-taking or lordly class extracts tribute from the peasants using coercion.[11] The tribute-taking class lives off the surplus peasants produce beyond what they need to survive. In capitalism, by contrast, producers without their own means of production sell their labour power to capitalists who possess such means. Capitalists direct the labour process, sell what is produced, and appropriate any surplus received above the wages paid (and other costs) as a profit. Unlike tributary peasants and lords, both capitalists and workers are generally subject to the 'imperatives of competition … [and are] obliged to enter the market for access to their means of subsistence and reproduction'.[12]

The foregoing brings me to two fundamental questions faced by all social and historical theorists. First, what does fundamental historical and social change entail? Second, what mechanisms drive such change?

These two questions have generated deep and complex divisions among contemporary theorists – not only between theorists who attend to social-property relations and those who do not, but also among social-property relations theorists themselves. These debates, in my assessment, are conducted across three major dividing lines. First, there is a division between theorists who understand historical change as a transformation of social-property relations, and those who do not. By clearly defining different types of social-property relations, and using these to distinguish different modes of production, the social-property relations approach insists that fundamental historical change involves a transformation of social-property relations.[13] Second, there is a division between social-property relations theorists who see social-property relations as transformed endogenously – through the very process of their reproduction – and those who believe exogenous forces transform social-property relations, as it were, 'from the outside'. Third, there is a division between all manner of theorists over whether social change is driven by agents – be these individuals, states, or social classes – or, alternatively, by structural forces.

In this study, I draw on other social-property relations scholars to propose a model of historical change that critically addresses all three of these divisions. I call this model 'endogenous transformation'. It consists of three basic propositions: first, that fundamental historical change requires a transformation of social-property relations; second, that social-property relations are transformed endogenously, through the process of their reproduction; and third, that the reproduction of social-property relations involves a dialectical interplay of structure and agency. I will explain and defend each proposition in detail.

After elaborating the concept of 'endogenous transformation', I will use it to distinguish and critique three common alternative models of social and historical change. First, I will critique 'non-transformation' models. These models fail to link fundamental change to transformations of social-property relations. Next, I will critique models of 'exogenous transformation'. These recognise historical change as a transformation of social-property relations, but mistakenly locate the cause outside the process by which social-property relations are reproduced. Finally, I will critique 'agent–structure dualism'. This approach misses the internal relations between agency and structure, and so cannot formulate historical explanations that accommodate both. All three common approaches, I argue, fall short in the task of social and historical explanation.

HOW SOCIAL-PROPERTY RELATIONS ARE REPRODUCED

My claim is that social-property relations are transformed endogenously – through the same process that reproduces them. The first task in explaining this claim is to outline what I mean by 'reproduce'. To do this, I will draw on Robert Brenner's account of 'rules of reproduction'. Going beyond Brenner, however, I will draw on the ideas of Andreas Bieler and Adam Morton (and others) to argue that social-property relations are reproduced through a *dialectical* interplay between agents and social structures.[14] 'Dialectical' means 'internally related'. My claim, in other words, is that we cannot define our capacity for agency without understanding the social structures we live in. The reverse is also true. Structure and agency, I claim, are internally related or co-constitutive. They are always interacting and always at play simultaneously. And this, we will see, has profound consequences for understanding history and society.

The social-property relations approach views social-property relations as the most fundamental social structures. It contends that of all the social structures at play in any historical epoch, social-property relations are the most 'deeply embedded', providing 'the overall framework of action during a particular historical period'.[15] The approach posits that social-property relations constitute individuals into classes with particular intra-class and inter-class relations.[16] The approach entails that, as social structures go, social-property relations are 'the most unlikely ones to change'.[17] The approach focuses on social-property relations precisely because, as the deepest social structures, they have the greatest explanatory power. Nothing less explains more.

Understanding agency and structure dialectically, I contend that what social-property relations structure, fundamentally, is our agency itself.[18] As Bieler and Morton write: 'agency is located in structure, but not determined by it'.[19] Despite being fundamental social structures, social-property relations do not extinguish agency by dictating what agents must do. Within particular social-property relations, all individuals and classes generally have many options for action and agency, and for defining their individual interests and identities.[20] What social-property relations do, however, is 'define the framework within which agents can choose several alternative strategies'.[21] One way social-property relations structure agency is by constraining action. Within any given set of social-property relations, individuals and classes will face real limits on what they can achieve.[22] But social-property relations do not just constrain agency; they enable it. Indeed, the prevailing social-property relations endow individuals and classes with definite social powers and opportunities, and these constitute much of their capacity for agency.[23] In any time or place, the simultaneously constraining and empowering *structure* of social-property relations is constitutive of both individual and class *agency*. My ancestors, medieval Cypriot peasants, could decide who their children would marry, but could not choose to invest their savings in technology stocks. Today, I can choose to drive a car or take a bus. Yet I cannot choose whether or not to resist the brutal Knights Templar, as my twelfth-century ancestors had to. Every agent, however creative or determined, faces a suite of options furnished and constrained by the prevailing social-property relations. The strategies employed by agents, therefore, 'cannot be analysed in isolation of [the prevailing social] structure'.[24]

The prevailing social-property relations always furnish agents with a set of archetypical strategies, from which they can choose. Every agent, whether an individual or a class, is, of course, to some extent unique and differently situated within the prevailing social-property relations. To that extent, every agent will have unique opportunities, constraints, capacities, and interests, and each will adopt unique strategies to pursue their interests. But many agents will have similar basic interests and capacities and face similar structural constraints under the prevailing social-property relations. To that extent, we can speak about classes of agents that face similar sets of options. For each set of social-property relations, it is possible to identify certain archetypical strategies, roles or identities that classes of agents will, on average, tend to adopt. Robert Brenner's term for these archetypical strategies is 'rules of reproduction'.[25]

'Rules of reproduction' are more like rules of thumb than legal rules. To emphasise a point Brenner makes somewhat casually: agents always *choose* their rules of reproduction.[26] Rules of reproduction do not represent structural diktats. They represent common paths, or paths of least resistance, that agents commonly choose to follow through the field of structural opportunities and obstacles their social-property relations present. Indeed, the structuring conditions of social-property relations usually offer agents choices between *multiple* 'rules of reproduction' or paths of minimal resistance. Under tributary social-property relations, for example, a peasant may face a choice between marriage and monastic life. Either strategy, in its own way, represents a path of minimal resistance.

And it is always possible for agents to 'break' the rules of reproduction – to choose paths of *greater* resistance. Just as there are archetypical rules of reproduction, there are archetypical resistance strategies. Factory workers can strike; peasants can revolt. But the opportunities and constraints faced by agents who choose resistance are likewise structured by the prevailing social-property relations. Under particular social-property relations, some forms of resistance will be more or less costly or effective.

Endemic resistance, however, tends to be episodic; agents usually adopt the paths of least resistance under the prevailing social-property relations, and it is precisely this which *reproduces* those social-property relations. The cumulative exercise of structured agency has a structuring effect on all agents. In a reflexive way, structure is *constituted* by agency. For example, when people face the structuring constraints and opportunities of tributary social-property relations, they tend to adopt the archetypical strategies of lords or peasants in response. And by acting as lords and peasants typically do, tributary agents cumulatively reproduce the structuring conditions of tributary social-property relations. The structuring effect of agency, which reproduces social-property relations, is never due to the agency of any particular individual or class, even the ruling class or state. Nor is it a reflection of some collective or general will, a common intention shared by all agents. It is rather the cumulative result of classes of similarly situated individuals tending to exercise their similar capacities for agency in archetypical and interlocking patterns, in response to the structuring conditions of the prevailing social-property relations.

Social-property relations, then, are not reproduced solely by agents or solely by structural forces. They are reproduced by an ongoing *interplay* of structure and agency, where each of these two elements constitutes the other. 'Rules of reproduction' represent structured agency, and 'social-property relations' represent agent-generated structures.

ENDOGENOUS TRANSFORMATION

We have seen how social-property relations are reproduced, but how are they transformed? How does one social order give way to another?

I claim that the transformation of social-property relations is endogenous. The word 'endogenous' comprises the prefix 'endo', with a Greek root meaning 'inside', 'internal', or 'within'; and the suffix 'genous', with a Latin root meaning 'born' or 'produced'. Something endogenous develops within. Something exogenous is produced by outside forces. As human beings, we all develop endogenously – from and within others of our kind. We are not, as it were, delivered by the stork. I claim this is true of our social-property relations too.

But what does this mean specifically? How can a new society grow within an older one? Social-property relations transform endogenously, I claim, because the dialectic of structure and agency that reproduces them is not circular. It does not return precisely to its starting point. It has a spiral form, a directionality. Brenner has explained the process. '[G]iven the prevalence of certain given social-property relations', he writes, 'people can be expected to make the choice for certain given rules for reproduction, [and] it follows that when those choices are made in aggregate, they give rise to certain corresponding overall developmental patterns, which Marx called … laws of motion'.[27] These society-wide patterns are also sometimes referred to as 'macro-dynamics', 'secular trends', or simply 'tendencies'.[28] Different forms of social-property relations generate different tendencies. Capitalism, for example, generates rapid technological development. Tributary societies, by contrast, generate large families and population growth.

In this sense, each set of social-property relations has its own dynamic logic that unfolds over time. This logic, however, is not purely structural, and it is not deterministic. It reflects, rather, intelligible and potentially predictable patterns in the *interplay* between the typical ways agents act within structures (their rules of reproduction) and the structuring conditions their actions cumulatively produce (social-property relations; tendencies).

As Brenner observes, the tendencies that different social-property relations generate can also culminate in 'society-wide forms of crisis'.[29] Indeed, under any form of social-property relations, we can distinguish between two broad states of society: normality and crisis. If secular trends generated by the prevailing social-property relations have not fundamentally altered the conditions agents face, then agents will usually stick to their trusted rules of reproduction. This is normality. However, if the macro-dynamics of the prevailing social-property relations have materially altered the conditions agents face, they may find themselves developing new or modified rules to cope.[30] These moments are crises. If agents respond to a crisis by adopting new strategies *en masse*, they may generate a new or altered structure of social-property relations.

In this story, every crisis has a unique structure. Crises are not 'structural breakdowns' where agents can assert their wills without constraint. During crises, the prevailing social-property relations confront agents with definite constraints and opportunities, just as they do in normal periods. What distinguishes crises, however, is that tendencies have developed enough to materially change the field of constraints and opportunities agents face. A crisis is the moment when conditions have altered enough that agents find their old rules of reproduction unsatisfactory. Crises prompt agents to respond *creatively* and to search for new strategies. They may repurpose once-marginal strategies to sudden effect, or they may try something entirely new. As Martijn Konings has observed, this can be 'a dynamic and often painful process of trial and error taking place right within the very social context that had produced the lived contradictions and problematic experiences motivating the search for new strategies in the first place'.[31]

While a society-wide crisis can prompt agents to adopt new rules of reproduction, which can generate new social-property relations, this outcome is not guaranteed. Agents can only choose strategies that the particular crisis places 'within reach'. Each crisis has a structure that presents agents with unique opportunities and constraints. In some crises, agents find no better alternatives to their old strategies. They 'muddle through'. They reproduce the same social-property relations through the crisis period, until some countervailing macro-dynamic asserts itself, and conditions normalise. Alternatively, the structural conditions of a crisis could be fatal, leaving some or potentially all agents with no viable rules of reproduction. Crises can become tragedies.

The endogenous transformation model, then, can be summarised as follows. Social-property relations structure the agency of individuals and classes, specifying their opportunities and constraints. Agents navigate these opportunities and constraints with certain archetypical strategies, or 'rules of reproduction'. Adopting these rules *en masse* has a structuring effect; it reproduces the prevailing social-property relations. This reproductive cycle is a spiral, not a circle. It has directionality. Over time, it generates societal tendencies which develop and interact, occasionally resulting in crises. These crises present agents with altered constraints and opportunities, prompting a search for new strategies or rules. If the opportunities and constraints of the crisis are just so, agents may adopt entirely new strategies or rules of reproduction, and this could generate entirely new social-property relations. And with these come a new framework for agency, and new tendencies, contradictions and crises. Every moment of this transformative, spiralling process involves an interplay of structure and agency.

This logic of endogenous transformation is rarely spelt out. But it is implicit in the metaphors many social-property relations theorists use. Ellen Meiksins Wood, for instance, wrote that the transition to capitalism was driven by 'a dynamic internal to feudalism'.[32] More famously, Marx captured the idea with his so-called obstetric metaphor.[33] '[N]ew, higher relations of production', wrote Marx, 'never appear before the material conditions of their existence have matured in the womb of the old society itself'.[34]

Endogenous transformation is a powerful model of social and historical explanation. One of this book's central aims is to demonstrate that power. For people living by society's conventions, social change can seem inexplicable. Yet the endogenous transformation model shows how conventional behaviour itself generates social change over time. To follow traditional 'rules of reproduction' is to reproduce the prevailing social-property relations, and also to animate their tendencies and contradictions. Through careful attention to social-property relations, and how they are reproduced, the social-property relations tradition seeks to understand not only why societies change but the nature and direction of that change. This was the approach Marx followed, placing the capital relation at the centre of his analysis. He enumerated capitalism's rules of reproduction, its structuring conditions, and its laws of motion, and he strove to understand its potential for endogenous transformation. This book follows the same approach, centring not capital but its mother. We will see, step by step, how the old tributary rent relation transformed internally, through its own dynamics, and thereby gave birth to capital.

But to tell the story well, I must first explain how my tale will depart from the usual accounts. I must distinguish endogenous transformation from three more common ways of explaining historical and social change. I call these 'non-transformation', 'exogenous transformation', and 'agent–structure dualism'. These three approaches encompass not only most mainstream economic-historical accounts of the rise of capitalism, but also many Marxist accounts, and some in the social-property relations tradition itself. All three of these approaches, as I will show, fall short of their ambitions.

NON-TRANSFORMATION

'Non-transformation' accounts present social change as a simple extension of past phenomena. They tend to be teleological stories, seeing history as moving straightforwardly towards a particular endpoint. They also tend to be structuralist, explaining historical change as the unfolding of structural forces, excluding or downplaying the role of agency in historical change.

In explaining the birth of capitalism, non-transformation approaches tend to proceed by identifying some feature or features of pre-capitalist society as 'proto-capitalism'.[35] They explain the advent of capitalism as an extension of whatever they have identified as proto-capitalism. Non-transformation accounts usually trace the origins of capitalism to some aspect of pre-capitalist commerce. Various aspects of pre-capitalist commerce have been posited as 'proto-capitalist', for example, money, trade, markets, merchants, a bourgeoise or town-dwelling class, urbanisation, or petty commodity production by peasants or artisans. For this reason, non-transformative accounts are often referred to as advancing a 'commercialisation thesis'.[36]

But the essence of non-transformative accounts is not their focus on commercialisation, but their failure to see that epochal change involves a transformation of social-property relations. Indeed, there are variants of the non-transformation approach that do not focus on commercialisation at all. Macfarlane, for example, identifies the transition to capitalism with the extension of pre-capitalist individual property, particularly landed property, rather than commerce. Consistent with the non-transformation approach, however, he denies any transformation of social-property relations. He insists there was 'no revolutionary change from one, pre-capitalist, economic formation, to another, capitalist one'.[37]

As Ellen Wood has shown, non-transformational accounts fail in the task of historical explanation because they beg the question. In explaining capitalism's birth, she observes, such approaches treat capitalism as 'a presupposition, whose unexplained existence in embryo must be assumed in order to account for its coming into being'.[38] Non-transformation approaches 'assume what needs to be explained' and shirk the task of historical explanation.[39]

Wood identified another variant of the non-transformation account, with similar flaws. This variant posits that capitalist social-property relations arose due to historical actors pursuing capitalist strategies to reproduce themselves – for instance, the strategy of specialising in market production.[40] Rather than assuming the existence of capitalist social-property relations, this variant assumes (without explanation) that agents follow capitalist rules of reproduction. It forgets that pre-capitalist social-property relations have their own distinctive rules of reproduction, and that the adoption of radically different rules itself must be explained. It begs the question in a different way, projecting 'capitalist principles back into pre-capitalist societies'.[41]

The non-transformation approach – and particularly the commercialisation thesis – encompasses not only most mainstream economic-historical accounts of the rise of capitalism, from Adam Smith onward, but also many Marxist accounts.[42] Indeed, when Brenner made his pathbreaking critique of non-transformation accounts, he labelled them 'neo-Smithian Marxism'.[43] Contemporary social-property relations theorists, especially Political Marxists, who insist on clear distinctions between different social-property relations and their archetypical rules of reproduction, have generally been the harshest critics of non-transformation approaches.

EXOGENOUS TRANSFORMATION

Exogenous transformation is my term for another broad approach to explaining historical change. These accounts recognise that fundamental historical change involves a transformation of social-property relations, but they posit, implicitly or explicitly, that social-property relations are transformed by outside forces. These exogenous forces are often framed as what Lafrance and Post term 'universal laws of historical development'.[44] These forces are posited as the prime movers of history. They are believed to exert a constant, universal transformative influence on the development of social-property relations, regardless of the historical epoch or its prevailing social relations.

Both mainstream and Marxist social theorists have proposed models of exogenous transformation. Numerous phenomena have been nominated as the main exogenous force that transforms society. Candidates have included: a tendency for the forces of production to develop; urbanisation; commercialisation; a human propensity to 'truck, barter, and exchange'; cyclical demographic patterns; military conflict; historical accident; the originary violence of 'primitive accumulation'; and a secular tendency to rationalisation or enlightenment.[45] Epstein, to multiply examples, refers to the Black Death as an 'exogenous event' that set off the 'higher growth path' of capitalism.[46]

More recently, theorists of Uneven and Combined Development have proposed 'the transhistorical fact of unevenness' as a force that intervenes upon social-property relations to transform them.[47] These theorists insist Uneven and Combined Development should be treated as 'an ontological premise that is irreducible' to social-property relations – in other words, an exogenous force.[48]

Another variant of the exogenous transformation approach treats class struggle as the prime mover of history. Political Marxists defend such an account, which I will critique later.

Accounts of exogenous transformation share flaws that undermine their explanatory power.

First, the unified transhistorical forces they posit generally turn out to be several distinct and consecutive phenomena. These phenomena typically belong to different historical epochs and bear only a superficial resemblance. For example, as Wood has shown, and as I will show in Chapters 2, 3, and 5, beneath superficial similarities, capitalist and tributary commerce operate on different principles, because different social-property relations generate them.[49]

Second, transhistorical forces are usually framed as having a universal and uniform influence, and this makes it difficult to explain why different societies develop so differently.[50]

Third, exogenous forces are a weak explanation for historical change because they themselves require explanation. Most exogenous transformation accounts do not explain the exogenous force they posit – it is treated as a 'prime mover' or 'uncaused cause'. Such explanations often reach a bedrock that consists of mere 'historical description, not analysis or explanation'.[51]

Fourth, we should be suspicious that theorists have posited so many different candidates as the exogenous 'prime mover' of history. This suggests each candidate is unsatisfying on its own, leaving historical change underexplained. Each force accounts for some but not all the historical change we see. The approach is too reductive. And if this reductivism is corrected by adding additional forces to the story, historical explanation becomes increasingly *ad hoc*.

The *endogenous* transformation model, by contrast, posits that when we see an apparently exogenous force transforming social-property relations, it is likely a tendency generated by the social-property relations themselves. What appears as a singular external cause turns out to be one of several internal tendencies. The force only appears to be singular and external because it has been abstracted from the process that generated it.

By insisting that history is explained by a single exogenous force, the exogenous transformation model generates endless, unsatisfying debates. Consider the perennial debate among Marxists over whether the motor of history is class struggle or the developing forces of production. Each side can summon compelling examples to counter the other, because each has grasped something real and important. Their debates never end, however, because they focus on where they disagree, and not their shared but mistaken belief that a single exogenous force drives history.

The endogenous approach, by contrast, recognises that the reproduction of particular social-property relations will generate *multiple*, simultaneous, historically specific tendencies that can interact in complex ways. And these tendencies and interactions can transform social-property relations themselves. Instead of isolating a favoured tendency and giving it a privileged transhistorical role, the endogenous approach strives to identify all the macro-tendencies of an epoch. It then tries to identify how they emerge from the interplay between the epoch's structuring social-property relations and its archetypical rules of reproduction.

Let us examine two concrete examples of how apparently exogenous historical forces may be re-read as endogenous. I will explore each in more detail later. These two forces are Uneven and Combined Development, and the Black Death.

As Sébastien Rioux argues, the inter-societal dynamics of Uneven and Combined Development need not be interpreted as reflecting a transhistorical force. Instances of Uneven and Combined Development can always be read as 'the spatio-temporal outcome of specific social and historical processes' – or, in my terms, as a result of the reproduction of specific social-property relations.[52]

In Chapter 2 of this book, for example, we will see how under tributary social-property relations lords often pursued strategies of conquest. Conquest undoubtedly produced Uneven and Combined Development that transformed the affected social-property relations. We will see how this happened in England after the Norman Conquest. But the Norman Conquest was not an exogenous event. As we will see, it emerged from the reproduction of tributary social-property relations in Normandy.[53] Conquerors may be exogenous to the territories they conquer, but the phenomenon of conquest is endogenous to social-property relations. As we will see in this book's final chapter, tributary societies are not the only ones that generate dynamics of Uneven and Combined Development. Such dynamics also emerge when capitalist and tributary societies come into contact. Uneven and Combined Development looks different in each case, reflecting different social-property relations at play. We are not dealing with a uniform transhistorical force.

Let me give another striking example of how an apparently exogenous force can turn out to emerge from the reproduction of social-property relations. Look at humanity's greatest pandemic, the Black Death of the fourteenth century. Some theorists regard the Black Death as an exogenous event *par excellence*, a bolt from the blue. In Chapter 3 of this book, however, I argue that its appearance and impact in Europe can be traced directly to tributary dynamics. Tributary social-property relations, I argue, have an immiserating tendency that primed the populations of Europe to be devastated by the Plague. At the same time, the commercialising tendency of tributary societies produced an intricate network of trade routes that transmitted the Plague all the way from China, along the Silk Road, into every corner of European society. The bacterium *Yersinia pestis* may have been a natural agent, but the transformative historical event known as the Black Death was endogenous to tributary social-property relations.

We cannot take for granted that natural events or agents are exogenous to social-property relations because social-property relations are not only relations between people, but between people and nature. It is beyond this book's scope to explore the various natural events that social-property relations have influenced. But human-made climate change provides a central example. A burgeoning literature now traces global climate change, and other changes to the global environment, to capitalist dynamics.[54] As another example, Mike Davis argues that a series of contemporary zoonotic pandemics, like Avian flu and COVID-19, trace back to capitalist dynamics, like industrialised animal agriculture.[55]

In summary, perennial debates over the 'prime mover' of history trace to a flawed way of explaining history that I call 'exogenous transformation'. It is unsatisfactory to posit that a 'prime mover' or 'uncaused cause' drives history, regardless of which force we nominate for that role. The forces that transform one epoch into another can seem exogenous, but they invariably stem from the reproduction of that epoch's social-property relations. Understanding social transformation is not about identifying a single engine of history. It requires a concrete analysis of the interplay between the prevailing social-property relations and the rules of reproduction agents adopt in response. If history has an engine, it is the ongoing dialectic between our choices and the social structures they reproduce.

AGENT–STRUCTURE DUALISM

Agent–structure dualism is the final major approach to historical and social explanation that I will critique. Instead of understanding agency and structure as interrelated and always both at play, this approach treats them as separate and isolated forces. As a result, it cannot explain history in a way that fully accounts for both agency and structure. It privileges the role of one or the other. When agency is privileged, it becomes untethered from structural constraints, resulting in 'voluntaristic' explanations of social change. When structures are privileged, agency is crowded out, resulting in mechanical or deterministic stories. As I will show, because neither approach is satisfactory, each approach tends to collapse into its opposite. Accounts that privilege agency collapse into determinism, and structuralist accounts collapse into voluntaristic ones.

'Agent–structure dualism' is not separate from the other two forms of historical explanation I have critiqued. Both 'non-transformation' and 'exogenous transformation' stories fall into the trap of agent–structure dualism. Non-transformation accounts tend to privilege structure over agency. They explain historical change as the extension of *structures* already present in the past. Stories of exogenous transformation, on the other hand, divide into those that privilege agency and those that privilege structure. Those who think exogenous forces drive history are structuralists. Those who fix on *class struggle* as the exogenous driver of historical change, by contrast, privilege agency, and they tend towards voluntaristic accounts.

A critique of agent–structure dualism is crucial because contemporary social-property relations theorists are increasingly divided into structuralist and agent-centred camps, with the latter camp calling themselves Political Marxists. I will argue, however, that both camps fall into the trap of agent–structure dualism.

Agent–structure dualists have prosecuted a long-running debate over whether structure or agency transforms social-property relations. The debate turns largely on how they interpret Robert Brenner's pathbreaking work on social-property relations. I defend a dialectical interpretation of the relationship between structure and agency in Brenner's work. But his watershed writings on the origin of capitalism, published in the 1970s, were widely received as privileging the role of agency over that of structure. Guy Bois famously labelled Brenner's approach 'political Marxism'.[56] According to Bois, Brenner had a 'volontarist vision of history in which the class struggle is divorced from all other objective contingencies'.[57] Callinicos summarised this problem of 'voluntarism' in more general terms. '[T]he prioritisation of agency', he writes, 'leaves it difficult to discern how the agency of social movements ... is structurally conditioned and contingently articulated'.[58] To preserve the role of agency in historical explanation, voluntarism denies or minimises the structural constraints agents face.

Notwithstanding the critique of voluntarism, a group of contemporary social-property relations theorists have embraced Bois' label of 'Political Marxism' and apply an agent-centred approach to critique structuralism.[59] Political Marxists Samuel Knafo and Benno Teschke identify various problems of structuralist accounts, including: a denial of agency and presentation of class struggle as a mere 'passive manifestation of a deeper structural logic'; a focus on structures to the neglect of 'the specific circumstances that define historicity'; a tendency to lapse into economic determinism or economism; and a bias toward forecasting terminal structural crises, wherein social-property relations cannot overcome their 'internal contradictions'.[60] Knafo adds that structuralism: tends to reinforce 'assumptions about the world by reifying it';[61] assumes that 'structures always have the same effect', failing to account for the divergent historical paths of different societies;[62] and over-emphasises 'the restrictive nature of structures' in a way that 'downplays' how agents 'leverage' structures to achieve their ends.[63]

While each side of the agency-structure divide offers powerful critiques of the other, each runs into trouble when attempting to articulate a positive model of historical change. Knafo and Teschke, for instance, formulate their positive approach in terms of 'radical agency'.[64] They argue for a methodological focus on the opportunities agents face in particular class struggles – with agency used as 'a principle of critical rigour to historicise'.[65] While historicism and attention to agency are laudable, as with all dualistic approaches, Teschke and Knafo cannot stably reconcile agency with the role of structure in historical explanation. Knafo explicitly rejects 'dialectical' approaches to agency and structure, insisting it is 'impossible to have it both ways' and that 'there will always be a choice to be made even if it is a reluctant one'.[66]

The decision to privilege agency causes problems, however, as it leads Knafo and Teschke directly to an exogenous model of how social-property relations are transformed. Emphasising agency, they posit class struggle as a prime mover or 'decisive explanatory differentia specifica' of history.[67] As I have argued, however, while class struggle does transform social-property relations, it does not stand above or outside them. In Post's words, 'the structure and dynamics of the dominant social-property relations … shape the variety of possible outcomes of class struggle'.[68] Nor is class struggle the only significant historical force; it is one of various macro-social tendencies that can be generated by different social-property relations. And class struggle can take very different forms depending on the social-property relations in question and the degree to which their other tendencies have developed.

The effort to prioritise agency leads to further problems. Knafo's efforts to eliminate structure by *reducing it* to agency have had paradoxical results. '[W]hat appears to be a product of structural constraints', Knafo argues, 'should … be analysed as a product of agency'.[69] The purpose of structures, he writes, 'is precisely to create agency (for some), not simply to close it off (for others)'.[70] While Knafo's approach effectively eliminates structure in favour of agency, it does so by reducing structures to tools created and used by powerful agents. Powerful agents become structural legislators, the masters of structure. But this misses that *all* agency is structured. The agency of the weak is certainly structured by that of the powerful, but the inverse also applies. Reducing structure to agency, while intended to eliminate structural determinism, paradoxically results in a 'voluntarism of the powerful'. It exaggerates the agency of the powerful and neglects that of the weak.

Knafo and Teschke try to avoid predictable charges of voluntarism by supplementing their focus on agency with historicism. Instead of identifying deep structures that explain the limits and opportunities all agents face, they argue that the limits and opportunities for agency lie in the peculiarities of each historical struggle, and these can be revealed only by historical investigation.[71] Through historicism, they hope to avoid the determinism of structuralist approaches, without descending into voluntarism.

Yet, I contend, historicism cannot substitute for analysing structures, nor is it a good way to avoid determinism. Historicism is indeed a crucial method for uncovering the choices historical agents faced, and hence their capacity for agency, but it is unclear why it should not also uncover structural constraints. Knafo and Teschke eschew this conclusion by insisting every class struggle is 'irreducibly distinct'.[72] But the fact that no two historical situations are alike does not preclude the discovery of persistent structures that condition class struggles. As Post identifies, Knafo and Teschke's insistence on substituting contextual peculiarities for persistent structures leads to a 'random (not necessarily more historical or historicist) understanding of the historical process'.[73] In seeking to avoid *structural* determinism, Knafo and Teschke paradoxically end up with something like *contextual* determinism or random determination.

While Knafo and Teschke's agent-centric approach is haunted by determinism, Post posits a structuralist account that is haunted by agency. Post rejects the label of Political Marxism, which has agent-centric connotations, and argues for a 'structuralism that allows us to understand the limits and possibilities of historical evolution and variation'.[74] Only structuralism, he argues, can 'account for the regular patterns of growth and crises' observed under different social-property relations.[75] Advancing a structuralist interpretation of Brenner's work, Post argues social-property relations have 'strong rules of reproduction ... that determine forms of expansion and crisis and of class struggle'.[76] But structural accounts always struggle with the role of agency. For Post, agency reappears in crises. Post interprets crises as moments of structural breakdown. Rather than seeing these breakdowns as terminal, he sees them as moments where agency radically reasserts itself, able to rewrite social-property relations. The resolution of a crisis, he writes, is 'dependent upon the unpredictable outcome of the class struggle'.[77] Post's structuralism paradoxically culminates in its opposite: a moment of voluntarism.

To summarise, despite occupying different sides of the agency-structure debate, Post, Knafo and Teshcke are all united by a common commitment to agent–structure dualism. Because dualism is ultimately incoherent, dualist accounts all display an unstable lurching between determinism and voluntarism. Knafo and Teschke's agent-centrism devolves into contextual determinism, whereas Post's structuralism leads him to posit moments of voluntarism or radical agency during crises.

Agent–structure dualism, whether it is structure-centric or agent-centric, is incompatible with the endogenous transformation approach. Structuralist accounts describe historical change in non-transformative terms. They attribute historical change to structures already present in the past, or to impersonal transhistorical forces that transform social-property relations exogenously. On the other hand, agent-centric stories conceive class struggle as the 'prime mover' of history and abstract these struggles from the structures that condition them.

Prioritising agency presents history as a series of radical breaks, where social-property relations are re-legislated *ab initio* by the victors of class struggles. Prioritising structure, on the other hand, captures the continuity of history, but either denies that social-property relations transform at all (as in non-transformation accounts) or invokes unexplained transhistorical forces to account for the transformation (as in exogenous transformation accounts).

The endogenous transformation model I defend privileges neither agency nor structure. It interprets Brenner's conceptual schema as a dialectical relationship between rules of reproduction (structured agency) and social-property relations (agent-generated structures). In this way, the approach breaks with most who have built on Brenner's pathbreaking analysis. Some have interpreted Brenner's attention to political struggles as an agent-centred approach to history. Others read his concept of 'rules of reproduction' in structuralist terms.[78] Post defends the structuralist interpretation, while Political Marxists like Knafo and Teschke defend a voluntarist one. Neither side recognises that Brenner's 'rules of reproduction' are not structural diktats, but rules of thumb agents adopt voluntarily to navigate their structural constraints and opportunities. Brenner's work need not be read as structuralist or voluntarist. Brenner exposed a social *dialectic*, a dynamic interplay of structure and agency, of social-property relations and rules of reproduction. Theorists who miss this are balkanised by a fruitless debate where agency excludes structure and vice versa.

Social-property relations and endogenous transformation are the framework of this book. In the following chapters, we will see exactly how feudal social-property relations transformed endogenously into capitalist ones – how rent gave birth to capital. And as we trace this transformation over eight centuries, we will see that social-property relations and endogenous transformation are not new ideas. They are part of an intellectual tradition that dates back at least eight centuries.

2
The tributary rent relation

The rent relation organised medieval European society according to a tributary mode of production. Wolf, drawing on Marx, defines the tributary mode as one where 'the primary producer ... is allowed access to the means of production, while tribute is exacted from him by political or military means' by a tribute-taking class.[1] Wolf observes that tributary relations can be centralised or localised. Under *centralised* tributary relations, local tribute-takers are subordinated to a central tributary authority like a monarch. Power, tribute, and the tribute-taking class are centralised. In contrast, under *localised* tributary relations 'power is held largely by local overlords and the rule at the apex is fragile and weak' (or non-existent).[2] According to Wolf's schema, European absolutism is a centralised form of the tributary mode, whereas European feudalism represents a localised form.[3]

The tributary social-property relations and tributary mode of production of high-medieval Europe was structured by a localised tributary relation I call the rent relation. The tributary rent relation constituted society into two main classes: peasants who possessed means of production, and lords who possessed means of coercion. Following the basic tributary pattern, lords applied coercion to exact tribute or rent from peasants. Lords used tributary rents to reproduce their means of coercion. Lords also used their coercive power to uphold peasant property in the face of intra-peasant disputes and external threats. By backstopping peasants' access to means of production, lords enabled peasants to produce both their own subsistence and tributary rents. The tributary rent relation was localised in that it was largely constituted and reproduced on a local level, with local lords enjoying a high degree of autonomy. Political power was 'parcellised'.[4]

As a form of tributary social-property relations, the rent relation structured both the productive class and production. As subsistence producers with their own means of production, peasants had strong incentives to diversify production to hedge against the uncertainties of bad harvests and market fluctuations.[5,6] They also had strong incentives to cooperate, both as social insurance against the risks of subsistence life and to resist lordly demands for tribute. The peasant property reproduced by tributary power was ultimately *private* property – whether held as individual plots or as shares in a village commons. Peasant society was thus always divided, latently or patently, into antagonistic interests – the rich, the poor, and the dispossessed.

As with all tributary social-property relations, lords responded to the rent relation by adopting strategies of 'political accumulation'. Brenner coined the term political accumulation to contrast lordly strategies with the economic strategies capitalist agents use.[7] I interpret political accumulation to include all strategies where lords apply tributary-coercive power to reproduce it on an expanded scale. Political accumulation could take three major forms: First, lords could squeeze more tribute out of existing peasants. This strategy was limited by the lords' coercive faculties and peasants' productivity and resistance. Second, lords could promote population growth in the peasantry, proliferating tributaries. This strategy was limited by the available land and its productivity. Third, they could conquer new territory and subordinate other lords' tributaries.[8] This strategy was limited by resistance from neighbouring tributary potentates (lords, monarchs, emperors, etc) and by resistance from potential tributaries.

In pursuit of political accumulation, lords had incentives to both cooperate and compete.[9] By cooperating, lords could buttress their individual coercive powers to more effectively counter peasant resistance and mobility, more effectively repel external threats, and seize opportunities for conquest.[10] On the other hand, the logic of political accumulation constantly drew lords into military competition for tributaries.[11] The prevailing incentive depended on the balance of conditions, threats, and opportunities facing each tributary lord.

Where lords cooperated, they tended to do so by establishing hierarchical and territorial relations with each other. Hierarchy established vertical relations of dominance between lords, obviating constant warfare. Hierarchy regulated the distribution of tribute between lords, and synchronised lords' political-accumulative targets. Territorial relations divided the labour of extracting tribute between lords and allowed for collective sanctioning of lords who tried to poach each other's peasants. To the extent that local lords established recognised hierarchical and territorial relations, these became inscribed in the rent relation itself – taking the form of recognised estates, ranks, laws, customs, and reciprocal fealties and intra-lordly obligations.

Tributary social-property relations generate oscillating dynamics of centralisation and localisation. As Brenner has observed, in localised tributary relations, dynamics of intra-lordly competition and lord-peasant struggle drive a centralising tendency, selecting for 'ever larger, more complex, and more coercively effective states'.[12] This tendency, however, tends to drive centralisation to unsustainable heights. When centralised tributary power surpasses the maximum scale at which it can effectively reproduce itself, intra-lordly competition and lord-peasant struggle produce a countertendency to fragmentation and relocalisation.

These oscillating dynamics explain the emergence and development of European feudalism. European feudalism arose as a generalised fragmentation of the more centralised tributary relations of the Carolingian great estates of circa 400–900 CE.[13] Once tributary fragmentation had reached its apogee in feudalism, however, the centralising tendency reasserted itself in a long-term process that would lead to early modern era absolutism.[14]

The ambivalent incentives of political accumulation explain, at least in part, Wolf's observation that 'historical societies predicated upon the tributary mode … tend toward centralization or fragmentation, or oscillate between these two poles'.[15] Where opportunities for political accumulation led tribute-takers to cooperate through orderly hierarchical and territorial relations, tributary power tended to centralise. Conversely, where lords saw their best opportunities for political accumulation in infighting, tributary power tended to fragment and further localise.

ENGLAND'S FEDERALISED RENT RELATION

Although the rent relation, as a localised form of tributary social-property relations, was endemic to medieval Europe, its successful mutation into a capitalist relation, as I will show, was peculiar to England. In the early modern period, as capitalism emerged in England, the tributary social-property relations of continental Europe were centralising. Local tributary rents were being consolidated into central tributary taxation. Feudalism was becoming absolutism. But the continental mode of exploitation remained the same: coercive extraction of tribute from peasants who possessed their own means of production and produced their own subsistence.

Yet, in England, a peculiar variant of the tributary rent relation would encounter some peculiar metamorphic forces. The result would be a different evolutionary path.

The English rent relation was an unusual hybrid of localised and centralised tributary relations, which I describe as 'federalised'. As in high-medieval feudalism, England's tributary relations were largely reproduced at a local level. Individual lords retained and reproduced localised means of coercion. Unlike high-medieval feudalism, however, the Crown had an unusually ample power to subdue intra-lordly disputes and coordinate warfare. Yet, unlike fully centralised forms of tributary relations, like continental absolutism, the English Crown could not reduce lords to mere courtiers or salaried officials, instruments of a central tributary apparatus. The Crown's limited arbitral authority reflected lordly integration rather than central dominance.[16] Brenner describes this situation as a 'centralized buttressing of decentralized lordship'.[17] The centrifugal power of local lords kept the centripetal power of the Crown in check, forming a 'homeostatic mechanism' where neither local nor central power attained supremacy.[18]

The peculiar, federalised structure of England's tributary rent relation developed as an adaptation to English conditions. Localised tributary social-property relations – the tributary rent relation – arose in England through the fracturing of the Anglo-Saxon great estates into smaller manors controlled by militarised knights.[19] England had followed the general European pattern of tributary fragmentation. From as soon as the eighth century, however, English tributary relations faced early and sustained adaptive pressure to re-centralise, to repel Viking raids and colonisation.[20,21] In the face of the Viking threat, English peasants acquiesced to heavier levies and feudal controls, supporting more knights. Likewise, pressured by an external threat, England's nobles and knights acquiesced to be organised under increasingly powerful Anglo-Saxon kings. They established and enforced cooperative relations by ceding *limited* arbitral and coordinative powers to an overarching federal authority. They overcame the lure of infighting by tying themselves to the mast.

The Anglo-Saxon Crown's accrual of this 'federal' authority was reflected in various developments: the expansion of Wessex into a unified English Kingdom; provincial and local jurisdiction through royal shire and hundreds courts; the Crown's ability to convene national assemblies of nobles and landowners; the imposition of national taxes such as the *Danegelt*; royal enforcement of treason laws; acquiescence to the Crown's fragmentation of rival magnates' estates; and the royal monopolisation of castles, noble oaths of allegiance, the minting of currency, the right to wage war, and jurisdiction over high justice.[22]

The federalised structure of England's tributary rent relation was reinforced by the Norman Conquest. Prior to the Conquest, Normandy's lords had independently begun to federate their tributary powers. They had acquiesced to the Duke of Normandy assuming arbitral and coordinative authority extending to his right to confiscate rebellious lords' lands, control over castle-building, and jurisdiction over intra-lordly disputes.[23] It was precisely the prior federation of Norman lords' tributary powers which enabled them to undertake political-accumulative joint-ventures like the Conquest. Under the Duke's leadership, Norman lords invaded England and decisively defeated the Anglo-Saxon nobility in 1066. William's knights violently subdued England's peasants and supplanted the previously Anglo-Saxon nobility.[24] Having secured Pope Alexander II's backing for his invasion, William likewise subordinated the spiritual fraction of England's nobility by restaffing the English Church with Norman bishops.

England's new Norman lords retained the extant federal institutions of Anglo-Saxon tributary power discussed above, melding them with those they imported from Normandy, and cementing the federal structure of the English tributary rent relation.[25] They did this from material necessity: upholding a unified English Kingdom and subduing a hostile Anglo-Saxon peasantry required strong lordly solidarity in the long term. By the middle of the twelfth century, the Norman Crown's federal authority over English lords was well established, except in the remoter parts of Wales and Scotland.[26] The enlarged resources of a federalised lordship enabled ploys to expand the federation. Welsh lords were incorporated through English conquests in the late thirteenth century, and Scotland's lords would fend off similar gambits for centuries to come.

England's federalised rent relation embedded a relatively stable balance between local and central tributary power. Because English lords still possessed their own means of coercion, they could effectively counter the Crown's power if they acted together. Moreover, by integrating themselves into the machinery of the Crown, lords ensured it could not exercise authority without a preponderance of lordly cooperation. As Brenner has observed:

> The feudal lords, led by the magnates, operated all levels of English royal administration, from the immediate entourage of the king (the Curia), on down through the perambulating courts, to the county sheriffs; they provided the core of the monarch's military organization; and they ultimately guaranteed the crown's financial wherewithal. As a result, the construction of an increasingly effective feudal state required the aristocracy's acquiescence and backing, and reflected their interest.[27]

While lords relied on the Crown to guarantee their unity, the Crown relied on lords to guarantee its authority. The federal balance of lords and Crown meant they could only advance mutually.

England's federalised rent relation rapidly reattained institutional solidity following the upheavals of the Norman Conquest. In the first instance, William the Conqueror confiscated vast estates from the previous Anglo-Saxon nobility, asserting arbitral authority over all English territory. Implementing the Norman system of tenure, the King allocated great estates to his closest followers – who became barons. Barons granted subsidiary tenures to their followers.[28] Through subinfeudation, each lord was granted exclusive, local, territorially circumscribed seigneurial powers and immunities in return for duties of loyalty, service, and tribute – rental obligations. Tenurial grants and obligations established a hierarchical distribution of the coercive labour of extracting tributary rent from peasants, and a hierarchical distribution of the rent surplus.

The Crown exercised its federal arbitral authority through a system of royal law. From the time of the Conquest, the Crown strove to project royal power to arbitrate territorial and hierarchical disputes between lords, and between lords and the upper strata of the peasantry. It sent assizes into the counties and asserted control over the regional hundred courts.[29] English lords' drives to internecine political accumulation henceforth generally played out in the royal courts rather than on the battlefield. The political-accumulative energies generated by the rent relation could be focused on external targets selected by the Crown, not squandered on local internecine disputes.

Regulated by royal authority, intra-elite rents settled into an increasingly solid juridical form. The Domesday Book of 1086 systematically recorded William's tenurial grants, helping to embed England's new hierarchy of estates.[30] As the Crown issued arbitral rulings in tenurial disputes, the powers, immunities, duties, and obligations that constituted the rent relation accreted into a body of judicial rulings. Legal doctrine came to posit a chain of sub-tenancies linking every English lord to a higher lord, and ultimately, to the Crown.[31] Lawyers began to impose legal classifications on land grants according to the different intra-lordly rental obligations attached.[32]

Rent was extracted by localised tributary power, seated in manorial or seigneurial courts. These courts exercised wide and intrusive powers, exercising executive, legislative, and judicial authority over peasants.[33] Under England's federalised feudalism, however, seigneurial authority was circumscribed by royal authority. Disputes between 'free' tenants – a legal category extending to both lords and the upper strata of the peasantry – were arbitrated by the Crown.[34] Lords did not have seigneurial jurisdiction over free men unless granted by royal franchise. The Crown protected free peasants from local lords, and free peasants formed a political base for the Crown, counterbalancing local lords' power.[35] By contrast, unfree tenants – villeins – were left to local lords' tender mercies. Royal power even backstopped lords' control over unfree peasants by guaranteeing their return if they escaped.[36] Within England's federalised rent relation, the juridical distinction between 'free' and 'unfree' marked the boundary between local and central tributary power.

THE FORMS OF TRIBUTARY RENT

In exchange for upholding peasants' customary tenure over agricultural land, enabling them to grow their subsistence, English lords demanded tributary rents. They demanded rent in the forms they found easiest to extract and use. Sometimes lords demanded in-kind rents such as grain, livestock, or chattels.[37] Mostly, however, they demanded cash.[38] To meet this demand, peasants had to produce a surplus crop and sell it for cash, which was then handed to the lord. The lord, in turn, used his money rents to purchase the subsistence, luxuries, materiel, or services needed to reproduce his lordship.

Unfree labour is the form of tributary rent most emblematic of English feudalism. Owing to their tight organisation and sweeping Conquest, Norman lords wrested personal possession of large swathes of English land, which became demesne land. Lords regularly granted unfree tenants customary tenure on the condition that they perform agricultural labour on the lord's demesne.[39] However, unfree agricultural labour was not used as intensively as often supposed.[40] Lords often used their money rents to pay labourers to work their demesnes, or simply leased their demesnes for money rents. Forced labour was deeply resented and difficult to extract. Dyer suggests lords resorted to demesne management and extracting labour rents not by preference but to protect the real value of rents during acute inflations, such as between 1180 and 1220.[41] Outside these periods, commuting labour rents into money rents was the secular trend.[42]

Peasants paid both regular and occasional rents. They paid aids, tallages, and other lump-sum rents on specified occasions.[43] Rents were extracted at key junctures of peasant family formation and succession, allowing the lord to influence decisions that might affect future flows of tribute. Merchet, for instance, was a rent demanded upon the marriage of a tenant's daughter. Heriot was a death duty.[44] Like their lords, peasants paid substantial entry fines on commencing a tenancy. Labour rents could be extracted as regular 'week-works' or as *ad hoc* 'boonworks' at harvest time. Peasants were also subject to the tithe – a regular ecclesiastical rent.[45] The tithe rate was customarily 10 per cent of a peasant's income.[46] The Anglo-Saxon nobility began enforcing the tithe in 901, and the Normans rolled it into the rent package following the Conquest.[47]

Seigneurial charges were another means of both extracting rent and reinforcing seigneurial control. Tenants could be forced to use their lord's mill, oven, or winepress, and to pay cash, grain, bread, or wine for the privilege.[48] Lords imposed tolls on peasant market transactions and trade.[49] Lords charged licence fees for permission to be educated, take holy orders, or enter an apprenticeship.[50] They levied leyrwite, a penalty for fornication, and childwite, a charge on children born out of wedlock.[51] Chevage or capitage was levied on landless manorial residents and peasants seeking temporary manorial leave.[52] Unfree peasants were also charged fees for the registration of land transfers.[53]

In summary, the aggregate rental surplus extracted from peasants was made up of a diverse bundle of tributary exactions. By the early fourteenth century, an average of 20 per cent of peasant rents were received as tithes, 13 per cent as seigneurial exactions, 30 per cent as demesne rents, and 37 per cent from customary tenancies.[54]

Senior lords in turn extracted rent from junior lords, reproducing an orderly hierarchy of tributary power and tribute distribution. Under serjeanty tenure, rent was extracted as personal services, including military services; fee farm was an agricultural tenure with regular rents in cash or kind; burgage was a town plot tenure with rents in cash, kind or service. Lords also demanded 'feudal incidents' from subordinate lords on specified occasions.[55] These were opportunities both to extract tribute and to influence decisions that could impact future rents. Incidents included fines on the succession of a deceased tenant's heir; 'wardship', the right of a lord to manage and enjoy a minor tenant's estate until the age of majority; and 'marriage', a tenant's payment for permission to marry his chosen spouse.[56] A lord could also protect his future rents by absorbing his tenant's entire estate if the tenant: died without heirs ('reversion'); failed to render service ('escheat'); or committed treason or a felony ('forfeiture').

The Crown extracted rents in forms that reproduced its preeminent authority and federal functions. As coordinator of lordly war-making, the Crown granted numerous military tenures, requiring lords to furnish trained knights, squires, and attendants, as well as provisions and equipment, on demand, for a set number of days each year.[57] Military tenures were also subject to *primer seisen*, a Crown rent payable upon succession.[58] Both lay and ecclesiastical lords held military tenures.[59] The limits on Crown demands for military rents were at first practical rather than juridical. In the thirteenth century, for example, the Crown tried to extend military obligations to every Crown tenant with a sufficient estate but was thwarted by lordly resistance.[60]

Aside from rents attached to tenure, the Crown demanded a range of *ad hoc* rents from lords. These often took the form of aids, loans, and benevolences.[61] Under the right of aid, the Crown could impose extraordinary rents in war or emergencies, which were frequent under feudalism.[62] Aid was often levied in the form of compulsory loans or obligatory gifts called benevolences. Demands for aid were calibrated to the size of a lord's estate.[63] The Crown also extracted *ad hoc* rents through its prerogative to collect the revenues of vacant ecclesiastical estates. The Crown could exploit this right opportunistically by delaying religious appointments.

In addition to extracting rents through the lordly hierarchy, the Crown drew rent directly from a segment of the English peasantry in the manner of a manorial lord. In 1086, the Crown directly possessed 18 per cent of England's land by value, and more by area. The royal demesne consisted of Crown estates strewn throughout England.[64] Peasants of royal demesne were Crown tenants, paying rent directly to the Crown.[65] They also paid tallage, an *ad hoc* Crown rent.[66] Demesne rents gave the Crown a crucial degree of autonomy from the lordly hierarchy and safeguarded its federal authority.

THE INTENSITY AND DISTRIBUTION OF RENT

The intensity of feudal rent extraction was determined by the balance of forces between peasants and lords. As noted, a lord had significant latitude to apply force to extract rent from unfree tenants, without fear of royal interference.[67] Lords did not, however, manage to extract every skerrick of peasants' actual or potential surplus.[68] As Hilton argues, seigneurial coercion was counterbalanced by peasant resistance, and this balance was crystallised in village customs.[69] The level of customary rents was, in practice 'a shifting compromise' between the two forces.[70]

Peasants had active and passive means of resistance. The peasantry's main strength in these struggles was possession of their own means of production.[71] To some extent, they could subsist while withholding tribute.[72] In England, however, this strategy may have been less effective because lords retained tight control of so much demesne land.[73] Peasants could also meet coercion with coercion, to some extent. There is evidence of violent conflict between villeins and lords dating to the mid-twelfth century, intensifying through to the fourteenth century.[74]

The balance of forces, and thus the level of rent, was also conditioned by the relative solidarity of lords and peasants. English lords had a high degree of solidarity compared to their continental counterparts. The Crown limited intra-lordly competition for tenants and ensured lords respected each other's exclusive seigneurial jurisdiction. Royal law gave lords the right to retrieve unfree tenants who escaped.[75] Lords could extract heavier rents from this more 'captive' tenantry. By immobilising the peasantry, however, lords effectively shielded local peasant tenants from outside competitors, facilitating local peasant organisation. While peasants could and did compete for local tenures, they had strong incentives to cooperate against seigneurial power.[76]

The intensity of rent extraction was uneven, varying between individual peasants and groups. Villeins of the royal demesne generally achieved lighter rents than manorial villeins.[77] The Church could generally squeeze more from its peasants than could temporal lords.[78] Because rent was a localised form of tributary social-property relations, the intensity of rent extraction varied according to the balance of power in each locality. In certain areas, notably in Kent, customary tenants effectively repulsed arbitrary rents, approaching the status of freeholders.[79] Unevenness between localities was compounded by unevenness within them. English peasant society was not egalitarian but stratified.[80] Wealth, landholdings, and social power varied significantly between individual peasants and different strata of the peasantry. A fortunate villein owned larger holdings and secured lighter rents than a less fortunate neighbour.

But villeinage was only half the story, with a full half of peasants being free.[81] Free peasants, who enjoyed the protection of royal jurisdiction, paid less than half the rent villeins paid and were free from forced labour.[82] Smallholders and landless individuals also faced lighter rents than their villein neighbours, although still high compared to their means. They were forced to work rich peasants' fields and lordly demesnes to obtain rent money and subsistence.[83] I will explain this tributary form of wage exploitation further in Chapter 3.

Just as rent was extracted unevenly from the peasantry, it was distributed unevenly among lords. The federalisation of lordly power meant the Crown commanded more rent than any other lord. Likewise, the stabilising hierarchical structure of the rent relation meant that great barons and bishops commanded vastly larger shares of the collective rental surplus than did minor knights and gentlemen. By the early fourteenth century, the top 5 per cent of lords – comprising a mere thousand – commanded around 47 per cent of all seigneurial income.[84] These outsized rent-takings both reflected and reinforced the hierarchical structure of feudal social relations.

3
Tributary tendencies and contradictions

In Chapter 2, I sketched the basic dynamics of the tributary rent relation and its rules of reproduction. I showed how the rent relation arrived in England through a process of political accumulation and adapted to local conditions by assuming a peculiar, federalised form, balancing localised lordly power and centralised monarchical power. Rent was extracted in the forms needed to reproduce lordly power and hierarchy, and the intensity of rent extraction varied with the balance of power between different groups of lords and peasants.

In this chapter, I will show how these rules of reproduction unfolded over time, drawing out the rent relation's secular tendencies and contradictions, as they ripened under English conditions. As will be seen, from the eleventh to the fourteenth century, the rent relation generated commercialisation, urbanisation, religious conflict, overpopulation, immiseration, and an endogenous crisis which sent the rent relation into retreat across Europe. As I will show, however, the English rent relation's peculiar, federalised structure mitigated this retreat, setting the stage for its unique development in subsequent centuries, and ultimately the birth of capitalism.

THE COMMERCIALISING AND URBANISING TENDENCY

Societies organised along tributary lines inherently tended to commercialise, and England, organised by the rent relation, was no exception. I use the term 'commercialisation' to denote a group of interrelated tendencies. These include the growth of commodity markets, the production of goods and services for trade, the extension of trade over distances, the use of money and the growth of urban centres of trade and commodity production. These tendencies were evident in England by the eleventh or twelfth century.[1]

Following Wolf and Hilton, I argue that commercialisation grows 'directly out of the operations of the tributary mode'.[2] Tributary rulers extracted subsistence goods from peasants, which they usually exchanged for more sophisticated means to reproduce their power. These included status goods and services (luxuries), as well as military services and materiel (means of coercion). Wherever tributary rulers began to enhance their powers via exchange, the competitive logic of political accumulation forced their peers to do the same. Tributary exchange corresponded to new classes: artisans, servants, tradesmen, and mercenaries. These classes reproduced themselves by producing the luxury and military goods and services lords coveted, in exchange for a share of the subsistence goods lords extracted from peasants. Merchants emerged too, facilitating tributary exchange for a cut of the tribute.[3] These new classes accreted in urban centres. Tributary exchange, hence, also drove urbanisation.

Tributary commercialisation in England can be tracked by the ubiquity of money rents. While lords could accomplish tributary exchange by bartering in-kind rents for useful goods and services, money was generally the most convenient medium of exchange. Lords could monetise their rents in three main ways: by selling tribute extracted in-kind; by selling produce they produced using forced labour (labour rents); or by demanding rents be paid in cash. Lords employed all three methods, but the last was usually most convenient. As I emphasised in the previous chapter, even at the outset of English feudalism, lords already demanded a preponderance of rents in cash. Even where commerce was limited, cash could still buy political services through the distribution of largesse and the engagement of retainers.[4]

As tributary commerce and its classes developed, more goods and services became available, and lords' thirst for money rents increased. Accordingly, customary entry fines were increasingly demanded in cash from the thirteenth century.[5] Labour rents reached their zenith at the end of the thirteenth century, after which they were progressively commuted to demands for cash.[6]

Lords who had farmed their demesnes in the thirteenth century – whether using forced or wage labour – began shifting to leasing them for money rents in the fourteenth century.[7]

The Crown similarly tended to demand rent in cash. Effective military competition increasingly required professional armies and mercenaries rather than knights. In the twelfth century, with lordly acquiescence, the Crown converted its rents from in-kind to monetary forms.[8] Most significantly, the practice of scutage allowed military tenants to pay money *in lieu* of knights' service.[9] The Crown's demands for cash rents from lords translated into lordly demands for cash rents from peasants. In later centuries, as Crown rents were superseded by taxes, the Crown's demands for cash only grew.

Lordly demands for cash rents drove a limited commercialisation of the peasantry. As I argued in Chapter 2, peasants had strong incentives to operate as subsistence farmers, diversifying production and avoiding the risks of market specialisation. However, increasing demands for money rents forced them to devote the tributary portion of their labour to cash-cropping – producing whatever would sell for the highest price. By the thirteenth century, peasants increasingly engaged in market-oriented production and exchange.[10] Exchange took place both within and between villages, and between rural areas and thriving urban centres. Commodity exchange was accompanied and facilitated by the growing ubiquity of money, credit and debt.[11] To facilitate peasants' acquiring cash for rent, English lords promoted and regulated commerce.[12] In the twelfth and thirteenth centuries, lords prolifically established seigneurial markets.[13]

As the tributary rent relation commercialised, it drove a concomitant process of urbanisation. Between 1100 and 1400, the proportion of the population living in towns and cities was low but growing.[14] Hilton emphasises that urbanisation was an 'integral part of the feudal-seigneurial economy'.[15] Hilton places medieval towns in two categories, based on how they served the rent relation.[16] The first type provided markets for peasants to transform agricultural produce into cash for paying rent. These tended to be small towns centred around produce markets and petty crafts. Lords founded such towns to facilitate the payment of cash rents.[17] By the end of the thirteenth century, small market towns accounted for up to three-quarters of all English towns and contained over half the urban population.

The second type of urban centre provided places for lords to spend their rents. These tended to be larger seigneurial or royal towns where local, regional, and international merchants marketed a wider array of goods. These were also places where artisans produced luxury goods and trades forged materiel, both marketed at lords. Urban development and the rent relation influenced each other. Lords' expenditure of rents in towns supported the expansion of urban populations, trade and industry. Conversely, the development of urban manufacturing enabled lords to transform money rents into an ever-expanding array of goods and services that could enhance the tributary power essential to the rent relation.

THE DEVELOPMENT OF FEDERALISED TRIBUTARY POWER

As we saw in Chapter 2, England's rent relation had a federalised structure, with the local and central poles of tributary power balanced in a rough equality. This balance would endure for centuries, even as its institutional forms evolved. Counterbalancing the central power of the Crown, local lords' countervailing collective power would gradually crystallise in the form of England's Parliament. In its earliest form, the nascent House of Lords gave the great barons a means to organise and represent their common interests to the Crown – haggling, for instance, over feudal aids and scutages.[18] When negotiations failed, however, the balance of power was maintained by force. The First Barons War erupted in 1215 when a group of rebel lords challenged King John's escalating programme of taxation and Crown rent extraction.[19] In a series of struggles, the rebel barons forced the Crown to accede to the Magna Carta. The charter institutionalised limits to the Crown's power to demand arbitrary rents from lords.[20] It restricted the Crown's right to seize land or rents in payment of a debt, except as a last resort.[21]

Crown authority was further circumscribed in the Second Barons War (1263–1267). During the war, in 1265, the rebel baron leader Simon de Montfort called a Parliament that mobilised not only the barons but the knights and burgesses against the Crown. While he nominally won the war, Edward I was forced to concede that the Crown could no longer exact military rents without the consent of both nobility and gentry. He was also forced to adopt de Montfort's Parliamentary model, in which the gentry had permanent representation.[22]

By the thirteenth century, the English Parliament was solidly bicameral, with barons represented in the House of Lords, and gentry in the House of Commons. Bicameralism reflected both common interests and divisions between lords. While barons and gentlemen shared a common interest in restraining Crown domination, great and minor lords' interests could also diverge. The great lords were more proximate to royal power and tribute than the gentry, and so, over time, the Commons would tend to break more sharply with the Crown than the Lords.

Aside from waging or threatening civil war, the key strategy lords used in their collective struggle to contain the Crown's demands for rent was to bargain away their Crown rent obligations in exchange for taxes raised by Parliament.

Parliament's preferred form of taxation was called the 'subsidy': a levy on all subjects' rents and moveables.[23] Lords preferred raising subsidies to paying Crown rents for several reasons. The Crown could demand Crown rents arbitrarily, but subsidies could not be levied without the lords' collective consent through Parliament. And since the Crown had no direct means of collecting taxes, subsidies also required local lords' further consent to act as tax collectors.

The subsidy was also lighter on lords than Crown rents, by design. The Crown demanded rents from lords in a lump sum on the assumption that they would recover this from tenants. But any shortfall in recovery had to be met by the lord personally. By contrast, subsidies were levied at a flat rate (e.g. 10 per cent) on every subject. A lord contributed the same proportion of his means to a subsidy as his tenant, and he was not liable if his tenant fell short. Lords indeed paid a smaller proportion of their means compared to other subjects because Parliament exempted from assessment lords' land, buildings, and goods deemed essential to lordly status.[24]

During the thirteenth century, the landed class leveraged its administrative integration with the Crown, its collective voice in Parliament, and its capacity for military resistance, to divert the Crown into a new modus vivendi. Local lords granted liberal subsidies and in return the Crown abated its arbitrary demands for rents from lords.[25] As the English Crown expanded, it grew increasingly reliant on subsidies, and hence Parliamentary consent, especially for making war.[26] The subsidy was thus a federal financial institution. It allowed the central power of the Crown to expand to meet external political threats and opportunities for conquest that local lords could not otherwise tackle, but without such expansion overwhelming the localised power of lords.

Over time, lords further circumscribed the Crown's unilateral authority by extorting formal veto rights over certain formerly arbitrary Crown rents. In 1297, with the statute Tallagio non Concedendo, the Crown conceded its right to levy aids without Parliament's consent.[27] Royal tolls became subject to Parliamentary consent in 1297, customs on wool and leather in 1362, and customs on wine and other goods in 1373.[28] The Crown's residual prerogatives were placed in 'cold storage'.[29] They would no longer be used to extract rent, but as a credible means of retaliating should Parliament refuse to grant subsidies. I will discuss this further later.

In summary, the federalised structure of the English rent relation ensured that the central power of the Crown developed in tandem with the local power of lords. The Crown's ambitions to centralise the rent relation were checked by lords' political and military resistance. As the Crown grew, so too did institutions, laws and constitutional conventions expressing the countervailing collective power of local lords, none more central than Parliament.[30] The Parliamentary subsidy in particular was a crucial federal financial institution, resourcing the Crown to expand and engage external political threats and opportunities, but without dominating England's local lords.

HERESY, OR TEMPORAL VERSUS SPIRITUAL RENT

England's kings and feudal lords upheld the rent relation with steel, whereas its bishops did so with preaching and alms. The Church's crucial ideological role in upholding the rent relation will be explored in the next chapter. Here I will explain why, despite that role, and despite the Church being fully part of the lordly class, the rent relation's structure nevertheless also placed spiritual and temporal lords in a long-simmering conflict.

Like other feudal lords, England's clergy held territorial estates where they exercised seigniorial power, extracting tributary rents from peasants. The Crown's arbitral jurisdiction mitigated territorial conflicts between ecclesiastical and temporal lords. But unlike temporal lords, the clergy also extracted rent in the form of tithes. These tithes applied universally and cut across the otherwise exclusive territorial jurisdictions of England's temporal lords. This effectively made the Church a competitor for the peasant surplus within every lordly and royal estate. There was also latent political competition between the Church and Crown, as the Church also represented and exercised the more distant tributary power of the Papacy. By the fourteenth century, political conflicts between Rome and local feudal monarchs were manifesting across Europe.[31] At such moments, the local Church became a threat to the local monarch, using the pulpit to promote Papal interests over local ones.

In the final years of the fourteenth century, the latent antagonism between England's Church and its temporal hierarchy assumed a definite ideological form: the heresies of John Wycliffe and the Lollards. The Twelve Conclusions of the Lollards appeared in 1395, in circumstances where the rent-take had collapsed and lordly solidarity was under great pressure.[32] Though framed in theological terms, the Twelve Conclusions amounted to a manifesto denying the Church's legitimacy as a fraction of England's lordly class. The Twelve Conclusions denounced the Church's sanction of foreign conflicts; its political connections to the Papacy; its lucrative business of pilgrimage; its monopolisation of theology and ministry; clerics holding temporal offices and manorial estates; and its wealth and military power.

Lollardy was the ideological expression of English lords' ambition to expropriate the Church's share of tributary rent. The Church called Lollardy heretical, but as Hilton and Fagan rightly observe it did not critique 'fundamental Catholic doctrines'.[33] Rather, it mobilised Catholic doctrine to attack the institutional Church. Lollardy is often misleadingly connected to the Peasant Revolt of 1381. But whereas the Revolt represented a subaltern struggle against rent itself, Lollardy was narrowly focused on which elites got the rental surplus. The Lollards were mostly members of the lay gentry, not peasants.[34] Wycliffe's work also appeared too late to have influenced the Peasant Revolt, and Wycliffe himself condemned it.[35] Moreover, Lollardy's blistering attacks on clerical lordship and clerical rents conspicuously avoided any generalised attacks on lordship or the rent relation per se. '[L]ords have power ...' Wycliffe affirmed, 'by God's law to compel men to do here service and pay rents, but by the gospel ... priests have not such power'.[36]

Sensing its vulnerability to being isolated from, and cannibalised by, other fractions of the lordly class, the Church doubled down on its traditional ideological role. It denounced Wycliffe as a heretic. It exhorted lordly solidarity and highlighted the common interest of ecclesiastical and temporal lords in subordinating the peasantry and extracting rent. It presented the rent relation and ruling-class hegemony as natural and eternal. The Church's position on Wycliffe is neatly exemplified in the following anonymous poem:

> Rightly so God has disposed the common people
> To labour for Holy Church and lordships also.
> ...
> But since that wicked worm – Wyclif be his name –
> Began to sow the seed of schism in the earth,
> Sorrow and ruination has awakened everywhere,
> In lordship and prelacy has grown less grace.
> ...
> The sun is Holy Church and lordship the moon,
> The stars being the commons, as I said before.[37]

Despite the fractures, solidarity between Church, lords and Crown would continue to hold until the sixteenth century. The clerical fraction continued to provide ideological support for the Crown and lay lords, and lords continued to back the Church. Church and Crown treated heresy as a threat to society and the state.[38] Yet, despite suppression, heretical denunciations of tithes and priesthood continued.[39] But heresy expressed the tension between temporal and spiritual rent only at the level of ideology. As Chapter 5 will show, the Reformation would resolve it in practice.

TRIBUTARY PROLIFERATION AND IMMISERATION

As I noted in Chapter 2, supporting population growth was a key strategy of political accumulation available to lords within the rent relation. More tributaries generally meant more tributary rent. In this section, I will show how this strategy intersected with peasant reproductive strategies, resulting in a broader tendency I call tributary proliferation. Tributary proliferation, I argue, resulted in widespread immiseration in England, as it did across Europe.

Within the tributary rent relation, a key mechanism by which lords could incite population growth, and therefore boost their rents, was by creating new tenures. Because peasants produced using family or domestic labour, the occupation of a new tenancy corresponded to the formation of a new family and, all things being equal, additional children.

One way of creating new tenures was to colonise unoccupied land. As Brenner writes, the 'twelfth century was the great age of colonization, assarting and the foundation of new villages'.[40] English lords offered incentives such as free status and fixed rents to peasants willing to farm marginal or contested land.[41] Lords regularly led projects of assarting, which involved 'scratching out new arable land from forests and wastes'.[42]

Lords could also generate new tenures by encouraging peasants with surplus land to alienate or subinfeudate it. Peasant land markets appeared by the late twelfth century, with transfers permitted by lords and recorded in the rolls of the manorial court.[43] Through subinfeudation, wealthier peasants could enjoy a share of the additional tributary rent generated by their new tenants.[44] Lords, however, appropriated the rest through heavy entry fines for subinfeudation or alienation, and proportionately higher rents that could be levied on the smaller plots.[45] Consistent with this process, peasant holdings fragmented over time.[46]

Tributary proliferation was equally a product of the strategies peasants pursued within the rent relation. Within tributary social-property relations, peasants had strong incentives to 'have large families to ensure security in old age; and where the size of holdings allowed … to subdivide holdings … to provide the means for young heirs to get married early and set up for themselves'.[47] By encouraging early marriages, peasants foreshortened the burden of childrearing and set their children up with independent means to care for themselves and their parents, but simultaneously encouraged their children to reproduce earlier, resulting in even larger families.[48]

The effects of tributary proliferation in England, as elsewhere, were striking. In the thirteenth century, the English gentry tripled in size, while its members maintained stable real incomes. The ranks of the magnates grew by only 25 per cent, but they doubled their real per capita incomes. The overall population, mostly comprised of peasants, likewise doubled or tripled between the late eleventh and early fourteenth centuries.[49]

As the rent relation encouraged proliferation, however, it generated declining labour productivity. Brenner has identified several features of the rent relation that limited agricultural productivity growth: tributary rent extraction limited peasants' capacity to accumulate capital; lords controlled peasant mobility and land transfers; peasant production was primarily oriented to subsistence rather than the market; and labour rents limited the scope for innovation on the demesne.[50] Incentives for political accumulation also diverted lords from improving agricultural productivity. As Hilton has observed, lords invested little of their rents in agricultural improvements.[51] Their efforts to increase the population encouraged tenurial fragmentation rather than economies of scale. With limited opportunities to implement labour-saving strategies, peasants adopted labour-intensive techniques that squeezed maximal food from increasingly scarce land. This strategy entailed diminishing marginal returns to labour. As tenures fractured and the population grew, land productivity (total output) rose, but labour productivity (output per hour) declined, reaching historical lows in the early 1300s.[52]

In the face of stagnant labour productivity and limited land, tributary proliferation immiserated the peasantry even as it grew. The steady fragmentation of peasant holdings meant that by 1280, only 32 per cent of peasant families held the minimal six hectares required to produce subsistence and pay rent;[53] 42 per cent held half the subsistence minimum, or even less.[54] While England had experienced strong population and economic growth in the twelfth and thirteenth centuries, by the late thirteenth century stagnation had set in.[55] Population growth likely faltered in the period 1260 to 1315.[56] Poor agricultural conditions led to sustained agrarian crises from 1315–1322, and in 1346.[57]

Other lordly avenues of political accumulation, including conquest and squeezing, further immiserated the peasantry.[58] English lords' overall ability to squeeze the peasantry is evidenced by how effectively they managed to raise nominal rents to keep up with persistent inflation during the thirteenth century.[59] As peasants' capacity to produce surplus dwindled, the extraction of rent, if anything, became more intense.[60] *Ad hoc* rents extracted for war-making placed further pressure on peasant subsistence. The early fourteenth century saw a heavy burden of war taxation with the commencement of the Hundred Years War in 1337.[61]

The logic of tributary proliferation generated growing underemployment and unemployment – a population with insufficient holdings (means of production) to produce a full subsistence and pay rent. Tributary society had several mechanisms for reabsorbing or managing the surplus population. The Church distributed spiritual rents to the unemployed through almsgiving. Surplus persons migrated to urban centres of commerce and production.[62] There they provided goods and services to lords, thereby partaking in tributary rent. Many joined the clergy, reproducing the ruling-class ideological apparatus and partaking in spiritual rent.[63] Finally, and most importantly, surplus labour could seek employment, either on lords' demesnes or with richer peasant families.[64] By the thirteenth century many smallholders were supplementing subsistence farming by selling crafts and their labour.[65] The labour market became deeper and more competitive over time.[66]

The appearance of tributary wage labour, however, should not be mistaken for nascent capitalism. Wage labour was generated by a tributary dynamic which, for the most part, proliferated and immiserated peasants *on* the land, rather than forcing them off it. Although rich peasants and lords became employers, they did not become capitalists. Rich peasants had little room to implement capitalist strategies of consolidated farming, specialisation, capital intensification, or labour-saving methods. On the contrary, the tributary rent relation fostered fragmented holdings, diversified subsistence farming, and labour-intensive methods. In a context of declining labour productivity, the surpluses rich peasants and lords could extract from wage labourers were bound to grow ever smaller, even as wages fell. To the extent rich peasants extracted surpluses from wage labourers, they used these for peasants' purposes: to support larger families in greater comfort. To the extent they acquired larger holdings, these tended to be re-fragmented by partible inheritance.[67] Likewise, lords spent surpluses they extracted by wage labour in the manner of lords: reproducing tributary power, not economic investment.

THE ENDOGENOUS CRISIS OF TRIBUTARY RENT

The proliferative and immiserating dynamics of the tributary rent relation generated, to use Brenner's words, the 'conditions for catastrophic crises'.[68] In 1348–1349, crisis arrived in England in the form of the Black Death. The first wave of Plague killed perhaps 40 per cent of the English population.[69] The Plague struck again in 1361, wiping out another 10 to 20 per cent of the already devastated population, and on a further 15 occasions between 1369 and 1480.[70] The Plague ushered in an era of low and stagnant population, falling prices and rising living standards, that lasted until the late fifteenth century.[71]

Despite its apparent exogeneity, the Plague can be traced to the internal dynamics of the tributary rent relation. Anievas and Nişancıoğlu have emphasised transmission of the Plague to Europe from China along the Silk Road as an instance of combined development – contact between unevenly developed societies.[72] The transmission of the Black Death can equally, however, be related to the shared commercialising tendency of all societies structured by tributary social-property relations, to which England was no exception. The complex network of European trading routes along which the Black Death travelled from the East, and which conveyed it to every corner of England, were generated by the internal dynamics of the tributary rent relation. Likewise, the catastrophic *impact* of the Black Death in England, as elsewhere in Europe, can be attributed to the immiserating tendency of the tributary rent relation, which had generated large and weakened populations.

The Black Death massively disrupted the balance of power between lords and tenants, forcing an adjustment in the quantity and quality of rent extraction. The population collapse created a dire shortage of tenants. Previously landless peasants now had their pick of vacant tenancies. Existing tenants were able to force reductions in customary rents through rent-strikes.[73] Desperate to attract and keep tenants, lords resorted to offering more attractive customary tenures with low entry fines, money rents, and no labour obligations. There is anecdotal evidence of entry fines falling from 1350 and a clear trend from 1380, reaching their nadir between 1430 and 1470.[74] Lords' incomes contracted by 20 to 30 per cent in the first half of the fifteenth century alone. As the new customary tenures were free of labour services, they anointed their holders as legally free. These tenures became known as copyholds.[75] Copyholds were granted heritably, or for terms of years or lives. Copyhold tenure rapidly superseded unfree villein tenure. Villeins whose lords would not grant a copyhold fled *en masse* to lords who would.[76] In 1300, around half the population was unfree, whereas by 1500 servile status was rare.[77]

Following Brenner and Dimmock, I argue that the peculiar, federalised structure of the English rent relation mitigated the collapse of lordly solidarity and tributary power in the face of the rent relation's endogenous crisis.[78] Collapsing rents posed a dire threat to lords' capacity to reproduce their tributary power. Under such stress, lords found the political-accumulative strategy of poaching each other's tributaries irresistible. Common interests – even backed by a royal prohibition – were insufficient to restrain them. The Crown's federal authority was, however, sufficient to prevent competition from degenerating into outright intra-lordly warfare. Crucially, too, the Crown backstopped lordly power against peasant inroads, a function it dramatically demonstrated by crushing the Peasants' Revolt of 1381. To a greater degree than their less united continental counterparts, England's federalised lords retained control of the land.[79] This control manifested in several institutions: their retention of broad manorial demesnes; their power to resume vacant land; their ability to time limit many copyholds to terms of years or lives; and their ongoing legal jurisdiction over peasant property through manorial courts.[80]

In precipitating a crisis and demographic collapse, the rent relation effectively reset its proliferative and immiserating tendencies back to zero. The lordly class, which had inflated on the back of tributary proliferation, deflated precipitously. Between the beginning of the fourteenth century and the end of the fifteenth, the number of knights was slashed by more than half, and the number of magnates shrank even more dramatically, from 200 to just 60.[81] Demographic collapse had reversed the tributary proliferation process and the immiserating effects of land scarcity. Between 1350 and 1450, a free middle peasantry flourished under light rents and with abundant land.[82]

While the tributary power at the base of the English rent relation contracted, its commercialising tendency did not. The massive turnover of customary tenures further entrenched money rents.[83] Analyses of the West Midlands and Lincolnshire indicate that while the number of village markets halved, roughly proportionate to the population decline, small urban markets persisted in their pre-Plague numbers.[84] As Dyer has observed, 'ingrained habits of marketing and the employment of credit and money continued' despite the massive economic contraction.[85]

Likewise, the crisis did not upset the rent relation's federalised structure, and accordingly Crown and lordly power continued to develop in tandem. Between 1350 to 1450, the lords facilitated an expansion of the Crown-cum-state machinery, while integrating themselves ever more deeply into that machinery.[86] Parliamentary subsidies facilitated the Crown's expansion, but only on Parliament's terms. The Crown developed a central civil service, but one heavily staffed by nobles. In the provinces, the Crown appointed local gentlemen as Justices of the Peace, centrally coordinating and regulating provincial administration in a way that buttressed local lordly authority rather than displacing it. The development of the English state in the wake of the Black Death thus represented the recuperation and further development of local and central tributary power in tandem. This federalised path reflected the unique structure of the English rent relation, and contrasted starkly with the nascent absolutisms of continental Europe, which reflected a one-sided centralisation of tributary power.[87]

To conclude, this chapter traced how the dynamics of England's tributary rent relation unfolded between the Norman Conquest and the Black Death. I showed how the rent relation's tributary logic drove commercialisation and urbanisation. I demonstrated how its federalised structure ensured the central powers of the Crown developed in tandem with the countervailing power of local lords, through institutions like Parliament. I showed how the structure of England's rent relation embedded a latent conflict between temporal and spiritual rent, generating a simmering tradition of heresy. I argued that the rent relation incentivised both lords and peasants to use proliferative strategies that immiserated the English peasantry even as it swelled. Finally, I argued that the immiserating and commercialising tendencies of the rent relation intersected to precipitate an *endogenous* crisis, which sent the rent relation into retreat across Europe. I concluded with the argument that the federalised structure of England's rent relation ensured that while English lords lost control of peasants' persons, they retained control of the land to a unique degree.

4

Tributary ideology, resistance, and critique

In this chapter, I will argue that the tributary rent relation's logic generated both consent and resistance. In the first part, I show how the rent relation gave rise to ideological conceptions of rent grounded in ideas of reciprocity and divine will. I will show how these promoted peasant consent to lordly leadership and furnished lords with practices for reproducing their power and managing peasant resistance. In the second part of the chapter, I show how, despite these self-stabilising mechanisms, the rent relationship's long-run tendency towards crisis nevertheless fermented the conditions for peasants to mount a generalised challenge to lordly power, threatening the rent relation itself. Finally, I will show how these peasant movements produced both theological and lay critiques of rent, which sought to dismantle lordly and Church ideology, and characterise rent instead as the fruit of forced labour.

Tributary relations between English lords and peasants were, by definition, coercive. Yet lordly rule was not maintained solely or, even regularly, by the exercise of force. Outright violence between lords and peasants, or between Crown and lords, was only sporadic. For the most part, the orderly functioning of tributary relations relied upon elites maintaining robust social ties with subalterns. Lords devoted much energy to cultivating subordinates' acquiescence, consent and, ideally, loyalty. They sought to establish stable hierarchical relationships and used both coercive and non-coercive means to do so. This required them to cultivate, maintain, and exercise social leadership or hegemony.

Ideology was indispensable to lordly hegemony. Driven by the imperative to reproduce their tributary power, England's lords developed, internalised, and disseminated concepts and practices which promoted and guided their leadership. Ideological concepts – such as 'honour', 'loyalty', and 'sin' – helped guide and coordinate lordly behaviour, promote lordly solidarity. They helped the lordly class navigate the world it faced.[1] Conversely, lordly ideology conditioned subalterns to their own class roles and provided an accepted language and framework for inter-class dialogue and negotiation. As with all ideas, the ideas that comprised tributary ideology bore the marks of their producers and conditions of production. Litterateurs, lawyers and priests were the principal ideologists of England's tributary society.[2] Accordingly, the ideology of the tributary rent relation expressed itself in literary, juridical and theological forms.

For lords, rent was a central ideological concept. I call their concept of rent 'rent as reciprocity' and will explain it further below. At the outset, however, rent as reciprocity must be distinguished sharply from any social-scientific definition of rent as a tributary social-property relation. Lords were not social scientists. Their objective in conceptualising rent was not to publicise its essential nature but to reproduce their ability to extract it. Hence, when they defined rent, they did so solely in terms of practices and ideas that helped promote their tributary authority and secure peasant deference.

A colourful literary illustration of rent as a feudal ideology comes from the medieval romance *King Horn*, composed circa 1225. In this story, the King offers his daughter in marriage to Horn, a promising knight. Horn refuses the King's offer on the basis that he is undeserving. Instead, he proposes that by the completion of seven years' service to the King, he could earn the princess' hand as a rent.[3] The story shows how ruling-class mores rejected the idea of rent as an unearned or unilateral benefit. A benefit could only be rent if the recipient rendered concomitant services to his superiors; rent without reciprocity was taboo. King Horn is the oldest surviving instance of the use of 'rent' in this sense of 'recompense' or 'reward'.[4] Rendering services to superiors, of course, reinforced the hierarchy of lordly power that made rent extraction possible. The idea of rent as reciprocity helped inculcate lords with practices that reproduced the rent relation.

While *King Horn* captures the ideology of rent as it operated within the lordly strata, the medieval allegorical poem *Piers Ploughman* demonstrates its application between lords and peasants. The poem's protagonist, a fictitious ploughman, spouts ideas that English lords wanted real ploughmen to internalise. In a speech to his lord, Piers says:

I will sweat in thy service, and tow for us both,
For thy love will I labour, while life shall endure,
In covenant that thou keep holy kirk and myself
From wasters and wantons, this world that destroy.[5]

Piers' words iterate another version of rent as reciprocity. He exhorts peasants to produce surplus and pay rent. But he links payment to reciprocal benefits provided by the lordly class, chiefly, protection from invaders and disorder. By presenting the rent as a 'covenant' rather than as a relation of exploitation, ideology promoted acquiescence to rent and lordly hegemony.

Piers' words were intended as much for lords as for peasants. For lords, the same 'covenant' linked the receipt of rent to the hegemonic practices by which the rent relation was protected and reproduced. Piers' words encouraged lords to maintain their military strength, protect the peasantry and cultivate its affection and loyalty, and to support the Church, which, as will be seen, was the principal ideological apparatus of the lordly class.

The ideological conception of rent as reciprocity also embedded practices for managing subaltern resistance. It encouraged peasants to understand lordly oppression as a deviation from the rent relation, rather than as inherent to it. It channelled peasant discontent toward efforts to restore reciprocity within the rent relation, and away from efforts to dismantle rent. *Piers Ploughman*'s entreaties to his lord provide a template for this sort of 'constructive criticism':

One point yet … I would pray you to grant!
O'ertax thou no tenant, save Truth will assent!
And though thou amerce them, let Mercy be taxer!
Be Meekness thy master, let Meed go unheeded;[6]

As Hilton observes, in *Piers Ploughman* '[t]he relationship between lord and tenant is accepted, though it must be observed in a spirit of justice'.[7] Anti-lord sentiment is transmuted into calls for more virtuous lordship. Anti-rent sentiment is transmuted into calls for lighter rents.

Conversely, by presenting mercy and moderation as inherent to the rent relation, ideology instilled lords with constructive strategies for responding to criticism. When criticism could not be suppressed, lordly ideology gave them tools for stabilising their power by transmuting criticism into calls for renewed reciprocity.[8] It is no coincidence that the domesticated critique promoted by *Piers Ploughman* was disseminated just as lords were scrambling to stabilise their tributary power in the wake of the Black Death.

While lords had an ideology of reciprocity, their most powerful ideological apparatus was the Church. The significance of the Church's ideological role and contribution to reproducing lordly hegemony is betrayed by the enormous share of rent it commanded. The Church exacted 37 per cent of all seigniorial rents, not including tithes. It achieved this share, in part, by virtue of its capacity to exploit villein labour more effectively than lay lords.[9] The Church received still further income from the tithe, which made up a fifth of the total rent pool.[10] Tithes were spent on maintaining the episcopate, churches, ecclesiastical courts, monasteries and nunneries, parish priests and the system of alms.[11] By 1300, England's vast ecclesiastical apparatus consisted of 50,000 secular clergy, and a further 25,000 monks and nuns.[12]

Ecclesiastical personnel were recruited from the ranks of the peasantry itself, achieving three hegemonic functions: employing and therefore pacifying many landless peasants; coopting the peasantry's most talented intellectuals and organisers, sapping the peasantry's capacity for self-organisation; materially bonding the peasantry to the Church, enhancing the latter's ideological authority and capacity to lead the former. If England's lords exercised hegemony through seigneury and warfare, the Church exercised it through sermons and alms.[13] Hilton describes the Church as 'responsible for the ideas of official society as a whole', and Hill, in similar terms, calls it England's 'main opinion-forming body'.[14]

The ecclesiastical machine tirelessly used its influence to support lordly hegemony. The key functions of the Church, in Hill's words, were to:

> soften the bitterness of class hatred, to keep the lower orders peaceful and subordinate, to stress the religious considerations which united a hierarchical society against the economic facts which so visibly divided it, to console the desperate.[15]

As in the literary exemplars discussed above, feudal theology conceptualised rent in terms of symmetrical duties owed by lords and peasants. Rather than presenting the rent relation in terms of a 'covenant', however, theology portrayed it as a 'reflection of the heavenly hierarchy'.[16] For those at the bottom of the divine order, the payment of rent was a 'holy obligation'.[17] Obedience to God required obedience to lords. Conversely, lords were measured according to godly virtues such as mercy, justice, and charity: social practices which eased class tensions and reinforced lordly hegemony. Social conflict was understood, in Hilton's words, as 'sinful departure, usually (though not invariably) by the ruled, from obedience in their allotted tasks'.[18] At times of social conflict, then, the social and spiritual sanctions on 'sinful' behaviour pressured peasants to return to the rent relation. Those same sanctions were used to cajole lords to comport themselves in ways that stabilised their hegemony. During the crisis of the late fourteenth century, establishment sermons were often critical of the lordly classes.[19] Such criticism recognised peasant discontent, but channelled it into calls for a return to lordly virtue. It transmuted criticism *of* the rent relation into criticism *within* the rent relation.

RESISTANCE TO TRIBUTARY RENT

In the last chapter I showed how localised resistance was part of the tributary rent relation. The level of tributary rent was determined by a political struggle between lords and peasants at the level of the manor. Peasant resistance in each locality yielded a local rent settlement, crystallised in manorial custom and administered by local manorial courts. But localised resistance always had the potential to become generalised, and in late fourteenth-century England it did.

Scholars like Hilton have argued that mass peasant resistance in the fourteenth century had a major role in reshaping the rent relation. The argument goes that peasant resistance ended English serfdom and caused rents to collapse.[20] According to this argument, this pivotal change in the tributary rent relation stems from the exogenous agency of peasants, not from the rent relation's own endogenous dynamics.

I dispute such arguments on both theoretical and empirical grounds.

As I argued at the outset of this book – social-property relations transform endogenously. Agents do shape their social-property relations. But their prospects and options for doing so at any moment are heavily conditioned by the social-property relations they find themselves within. Accordingly, I contend that if we see the emergence of generalised peasant resistance to rent in the fourteenth century, we should expect this to be at least partly a *consequence* of the rent relation's own dynamics, not an intervention over and against them.

My theoretical argument is supported by the latest scholarship. Bailey's revised chronology indicates that the momentous transformations in the rent relation seen in the fourteenth century came *before* the upsurge in peasant resistance, not after.[21] Likewise, Scheidel recently concluded peasant resistance in the fourteenth century reflected 'the desire to preserve gains' they had already made, not to win them in the first place.[22]

Indeed, we have already seen exactly how the rent relation created the conditions for mass peasant resistance. As I showed in Chapter 3, the tributary rent relation had a long-term endogenous tendency to generate immiseration, disease transmission, and crisis. In the fourteenth century, just such a crisis sent rent-takings, the lordly population, and seigneurial control over peasants' bodies into retreat, creating fertile conditions for generalised peasant resistance to lords' tributary authority and the rent relation itself.

The most acute example of generalised resistance to England's tributary rent relation was the Peasants' Revolt of 1381. The Revolt's proximate causes were grievances about corruption, taxation, the administration of justice, forced employment, and a slump in grain prices, which depressed peasants' market incomes from the mid-1370s (making money rents more burdensome).[23] Every one of these gripes went to the lords' authority within the tributary rent relation. The rebellion was led by Wat Tyler, likely a tiler by trade; Geoffrey Litster, a dyer; and the dissident clerics John Ball and John Wrawe.[24] The rebellion arrayed, on one side, the mass of the peasantry, and on the other, lords, the Crown, the Church and the tributary bourgeoisie, including lawyers and bureaucrats.[25] The Revolt united rich and poor peasants alike.[26]

The Revolt sought a generalised but limited curtailment of the English tributary rent relation. Chief among its leaders' demands was a blanket end to serfdom – an institution which, as I have shown, was already collapsing.[27] Another demand included a general limitation of rents to fourpence an acre.[28] Both demands sought to curtail the reproduction of lords' tribute extracting power, and hence to curtail the rent relation itself.

The Revolt did not oppose itself to the entire rent-taking class, but instead sought to divide it. The rebels made a significant assault on the Crown's bureaucracy, assassinating the Archbishop of Canterbury, Simon Sudbury, who was the King's High Chancellor, as well as the Lord High Treasurer, Robert de Hales, both architects of a hated poll tax. Likewise, the rebels called for 'slaying the lawyers, justices and jurors' – Crown servants who enforced repressive labour laws and wage regulations.[29]

But the peasants did not seek to overthrow the King or the monarchy itself; instead, they appealed to the King for support against the lords and clergy.[30] This tactic had some logic. As Wolf has observed, in tributary societies 'central rulers and peasants are linked by a common antagonism against power-holding and surplus-taking intermediaries'.[31] But as I showed in Chapters 2 and 3, however, England's federalised rent relation put lords and the Crown in a tight lockstep. A peasant–Crown alliance to oust England's lords was chimerical. The Crown, while appearing to entertain the peasantry's demands, ultimately supported England's lords and clergy to put down the Revolt and execute its leaders.[32]

Generalised resistance to the tributary rent relation found a related expression in anti-clericalism. Anti-clericalism was a rejection of the Church both as a major fraction of the rent extracting elite and as its chief ideological apparatus. A current of anti-clericalism can be traced as early as the twelfth century, often expressed as derision toward the opulence and hypocrisy of abbots and monks.[33] This current surfaced in 1381. The leaders of the Peasant Revolt displayed a sharp anti-clericalism in their demands, seeking the abolition of all but one bishop and two monasteries, the distribution of Church estates to the peasantry, and a radical curtailment of tithes and clerical benefices.[34] These demands entailed the extinguishment of the spiritual rent relation and the liquidation of the ecclesiastical class which subsisted upon it.

Paradoxically, anti-clericalism often originated within the Church. Heretical clerics tended to be unsalaried – hence, *declassee*. Denied a share of the Church's rent-takings, these clerics' affiliation reverted to the peasantry from which they were recruited. An intensification of clerical heresy can be directly linked to the fourteenth-century crisis of the rent relation: with the Church's rent-takings drastically reduced, the pool of unbeneficed clerics increased, producing more potential heretics like the rebel leader John Ball.[35] Heretical clerics like Ball were fierce and articulate. The Church had bestowed them with a general education, skills of oratory and organisation, and a deep knowledge of Christian teachings. They used these tools to organise the peasantry and to reconstruct Christian doctrines to express peasants' material interests.

THEOLOGICAL AND LAY CRITIQUES

Thus far I have distinguished two entwined social tendencies that expressed generalised resistance to the tributary rent relation: the movement to curtail rents and anti-clericalism, both manifesting acutely in the Peasant Revolt of 1381. I have shown how both movements can be traced to the internal dynamics of England's tributary rent relation, including its lord-peasant antagonism and its tendency to crisis. Now I will turn to these movements' key ideas or theories: the theory of the Norman Yoke and the theological critique of lordship.

The theological critique of the tributary rent relation grounded itself in an egalitarian interpretation of the Christian Genesis narrative. This is exemplified in the chronicler Walsingham's account of the Peasants' Revolt, wherein John Ball argues 'from the beginning all men were created equal by nature, and that servitude had been introduced by the unjust and evil oppression of men, against the will of God'.[36] Froissart's chronicle of the rebels has them expressing similar views: 'in the beginning of the world, they said, there were no bondmen ... for they were neither angels nor spirits, but men formed to the similitude of their lords'.[37] Egalitarianism was a common message in radical fourteenth-century sermons, and egalitarian theology was a common feature of medieval European peasant movements.[38]

Taking divinely endowed human equality as its point of departure, the theological critique posited unnatural and coercive social-property relations as the basis of rent. In Froissart's account of the Peasants' Revolt, the peasant rebels put the following argument to their masters:

> whereby can ... [lords] say or shew that they be greater lords than we be, saving by that they cause us to win and labour for that they dispend? ... by that [rent] that cometh of our labours they keep and maintain their estates: we be called their bondmen, and without we do readily them service, we be beaten.[39]

Negating the proposition that lordship, bondage, and rent extraction are natural and godly, the theological critique posits an alternative. Lordship, according to the theological critique, is lordly command over peasant labour by means of violence. Rent was the fruit of lordship, consisting of the products of forced labour. The theological critique of lordship advanced from the norm of equality to an alternative analysis of social-property relations, emphasising the fundamentally coercive nature of the tributary rent relation.

Having diagnosed lordship and rent as ungodly and coercive, the theological critique prescribed peasant self-emancipation as the cure. As Froissart records, the peasants reached a simple conclusion: that 'none ought to be bond'.[40] The leader John Ball proposed 'that we may be all uni[t]ed together, and that the lords be no greater masters than we be'.[41] As another source put it '[w]e'll be lords, my masters, every one'.[42] As Hilton has observed, the demand 'that lordship should be enjoyed proportionately by all men' constituted a 'general demand for an end to lordship'.[43] Lordship was not merely to be equally distributed, but dissolved. And peasants would emancipate themselves, violently. Ball proposed 'killing the great lords of the realm'.[44] Liquidation of the lordly class would end tributary labour and the rent relation itself.

The theological critique imagined an alternative peasant society, without lords or rent. Ball, in Walsingham's account, imagined 'equality of liberty and nobility, as well as of dignity and power' once 'the great ones had been removed'.[45] In Froissart's account, Ball speaks of a society where 'everything be common, and that there be no villains nor gentlemen, but that we may be all uni[t]ed together'.[46] It bears emphasis that Ball here envisaged a society of *commoners*, rather than a society of common property. As Hilton clarifies, the imaginary attached to the Peasant Revolt remained one of 'family ownership of peasant holdings and artisan workshops, with the large-scale landed property of the Church and the aristocracy divided among the peasants'.[47]

In its attachment to peasant property, however, the theological critique showed the limits of its imaginative capacity to transcend lordship and the rent relation. To reproduce itself as a class of peasant proprietors, the peasantry needed an overarching authority capable of defending property from both internal rivalries and external threats. The rebels accordingly envisaged the retention of what Hilton has called 'a people's monarchy'.[48] The Crown would 'remain intact ... as an institution standing above individuals and classes, capable of dispensing even-handed justice'.[49] The retention of the Crown implied the retention of Crown rent and thus the rent relation, however attenuated, and hence the limits of the peasant critique of rent.

Alongside the theological critique of lordship was a lay critique, historiographically dubbed 'the Norman Yoke'. In Hill's concise formulation, the Norman Yoke was the proposition that:

> Before 1066 the Anglo-Saxon inhabitants of ... [England] lived as free and equal citizens, governing themselves through representative institutions. The Norman Conquest deprived them

of this liberty, and established the tyranny of an alien king and landlords.[50]

Hill describes the Norman Yoke as a 'rudimentary class theory of politics' which 'united the Third Estate against Crown, Church and landlords', asserting that 'the ruling class is alien to the interests of the vast majority of the population'.[51] It focused attention 'on the relation between force, property and the origin of the state'.[52]

The Norman Yoke critique was analogous to the theological critique in many ways. Like the theological critique, the Norman Yoke was grounded in an alternative account of the past.[53] It was also analogous in using 'alternative history' as a basis for contesting the justice and naturality of medieval social-property relations. Whereas the theological critique grounded itself in lost Edenic equality, the Norman Yoke posited lost historical liberties. Despite its different point of departure, however, the Norman Yoke theory arrived at remarkably similar characterisations of lordship and rent. According to the Yoke's central metaphor, the lordly class had trammelled upon ancient liberty by reducing peasants to domesticated beasts. Exactly as the peasants yoked oxen, lords had yoked the peasantry to exploit its productive energies. Just like the theological critique, the Norman Yoke story characterised rent as the fruit of forced labour.

Also, like the theological critique, the Norman Yoke was a counter-ideological and counterhegemonic weapon. It gave peasants a means to 'ridicule the pretensions to sacredness of any institutions which perpetuate the rule of a propertied class'.[54] It sought to break vertical bonds of lord-peasant fealty and direct peasants' attention to their common interest in uniting against the lordly class. It emboldened peasants to shrug off the Yoke and declare – as they did in the Revolt – that they would 'not longer suffer' to be 'kept so under like beasts'.[55]

Like the theological critique of lordship, the Norman Yoke theory had a long history.

Hill speculates it may date right back to 1066.[56] Unlike the theological critique, which sang its swansong in the transition to capitalism, the Norman Yoke proved so flexible that it thrived well into the capitalist epoch. From the seventeenth to the nineteenth century, it was appropriated by groups as diverse as the Diggers, Levellers, the nascent English working class, the aristocracy, the wealthy middle class, and waning small proprietors.[57] Any group that perceived an oppression could formulate its gripe in terms of the Norman Yoke. References to the Norman Yoke remained common even into the second half of the nineteenth century.[58]

5

From tributary to capitalist rent

Thus far I have laid out the general logic and tendencies of the tributary rent relation, the ideologies it generated, and the peculiar, federalised form it took in England. I have explained how the tributary rent relation generated commercialisation, urbanisation, and prolific population growth that culminated in immiseration, disease, and crisis. I have shown how the rent relation generated both local and generalised forms of resistance and critique.

With this groundwork laid, this chapter presents my central argument. Here I will show that England's transition to capitalism can be explained as an endogenous transformation of its tributary rent relation. In other words, I will show that rent is the mother of capital.

In this book's final chapter I will extend this argument, showing rent was the mother of capital not just in England, but globally. English capitalism, once born, would ignite an entirely novel world-historical process called tributary metamorphosis – a global process of capitalist transition that continues today.

But to pick up the thread from Chapter 3, by the fourteenth century, the tendencies and contradictions of the tributary rent relation had generated a crisis which sent tributary power across Europe into a deep recession. The tributary rent relation was everywhere forced to *mutate* to reproduce itself under the adverse conditions it had generated.

The more localised and fragmented tributary powers of continental Europe had to consolidate and centralise to survive. By acquiescence and force, weakened continental lords were progressively integrated into monarchs' tributary machineries as nobles or courtiers. Continental feudalism gradually mutated into absolutism.[1]

In England, by contrast, the rent relation retained its uniquely federalised structure. Local tributary power was buttressed by a strong but limited central authority. Local lordly power endured a diminution, but not a total rout. English lords lost control of peasants' bodies but retained strong control of the land. Under these conditions, English lords found they could reproduce their localised tributary power – and hence the rent relation – by granting tenures on competitive terms. Lords competing for tenants corresponded to a mobile peasantry, competing for the best tenures available. In adapting to an endogenous crisis, England's federalised tributary rent relation had mutated into a *competitive* relation.

England's competitive rent relation corresponded to three new classes: landlords, husbandmen, and yeomen. Chapter 3 traced how the first two classes emerged in the Black Death's wake. Having lost control of peasants' bodies but retained control of the land, lords had become landlords. Likewise, formerly unfree villeins secured long-term – though not indefeasible – customary tenures known as copyholds, with ample plots, lighter rents, and no labour services. These newly flourishing subsistence farmers became known as husbandmen.[2]

The third new class generated by the competitive rent relation, the yeomanry, has not yet been described. Facing high wage costs and unable to extract labour services, lords relinquished direct management of their demesnes, and leased them for terms of years.[3] In the decades around 1400, lords leased a massive 25 per cent of the cultivated area of manorial land.[4] Lords had to find persons with sufficient means to rent and use large tracts of agricultural land. Lords recruited, therefore, mostly 'middling and wealthy peasants', especially manorial office holders, but also 'artisans, merchants, clothiers, clergy and gentry'.[5] The new leaseholders became known as yeomen.[6] The competitive rent relation would propel yeomen down a very different path from the husbandmen.

Competitive leasing drove yeomen to shift from subsistence to capitalist farming. Yeomen, as Dimmock argues, found themselves with leases on farms that were far larger than required for subsistence farming, and too large to exploit using family labour.[7] To meet the rents on these large leaseholds, then, yeomen had to hire wage labourers and produce for the market.[8,9] As labourers were scarce and expensive, yeomen had a strong incentive to produce products with minimal labour inputs. Accordingly, in the fifteenth and sixteenth centuries, yeomen often became specialist capitalist pastoralists.[10] Pastoral products – wool, meat, and dairy – fetched higher market prices than the arable produce favoured by subsistence farmers, and required fewer labour inputs.[11] Dimmock locates the yeomanry's transition to market-dependence primarily in the years 1380 to 1420.[12] From the 1540s, grain prices rose, drawing yeomen into capitalist grain farming.[13] In order to turn a sufficient profit to meet competitive market rents, they had to economise on labour. They did so by implementing new, comparatively capital-intensive methods of arable farming.[14]

Yeomen could only pursue this strategy of market specialisation because the tributary rent relation, through its commercialising tendency, had already generated a vast network of local, national, and international markets. The goods yeomen sold into those markets, at least initially, were precisely the luxuries demanded by tributary elites both in England and abroad.

The rent relation's competitive mutation rewarded yeomen who adopted accumulative behaviours and punished those who did not. To keep his lease, a yeoman had to compete in the market and maximise his profit. As Brenner observes, in order to compete 'as effectively as possible', yeomen had to maximise profits by 'cost-cutting', 'specialising', 'innovating', and 'accumulating their surpluses'.[15] Without surpluses a farmer could not weather adverse shifts in the market. Brenner has also observed that yeomen tended to respond to market downturns with increased 'productive investment to enhance labour productivity and cost effectiveness'.[16] This was another key behaviour premised on the prior accumulation of surpluses. The yeomanry developed a culture of accumulation. Yeomen adopted 'a meticulous approach to accountancy and a focus on accumulation and productive expenditure'.[17] To enable intergenerational accumulation and prevent the fragmentation of fortunes, yeomen adopted primogeniture.[18]

The competitive rent relation induced capitalist behaviour in landlords too. Landlords' rents and livelihoods increasingly depended on how profitably yeomen could use their lands. This gave landlords 'incentives to encourage "improvement" … quite unlike the traditional rentier'.[19] Some landlords became leasehold-ing capitalist farmers themselves.[20]

THE PROLETARIANISING TENDENCY

By the middle of the sixteenth century, the new competitive rent relation had undeniably generated capitalist production in England. But the rent relation and the mode of production remained primarily *tributary*. Despite the presence of a capitalist yeomanry, the bulk of England's social product was still being generated by husbandmen – peasant subsistence farmers paying tributary rents from their surplus product.

In this section, I will show how the competitive rent relation, through its own logic, tended to uproot subsistence agriculture in favour of capitalist wage labour. The rent relation, I argue, pulled up its own tributary roots and re-grounded itself in capitalist social-property relations. Whereas a landlord's rent had once represented a flow of peasant tribute, it came to represent a share in capitalist surplus. The rent relation transformed thus, as I will show, through its *proletarianising* tendency, giving landlords and capitalists both the means and incentive to drive peasants off the land, transforming them into capitalist wage labourers.

The post-Plague competitive rent relation became fully capitalist through its tendency to drive enclosure. Customary land tenure gave peasants a diverse bundle of access rights to open fields, commons, and wastes. These rights, some exclusive, many *shared*, were the legal manifestation of subsistence production and peasant community life. Enclosure, by contrast, was the process of establishing *exclusive* legal rights to a defined piece of land, enclosing it legally and, in most cases, physically too.[21] Enclosure represented the legal and practical extinguishment of peasant production, and the establishment of the legal and practical conditions for capitalist agriculture. Some English land had always been enclosed, but enclosure became a secular trend in the fifteenth century.[22]

The competitive rent relation incentivised enclosure through the higher rental yields available on enclosed land. From the mid-sixteenth century, as the demand for land recovered from its post-Plague lows, growing competition for tenancies enabled landlords to impose higher rents and shorter lease periods, as demesne leases came up for renewal.[23] A significant differential opened between the rents on demesne leaseholds and those that husbandmen paid on multigenerational customary tenures. In this context, the competitive rent relation gave lords a strong incentive to increase rental yields by enclosing customary land and leasing it to capitalist graziers.[24]

An enclosure movement proceeded gradually from the fifteenth century, with a pronounced wave in the late sixteenth century.[25] The rate of enclosure reached its historical crescendo in the seventeenth century, at almost twice that of any other century.[26] By the middle of the seventeenth century, a tripartite system of capitalist agriculture consisting of landlord, farmer, and wage labourer was widespread.[27] Many landlords were now capitalist landlords – drawing a significant and growing proportion of their rents from capitalist agriculture. Yet enclosure still had far to run.[28]

The competitive rent relation gave landlords and farmers strong incentives to cooperate to enclose land. Enclosure allowed yeomen to expand their capitalist farms and make greater profits, which landlords shared in through the higher rents of enclosed land. Cooperation took several forms. A yeoman would, for instance, buy up and engross customary land, for a gentleman to buy and lease back.[29] The yeoman functioned as a buyer's agent for a landlord expanding his holdings, while the gentleman acted as a financier for the farmer, letting the farmer expand his enterprise onto new lands without his capital being sunk in that land. The landlord–capitalist alliance reflected a deep integration between rent and capital. The expanded reproduction of each reinforced the other. Enclosure expanded opportunities for profit, and the need to reinvest those profits stoked the demand for productive land, driving up rents and accelerating enclosure.

But the competitive rent relation did not just make enclosure attractive to lords; it furnished them with the means to enforce it. Landlords' tributary-coercive control of the land was the basis of the competitive rent relation. Lords could use that coercive authority to apply economic pressure to force customary tenants off the land. This often took the form of ratcheting up entry fines on heritable copyholds.[30] When peasants could not pay, landlords evicted them, engrossing their copyholds and converting them to leasehold.[31] Eviction was endemic to the English Midlands from 1485 at the latest.[32]

Whereas the tributary rent relation gave rise to manorial courts, the competitive rent relation swept them aside. Manorial courts were custodians of the historical tributary rent bargain in each locality. As such, they often upheld customary rents against the local landlord's desire for a higher market rent. In response, landlords turned their tributary-coercive power – once used to establish manorial courts – to the task of destroying them. One strategy was to boycott the court, rendering it defunct.[33] Another was to appeal to Parliament, which represented the collective power of all landlords.[34] A landlord could petition for 'ascertainment', wherein a Parliamentary surveyor would examine the manorial roll for evidence of a fixed customary fine.[35] Unless the custom was formally recorded, as it rarely was, Parliament would back the landlord to raise entry fines over and against the manorial court and customary tenant, leading to eviction.[36]

Alongside formal authority, enclosing landlords and lease-hungry yeomen used direct violence and intimidation to enclose.[37] Yeoman tactics included, for instance, sending cattle to destroy copyholders' arable, even while offering to buy them out.[38] Lords and farmers demolished bridges or allowed them to decay to block customary byways.[39] In other cases they obstructed commons and byways or over-stocked the commons on which peasants relied.[40] Farmers would extend their fencing to encroach on common land.[41] Where most plots in a village had been bought out, engrossed, fallen empty, or cleared out legally, the remaining peasants would be driven off the land.[42]

As the competitive rent relation drove landlords, in league with capitalists, to rack up local rents, evict peasants, and enclose, it manifested its *proletarianising* tendency. By separating peasants from the soil, the competitive rent relation simultaneously made them dependent on wage labour to survive. Once competitive rents had swept peasants into the proletariat, ongoing high rents corralled them in intergenerational landlessness. As Dyer points out, future population increases henceforth *automatically* added to the proletariat.[43]

The capitalist rent relation and proletarianisation were mutually reinforcing. By driving peasants off the land, the rent relation increased the labour supply, pushing wages down and profits up, stoking farmers' demand for new leaseholds, driving up rents, and creating further impetus to enclose. From the mid-sixteenth to mid-seventeenth centuries, the living standards of England's working population fell as those of landlords and farmers steadily rose.[44]

As the capitalist rent relation sloughed peasants off the land, the supply of wage labour grew and wages fell, making new, labour-intensive capitalist industries profitable.[45] Medieval manufacturing towns and their artisanal guilds, tributary relics, were bypassed for new rural industrial centres that processed the products of agrarian capitalism using rural proletarian labour.[46] Alongside clothiers appeared mills and breweries.[47] Early industrial capitalists produced both for export and to meet the growing domestic consumer demand from expropriated peasants now reliant on the market for necessities.[48] The nascent state saw industrial jobs as a solution to the unemployment and social dislocation attending these processes, so it promoted industrial diversification and import substitution.[49]

English commerce and industry had originally been animated by tributary rents, representing elite demand and consumption. The capitalist rent relation now supercharged commerce and industry with proletarian labour and proletarian consumer demand, radically expanding and transforming it. London became the chief distribution point for the new national consumer market, the largest urban centre of consumption, and the main gateway for foreign trade and colonialism.[50] Rural industrial districts established trade links directly with London, demoting the old medieval towns to 'internal distribution or import and export centres' for capitalist commodities.[51] All these processes trace to the proletarianising capitalist rent relation.

CAPITALIST RENT AND STATE FORMATION

The development of the English Crown into a state was deeply related to the emergence of the capitalist rent relation. Žmolek hints at the connection when he links English lords being 'increasingly dependent upon rents derived from strictly economic leases' to their willingness to demilitarise.[52] As lords pursued economic rents within the competitive rent relation, concomitantly fostering capitalist agriculture, old strategies of political accumulation became unattractive.

Intra-lordly militarism drained rents that could now be more profitably invested in enclosure or improvement. This was brought home in the late fifteenth century by the Wars of the Roses, an exceptional breakdown of English landed-class solidarity, in which lords squandered great resources battling over royal succession. When landlord solidarity finally recohered around the Tudors, the English nobility rapidly and finally demilitarised, allowing it to focus on economic accumulation through the new competitive rent relation.[53]

The capitalist rent relation encouraged lords to take actions which necessarily transformed the Crown into a modern state. As lords demilitarised to pursue economic rents, they implicitly ceded a military monopoly to the Crown. As landlords enclosed lands and disbanded their manorial courts, they concomitantly gave the King's assizes both a universal legal jurisdiction in property matters, and primary responsibility for enforcing the territorial control on which the rent relation rested.[54] Hence, the Tudor period was characterised by the development of state institutions and a growing central bureaucracy.[55] Tellingly, the term 'state' came into use – referring to an institutional totality of which the monarch was only one organ.[56]

As the capitalist rent relation generated an English state, it simultaneously generated a national civil society. When landlords demilitarised and abandoned manorial jurisdiction in pursuit of commercial rents, they implicitly dissolved the boundaries that had segmented feudal society. The political apparatus of the state became national, mediating relations between every subject in a universal, demilitarised, and hence 'civil', society.[57] The existence of a national civil society was expressed in property rights that held good throughout the kingdom. Whether a subject had property in land, capital, or just his own labour power, the national state would enforce his rights therein against all others, coercively guaranteeing 'civil' relations.

The Crown had a contradictory position in relation to the advancing capitalist rent relation. On the one hand, the capitalist rent relation drove upheaval that threatened the state and Crown. As Dimmock observes, the Crown feared enclosure would lead to 'public disorder due to starvation, dislocation and … invasion due to depopulation of coastal areas'.[58] Likewise, as Martin observes, dislocation compromised the Crown's ability to extract tallage and raise armies.[59] On the other hand, as I have shown, the capitalist rent relation was progressively consolidating the state's monopoly on force and expanding Crown jurisdiction.

Contradictory interests produced a contradictory posture. The Crown resisted enclosure, but weakly and transiently. Its efforts peaked in the late fifteenth and early sixteenth centuries.[60] From 1489 the Crown introduced statutes to prevent depopulation and excessive specialisation, but these were undermined by the lords and farmers on whom the Crown relied to enforce them.[61] During Henry VIII's reign, the royal courts developed legal remedies for copyholders, though few copyholders could access the royal courts.[62] The Crown also supported peasants by upholding clerical jurisdiction over enclosure disputes, but this only protected those who happened to be tenants-at-will.[63] Even as the Crown officially resisted enclosure, enclosing lords had great influence in the King's courts, and often in the royal household.[64]

Ultimately, the landed class also applied fiscal pressure, through Parliament, to coopt the Crown in advancing enclosure and capitalist rent. In the wake of the Reformation, the Crown's fiscal weakness forced it to sell clerical courts to landlords, who promptly dismantled them, along with the protections they offered to customary tenants. Likewise, as the Crown liquidated clerical lands for finance it acquiesced to these being enclosed.[65] The Tudor inflation – partly resulting from the Crown resorting to debasement as public finance – gave landlords additional incentive to rack rents and enclose.[66] Enclosures could not be legally effected without the Crown's consent, and yet it used this leverage not to block enclosure but to fill its coffers. In the fifteenth and sixteenth centuries, the Crown imposed fines on enclosures.[67] In the seventeenth century, the Crown granted enclosures in exchange for loans and political influence.[68] From the early seventeenth century, the Crown's financial desperation led it to effect its own enclosures – exploiting forests and common lands, and draining and farming wetland fens in the east of England.[69]

By the seventeenth century, then, the Crown was deeply entangled in the capitalist rent relation.[70] It was not only facilitating and sharing in the profits of lords' enclosure but also enclosing its own lands. As the productive base of society shifted from tributary to capitalist agriculture, Parliamentary taxation increasingly rested on capitalist rents, the profits of agrarian capital, and levies on proletarian consumers' goods, rather than peasant tribute. Enclosure progressively transferred jurisdiction over landed property from manorial to royal courts.[71] The rent relation's coercive foundations rested ever more heavily on the juridical and coercive apparatus of the Crown. The Crown became integral to the advance of capitalist rent, and, by extension, to capitalist social-property relations.

CAPITALIST RENT AGAINST CROWN RENT

Even as the capitalist rent relation relied on an expanded state, it was haunted by the spectre of absolutism. Absolutism was the perennial monarchical ambition to dominate local lords and build up the fiscal, bureaucratic, and military capacities of the state machine, as the basis of centralised *tributary* social-property relations.

Wood has highlighted the fundamental conflict between absolutism and capitalist rent extraction. Capitalist landlords, she observes, wanted 'a state that maintained order and sustained their own absolute property rights. They certainly did not want monarchs ... [with] their own economic interests and resources in competition with the landed class'.[72] The unrestrained demands of an absolutist monarch could sap landlords' rents and farmers' profits. It could drain the newfound circuits of capitalist economic accumulation by diverting social surplus into projects of political accumulation centring on the Crown. Absolutism could overwhelm the capitalist rent relation by reinstating a state-centred system of tributary social-property relations. By the sixteenth century, absolutist projects were ascendant across continental Europe.

On the surface, historical relations between England's lords and the Tudor and Stuart monarchies appear driven by contingent events and historical personalities, not least the monarchs themselves. In this section, however, I argue a deeper logic was at play: long-term relations between lords and Crown were driven by an existential struggle between the ascendant capitalist rent relation and the old tributary machinery of Crown rent. England's landlords, advancing under the standard of the capitalist rent relation, laid a multigenerational fiscal siege on the machinery of Crown rent, ultimately destroying that machinery through a regicidal republican revolution. With the material basis of the Crown's autonomy destroyed, along with the germ of tributary absolutism, monarchs could no longer threaten the capitalist rent relation. The Restoration monarchy and state, I will argue, was subordinated to the capitalist landed class, inaugurating the first project of truly capitalist statecraft.

In the English context, the danger of tributary absolutism issued partly from the logic of capitalist rent itself. As I have shown, landlords' pursuit of economic rents led them to demilitarisation and enclosure, which implied a relative expansion of the central state, militarily and juridically. Further, as landlords became dependent on world markets via their export-oriented capitalist tenants, they found themselves with a unique set of 'international military, commercio-colonial, and religious objectives'.[73] The attainment of these depended on a 'strong state', especially in military terms.[74] Inasmuch as the capitalist rent relation demanded a stronger state, it flirted with tributary absolutism.

To protect the capitalist rent relation from the threat of absolutism, the landed class had to extinguish the Crown's fiscal autonomy. Despite its fiscal reliance on Parliamentary subsidies doled out by the landed class, the Crown retained a substantial autonomous capacity to extract arbitrary Crown rents. England's capitalist landlords worried the Crown might parlay even the slightest fiscal autonomy into a tributary-absolutist apparatus, threatening the capitalist rent relation. The landed class thus set its sights on tightening its fiscal grip on the Crown and, ultimately, dismantling the machinery of Crown rent.

For similar reasons, the landed class challenged the Crown's autonomy on foreign policy. Even if fiscal discipline was imposed domestically, the Crown might build an absolutist machinery through contact with a continental tributary power – through alliance, agglomeration, subordination or conquest. Accordingly, in the century before the English Civil War the landed class disputed the Crown's foreign policy.[75] The landed class pressed for a Protestant foreign policy that would advance its capitalist commercial and proprietary interests, such as an alliance with Protestant and nascently capitalist Holland. The Crown, by contrast, was all too willing to countenance alliances with Catholic tributary-absolutist states.

Commencing its siege on Crown autonomy, from the mid-sixteenth to mid-seventeenth centuries, Parliament imposed a strict fiscal discipline on the Crown. Parliament increasingly made its financial support conditional upon the monarch's compliance with Parliamentary spending and foreign policy priorities. The Crown had become sufficiently dependent on Parliamentary taxation that Parliament could force it into a structural deficit, and thereby corral it fiscally. Bonney has found that despite 'modest economic progress' during both the Tudor and Stuart ages, 'the state appropriated and spent a declining share of the nation's income' from the Tudor age onward.[76] As Clay observes, revenue constraints on the Crown in this period were 'political rather than economic'.[77]

As the fiscal vice tightened on it, the Crown tried to squeeze more from the machinery of Crown rent. In 1540–1541, Henry VIII set up the Court of Wards and Liveries, tasked with systematically extracting dues from feudal tenures. Although hated by landlords, the Court's exactions were firmly grounded in tradition. Yet, even as the state tried to ramp up Crown rents, its capacity to extract them eroded. Most feudal incidents were fixed nominally and could not be adjusted without confronting the landed class. In an epoch of inflation, the Crown had chronic problems preserving the real value of its rents.[78] The Crown made matters worse for itself in exploiting its control of the currency. Between 1542 and 1551, the Crown heavily debased its coinage to fund military expenditure, contributing to rapid inflation between 1550 and 1560.[79] Debasement bought the Crown short-term military-fiscal autonomy, but it eroded that autonomy in the long term by inflating away the value of its rents.

The Crown bought short-term autonomy at long-term expense through land sales. The sale of monastic lands, commencing in 1539, met Henry VIII's thirst for military finance but represented the loss of vast potential rents. Lachmann suggests this was the Crown's final real opportunity to build an absolutist state.[80] This contention, however, implies an illusory freedom of action on the Crown's part. Due to the Crown's longstanding integration with the landed class, Henry could not have undertaken his Reformation without landed support, and liquidating monastic estates was the price. Thus blocked from augmenting the machinery of Crown rent, the Crown continued to supplement its revenues through sporadic land sales over the next 100 years. Including gifts to royal servants and courtiers, around 25 per cent of the land in England had been sold off by 1642.[81] Between 1558 and 1635, land sales afforded the Crown revenues of around £2,240,000.[82] While these divestments produced short-term windfalls, whether financial, military, or political, the Crown's capacity to extract demesne rents, and hence its autonomy from the landed class, was drastically reduced in the long term.

The period from the ascension of James Stuart in 1603 to the outbreak of civil war in 1642 was characterised by escalating conflict between the Crown and landlords.[83] The Crown's autonomy was the underlying matter of contention. Notwithstanding the Tudor fiscal stopgaps, and in Elizabeth's case her famous frugality, when the last Tudor died in 1603 the Crown was still in debt to the tune of £400,000. With Parliament rarely willing to grant subsidies, the Stuart Crown adapted by deploying its dwindling autonomous capacity to extract rents – its so-called 'prerogatives' – in creative but inevitably provocative ways. It ratcheted up its fines, especially on old military tenures, exploited its rights of wardship, imposed forced loans, shifted military costs onto landowners through billeting, demanded 'gifts' from wealthy individuals, and granted monopolies, patents, and licences on consumers' goods.[84] The Crown's ancient right to commandeer ships from coastal towns in emergencies became a de facto naval tax – so-called 'ship money'. The prerogative of purveyance – originally an obligation of hospitality to the travelling monarch – was exploited to provision the court. Customs revenues were collected more systematically.[85] Nevertheless, the structural deficit remained.

By the early seventeenth century, the Crown was ready to bargain. In 1610, the Crown offered to abolish the despised Court of Wards, in exchange for a one-off subsidy of £600,000 to retire its debts, plus a permanent annual income of £200,000, to be raised by a land tax.[86] James would not, however, offer up the Crown's autonomy in spending or foreign policy. The Commons rejected James' proposal, cleaving to the old doctrine that the Crown should meet its own ordinary expenses.[87] In retort it proposed a 'Great Contract' wherein it would purchase the Crown's prerogatives at face value.[88] The value of royal prerogatives, however, lay not just in the revenue they could raise directly, but in the inconvenience they could visit on the landed class as a means of extorting Parliamentary subsidies. The Crown would not, therefore, trade them at face value, and the bargaining foundered.

Following the failure of the Great Contract, a stalemate ensued, with the Crown's underlying fiscal position growing ever weaker and Parliament's hand ever stronger. Parliament increasingly attacked Crown prerogatives as illegitimate and made subsidies conditional on giving them up. The Crown tried to preserve its autonomy by ruling, so far as possible, without Parliament.

Parliament gained the upper hand, however, when the Crown became embroiled in the Thirty Years War. In 1624, desperate for finance, James summoned Parliament. The Commons granted only a fraction of what he sought, and passed legislation curtailing his power to grant monopolies and to pursue landlords encroaching on Crown land. In 1628, James' successor Charles again resorted to Parliament for war finance. This time, the Parliament presented the Petition of Right.[89] It asserted the illegality of key Crown prerogatives: non-Parliamentary taxation, forced loans, and billeting. Parliament also asserted the illegality of key mechanisms by which prerogative exactions were enforced: seizures of property, imprisonment, disinheritance, and martial law.[90] Desperate for finance, Charles agreed to give the petition legal effect.[91]

The struggle between Crown and Parliament for control of the state culminated in civil war. Charles ruled without a Parliament from 1629 to 1640, relying on a mixture of frugality, Crown rents, and avoiding foreign entanglements.[92] From 1637, however, he became mired in a complex set of conflicts that would escalate into civil war across his three kingdoms.[93] At the end of 1640, in dire straits, Charles called what would be known as the Long Parliament. In 1641, the King offered, in return for finance, to give up 'what parts of my revenue … shall be found illegal or grievous to the public'.[94] He conceded the extinguishment of ship money and his right to fine Crown tenants who failed to take up knighthoods.[95] Even this undertaking, however, did not move Parliament to provide finance. On 5 March 1642, Parliament passed an ordinance taking control of England's militia, and on 15 March, after the King refused Royal Assent, Parliament resolved that Royal Assent was not required 'in Case of extreme Danger, and of His Majesty's Refusal'.[96] This unprecedented assertion of Parliamentary sovereignty crystallised a constitutional breakdown that would play out in two civil wars between Royalist and Parliamentary forces (1642–1646, 1648–1649).

By the outbreak of civil war, the Crown was politically isolated. The measures it had taken to shore up Crown rents had been highly unpopular. From the early seventeenth century, the Crown's attempts to boost its rents had led it to enclose and exploit forests and common lands, and to drain and farm the wetland fens in the east of England.[97] As a result of landlords' tax evasion, the burden of such Parliamentary subsidies as the Crown could extract had come to fall ever more heavily on 'the lesser gentry, the commercial farmers and the artisans and tradespeople of the towns'.[98] Prerogative rents, like ship money, likewise fell heavily on the middling sort.[99] Finally, in the upper reaches of society, prerogative taxation fell not just on landlords, but on the overseas company merchants who were the Crown's traditional allies.[100] As Hill has observed, 'the financial measures to which … [the Crown] was forced to resort alienated its potential supporters no less than its enemies'.[101]

The English Revolution consisted most fundamentally in the landed class seizing the machinery of state from the Crown. In 1645, Parliament established the New Model Army.[102] It was composed of professional soldiers and conscripts, many drawn from 'the middling sort', and many with strong puritan and republican convictions.[103] The New Model Army, backed by what Brenner calls a 'socioeconomically and politically unified landed class', confronted a relatively isolated monarch 'and his limited number of supporters'.[104] After defeating the royalists between 1645 and 1648, however, the New Model Army asserted itself as an autonomous political actor.[105] It forcibly purged the Commons of members who favoured re-instating Charles.[106] Captured by the Army, the so-called 'Rump Parliament' put Charles to death in January 1649 and declared a Commonwealth in May. Parliament did not regain control of the Army until 1660, when the monarchy was restored. The landed class fell in behind Oliver Cromwell, a leading military figure who could mediate between landlords' interests, as expressed in Parliament, and the 'middling sort' whose power base was in the Army.[107] Cromwell dominated Parliament from 1649 to 1653 and ruled as Lord Protector from 1653 to 1659.

Having sidelined the Crown, the landed class was finally free to dismantle the institutional basis of the Crown's autonomy and its potential for absolutism: the machinery of Crown rent. In February 1646, the *Ordinance for Removing the Court of Wards* abolished all Crown rents applying to lands held directly by the Crown ('tenures *in capite*').[108] The administrative machinery of the Court was also abolished.[109] Knights fees, by which the Crown had for centuries extracted revenues from lords, were sweepingly converted to freehold titles ('Free and Common Soccage').[110] These measures negated the material basis of the Crown as an autonomous class fraction with the capacity to extract tribute. They represented the decisive victory of the capitalist rent relation over its tributary predecessor – the triumph of capitalist over tributary rent.

Having used its 'federal' fiscal-administrative integration to starve and seize the state, the landed class now used that same integration, and its capitalist rents, to reinvigorate the state.[111] Parliament imposed a land tax, channelling landlords' rents to support first the Parliamentary Army and later the republican regime. Clay estimates a 75–80 per cent increase in tax revenues from the 1630s to the 1650s.[112] Landlords who paid no tax in 1640 were paying a peak rate of 10–20 per cent by the late 1640s.[113] Because of its longstanding integration into England's tax machinery, the landed class could also exact tribute from the population at large. In 1643, for the first time, a wide range of domestically produced consumer goods – both luxuries and basics – were subject to excise duties.[114] Between 1646 and 1654, the Parliamentary and Commonwealth regimes also derived significant additional finance by disposing of land seized from the bishops, deans and chapters, the Crown and royalists. £5 million worth of land was confiscated and sold.[115]

England's landed class emerged from its showdown with the tributary Crown victorious but fractured. To break a centuries-old balance of power and fully subordinate the Crown, they had resorted to mobilising a volatile middle-class popular movement under the banner of republicanism. It was a risky and divisive strategy that cleaved landlords into radical and conservative camps.[116] Cromwell, with the backing of Parliament and landlords, had managed to mobilise the 'middling sort' while containing their more radical democratic ambitions.[117] But even a limited republicanism forced landlords to appease 'middling' interests in ways unnecessary when landlords had been united under the Crown.

Eventually, radical and conservative landlords recoalesced and brought down the republic. They used similar means as they had used to upend the monarchy, including a tax strike.[118] When the republic collapsed in 1659, Parliament invited Charles II to resume his father's throne. Charles promised no reprisals, and to leave the settlement of his rights to 'a free Parliament'.[119] By 1660, capitalist landlords were reunited under the banner of a domesticated monarch.[120]

While the monarchy was restored, the machinery of Crown rent was not. The *Tenures Abolition Act* of 1660 confirmed the abolition of feudal tenures, including military tenures, purveyance and the Court of Wards and Liveries.[121] The Crown's capacity to extract demesne rents was practically destroyed. Crown lands had yielded rents of £100,000 per year on the eve of the civil war.[122] To secure Restoration, the Crown conceded the preponderance of its demesne. In the eleven years following the Restoration, the Crown's total rents dwindled to just £12,000 a year.[123]

With the spectre of tributary absolutism destroyed, and the republican genie stuffed back in its bottle, Parliament could loosen the fiscal noose, beginning a project of truly capitalist statecraft. Parliament granted the Crown, now totally dependent fiscally, an annual income of £1,200,000 to meet the expenses of the state. This income would be raised not through a tax on rents – as James had once proposed – but through excises that fell on the general populace.[124] These vastly increased revenues did not represent a rising absolutism. The capitalist landed class, through Parliament, had become the sole arbiters of the Crown's capacity to exact tribute. Henceforth, the state could exact tribute only *in service* of the capitalist rent relation – and hence in service of capital – and not in competition with it.

CAPITALIST RENT AND THE PROTESTANT REFORMATION

As I showed in Chapter 2, the Church was part of England's lordly class, with vast estates and special ideological and international coordination functions. But Church tithes ate into landlords' rents, and the Papacy's international interests often clashed with those of England's landlords and Crown. These tensions fuelled a simmering tradition of anti-clerical heresy. With the arrival of English Protestantism, tensions boiled over. Here I argue that the development of the capitalist rent relation fed the English Reformation and vice versa.

Protestantism arrived in the 1530s, as the tense alliance between spiritual and temporal lordship decisively collapsed. Henry VIII broke with the Papacy and assumed leadership of the English Church. He confiscated monastic lands *en masse* between 1536 and 1540.[125] This dissolved the Church as an autonomous class fraction. The question remained, however, as to how the spoils would be divided among the Crown and lords.

England's capitalist landlords sought a Reformation that eliminated the Church's competing claims on their rents without augmenting the Crown's tributary power. Had the Crown retained England's vast monastic lands, its augmented rents could have provided a material basis for a tributary absolutism that threatened the nascent capitalist rent relation. However, as landlords operated the Crown's fiscal and administrative machinery, the Crown could not move against the Church without landlords' support. The price of that support was selling the seized ecclesiastical estates and tithe rights, mostly to the landlords.[126] Instead of augmenting its rents, the Crown attained only a cash windfall.[127] Unable to expand domestically, the Crown attempted to convert its windfall into new, foreign sources of rent through military adventures. These, however, came to nothing, and the Crown's tributary machinery would enter a terminal decline.

Once in landlords' hands, monastic lands were quickly metabolised by the capitalist rent relation. Tithes became 'a particular species of property, collateral to the land'.[128] The once-distinct streams of spiritual and temporal rent became increasingly comingled, flowing as one into landlords' coffers.[129] Whereas the Church spent rent and managed estates according to feudal ideological practices, which included 'hospitality and charity', as well as paying tribute to Rome, the landlords pursued competitive rents and 'returns on investment'.[130] Former monastic estates became 'the main sites of quick and drastic enclosures and evictions after the Reformation'.[131]

The Crown absorbed the episcopate, which became an ideological pillar of England's nascent capitalist state.[132] But the local parishes were sold off to England's landlords. Landlords purchased the right to appoint parish ministers ('advowsons'), as well as control of each parish church, parsonage and ministerial stipend ('benefices').[133] As Hill has shown, landlords bought these rights and used them to sponsor a puritan Protestantism that favoured improvement, defended landlords, was hostile to the poor, and opposed Crown and episcopal domination of the Church.[134] Protestant theology emphasised 'the duty of hard and regular work in one's calling, labour discipline, austerity, thrift, monogamy: the bourgeois virtues'.[135] Where Catholicism had defended feudal rent under the banner of lordship, Protestantism defended capitalist rent, capitalist property and state authority.[136]

To conclude, in this chapter I have shown that England's uniquely federalised rent relation underwent a unique endogenous transformation in the fourteenth century. It mutated to adapt to a crisis precipitated by its own dynamics. It mutated into a competitive relation, stimulating leaseholding yeomen to become capitalists.

The new competitive rent relation also supplied landlords with the means and incentive to enclose and evict husbandmen, proletarianising the English peasantry, and gradually universalising capitalist social-property relations in England. I extended the argument by showing that the modern English state was a direct outgrowth of the capitalist rent relation's expansion. I showed how the showdown between England's Parliament and Crown in the seventeenth century represented a final confrontation between capitalist and tributary rent, in which the residue of Crown rent and the germ of tributary absolutism were decisively extirpated. Finally, I explained how England's Protestant Reformation erupted from longstanding tensions in the tributary rent relation and fed capitalist rent's expansion.

These strands of argument combine to show that, in every important respect, England's transition to capitalism represented an endogenous transformation. Tributary social-property relations generated capitalism through their own dynamics. Rent is the mother of capital.

6

Resistance and critique in transition

Peasant resistance was widespread as the capitalist rent relation drove its wavefront of enclosure across the England countryside. In his case study of the Lydd area, Dimmock identified resistance to enclosure by 'highly committed individuals' from the middle of the fifteenth century.[1] He documented sixteenth-century efforts to resist enclosure, both through local and royal courts, as well as unlawful resistance such as 'hedge picking and sheep stealing'.[2] Resistance became widespread in the sixteenth and early seventeenth centuries, as peasants rioted against and razed local enclosures, and instigated occasional large-scale rebellions.[3] Across England there were struggles for forests, fens, and commons as landlords sought to enclose and exploit them.[4] Self-organised peasant armies put up stiff resistance to enclosure in the 1530s and 1540s.[5] Large-scale rebellions reached their peak in 1548–1549, when the ruling class was stretched by war and internal divisions.[6] However, even facing great uprisings such as Kett's Rebellion, the ruling class prevailed.[7] In the century after 1549, resistance took on a more muted expression in localised struggles.[8] In the seventeenth century, while the ruling class was divided by civil war, the peasantry successfully reclaimed some enclosures from the Crown.[9] But this was a swansong; resistance ultimately failed. Why though?

The peasantry's failure to halt enclosure traces to the rent relation's own reproductive logic, and especially to tributary-coercive power. While enclosure posed a fundamentally new kind of threat to English peasants, what lurked behind it was the same federalised tributary power which had bested them for centuries. Moreover, the capitalist rent relation propagated itself in ways that undermined strategies peasants had traditionally used to resist lordly power. As seen in Chapter 2, the tributary rent relation had functioned by immobilising the peasantry. Corralling peasants allowed landlords to extract greater tribute, but it also protected local peasantries from outside competition for tenancies. This resulted in a plethora of local political rent-bargains, crystallised in manorial custom. The capitalist rent relation, by contrast, was premised on competition and tenant mobility. By eliciting competition from wealthy outsiders, it circumvented local rent-bargains.[10] Moreover, even within localities, the competitive logic of capitalist rent undermined solidarity between poor and rich peasants. As it uprooted the former through enclosing and encroaching upon copyholds, it offered their richer neighbours, often freeholders, the opportunity to become leaseholding agrarian capitalists. Thus, the upper stratum of peasants rallied not to the aid of their poorer fellows but to seigneurial power, weakening peasant resistance and hastening the propagation of the capitalist rent relation.

LEVELLERS AND THE RENT RELATION

As the capitalist rent relation bifurcated the peasantry into capitalists and proletarians, market-oriented production and proletarian consumer spending supercharged growth in the commercial classes. With this new capitalist configuration of classes, subaltern resistance began to take on new and distinctively modern forms. As we will see, even as the capitalist rent relation corralled these classes into capitalist dynamics, it opened novel opportunities for resistance. As I argued in the last chapter, the turmoil of mid-seventeenth-century England was pivotal for the advancing capitalist rent relation. It was the climax of a long-building tension between capitalist and Crown rent, from which the former would emerge victorious. But until then, ruling class disunity would enable a brief and unique wave of subaltern resistance and critique. The 1620s to 1640s was a period of economic depression and hardship, characterised by 'intense social unrest and class conflict'.[11]

A key movement that challenged the capitalist rent relation in this period, albeit laterally, was the Levellers. The Levellers were thrust into the centre of England's political stage in the 1640s, as conflict between Parliament and Crown reached its climax. To overcome the Crown and its allies, key elements of the landlord-controlled Parliament allied with London's new-merchant establishment and 'a London mass movement composed of non-merchant citizens drawn from the ranks of retail shopkeepers, mariners, and artisans'.[12] Partnering with a mass movement was fraught for the landed class. As Brenner has argued, a mass movement could 'threaten hierarchy, endanger the oligarchic control of politics traditionally exercised by the landed classes and urban elites, and place new, unwanted programmes on the political agenda'.[13] One of those 'unwanted programmes' was that of the Levellers, who composed a crucial element of the mass movement.

At first blush, the Levellers' political programme seems quite removed from the capitalist rent relation. Levellers were primarily urban and political in their aims.[14] Chief among their political goals was a universal franchise. As Žmolek has argued, the Levellers' programme was a universalisation of the democratic governance practised among the urban craftsmen and London trading company men that made up the movement.[15] As middling urbanites, then, they had limited connections to rural society as it faced down the rent relation's proletarianising advance. Brailsford observes that the 'Agreement' of May Day 1649 – the most important manifesto of the Leveller programme – was entirely silent on 'the agrarian question'.[16]

Nevertheless, the Levellers threatened the capitalist rent relation indirectly. As I argued in Chapter 5, demilitarised capitalist landlords became reliant on the state to uphold landed property and extract rent. To secure the capitalist rent relation then, they were compelled to seek total control of the state and to wrest that control from a waning tributary Crown. In the throes of that struggle, however, the Levellers' interjected their own vision: a reformed, democratic state which, instead of advancing landed interests, would defend the middling sort against them. The Levellers rejected as 'tyrants and opressors' not only the Crown but the landlord-stacked Parliament.[17] In claiming for themselves the state machinery on which capitalist rent rested, the Levellers indirectly threatened the rent relation itself.

The threat became direct when the Levellers sought to ally with the ailing peasantry. Seventeenth-century English society was still predominantly agrarian. It was inconceivable that the

Levellers could propose a democratic franchise that excluded peasants, nor achieve their programme without peasant support. But the Levellers realised peasants' vulnerability to eviction would undermine any franchise granted them.[18] Insecure copyholders, in 'awe' of their landlords, would vote at their behest.[19] Democracy could only flourish if the peasantry was 'so securely planted on the soil that it ... dared to stand erect'.[20] For the Levellers, as Brailsford writes, '[t]he obvious solution was to turn the copyholder into a peasant owner'.[21] Moves in this direction were modest. One Leveller manifesto, for instance, proposed that copyholders be given the right to 'purchase themselves freeholders'.[22] This right did little to rally most peasants who were too poor to exercise it.[23] Another proposal – to rationalise heterogeneous tributary obligations into 'a certain rent' – was similarly modest.[24] Nonetheless, any move to strengthen peasant tenure directly obstructed the advance of capitalist rent.

The Levellers' political ambitions for the poor traversed the capitalist rent relation even more radically than their plans for the peasantry. In seventeenth-century England, 'the poor' increasingly comprised the growing class of landless wage labourers sloughed off the land by the advancing capitalist rent relation.[25] While not a proletarian movement, the Levellers recognised the imperative to incorporate this rapidly growing class into their democratic vision. In July 1647, the Leveller leader Richard Overton made the following proposal:

> That all grounds which anciently lay in Common for the poore, and are now impropriate, inclosed, and fenced in, may forthwith (in whose hands soever they are) be cast out, and laid open againe to the free and common use and benefit of the poore.[26]

Overton and other Levellers made similar proposals as long as the movement endured.[27] Security of peasant tenure would only have halted the capitalist rent relation's advance. Whereas resettling proletarians on the land, if successful, would have entirely routed the capitalist rent relation. It would have driven agrarian capital off the land and starved it of wage labour.

Levellers further traversed the capitalist rent relation by opposing the tithe. They resented the burden it placed on the middling sort. Radical Levellers called for the abolition of tithes, while moderates called for their replacement with 'a moderate and certain rent charge'.[28] Since the Dissolution of the Monasteries, spiritual rents had been subsumed into the overall rents extracted by capitalist landlords. To interfere with the tithe was to interfere with the rent relation.

Given Levellers' various insults to the capitalist rent relation, it is unsurprising that the landed class ultimately united to crush them. The Levellers had support in the city and that of freemen in the Parliamentary Army.[29] Civilian Levellers looked to their comrades in the Army to carry through their political programme.[30] While many soldiers were Levellers, the Army's officers, Cromwellian Grandees, had deep links with the landed class. Hence, once the Crown was defeated in the Civil War, the landed oligarchy no longer needed its alliance with an urban mass movement. Cromwell's Grandees could turn on the Levellers.

Had the peasantry and the poor rallied to the Levellers, they might have prevailed; as it was, however, the Levellers had done 'enough for the tenants' cause to provoke Cromwell and the gentry ... but not enough to mobilise the villages'.[31] The landed class and capitalist rent relation prevailed. It is telling that when, some years later, Cromwell reflected on the Levellers before Parliament, he focused not so much on their democratic ideals, or their quest for power, but on the threat they posed to rent. By reducing 'all to an equality', Cromwell observed, levelling threatened to 'make the tenant as liberal a fortune as the landlord'.[32] Cromwell had perceived in the Levellers a vivid threat to the capitalist rent relation, and the landed class had rallied to him.

THE DIGGER CRITIQUE

If the Levellers comprised an urban movement that flourished in the interstices of ruling class discord, the Diggers or True Levellers were its rural counterpart. The term 'Diggers' is indelibly associated with the group led by Gerrard Winstanley, but the conditions of early seventeenth-century England generated Diggers more than once. At moments when seigneurial authority slacked, groups of landless labourers organised spontaneously to dig, plant crops, and build houses on commons and wastes. An early Digger movement arose in 1607, only to be put down and its leader hanged.[33] In 1648–1649, rural Levellers in Buckinghamshire would express similar sentiments to Winstanley's Diggers.[34] Rural Levellers in Aylesbury declared their support for Winstanley, while Kent produced its own Digger colony.[35] Another group of Diggers sprang up under the leadership of Richard Smith in Wellingborough.[36] The Diggers, like the Levellers, were a 'temporary phenomenon'.[37] By the second half of the century the ruling class would reunify its factions and outbreaks of digging would be thoroughly suppressed.

As the experience of the St George's Hill Diggers illustrates, digging challenged the rent relation by directly confronting the coercive power at its foundation. In April 1649, amidst the chaos of civil war, Gerrard Winstanley and six landless comrades began digging and ploughing the commons at St George's Hill.[38] They paid no rent and sought no tenure. The group soon swelled to several dozen.

Local landowners quickly brought their means of coercion to bear. They brought state power to bear through legal suits and repeated arrests. They also exerted personal coercion, harassing and beating the Diggers, and seizing their livestock.

The Diggers soon abandoned St George's Hill and, in the same year, migrated to the commons of Cobham Manor, owned by the rector of West Horsley. They built four houses and tilled the soil. Again, the landed class used violence. In October and November, the rector called in troops to disperse Digger assemblies and pull down their houses. The Diggers persisted, and by April 1650 they had built seven new houses and raised eleven acres of corn. At Easter the rector sent a gang which destroyed one house and assaulted its pregnant occupant, causing her to miscarry. After a brief dialogue with Winstanley, the rector sent in another gang to burn the remaining houses. The Diggers were routed and the landed class had defended the land.

Winstanley and other Digger intellectuals produced a substantial body of thought. The significance of the Diggers to this book lies partly in their production of proletarian social theory and, specifically, their critique of the rent relation. At first blush, the Diggers' theological idiom militates against seeing them as social theorists.[39] But as I will show, Digger intellectuals used theological concepts to frame proletarian material interests. And they used theory in much the same way as the intellectuals of other subaltern movements: to orient their movement within their society, to articulate their interests and objectives, and to formulate strategies to achieve them. And in doing so, they developed the first proletarian theories of early modern social-property relations, including both rent and capital.[40]

The Diggers articulated the material interests of England's subaltern classes using theological concepts. From the theological concept of Sonship, the Diggers established universal equal freedom as a fundamental social norm or claim. Sonship was the idea that Christ, the Son of God, was within each human being.[41] Every human being, then, shared the same divine essence and dignity. While the doctrine was a common seventeenth-century heresy, the Diggers believed it had radical social implications: 'all men by Gods donation are all alike free by birth'.[42] Universal freedom implied an *equality* of freedom. Because mankind was 'created male and female after Gods own Image ...', Winstanley wrote, every man 'should walk in ... Equity towards his own kind'.[43] For the Diggers, Sonship was synonymous with the phrase 'equal freedom'.[44]

The Diggers used a further norm to articulate subaltern material interests: the right to the fruits of labour. They derived this right from the divine injunction to toil. As the Diggers of Wellingborough wrote, God had set man to 'till and dresse' the Earth, '[t]hat in the sweat of his brows he should eat his bread'.[45] Consistent with this divine injunction, the Diggers concluded, man had a right to the fruits of his labour. '[L]et every one injoy the benefit of his Creation', wrote Winstanley, 'to have food and rayment free by the labour of his hands from the earth'.[46] This was the positive dimension of the right to the fruits of labour. The Diggers also formulated this right in the negative: 'those that work not', Winstanley said, 'have no right to eat'.[47] For the Diggers, the right to the fruits of labour implied the duty to labour for one's subsistence.

Closely related to the right to the fruits of labour, the Diggers also asserted a universal right to the earth. 'God made the Earth', wrote the Wellingborough Diggers, 'for the use and comfort of all Mankind'.[48] In line with the equal freedom mandated by Sonship, the right to the earth was enjoyed by all humanity. '[F]or all men', wrote Winstanley, 'being a like priviledged by birth … enjoy the creatures a like without proprietie one more than the other'.[49]

The right to the earth and the right to the fruits of labour were closely related for the Diggers; indeed, the former derived from the latter. '[I]f man shall eat bread by his sweat', Winstanley inferred, 'then he must needs have ground to sow corn'.[50] In other words, the right to the fruits of labour, and the duty to labour for one's subsistence, together implied a right to the means of labour, that is, a right to the earth.

On the basis of Sonship, the right to the fruits of labour, and the right to the earth, the Diggers formulated a sophisticated theory of the rent relation, rooted in the concept of lordly power – which they referred to variously as 'lordly power', 'kingly power', 'tyranny', 'lordship', 'command', 'oppression', and 'the curse'. The Diggers understood lordly power in relational terms. Lordship was 'to lord or force any arbitrary power one over another, or to assume any priviledge above his brethren'.[51] Lordly power was salient to the Diggers precisely because it *violated* the equal freedom proper to man's Sonship. '[N]one', wrote the Digger Robert Coster, 'should Lord over his own kind'.[52] The Diggers argued lordly power was propagated by 'murder and theft, treading others under foot … by the sword'.[53]

The Diggers theorised that many forms of property, especially landed property, were based not in equal rights to the earth and the fruits of labour, but in the violence of lordly power. '[P]ropriety …' wrote Winstanley, 'was ushered into the Creation, by those two grand disturbers of our Peace, Murther and Theft'.[54] 'Lords of Mannours' he observed, 'hold claiming to their Copyholds, and to the Commons, under or from the King'.[55] '[T]hat Kings and Lordly power', he argued, 'is the power of the Conquest over the people'.[56] Every landlord, he wrote, 'lives in the breach of the Seventh and Eighth Commandements, *Thou shalt not steal, nor kill*'.[57]

Other forms of property too, the Diggers argued, were based on lordly coercion and violence. Winstanley declared that 'all Monopolizings, Encroachings, Inhancings, Licenses, Patents, Grants, Prerogatives, privileges, [are] unjust and unnatural, arbitrary and wicked … and the Scriptures do every where protest against it, calling it Oppression'.[58] As reflections of lordly power, all these forms of property violated the equal freedom mandated by Sonship, as well as the right to the earth.

Winstanley observed that buying and selling land obscured but did not change its basis in lordly coercion: 'For now saith the Buyer, this parcell of Land is mine, I have paid the fruit of my labours for it, to be properly my owne'.[59] But Winstanley rejected this appearance, arguing 'the land is our portion by creation as well as yours, and we give no consent to be shut out; therefore what authority had you to buy, or the other to sell{?]'.[60] Buying land 'with Money got by Trading …', Winstanley declared, 'doth not alter the Title of the Conquest'.[61]

The Diggers conceived lordly power as pervasive relations of domination, not only between the landed and landless, but between the state and its subjects. Winstanley surmised that the entire machinery of government – lawyers, judges, ministers, bureaucrats, and the King – had been 'brought up to … tyrannise &c. over the poor people'.[62] The function of state and law, he argued, was not justice but 'to uphold the conquering Sword, and to preserve his son Propriety'.[63] Kingly power was pervasive and distributed. Though 'the Emperial King is removed …' Winstanley wrote, 'other petty kings remain'.[64] 'Kingly power in that one particular is cast out'; he declared, 'but alas oppression is a great tree still … he hath many branches and great roots'.[65]

From their theorisation of lordly power, the Diggers derived a theory of tributary rent as forced labour. They saw rent as 'part of the Kingly power'.[66] The rent relation reflected the use of lordly power to command subaltern labour or appropriate its products as tribute. 'By murder and theft, treading others under foot'; wrote Winstanley, 'this power … rules over the labours and bodies of others'.[67] Accordingly, Diggers often compared or referred to rent as a relation of 'slavery'.[68] But they distinguished rent from slavery too: rent was extracted not through direct personal coercion but lordly power's capacity to exclude men from the land. '[T]he Younger brother', observed Winstanley, was forbidden to 'live in the Earth, unless he would work for, and pay his Elder brother Rent'.[69]

The Diggers further delineated the rent relation by the norms it violated. First, it violated the right to the fruits of labour and the duty to toil for one's bread. '[W]hen a man hath got bread … by his labor', wrote Winstanley, 'it is his bread; now the other that sweats not at all, yet makes this man to pay him tribute out of his labor, by Rates, Taxes, Rents, &c. it is theft, and so against the Commandment, Thou shalt not steal'.[70] Being based on the elder brother's power to exclude the younger from the earth, the rent relation also violated the right to the earth and the universal equality of Sonship. In this way, the Diggers used normative concepts to derive a positive analysis of rent as a social-property relation.

Understanding the state, clergy, and landed class as constituent parts of a unitary lordly power, the Diggers characterised tithes and Crown rents in identical terms to landlords' rents. Government rates, taxes, tolls, and customs, Winstanley argued, all consisted of the application of lordly power by 'oppressors' to 'extort away the labours of their poor brethren'.[71] Likewise, '[m]inistrie', declared Winstanley, 'is set up by craft and covetousnesse, how to draw the Earth, and the labours of men into the Clergies hands'.[72] '[T]he Tythes of Superiority', wrote the Diggers of Buckinghamshire, 'as King, Lord, &c. are from the devil'.[73] As extractors of the tithe, the clergy, like lords and state officials, violated the right to the fruits of labour. 'They neither plow nor sow …' wrote the Cobham Diggers, 'But Priests the people grinde: The tenth of all things they do crave; And thus each man is made a slave'.[74] Whereas Lords and Crown upheld lordly power by the sword, the clergy used sermons. '[T]he Priests …' wrote Winstanley, 'keeps thee in all ignorance and malice… and for their so bewitching thee they come by … fat Benefits'.[75]

Alongside their theory of tributary rent, the Digger intellectual community produced a distinctive conception of a *capitalist* rent relation. The most perspicuous Digger analysis of capitalist rent can be found in Coster's *A Mite Cast into the Common Treasury*. Coster's words bear quoting at length:

> For what is the Reason that great Gentlemen covet after so much Land? Is it not because Farmers and others creep to them in a slavish manner, proffering them great summes of money for such and such percells of it, which doth give them an occasion to tyrannize over their fellow Creatures which they call their Inferiours?
>
> ... And what is the Reason that Farmers and others are so greedy to rent Land of the Lords of Mannors? Is it not because they expect great gaines, and because poor men... creep to them for imployment, although they will not give them wages enough to maintain them and their Families comfortably: All which do give them an occasion to tyrannize over their fellow-Creatures, which they call their Inferiors.[76]

Coster's analysis clearly describes the emergent capitalist rent relation, encompassing landlord, tenant farmer, and wage labourer. In this account, rent is set by a competitive market in which 'Farmers and others' bid for the land, 'proffering great sums of money'. Tenant farmers, he reasoned, could only pay high rents because they expected 'great gains' or profits. These, Coster observed, were made by employing wage labourers to produce valuable commodities in return for subsistence wages. In the Digger account, then, capitalist rent was a share of the 'gain' or profit farmers realised by selling workers' produce, less the cost of subsistence wages. And coercive, lordly power – exerted through the monopolisation of land – was central to the account. Coster called both commercial leasing and wage labour an 'occasion to tyrannize'. The landlord used his control of the land to tyrannise the farmer, demanding rent for permission to use parcels of land. In turn, the farmer used his temporary control of land to tyrannise the landless labourer, demanding full disposal of his labour in return for bare subsistence.

In striking concordance with the thesis of this book, the Diggers explained the emergence of these capitalist social-property relations as an endogenous transformation of the tributary rent relation. On the one hand, they recognised the capitalist rent relation, and capitalist relations it relied upon, as a novel development. Winstanley referred to capitalist farmers, for instance, as a 'new (more covetous) Gentry'.[77] On the other hand, however, the Diggers insisted the new capitalist social-property relations were founded on a *continuation* of the same lordly power which had upheld the older tributary rent relation. '[T]he old Gentry', wrote Winstanley, 'and the new Gentry likewise, walking in the same steps, are but the successors of the Norman victory'.[78]

In the Diggers' perspective, capitalism emerged as lordly power shifted from exacting tribute to forcing peasants off the land. In the passage quoted above, Coster complained of capitalist farmers 'proffering ... great summes of money' for leases. His implication was precisely that peasants could not afford such 'summes'. It was common knowledge that peasants were being proletarianised by rack renting, enclosure, and foul play. Winstanley, for instance, observed the poor were not even 'suffered to plant the waste land for their livelihood, unlesse they will pay Rent to their brethren for it'.[79] '[M]any thousands', he wrote, 'are deprived of their rights... because of those forenamed oppressors, who have ... inclosed, monopolized, incroached'.[80] Elsewhere, Winstanley reported capitalist farmers would 'over-stock the Commons with Sheep and Cattle; so that inferior Tenants and poor Laborers can hardly keep a Cow'.[81]

Just as they identified how the capitalist rent relation was proletarianising the peasantry, they also recognised how landlessness forced proletarians into exploitative wage labour. '[T]he poor that have no land ...' wrote Winstanley, 'are shut out of all livelihood, but what they shall pick out of sore bondage, by working for others, as Masters over them'.[82] Coster wrote, in similar terms, of landless men going 'with Cap in hand, and bended knee, to Gentlemen and Farmers, begging and intreating to work ... which doth give them occasion to tyrannize'.[83] Winstanley linked this tyranny to exploitation. When men enclose the land, he wrote, 'all the rest [are] deprived and made their slaves'.[84] Wage slavery deprived man not only of the fruits of his labour, but the equality of Sonship. Winstanley thus decried 'working for day wages ... under our own brethren, with whom we ought to have *equal freedom*'.[85]

The Digger normative framework – comprising equal freedom, a right to the earth, a duty to labour for one's bread, and a right to the fruits of one's labour – was not just a tool to critique rent and capitalism. The Diggers applied their precepts to develop a radical post-capitalist social imaginary. Each man, 'by the righteous Law of our Creation', wrote Winstanley, 'ought to have food and rayment freely by … righteous labouring of the earth, without working for hire, or paying rent one to another'.[86] This meant guaranteeing each a 'just portion' of the earth.[87] For the Diggers, this could only be achieved by guaranteeing common access to productive resources, 'without proprietie one more than the other'.[88] The Diggers likewise believed that for labour to truly comport with freedom and equality, it had to be communal and universal. Thus, Winstanley wrote that 'to eat our bread with the sweat of our brows, neither giving hire, nor taking hire' required 'labouring the Earth in righteousnesse … working together'.[89]

With communal production came communal consumption. '[I]f any man or family want Corn, or other provision', Winstanley declared, 'they may go to the Store-houses, and fetch without money … Because the earth, and the labours thereupon, are managed by common assistance of every family'.[90] In accordance with the right to the fruits of labour, distribution was to be proportionate to the individual's contribution to the common labour. 'If I adventure my life, and fruit of my labour, equal with you …' wrote Winstanley, 'I should equally divide the Spoil with you'.[91] Labour and distribution were not only to be equitable, but free from coercion. '[C]ommunitie will force nothing from any one', he wrote, 'but take what is given in love, of that which others have wrought for'.[92]

The Diggers sought to abolish rent and capital and achieve their vision by a revolution to abolish lordly power.[93] This revolution would be peaceful, because the Diggers believed armed struggle against lordly power would only reproduce it. As Winstanley put it, '[f]reedom gotten by the Sword is an established bondage to some part or other of the Creation. … Victory that is gotten by the Sword, is a Victory that slaves gets one over another'.[94] The Diggers therefore sought not to fight but to transgress lordly power. Winstanley called for the productive classes to refuse 'to work for hire, for any Landlord, or for any that is lifted up above others'.[95] The Diggers bade wage labourers to occupy vacant land, asserting their right to the earth. '[T]he common People' wrote Winstanley, 'ought to dig, plow, plant and dwell upon the Commons, without hiring them, or paying Rent to any'.[96] '[T]ake possession of your own Land', he wrote, 'which you have recovered out of the hands of the Norman oppressour'.[97] The call to dig the commons was soon expanded to encompass 'Bishops Lands, Crown Lands ... Parks, Woods, Forrests &c'.[98] The great obstacle to this strategy against lordly power was, of course, lordly power itself. But the Diggers' tactics were driven by desperation rather than naivety: 'it were better for us that are living', Winstanley wrote, 'to dye by the Sword then by the Famine'.[99]

To conclude, this chapter has explained the nature of resistance and critique levelled at the rent relation as it drove England's transition to capitalism. It showed that peasants failed to overcome the capitalist rent relation because it advanced in a way that divided the peasantry, undermining traditional strategies of resistance. I explained the Levellers as an early urban movement whose democratic programme briefly challenged the ascendant capitalist rent relation during a moment of ruling-class division in the seventeenth century. And finally, I chronicled the Diggers, the first proletarian social movement. I showed, consonant with my general thesis, that the Diggers understood the rent relation both as a tributary relation and as the 'mother of capital'. They used rent theory to derive strikingly perspicuous analyses of both tributary and capitalist social-property relations in a period of transition. They theorised capitalist rent as both generating a proletariat and sharing in the profits of its exploitation. Finally, I demonstrated how the Diggers went further still, using their framework of norms to conceive a unique post-proletarian imaginary based on community of property, production, and consumption.

7
The political economy of capitalist rent

Under the tributary rent relation, the political and the economic were fused. Lords' ability to extract an economic income depended directly on their personal capacity to coerce peasants. As the tributary rent relation transformed itself into a competitive relation, landlords became enclosers, and the political and economic spheres peeled apart. Enclosing landlords demilitarised and dissolved their manorial courts. This gave them, and the rent relation, a new and distinctively economic appearance. Landlords no longer lived by the sword but by consensual lease agreements. Rent now appeared as a purely civil-social relation: a flow of income from an economic asset. But the political dimension of rent had not disappeared. It had simply been hived off into the state. The peaceable and consensual economic logic of capitalist rent now rested on a crucial coercive foundation: state-enforced control of the land.

Not only did capitalist rent rest on this political foundation, but so did capitalism more broadly. Competitive rents, enforced by the state, performed constitutive functions for capitalism. They delivered land into the hands of capitalist farmers, forming the basis for capitalist agriculture. Competitive rents priced the proletariat off the land and precluded any retreat to subsistence agriculture. This is what made them wage labourers, with no alternative but to sell their labour to capitalists, and consumers who purchased subsistence from capitalists too. In other words, the new state-backed capitalist rent relation backstopped the proletarianised conditions on which all capitalist production and accumulation rested. And because rent was now a constitutive element of capitalism, landlords became a constitutive fraction of the capitalist class.

The modern separation of rent's consensual economic logic from its coercive political preconditions reflected a more general disjunction between the political and the economic under capitalism. Capitalist societies, Wood has argued, are characterised by two distinct but interdependent sets of relations or spheres. There is a political sphere in which coercive relations manifest as 'a specialized public coercive institution, the state'.[1] And there is a civil-social or economic sphere, in which interactions have an apparently voluntary character and where 'a private appropriating class' directs production by wage labourers and appropriates a surplus as profit.[2] But, as Wood explains, these apparently separate spheres are in fact internally related and mutually constitutive. Capitalism's civil-social sphere relies on the political state to uphold its private property relations.[3] Conversely, the political state depends on the material support and political acquiescence of civil society to survive. State and civil society are constitutively interdependent.

Despite their interdependence, however, capitalism's political and civil-social spheres each exercise a kind of autonomy. The state's political autonomy manifests in its coercive powers of arbitration, legislation, and enforcement. The autonomy of civil society manifests in civil rights – at a minimum, those rights and freedoms implicit in the capacity to own means of production and to sell one's labour for wages. These two forms of autonomy generate capitalism's separation between public and private, or political and economic.

The autonomy of each sphere generates a potential for conflict or 'disjunction'. The state, in exercising its political authority, may impinge on the autonomy of civil society, including its rights of property. Classes and individuals in civil society, in turn, may exercise civil freedoms in ways that undermine the state – tax avoidance or civil unrest, for example. 'Disjunctions', Poulantzas observes, may arise not just between political elites and the labouring masses, but between the state and the dominant economic class.[4] If a disjunction between the political and economic spheres becomes severe enough, the survival of both is threatened.

The potential for 'disjunction' is particularly striking in the British case. It is a paradox that capitalism blossomed in the British Isles after 1660 despite an ever more dramatic 'disjunction' between Britain's economic and political classes. As agrarian and then industrial capitalism took off, capitalists everywhere assumed control of production, and concomitantly attained great economic power. But these capitalists did not begin to populate the ranks of the British political class until centuries later, when English capitalism was already mature. The question arises: how was this disjunction sustained? How were the political preconditions of capitalist social-property relations secured if the state was not controlled by capitalists?

I argue that, in the classical period of British capitalism, the disjunction between capitalism's political and economic spheres was bridged by the landed class, pursuing its interests in the capitalist rent relation. We have already seen that as English capitalism developed, the landed-class interest in protecting and advancing the capitalist rent relation drove it to wrestle with the Crown for control of the English state. The capitalist rent relation thus prompted a Janus-like transformation in the landed class. Even as the rent relation led the landed class to assume a distinctively modern economic identity as capitalist landlords, it also drove them to forge a new political identity as an aristocratic political class. Where hitherto there was a single politico-economic identity – lordship – now there were two, one economic, the other political. By working these two identities, I contend, the landed class not only protected the political preconditions of capitalist rent but orchestrated a broader comity between capitalism's political and economic spheres. The dual identity of the landed class guaranteed the alignment of politics and economics in Britain's maturing capitalism. In advancing the capitalist rent relation, I argue, the Janus-faced class in fact orchestrated the classical age of British capitalism.

ARISTOCRACY AND STATECRAFT

To constitute itself as an aristocracy, England's landed class had to wrest political supremacy from the Crown. This meant bringing England's state machinery fully under the control of Parliament and eliminating the Crown's capacity for independent action. In Chapter 5, I traced this project to its partial completion in

1660, when the landed class extinguished the Crown's autonomous capacity to extract rent. The landed class won this victory through a radical popular mobilisation, but at the cost of dividing itself into republican and royalist factions. The Restoration of the Stuart Crown in 1660 healed this fracture by deferring any final assault on the Crown's political autonomy. Checkmate was finally achieved, however, in 1688, when William III of Orange invaded England, seeking to secure English cooperation in a Dutch war against France.[5] The English nobility supported the Hanoverian takeover largely through acquiescence.[6] The tacit *quid pro quo* was Hanoverian accession to Parliamentary supremacy. Unlike earlier attempts, the Hanoverian takeover subordinated the Crown while maintaining landlords' unity.[7]

With the Crown subordinated, the wealthiest and most powerful noble families quickly monopolised political power, forming the core of a capitalist aristocracy. In preceding centuries, the Crown and the gentry had often united to check noble power. The subordinated Crown was no longer willing or able to perform this mediating role. Thus, the great nobles, who had always been closer to state power than the gentry, could now monopolise the state at the gentry's expense. As Beckett writes, 'the aristocracy came to control every aspect of government, both executive and legislative. They dominated the Cabinet, the highest ranks of the armed forces, the civil service and, to a lesser extent, the judiciary'.[8] Nobles used their economic power (bribery) and political power (corruption) to fill the Commons with their clients and nominees.[9] The Commons, hitherto a bastion of the gentry, was neutered. The House of Lords reigned supreme.

To further insulate itself, particularly against other fractions of capital, the aristocracy made it ever more difficult to attain the markers of aristocratic status: land and nobility. Before 1688, the creation of peerages had been a Crown prerogative. In the post-revolutionary era, however, the aristocracy began vetting new peerages on the basis of 'acceptability and securely independent means'.[10] The aristocratic state also passed laws restricting the purchase and sale of land. These restrictions 'had the effect of … making penetration [into the aristocracy] through size of estate wellnigh impossible'.[11] Class boundaries that had blurred during the tumult of the seventeenth century were resharpened in the service of a new capitalist aristocratic political order.

As a Janus-faced class, the aristocracy could call heavily on the economic resources of its landlord alter-ego to build up the British state. From 1693 to 1798, Parliament levied a land tax which diverted a significant fraction of rents into state coffers.[12] With the gentry as tax collectors, the landed class effectively collected tax from itself – a unique spectacle in the European context.[13] The landed class taxed itself heavily during the war years of 1692 to 1715.[14] Towards the end of the eighteenth century, as the British state struggled to manage an unfolding Industrial Revolution, landlords were again required to contribute through rising county and poor rates and property taxes.[15] During the wars with France in the period 1793 to 1815, the majority of the additional tax burden fell on the wealthy.[16]

The aristocracy expanded the British capitalist state through a project of fiscal-military statecraft. As Anievas and Nişancıoğlu have argued, external conflicts with the Netherlands and France from the late seventeenth to early eighteenth centuries generated 'a modern fiscal-military state capable of harnessing vast fiscal and social resources in forging war'.[17] In the face of real external threats, both the working and ruling classes deferred to the aristocracy as it expanded the British state.[18] A key part of this was an expansion of Britain's machinery of tax collection during the eighteenth century.[19] The project of statecraft found its material base in the incredible productivity of British capitalism. By the early eighteenth century, agrarian capitalism was yielding trade surpluses sufficient to support constant overseas military deployments.[20] By the mid-eighteenth century, as British imperialism yielded colonial possessions, aristocratic statecraft in Britain had translated into British hegemony over a world empire.[21]

LANDED HEGEMONY

To rule effectively, Britain's capitalist landlord aristocracy had to establish hegemony. Hegemony, as Poulantzas' defines it, is the process by which a 'dominant class or class "fraction"' organises 'subordinate and allied classes and fractions' under its leadership.[22]

The landed class had to organise a hegemony that spanned both the political and civil-social spheres of Britain's capitalist society, bringing them into alignment and managing their potential for disjunction. It had to orchestrate civil-social relations that endowed its political leadership with the consent, legitimacy, and the material support it required.

The aristocracy attained hegemony by cultivating a broader 'landed interest.'[23] This broad interest included everyone who lived off capitalist agriculture: landlords, tenant farmers, agricultural workers, non-agricultural rural workers, and domestic servants. Leading the landed interest allowed the landed class to conflate its peculiar interests with a broader social concatenation that crossed class lines. Given the agrarian basis of early capitalism, the landed interest encompassed most of society up to the mid-nineteenth century.[24] At the head of this interest, the aristocracy could champion the rising agrarian middle class, play off rural and urban society for political advantage, and present capitalist development as a national achievement without reference to its class character. In doing so, the aristocracy achieved what Beckett called a 'popularity in society which negated any underlying dissension.'[25]

To hold the landed interest together, landlords drew on the civil-social power they derived from the capitalist rent relation. As Olney observes, 'the landowner who chose to exercise political influence could normally rely on the support and cooperation of his tenants and dependants. The almost complete unanimity of voting on many estates was attributed by some to coercion, by others to the unthinking deference of the lower orders to their superiors' wishes.'[26] Landlords also secured political support by charging below-market rents, or by failing to collect arrears.[27] These practices, as with sponsoring local businesses and families, converted economic rent into political support.

The aristocracy also consolidated its landed interest by acting as its political benefactor. Once it wrested control of the state from the Crown, it began imposing protectionist limits on corn imports, boosting the profits of English agrarian capitalists, employment among rural labourers, and, of course, rents for the gentry and aristocracy. Benefiting all strata of the landed interest, the Corn

Laws helped the aristocracy bind the landed interest together as a political constituency.

The aristocracy buttressed this hegemony by coopting the Old Bourgeoisie. The Old Bourgeoisie consisted of various urban classes that sprang up under the old tributary social-property relations: all those who served England's lords and Crown for a share in the tributary surplus. It included the core political class – officials, judges, and the military – plus various state-adjacent class fractions like the legal profession, the London financial elite, and the Anglican clergy.[28] It also encompassed merchants and officials of the East India Company. In the century and a half after 1688, the aristocracy coopted the Old Bourgeoisie through patronage, using the financial and legal power of the state to grant the Old Bourgeoisie privileges, monopolies, sinecures, bribes and favours. The new middle classes would eventually decry these practices as 'Old Corruption'.[29] But no matter. In the long run, crass corruption was superseded by a more sophisticated nepotism. The aristocracy used its networks of patronage to implant its sons throughout the Old Bourgeoisie. By the middle of the nineteenth century, this practice had organically grafted the Old Bourgeoisie to the aristocracy.

Whereas the aristocracy used patronage and nepotism to coopt the Old Bourgeoisie, its alliance with the new industrial and commercial middle class was founded on common economic interests in the expansion of capital. This alliance found its political expression in the defence of private property. The middle class cleaved especially close to the aristocracy when property was threatened, whether from below, such as in the wave of radicalism that followed the French Revolution, or from outside, as in the Napoleonic Wars.[30]

Yet to maintain hegemony, the aristocracy also had to manage tensions with the middle class. In the economic sphere, landed and industrial capital perpetually struggled over the division of surplus between profit and rent. In the political sphere, they struggled whenever the aristocracy subordinated urban middle-class interests to its own (as with the Corn Laws), to the interests of other class fractions (like the Old Bourgeoisie) or to the interests of capitalism as a whole (through taxation). As the middle class flourished and its confidence grew, it threatened to become a rival hegemon. In the nineteenth century, the middle class began to organise politically, spawning movements like the crusade against Old Corruption, and sought greater representation in politics through electoral reform. Nevertheless, in the two centuries after the Glorious Revolution, through common interests and concessions, the aristocracy kept the middle class relatively quiescent in its political subordination.

Alongside the project of integrating the surplus-taking classes into its ruling coalition, aristocratic hegemony also required managing the working classes. In the economic sphere, this meant disciplining the labour force. In the political sphere this meant suppressing working-class politics. Noting that these two aspects are interrelated, I will focus on the political aspect here, returning to the economic aspect later in this chapter.

In the early days of Britain's capitalist aristocracy, the working class was not yet a political force. In 1691, John Locke could observe that 'the labourer's share, being seldom more than a bare subsistence, never allows that body of men time or opportunity to ... struggle with the richer for theirs ... as one common interest'.[31] Aside from sporadic riots over food shortages, the early eighteenth century saw no political movement against property.[32] Over time, however, capitalist development brought technological and social changes that made political organisation easier.[33] Daily and weekly newspapers began to appear from the late seventeenth century, as did scientific, political and other societies.[34] By the eighteenth century, mass literacy had arrived.[35]

In the 1790s, the aristocracy had its first major confrontation with the working class, as the French Revolution set off a wave of radicalism. The aristocracy used state coercion to suppress working-class politics. Radical meetings, organisations, newspapers and pamphlets were deemed seditious.[36] The aristocracy deployed its ideologues against working-class propaganda. In his *Reflections on the Revolution in France*, for instance, Burke insisted that expropriating Britain's landlords would unravel its social and economic fabric.[37] Exhorting stability, the aristocracy and its proxies appealed to 'veneration for the monarchy, the Church, the Peerage, the City'.[38] The aristocracy formulated cross-class interests under the banners of 'loyalism' and 'conservatism', providing a highly successful answer to working-class radicals.

Working-class political activity spiked again from the late 1830s in the form of Chartism. Through Chartism, millions of working-class people pressed for representation of their interests within the British state. Chartists demanded political reforms, including annual Parliaments, the secret ballot, new electoral boundaries, the abolition of property qualifications for MPs, the payment of salaries for MPs, and universal male suffrage.[39] The Chartists were largely peaceful, holding massive rallies and presenting petitions with millions of signatures to the Commons. Chartism provided a political complement to the economic demands workers had begun to express through trade unions.

The aristocratic state responded with brutality and steadfastness. It deployed spies, police and the military to suppress any Chartist who resorted to force. Chartist leaders were arrested and prosecuted. When the working class was finally granted political representation in the late nineteenth century, it would be on the aristocracy's terms, with Chartism long defunct.[40]

THE DYNAMICS OF CAPITALIST RENT

In the period between the Restoration of 1660 and the Glorious Revolution of 1688, the competitive rent relation continued to dismantle Britain's tributary social-property relations and drive a capitalist transition. As chronicled in previous chapters, the seventeenth century's upheavals accelerated enclosure and leasing to capitalist farmers, displacing tributary lord-tenant relations.[41] Peasants became proletarian wage labourers. Capitalist agriculture combined with mercantile imperialism to generate an economic boom in the late seventeenth century.[42]

As capitalist agriculture developed, the rent relation marketised steadily. Lease periods became shorter and rents became more sensitive to market conditions. By the first half of the nineteenth century, most leases were annual or at-will.[43] Large farms tended to yield higher rents, so farm sizes grew steadily from the early eighteenth to the early nineteenth centuries.[44] Meanwhile, a shrinking rump of husbandmen clung to copyholds and life leases on submarket rents, particularly in the north and west of England.[45]

The rent relation's marketisation accelerated agricultural commercialisation. Landlords' demands for market rents forced agricultural tenants to produce and sell the most profitable crops. To acquire cash for rent, even former subsistence farmers were forced to become commodity producers and to compete with agrarian capitalists in the agricultural market. The city of London formed the epicentre of an emerging national agricultural market. By the middle of the eighteenth century, English agricultural production was highly commoditised.[46]

The marketisation of rent also drove agricultural productivity. As more landlords demanded market rents, the option of subsistence farming was progressively closed off, pushing farmers to produce for the market, and, crucially, to compete. Exposure to the relentless force of competition, in both the agricultural market and the market for leases, gave farmers an inexhaustible motive to improve their productivity, adopting labour-saving and capital-intensive methods. In the period 1600 to 1800, England experienced an agricultural revolution. Agricultural productivity doubled, compared to an increase of only 20 per cent in France.[47]

The discipline of competitive rent was not the only driver of agricultural productivity, of course. Wrigley, for instance, argues that London provided a unique impetus to agricultural productivity. A bourgeoning centre of national consumption and international mercantile trade, by the mid-eighteenth century, London had become Europe's largest city and provided an unusually deep and competitive national market for English agricultural commodities. This encouraged both efficiency and scale in English farming. But I would insist that demand, on its own, is not enough to drive productivity growth. As we saw in previous chapters, late medieval society responded to the demand of its swelling population not with capital investment and labour-saving techniques, but with capital-depleting tributary rents and the immiseration of ever more labour-intensive cultivation. Tributary megacities like Rome and Constantinople had rivalled London in size before, but neither sparked an agricultural revolution. The demand of a large consumer market only induces productivity growth when the prevailing social-property relations incentivise and reward that response. It took the birth of England's peculiarly competitive, proletarianising, capitalist rent relation to ensure the nation's elites were rewarded for meeting rising consumer demand with rising agricultural productivity.

Indeed, the capitalist rent relation was itself a driver of England's spectacular urbanisation. We have seen that under feudalism, the expenditure of tributary rent in towns drove a degree of urban development. As Wrigley observes, a society's capacity to feed an urban population is limited by its agricultural productivity.[48] By rewarding sustained, profit-driven improvements in agricultural productivity, competitive market rents unleashed a tsunami of cheap food on urban markets, overcoming previous limits on urban population growth. As capitalist production spread, the lavish expenditures of England's flourishing capitalist landlords continued to fuel the growth of English towns and cities, but their largesse was joined and later surpassed by a new flow of luxury spending derived from capitalists' profits. A substantial non-landed elite began to appear in urban areas, particularly London.[49] By 1800, 28 per cent of the English population lived in urban centres, compared to just 11 per cent in France.[50] By the mid-nineteenth century, the urban population had surpassed that of the countryside.[51]

As it deepened marketisation and capitalist production, the capitalist rent relation became increasingly sensitive to technological changes prompted by capitalists' search for profit. During the seventeenth century, new agricultural techniques – more productive and profitable for farmers – favoured light soils, whereas the old ones had favoured clay. This resulted in a mass conversion of once-high-rent cropland into low-rent pasturage, and vice versa.[52] For good and ill, profit-driven technological change reversed the fortunes of many capitalist landlords.

The rent relation responded to market forces on an even larger scale during the Industrial Revolution. Industrial capitalism grew exponentially during the eighteenth century, with a full-blown Industrial Revolution ensuing around 1780.[53] As the economy industrialised, the role of agriculture declined proportionately. By the turn of the nineteenth century, less than a third of the workforce worked in agriculture.[54] The nineteenth century was characterised by low rents on agricultural land.[55] But this was not a waning of the rent relation itself. While agricultural landlords experienced a secular decline, those with urban and mining land flourished.[56] As agricultural capital gave way to industrial capital, the rent relation shifted its weight onto the latter.

LANDLORD-LED CAPITALISM

Here I want to make an unlikely argument: the world's first Industrial Revolution was led not by industrialists searching for profit but by landlords thirsting for rent. The idea of 'landlord-led capitalism' may sound perverse. Britain's first industrialists were famously creative and diligent, while its landlords had a reputation as idlers, absentees, and feudal relics. Undeniably, landlord absenteeism was common and increased steadily from the last decade of the seventeenth century.[57] I must therefore put absenteeism in context before explaining how landlords led Britain's Industrial Revolution. My argument, essentially, is that absenteeism reflected not idleness, but the opportunity cost the landed fraction of capital paid for political monopoly.

Absenteeism was a byproduct of the landed class concentrating itself into an aristocracy. As a small elite of wealthy magnates managed to monopolise land after the Glorious Revolution of 1688, they inevitably found themselves managing far-flung estates remotely.[58] Family alliances, strategic marriages and primogeniture also tended to concentrate distant possessions in the hands of a single landlord.[59] Absenteeism became inevitable. Compounding this, the daily demands of political aristocracy made absenteeism a necessity. In their capacity as aristocrats, landowners needed to reside in urban centres, close to the seats of government and finance, distancing them from their estates.[60] Most aristocrats dealt with the demands of their political roles by becoming rentiers, acting as non-executive directors of their estates.[61]

Absenteeism imposed a considerable cost on Britain's capitalist landlords. Roebuck identifies the principal costs of absenteeism as 'uncertainty, indecision, and neglect'.[62] Absenteeism inevitably affected rental returns. Stewards and land agency firms appeared from the mid-eighteenth century, but only partially mitigated the problem.[63] Neglect was expensive, but so were trustworthy and competent managers, if they could be found at all.[64] Most landlords remained as involved as they could be, since unmonitored stewards could spell disaster.[65] Absenteeism also had political consequences. A landlord who neglected his responsibilities risked eroding the civil-social support that formed an important basis of his political influence.[66]

Absenteeism was the unavoidable economic price landlords paid for maintaining their political-aristocratic alter egos. Neither identity could exist without the other. Political hegemony was a precondition of the capitalist rent relation and the maturing capitalist system more generally. Notwithstanding a degree of absenteeism, however, there is strong evidence that landlords proactively fostered capitalist development. The dynamics of the capitalist rent relation, I argue, left them few options but to do so.

The capitalist rent relation drove landlords into a partnership with their capitalist inferiors. As land was progressively enclosed, landlords were constantly looking for quality tenants to take up leases,[67] especially those competent to operate the larger, high-rent farms.[68] As leases grew larger and fewer, landlords relied more and more on cordial relations with a handful of key tenants.[69] Landlords regularly restrained their rental demands to retain good tenants.[70] One testament to the success of the landlord–capitalist alliance is the scale of their collective surplus-taking. Between the mid-sixteenth and late eighteenth centuries, property-owning classes increased their share of the product sixfold compared to workers.[71]

Once capitalist dynamics had taken root, a major field of entrepreneurial activity opened for the landed class under the banner of 'improving' the land. As the rent relation marketised, landlords were forced to compete for quality tenants. To attract productive tenants who used the most advanced techniques – and could sustain the highest rents – landlords had to finance improvements to their estates. These included the construction of buildings, fences, drainage, roads, and gates.[72] The capitalist rent relation drove landlords to become infrastructure capitalists. By the nineteenth century, a substantial portion of the national rental take was being recycled into improvement.[73] Repairs and improvements represented as much as a quarter of gross rents.[74]

Landlords also absorbed a considerable burden of entrepreneurial risk. Where they lacked the wherewithal, they borrowed, seeking private or public finance.[75] By the early 1840s, 'land improvement companies' appeared, specialising in finance for improving landowners.[76] Such investments carried considerable risk, and it was not uncommon for landlords to be ruined when leveraged investments failed during agricultural downtowns.[77] The rate of return on improvements appears to have been quite low by the nineteenth century,[78] indicating, if anything, that landlords tended to overcapitalise, effectively subsidising capitalist agriculture. Landlords also absorbed entrepreneurial risk and encouraged capital deepening through the practice of 'tenant right' – compensating outgoing tenants for any unexhausted improvements made to the land.[79] The practice originated in the middle of the eighteenth century and was widespread by the middle of the nineteenth century.[80]

Enclosure was a further field of landlord investment, driven by the dynamics of the capitalist rent relation. As capitalism continued to develop in the wake of the English Revolution, the market demand for commercial tenancies steadily grew.[81] Capitalist tenant farmers valued enclosed land highly because it was unencumbered by customary rights and regulations. Over the eighteenth century, for example, enclosed land yielded upward of double the rent of unenclosed land.[82] This rent differential provided a strong incentive for landlords to shoulder the regulatory, political and commercial risks of enclosing. The rent relation shepherded the landed class into a form of regulatory entrepreneurship, analogous to that undertaken by contemporary property developers attempting to have land rezoned. Enclosure was also entrepreneurial in that it often required a significant capital outlay. Enclosures from the late seventeenth to early eighteenth century, for instance, uniformly show landlords buying out local freeholders *en masse*.[83]

Beyond being a type of entrepreneur, enclosing landlords collectively and indirectly propagated the general preconditions of capitalist development. The mechanisms by which they did so have been outlined already. Enclosure progressively squeezed out small and customary tenants, closing off avenues for non-capitalist, subsistence production. As evicted smallholders were forced into wage labour, enclosure inexorably deepened the workforce available to capitalists.[84]

ARISTOCRATIC ECONOMIC POLICY

Having discussed how landlords contributed to capitalist development in their economic guise, I will now turn to their interrelated political contributions. Moonlighting as aristocrats, landlords applied the state's coercive power with great determination to promote and guarantee both the capitalisation of the rent relation and the capitalist foundations on which rent increasingly rested.

In his *Reflections on the French Revolution*, Edmund Burke perfectly captured the capitalising mission of Britain's aristocratic regime: '[t]he only concern of the state is, that the capital taken in rent from the land, should be returned again to the industry from whence it came'.[85] Accordingly, the aristocratic state, anxious to expedite the conversion of rent into capital, did much to beat a path for improving landlords. In 1660, Parliament confirmed the right of landowners to evict customary tenants.[86] In 1677, Parliament passed legislation that reduced small freeholders to the legal position of copyholders, making it easier for landlords to enclose.[87] After the Glorious Revolution, Parliament actively promoted the exploitation of mineral resources.[88] In the mid-nineteenth century, Parliament passed laws to enable landlords to borrow against their estates for improvements.[89] Likewise, the aristocratic Parliament oversaw all locally significant economic developments, including enclosures and transport infrastructure.[90]

Enclosure is probably the most dramatic case in which the aristocracy applied state power to press the case of improving landlords. By the middle of the eighteenth century, private strategies of enclosure were yielding diminishing returns.[91] Enclosing landlords were running up against complex negotiations, residual legal uncertainties and intransigent neighbours.[92] Remnant freeholders were not as easy to dislodge as copyholders had been.[93] It was at this point that the landlord-controlled Parliament began passing bills to compel enclosures at the behest of interested landlords.

Enclosure bills became ubiquitous, with over 5,000 passed between 1730 and 1870.[94] The pace of Parliamentary enclosure was particularly furious in the late eighteenth and early nineteenth centuries.[95] The aristocratic state successfully dampened opposition to Parliamentary enclosures by developing norms regarding 'good practice', compensation and hearing minority objections.[96] Parliament enclosed 6.5 million acres between 1760 and 1914, by which time enclosure was effectively universal.[97]

While the aristocracy gave closest attention to landed-class interests, it certainly applied its political power to cultivate other fractions of capital. As Žmolek argues, by legislation such as the Riot Act of 1715, and the Combination Act of 1799, the landed state intervened to dissolve the customary regulations and self-activity of craft workers, making way for industrial capital.[98] The artisans endured further blows when the royal courts ceased regulating wages and Parliament abolished apprenticeship protections. The aristocracy also took active steps to cultivate merchant capital. As Brenner describes, after 1688, Parliament 'assumed a central position in regulating trade and chartering commercial companies and immediately took measures to allow for freer and greater mobilization of capital in an overseas enterprise'.[99]

Some aristocratic contributions to capitalist development were unintentional. As already explained, the aristocracy placed legal restrictions on the sale of land to consolidate its position as a political class. By the middle of the eighteenth century, it was rare to convert non-landed wealth into acreage, whereas before it had been common.[100] The aristocracy had effectively closed off the traditional avenue for 'parking' a financial fortune. In the eighteenth and nineteenth centuries, as capitalism flourished, the emerging middle class was thus forced to invest in activities more closely related to production and improvement, such as mortgage lending, commerce and banking.[101] Government securities provided another non-landed investment option, likewise fuelling the expansion of the British state and its mercantile empire.

The aristocracy made another key contribution to capitalist development by its management of the working class. Earlier in this chapter I discussed aristocratic efforts to exclude the working class from political power. Though largely excluded, the working class nevertheless found ways to prosecute its interests outside the political sphere. Workers found they could assert their interests by challenging capitalist control of the labour process: by striking, or by taking control of the product or the workplace. Unionism and strike activity grew steadily in Britain from the mid-eighteenth century.[102] By the early nineteenth century, workers were increasingly capable of organised resistance, with notable spikes in 1819–1820 and 1831–1832.[103]

As soon as it gained decisive control over the state, Britain's capitalist aristocracy began applying the state machinery to discipline the working class. In the late seventeenth century, Parliament introduced the death penalty for many property offences.[104] Over the course of the eighteenth century, the aristocratic state oversaw the development of a more sophisticated system of criminal laws and policing.[105] The state helped manage the problem of surplus workers through policies of emigration and colonial transportation.[106] When workers' industrial activism spiked in the nineteenth century, the aristocracy came down heavily, mobilising military and state intelligence resources to surveil and suppress.[107] By suppressing working-class industrial activity, the aristocratic state defended both the capitalists' profits and the landlords' share in them.

In conclusion, capitalist rent relation powerfully shaped the development of Britain's capitalist political economy. As the British rent relation became capitalist, Britain's once-feudal lords were transformed into a Janus-faced class: capitalist landlords in the economic sphere, and the aristocrats of Britain's capitalist politics. Thus, transformed, they could defend and advance the political preconditions of capitalist rent, while orchestrating a delicate comity between capitalism's political and economic spheres in a crucial phase of British capitalist development. At every stage of the process, the landed class leveraged both state power and civil-social power derived from the rent relation.

The capitalist rent relation, tended to by its Janus-faced class, was the engine of Britain's classical period of capitalist development. The dynamics of enclosure and competitive leasing inexorably advanced proletarianisation, capitalist production, urbanisation, commerce, competition, capital intensification, and technological development. The rent relation spurred the Janus-faced class to practice a 'landlord-led capitalism' whose dynamics generated an agricultural revolution, then an industrial one. In the political sphere, the aristocracy's efforts to advance the capitalist rent relation led it to apply state power systematically to support and accelerate capitalist development. Behind every moment of classical British capitalism lurked the dynamics of rent.

8

Resistance to rent under capitalism

In the eighteenth century, as the project of enclosure was taken up by Britain's aristocratic state and neared its practical completion, resistance to the capitalist rent relation took a new form. It shifted from concrete struggles over land and enclosure, fought by a dwindling peasantry, to a two-front struggle fought by a landless working class. On the political front, the working class struggled against the aristocratic state, and in the workplace, it struggled against industrial capital. Whereas the anti-enclosure movement resisted rent directly, each front of the new struggle resisted rent *indirectly*. In the economic sphere, working-class industrial activity threatened capitalists' profits, and thereby the landlord's share of them. In the political sphere, working-class politics threatened aristocratic control of the state that upheld capitalist private property, including landed property.

As we saw in the last chapter, the Janus-faced landed class was ultimately successful in subordinating Britain's workers. This chapter, however, returns to the struggle from a working-class perspective. Many have recognised that political and economic struggles over industrial conditions in eighteenth and nineteenth-century Britain were expressions of a struggle against capital.[1] I will show, however, that precisely because Britain's working class could trace proletarianisation and aristocracy to the capitalist rent relation, working-class politics were also greatly preoccupied with questions of land and rent.[2]

The connection between rent and working-class politics was evident from the late eighteenth century. The 1790s saw a wave of radical opposition to aristocratic government following the French Revolution. English radicalism found its class basis in the upper reaches of the working classes: artisans, tradesmen and small masters.[3] Opposition to aristocracy was often expressed through the Norman Yoke trope.[4] The formulation was significant because, due to its feudal origin, it drew no distinction between the political and the economic. As an intellectual rubric, the Norman Yoke was well suited to framing a radical critique that connected political aristocracy to economic landlordism and could shift its attack between either target.

The thought of Thomas Paine (1737–1809) typified this target shifting. Paine's *Rights of Man* (1791), defending the French Revolution, sold 200,000 copies in Britain, notwithstanding state censorship and repression.[5] In it, Paine set his sights on aristocracy, attacking the monopolisation of political power by 'the mere consumers of rent'.[6] Paine did not attack rent per se, just its aristocratic manifestation, denying the aristocracy's claim to 'distinct and separate representation from the general interest'.[7] Later, however, in his *Agrarian Justice* (1797), Paine set his sights squarely on the economics of rent, and particularly its proletarianising tendency. '[T]he landed monopoly …' he wrote, 'has dispossessed more than half the inhabitants of every nation of their natural inheritance, without providing for them, as ought to have been done, an indemnification for that loss'.[8] Paine stopped short of calling for rent's abolition or deproletarianisation, but he demanded a radical political settlement. All citizens, he argued, should receive an inheritance funded from a property tax.[9] In Paine's vision, the rent relation would continue and workers would remain landless, but the rent surplus would be shared and the landed class eliminated.

Contemporary with Paine but less prominent was Thomas Spence (1750–1814). Like Paine, Spence's followers hailed from the lower middle and working classes.[10] Spence agitated in the most vitriolic terms for the abolition of the Janus-faced class – both landlords and aristocrats. He proposed that land be confiscated and democratically managed at the parish level, with parishes federated into a democratic national government. Spence envisaged parishes renting productive land in small lots to citizen-farmers, with the rent being used for state services. Spence was an important contributor to critical rent theory, and I will discuss his theories further in Chapter 10. Although Spence's ideas remained marginal, they regularly resurfaced in the early nineteenth century, through figures like Allen Davenport and George Petrie.[11] They manifested again in Chartism's land nationalisation tendency, discussed further below.

In the nineteenth century, working-class struggles against capitalism continued to be expressed as attacks on aristocracy and landlordism. As Winch writes, 'the fundamental divide in British politics' centred 'more on the ownership of land than capital'.[12] In the first half of the nineteenth century, British working-class politics found their sharpest expression in the Chartist movement. While the Charter itself contained a set of purely political demands, Chartists saw democracy as a means to economic ends. These ranged from 'fair wages' to a comprehensive reorganisation of class society.[13] As will be seen, proposals to alter the balance of landed property – with consequences for the rent relation – were common in Chartist politics throughout the 1830s and 1840s.[14] Alongside Chartism, Owenite socialism also captured working-class interest, expressing ambitions to escape not only the rent relation but capitalism more generally.

While middle-class voices also called for land reform, middle- and working-class interests in the 'land question' diverged. As we have seen, despite antagonisms over the distribution of surplus, landlords and capitalists were fundamentally economic partners. The middle class was largely content with landed political hegemony. Industrial capital certainly resented aspects of aristocratic statecraft, like patronage, monopolies, heavy taxes and military expenditures. But it was largely appeased by reforms to restrain Old Corruption. Middle-class commitment to radical anti-aristocratic positions like 'free trade in land' was typically shallow. Even if it had been deep, 'free trade in land' had little appeal to a working class that could not afford land anyway.[15] Conversely, more radical attacks on landed property appealed to workers but tended to divide the middle class.[16] Thus, as Martin has argued, middle- and working-class unity on land reform concealed significant 'class antagonisms'.[17]

CHARTISM

I will examine two tendencies within working-class Chartism that addressed themselves directly to the land question, challenging not only the aristocratic state but the capitalist rent relation itself. The first strand, and by far the most prominent, was the peasant proprietorship tendency championed by the Chartist hero Feargus O'Connor. The second strand was the land nationalisation tendency associated with Bronterre O'Brien. Ultimately, neither tendency threatened the Charter's status as the central focus of Chartist politics. Other Chartist leaders, by and large, scorned efforts to address the land question, especially O'Connor's, as a 'distraction of energy and attention from the main political drive at a crucial stage'.[18] Nevertheless, the very fact that the land question could 'distract' Chartists shows how readily working-class people connected aristocratic politics to economic landlordism. As with eighteenth-century radicalism, Chartism often framed its critiques using the rubric of the Norman Yoke.[19] This usefully ambiguous trope supported attacks on both political aristocracy and economic landlordism.

Chartists generally strove to achieve working-class political power without violating the mores of capitalist civil society. Even the so-called 'physical force' Chartists primarily employed only violent rhetoric, and for good reason. On the rare occasions Chartists resorted to force, such as in the Newport Rising of 1839, they were brutally put down by the state. Rather than challenging the state's monopoly on force, Chartism generally pressed for political power by challenging the legitimacy of the aristocracy through civil mechanisms, like demonstrations and petitions to Parliament. As we have already seen, aristocratic hegemony held firm.

By the 1840s, facing an intransigent Parliament, Chartist leaders had begun to consider alternative civil-social levers for attaining political power. Feargus O'Connor was one such leader – a major hero of the Chartist movement, with millions of followers.[20] In 1842, O'Connor mooted the idea of achieving Chartist political goals by 'a plan for settlement of large numbers on the land, each man holding freehold property of the minimum annual value of 40s required to qualify for a county vote'.[21] Better-off members of the working class would thus establish a beachhead of enfranchisement from which to press for universal suffrage.[22]

O'Connor's target, however, quickly shifted from the political to the economic. By 1843, O'Connor had fixed on the idea that land settlements could provide 'independence from employer and landlord'.[23] He invoked the Norman Yoke, a stick as well suited for beating landlords as aristocrats. 'Kings, princes, lords and citizens', he wrote, 'have stolen … [the land] from the people. Usurpation is the work of the rich and powerful'.[24] O'Connor presented his Land Plan to the Chartist annual conference in 1845, confidently promising that:

> An industrious person, of very moderate strength, will be enabled to support himself, a wife and three children, upon an average of six hours' labour of each day throughout the year upon four acres of land, and will have a surplus in each year of £100, after the best of living and the payment of all expenses.[25]

O'Connor's Land Plan, then, was to overcome the exclusory capitalist rent relation and re-establish the worker on the land, so he could 'live upon his own resources, and enjoy the entire sweets of his own industry'.[26] The labourer's dependency on wages, and vulnerability to capitalist exploitation, would be overcome. The Land Plan, O'Connor believed, would also render those who remained in the labour market immune to exploitation. If faced with a 'competitive labour surplus' workers could avoid low wages and unemployment by retreating to the land.[27] The backstop of peasant proprietorship, O'Connor argued, would give 'the working classes, when offering their labour for sale … some scale by which to judge of its value'.[28] The value of labour would no longer be determined solely by the capitalist's willingness to pay.

For the Land Plan to achieve its ambitions, however, it needed a means of overcoming the rent relation, which stood between the worker and the land. O'Connor was convinced that by adopting labour-intensive spade-farming, in place of the labour-saving plough-farming used by capitalist farmers, the productivity of the land (though not of labour) could be raised threefold.[29] Even if workers could only establish themselves on poor, cheap, marginal land, O'Connor believed, their labour could make it productive enough for subsistence.[30] O'Connor would thus form a company to buy large estates and subdivide them into small lots.[31] The company would be funded by subscriptions from Chartists and the public at large.[32] O'Connor envisaged subscribers renting plots at first, but saving enough to buy them outright in five years.[33] The company would reinvest its income from those renting and buying lots, thus planting ever more workers back on the land.[34]

O'Connor's scheme captured working-class imagination but ended in disaster. At its peak, around 1847–1848, O'Connor's Land Company had over 20,000 shareholders, 70,000 weekly subscribers making payments towards shares, 600 branches across Britain, and had purchased five estates.[35] Yet the scheme had problems from the outset. Subscribers' funds were too meagre to furnish all with the promised land and house. O'Connor responded to the shortfall by allocating allotments by lottery.[36] As a subsequent Royal Commission found, however, the allotments, for those who got them at all, were too small to be self-supporting, even before rent was imposed, and those who farmed them were unskilled in agriculture.[37] By 1848, the scheme had collapsed, greatly damaging the reputation of both O'Connor and Chartism.[38]

The Land Plan episode shows how British working-class movements understood they were 'boxed in' by the capitalist rent relation, both politically and economically, and how they oscillated between economic and political strategies of self-liberation. First conceived as a vehicle to gain the franchise and end political aristocracy, the Land Plan morphed into a vehicle to overcome the landless condition of proletarian workers. O'Connor's target, in other words, had shifted from the politics of rent to its economics. O'Connor argued compellingly that British workers were vulnerable to exploitation because they were landless. Yet, in the Land Plan, O'Connor and thousands of other workers pinned their hopes on the unlikely theory that they could reverse this situation by using their meagre wages to rent the land back. The failure of the Land Plan demonstrated, abjectly, that the working class could not overcome the exclusory capitalist rent relation by operating within its economic logic.

If the Land Plan had promised Chartists a civil-social exit from the rent relation, Chartism's land nationalisation wing offered a political path. As Claeys highlights, Chartist radicals had always seen the Charter as a means for effecting economic change, especially an equalisation of wealth.[39] For the Chartist leader James Bronterre O'Brien (1804–1864), political power could produce economic liberation through currency reform and land nationalisation – policies drawn from Owen and Spence respectively. O'Brien developed a polemic in favour of land nationalisation between 1833 and 1835.[40] In doing so, he rejected narrower political critiques focused on aristocratic privilege and economic critiques limited to opposing Old Corruption:

> Enormous taxation is no doubt an evil; but it is only one of a number of evils, many of them equally oppressive as taxation, and all growing out of, and equally inseparable from, the present constitution of society ... RENTS, and TITHES, and INTEREST of money, and tolls, and above all, of the *profits realized on Capital*, which is greater than all the other burdens put together.[41]

Under O'Brien's plan, the state would buy out each landlord upon his death, his heirs receiving the financial value of their lost inheritance.[42] The state would then lease land to the highest bidder, to be privately farmed.[43] O'Brienite land nationalisation did not seek to abolish the rent relation, nor to reunite landless wage labourers with the land. Rather, it sought to establish a single democratic 'landlord state' to extract and distribute rent for the community's benefit.

Land nationalisation failed at multiple levels. As Chartism never attained political power, it never became a practical possibility. And even among those Chartists who prioritised the land question, nationalisation was never the most popular approach. Nationalisation also tended to compete with, not complement, other approaches. O'Brien, for instance, attacked O'Connor's more popular Land Plan. He argued that turning Chartists into small proprietors would make them conservative and anti-nationalisation.[44] Nevertheless, proposals for land nationalisation continued to circulate in Chartist circles into the 1850s.[45]

OWENISM

Owenism represented another working-class project that, like the Chartist Land Plan, sought a civil-social path to liberation from rent and capital. Robert Owen was a self-made businessman in the cotton milling industry, who made a fortune in the 1790s. He became the manager of the New Lanark mills in Scotland in 1800, and for the following quarter century undertook 'experiments in factory reform that gradually evolved into experiments in comprehensive social planning'.[46] From 1817 his communitarian ideas firmed up, and he became 'a propagandist to the masses of men'.[47] Owenism soon became 'extraordinarily influential in forming the economic views of large sections of the working classes'.[48] Owen's influence inspired a strong cooperative movement in Britain from 1824 to 1829.[49] He applied wealth and energy to bring his vision to life, founding cooperative communities in both Britain and America. By 1829, these had failed. But between 1829 and 1834, the Owenite movement nevertheless took on a life of its own, as Owen's own intellectual dominance was eclipsed.[50]

Owen's communitarian vision involved forming productive rural communities with a maximum population of 2,500.[51] These communities were to be both agrarian and industrial. Owen believed human 'health and happiness' required combining manufacturing with agricultural labour. Communities were to produce using the most advanced agrarian and industrial techniques and machinery. Owen's vision was for cooperation in both production and social life, so he envisioned communities living in a central group of buildings rather than in isolated cottages. Exchange and distribution was likewise to be regulated on a communitarian basis, eliminating merchants and middlemen.

In theory, Owen's vision would supersede both aristocracy and capitalist production. Owen originally proposed his rural communities as a remedy for unemployment.[52] But his ambitions grew more radical, especially from the mid-1820s to the mid-1830s.[53] In 1830, in his *Lectures on an Entire New State of Society*, Owen spoke against private property, commercial competition, and advocated equality of condition.[54] He imagined his landed communities replacing capitalist firms and abolishing the distinction between rich and poor.[55] These ideas were as attractive to workers as they were threatening to capitalists, landlords and aristocrats.

But despite Owen's radical vision, he made few overt efforts to challenge the class system.[56] Owen was resolutely opposed to violent revolution.[57] Nor did he seek, except fleetingly, to achieve change through legislation. Instead, he championed the notion that a communitarian social revolution could grow peacefully within civil society, funded by worker cooperatives or rich benefactors like himself. Even within his planned communities, Owen was not committed to the immediate abolition of class. Aside from in his middle period, Owen's communitarian schemes were explicitly class segregated – with participants formally divided into four class categories.[58] What rendered the Owenite path to socialism plausible, however, despite its eschewal of violence and deferral of class abolition, was technology.[59] Advanced methods of production, Owen believed, would produce an abundance of both products and leisure time, eventually rendering relative wealth and class irrelevant.[60]

So despite its radical vision, Owenite communitarianism did not pose an immediate challenge to the rent relation or the capitalist order. As Bush observes, 'communities were planned and sometimes founded in which aristocracy had no place, while the aristocracy was allowed to dominate unchallenged society at large'.[61] Owenism formed what Claeys calls the 'moral self-help wing of working-class movements'.[62] Like the Chartist Land Plan, its results demonstrated the limits of civil-social self-help. Although Owenite socialism provided only an 'in principle' threat to the rent relation and capitalist social-property relations, however, it did provide a rich intellectual context for the critique of both. As will be seen in the following chapters, Owenites made powerful contributions to Critical Social Theory, fundamentally challenging mainstream political economic analyses of rent and capital.

In summary, in this chapter, I have shown the deep connection between the working-class politics of classical British capitalism and the capitalist rent relation. I showed how working-class movements confronted the relation as two distinct but interrelated forms of oppression: aristocratic rule and landlessness. Working-class movements responded by slipping between political and economic strategies – between the struggle for democracy and 'the land question'. Working-class movements proposed various answers to the land question, but all ultimately demonstrated the limits of civil-social self-help strategies that sought to transcend rent and capitalist social-property relations from within their own civil-social logic. But these early movements did leave a legacy. As will be seen, they sparked a new, proletarian social science that developed a perspicuous critique of both the rent relation and capital itself.

9
The critical social theorists

Over the next few chapters I will unearth the neglected body of social science that I call Critical Social Theory, and I will show how it developed sophisticated yet now forgotten analyses of the capitalist rent relation and of capitalist social-property relations. But before I do this, I must explain what Critical Social Theory was and who developed it. Critical Social Theory, I argue, was constitutively related to a better-known though perhaps equally misunderstood intellectual tradition: political economy. I contend that Critical Social Theory and political economy were dialectically related and hence neither can be understood fully except in relation to the other. Thus, in this chapter, I will first explain what political economy was, arguing for a materialist conception of political economy as a historical project of scientific statecraft, a project that continues today under the banner of economics. I will then outline Critical Social Theory as a contemporaneous intellectual tradition, premised upon the scientific critique of political economy from a proletarian perspective. I will then show how intellectual historians have egregiously mischaracterised Critical Social Theory with reductive labels like 'utopianism', 'Ricardianism', and 'proto-Marxism', which have hitherto obscured its insights.

In material terms, the story of Critical Social Theory begins with political economy, a creature of the capitalist state. I have already shown that as the capitalist rent relation propagated itself seigneurial power was gradually transferred from the manor to the English Crown, unifying England's fragmented jurisdictions. As the Crown's autonomous capacity to extract rent was gradually extinguished, and its tribute-taking was curtailed to such taxes as the landlord-controlled Parliament authorised, a modern state emerged. As I have argued, this unitary state apparatus was constitutively related to an emerging capitalist civil society. The unitary state upheld the property rights that constituted capitalist civil-social relations – rights over land, labour power, and capital. It backstopped the political preconditions for capitalist production. Reciprocally, to enable the state to uphold capitalism's political preconditions, capitalist civil society rendered to the state a portion of its social product in taxes and other forms of tribute.

To reproduce its authority and existence, the emerging central state had to actively manage the turbulent and dynamic relations of an increasingly capitalist civil society. To reproduce its political authority, the state had to 'weld … disparate and competing group interests into a single common interest'.[1] To uphold and reproduce capitalist social-property relations, the state had to uphold not only property rights, but also 'encourage cooperative labor' and promote 'social harmony and tranquillity'.[2] Managing, stabilising, and reproducing the relations of capitalist civil society confronted the state with questions of policy spanning: 'property, finance, taxation, productivity, consumption, farming, enclosure, manufacture, trade, exports and imports, labor, unemployment, poverty, prices, inflation, wages, acquisition, usury, and other such topics'.[3] Much of the fledgling state's energy was devoted to upholding civil-social order in the face of the immense social dislocation being wreaked by the advancing capitalist rent relation, as enclosure ramified into unemployment, rural depopulation, poverty, crime, and civil unrest.

The managerial role of the emergent capitalist state found its first intellectual expression in a tradition of Tudor statecraft. In his *Foundations of Political Economy*, Neal Wood has traced the emergence of this intellectual tradition.[4] Tudor statecraft was characterised by 'meticulous and exhaustive inquiry' and 'the realistic empirical observation of social and economic conditions'.[5] On the basis of systematic analysis, Tudor statesmen recommended 'state measures to remedy the economic and social defects so revealed'.[6] They also turned their attention to the functioning of the state's internal relations, developing an intellectual tradition of 'improvement and governance'.[7] Tudor statecraft strove towards a vision of enlightened, prudent, and long-term government, contrasted with a grasping or short-sighted approach to policy.[8] It focused on governance for the 'long-term advantage' of the ruler.[9]

As the tradition of Tudor statecraft coalesced around a distinctively scientific mode of inquiry, it matured into political economy. The authority and influence of the discourse of Tudor statecraft depended on its ability to demonstrate alignment with the state's interests. Tudor statesmen had to distinguish their intellectual products from the special pleading of various civil-social and political interests that sought to influence state action. In response to this problem of intellectual authority, Tudor statesmen adopted a self-consciously scientific approach. Edmund Dudley (1462–1510) pioneered the practice of supporting claims either by reference to empirical evidence or by deducing conclusions from demonstrable or self-evident premises.[10] Later, Francis Bacon (1561–1626) promoted inductive empiricism, contributing 'a taste for economy in analysis, an abhorrence of *ad hoc* explanations, [and] a determination to explain as wide as possible a range of phenomena in terms of just a few simple principles'.[11] Their approaches were notable for their eschewal of appeals to authority.[12] As intellectuals such as William Petty (1623–1687) and John Locke (1632–1704) began to rigorously apply the Baconian methods to matters of policy, the enlightened discourse of the Tudor statesmen became a project of scientific statecraft, known as political economy.[13]

The discourse of political economy spanned around two centuries.[14] Its first major figure was Petty, with his *Treatise of Taxes and Contributions* (1662), and its last was arguably John Stuart Mill (1806–1873), with his *Principles of Political Economy* (1848). After Mill, political economy entered a period of decline before the marginalist revolution of the 1870s, after which it was reborn as economics.[15] This latter transformation lies beyond the scope of this book. Unlike modern economics, political economy did not have a 'tight sociological structure'.[16] Significant figures with respect to rent theory, without repeating those mentioned already, included: Richard Cantillon (1680s–1734) James Steuart (1711–1776); Adam Smith (1723–1790); James Anderson (1739–1809); Thomas Robert Malthus (1766–1834); David Ricardo (1772–1823); James Mill (1773–1836); David Buchanan (1779–1848); John Ramsay McCulloch (1789–1864); William Nassau Senior (1790–1864); Richard Jones (1790–1855); Samuel Bailey (1791–1870); Edward Wakefield (1796–1862); Mountifort Longfield (1802–1884);[17] and

Samuel Read (active 1816–1829). German scholars, such as Johann Heinrich von Thünen (1783–1850), also influenced the Anglophone political economic discourse, primarily via Senior. French writers likewise exerted influence, especially François Quesnay (1694–1774); Jean-Baptiste Say (1767–1832); and Frédéric Bastiat (1801–1850).

Despite its more scientific trappings, political economy was fully contiguous with Tudor statecraft in analysing society from the vantage of the state. In Petty's seminal writings, for example, he adopted the literary persona of a statesman-scientist advising the sovereign on how to increase the 'number, art and industry of his people, well united and governed'.[18] Over a century later, Smith, who brought political economy to fame, would define political economy as 'a branch of the *science of a statesman or legislator*'.[19] Half a century later, at the height of its prestige, McCulloch would surmise that political economy was 'to the State what domestic economy is to a single family'.[20]

In their efforts to manage capitalist civil society scientifically, political economists developed theoretical conceptions of its constitutive relations, including the rent relation. The complexity and variety of political economy's contributions to rent theory merits a more detailed treatment than I can offer here. Doing justice to the contributions of the political economists I have recited above would require a lengthy study of its own. I must leave this to others as I attempt to throw light on an even more neglected tradition: Critical Social Theory. The succeeding chapters will, however, sketch political economy's most prominent contribution to rent theory – the differential theory of rent – precisely because it was a key target of critique for Critical Social Theory, even as Critical Social Theory elaborated its own theories of the rent relation.

Critical Social Theory was largely structured around the critique of political economy from its margins. Political economy proceeded primarily through internal debates among theorists who recognised each other's standing as political economists and as participants in a shared scientific enterprise. Critical social theorists, by contrast, proffered views that marked them as outside the bounds of political economy. Political economists typically responded to critical social theorists with a studied ignorance, interspersed with occasional swatting in the form of refutations and apologia.[21] Despite their marginalisation or exclusion, and often because of it, critical social theorists often structured their works as critiques of political economy. Their works were strewn with references to figures like Smith and Ricardo. In this sense, Critical Social Theory was structured as a *negative* intellectual community: its theorists were united not so much by collaboration or ideological unity, but by a common orientation toward critiquing political economy from the outside.

Whereas political economy's scientific statecraft was an intellectual outgrowth of the capitalist state, Critical Social Theory was an outgrowth of the working classes, and especially the swelling proletariat. As will be seen, critical social theorists often had subaltern or proletarian backgrounds. Others, hailing from the middle and upper classes, explicitly declared proletarian sympathies – and often wrote anonymously, to avoid the repercussions of their class treachery. Critical Social Theory often had a working-class audience. The work of leading critical theorists like Thompson, Hodgskin, and Gray was taken up by the working-class presses, particularly in the 1820s and 1830s.[22]

Critical social theorists often understood themselves, explicitly or implicitly, as appropriating and reorienting the social insights of political economy to serve proletarian interests. Hopkins, for instance, argued that political economy should become 'the science of the poor man'. Its proper focus, he argued, should be 'those causes which affect and regulate [the condition of] all those who … procure their subsistence by the sweat of their brow'.[23]

Like political economists, critical social theorists were assiduously scientific. Indeed, the term 'social science' was itself coined by the critical social theorist William Thompson in 1824.[24] Critical social theorists generally eschewed appeals to scholastic or divine authority, and aspired to support their claims by empirical proof or deductions from demonstrable or self-evident premises. As Bailey wrote, the 'science of society' should be 'founded on demonstrable facts'.[25] '[A]bstract truth', he argued, 'can be obtained only by patient and elaborate inquiry … accurate scrutiny of the phenomena … and a mind free from prejudice, calm, and dispassionate … [in] the true spirit of the inductive philosophy'.[26]

Critical Social Theory attacked political economy for its myopic focus on problems of the state and propertied classes, and its neglect of proletarian interests. Dove noted that political economists 'strenuously adhered' to a 'restricted' understanding of their science as 'an exposition of the laws according to which man creates or produces wealth'.[27] '[T]his wealth', he noted, '... is the wealth of the land owner, the mill owner, the iron master, &c., and not the wealth of the multitude of human laborers'.[28] Sismondi likewise noted political economy's monotonous focus on 'adding ever greater sums to the balance sheet of the nation'.[29] Dove called for replacing political economists with men 'who take a wider range of investigation'.[30] Social science, Thompson wrote, should focus on 'the situation of the industrious classes, as compared with that of the idle'.[31]

The ambitions of Critical Social Theory were often framed in utilitarian terms. Edmonds, for instance, called for a science that served '[t]he greatest Happiness of the greatest Number'.[32] Dove called for a 'science of social utility, of which the production of wealth is only the first and simplest embranchment'.[33] Hopkins argued political economy should examine not 'what leads to the greatest opulence, but what would give humanity the greatest happiness through opulence'.[34]

WHO WERE THE CRITICAL SOCIAL THEORISTS?

Reflecting on some major figures of Critical Social Theory, Prum has aptly summarised the project's material basis. To borrow his words, critical social theorists

> differed in nationality, occupation, inspiration ... Although they hardly knew each other, they shared some essential ideals ... They all criticized the rising industrial capitalism and classical political economy; they all defended the claims of the working class, trying to turn the very weapons of the economists against the 'dismal science'.[35]

So who were they? I will now briefly outline the identities, biographies and writings of key contributors to Critical Social Theory, focusing on those who theorised rent.[36] These include Ogilvie, Hall, Spence, Sismondi, Hopkins, Thompson, Hodgskin, Mudie, Gray, Edmonds, John Francis Bray, Charles Bray, Dove, and Ravenstone. Robert Owen, whose biography I sketched in the previous chapter, requires a special mention. While not a notable theorist of rent, his ideas loomed large in the discourse.[37]

William Ogilvie (1736–1813) attended Glasgow University in the winter of 1761–1762, while Adam Smith was Professor of Moral Philosophy.[38] Beyond Smith, Ogilvie was also likely influenced by Locke.[39] Ogilvie went on to become a celebrated professor of Humanity at King's College, Aberdeen, from 1765 to 1817. In 1781, five years after Smith published his *Wealth of Nations*, Ogilvie penned his contribution to Critical Social Theory: *An essay on the right of property in land*. Ogilvie was a landlord with close connections to the Scottish aristocracy.[40] He had much to lose, which is likely why he published his essay anonymously.

Charles Hall (1740–1825) was a physician whose primary contribution to Critical Social Theory was his *The Effects of Civilisation on the People in European States* (1805). Hall's critique was framed by debates with mainstream figures like Malthus and Smith, with Smith serving both as Hall's interlocutor and his principal intellectual influence.[41] Although he read Ricardo, Hall's contribution to rent theory antedates that of both Ricardo and Malthus. Hall was a friend and contemporary of another important early figure of Critical Social Theory: Thomas Spence.

Thomas Spence (1750–1814) was a working-class autodidact, radical bookseller, and author of perhaps the first major contribution to Critical Social Theory. Spence read thinkers such as Harrington, Locke, Swift, Priestley, and Godwin.[42] In 1775, he published his *The Real Rights of Man*, which, alongside its economic analysis, proposed that land be publicly owned at the parish level. Radicalised by the French Revolution, Spence later combined his land plan with calls for a violent insurrection.[43] He was repeatedly imprisoned on charges including treason and seditious libel.[44] By the 1790s, his works gained a following among radical working-class Londoners. Spencean Clubs sprang up following Spence's death, and Spenceans were behind two abortive insurrections in 1816 and 1820.[45] Speanceanism became 'part of the intellectual matrix of working-class culture that was emerging in the early nineteenth century'.[46]

Jean Charles Léonard de Sismondi (1773–1842) is unique among critical social theorists because he defected from political economy. Sismondi, a Genevese historian and landowner, made his entrée into political economy with his *De la Richesse Commerciale* (1803). The book established Sismondi's reputation as a Smithian free trader resolutely opposed to state intervention.[47] In the following years, however, Sismondi's scholarship and observation of the Industrial Revolution led him to repudiate *laissez faire*.[48] Oblivious to this conversion, the Edinburgh Encyclopedia commissioned Sismondi to write an introduction to political economy in 1815. The article, entitled 'Political Economy', was profoundly heterodox.[49] By 1819, Sismondi had expanded the article into his magnum opus, *Nouveaux principes d'économie politique*.[50] In it, he set himself against luminaries like Say, Ricardo, Malthus and McCulloch.[51] He rejected Say's Law,[52] asserting that capitalism caused 'unforeseen crises' and 'unheard-of suffering'.[53] He critiqued Ricardo's doctrine of comparative advantage and defended protectionism.[54] He rejected Ricardo's formulation of the differential theory of rent and rejected capitalist agriculture in favour of peasant proprietorship.[55]

Political economy treated *Nouveaux principes* as an act of treachery. The fact that the critique was penned in French only added to the insult. It was reviewed excoriatingly in *The Edinburgh Review*.[56] An English translation of its foreword appeared in 1847,[57] but polyglot English intellectuals read it in French before that.[58] Though effectively excommunicated, Sismondi never styled himself as an outsider, insisting he remained fundamentally 'Smithian'.[59] While his views took him beyond the pale of political economy, he retained personal connections with figures like Ricardo.[60]

Sismondi's ideas ramified through Critical Social Theory via several channels. Early Owenite thinkers read and discussed his work.[61]

Sismondi strongly influenced the writings of the critical social theorist Thomas Hopkins (active 1811–1840). I have been able to discover little about Hopkins, but aspects of his work are unmistakably Sismondian, particularly his critique of differential rent and his promotion of peasant proprietorship. Like Sismondi, Hopkins framed his work as a critique of Ricardo, James Mill and McCulloch.[62] Hopkins was not, however, *just* an Anglophone Sismondian. He made important contributions to Critical Social Theory in his own right.

William Thompson (1775–1833) was perhaps Critical Social Theory's greatest figure before Marx. Thompson was a remorseful Anglo-Irish landowner, heir to the fortune of a prominent Cork merchant family. When he died, he willed his fortune to Britain's burgeoning cooperative movement, in which he was a leading figure, second only to Robert Owen. He was a friend of both Jeremy Bentham and David Ricardo.[63] Thompson published several major contributions to Critical Social Theory, most notably *Labour Rewarded* (1827), which he published anonymously, signing as 'One of the Idle Classes.' Thompson was influenced by Smith and took mainstream writers like Malthus, James Mill, and Martineau as his interlocutors.[64] He was an acquaintance of the young John Stuart Mill and debated with him.[65]

Thomas Hodgskin (1787–1869) is one of the best remembered critical social theorists, via his status as one of the principal 'Ricardian Socialists.' He was a journalist with working-class roots, rising to prominence in the 1820s and in later life writing for the *Economist*. His tract *Labour Defended* (1825) was framed as a riposte to James Mill's *Commerce Defended* (1808). Hodgskin was influenced by figures like Say, Smith, Locke and Rousseau.[66]

George Mudie (born in 1788) was a Scottish printer and journalist, and one of the earliest proponents of Robert Owen's social philosophy.[67] Mudie made journalistic contributions to Critical Social Theory over many years, including as printer of the *Economist*, which he founded to popularise Owenism and to offer an Owenite critique of political economy. Claeys describes Mudie as Owen's 'first radical sympathizer … of any note.'[68]

John Gray (1799–1883) was a former factory worker and newspaper printer who made significant contributions to critical social theory.[69] He was a student of Smith and Ricardo. Gray met Robert Owen in 1823, first extolling but later rejecting Owen's social philosophy.[70] Gray was active from the mid-1820s to the late 1840s.

Thomas Rowe Edmonds (1803–1889) was a town clerk and actuary. His principal contribution to Critical Social Theory was his *An Enquiry into the Principles of Population* (1832). In it, he proposed a 'system of regulations' framed to redress 'the evils which have hitherto pressed upon the labouring classes of society'. Tellingly, Edmonds published this work anonymously.

John Francis Bray (1809–1897) was born in the United States of America into a family of clothiers and farmers. He trained as a printer and became a working-class activist, associated with the Chartist movement. Bray's principal contribution to Critical Social Theory was his *Labour's Wrongs and Labour's Remedy* (1839). Marx described it as a 'remarkable work' and quoted it at length in his *Poverty of Philosophy* (1847).[71]

Another Bray, Charles Bray (1811–1884), was a wealthy ribbon manufacturer, proprietor of the *Coventry Herald*, and social reformer. He established and promoted a non-sectarian school for infants in a poor neighbourhood in Coventry.[72] He was a follower of Robert Owen, a member of the Rosehill Circle, and a friend of George Eliot's. His principal contribution to Critical Social Theory was his *Philosophy of Necessity*, published in two volumes in 1841.

Patrick Dove (1815–1873) was a member of the Scottish gentry, whose family had roots in the navy and clergy. His principal contribution to Critical Social Theory, *The Theory of Human Progression* (1850), was published anonymously.

John Watts (1818–1887) was from a working-class background, and worked as an Owenite social missionary, lecturer and teacher in the early 1840s, before retreating to liberal, Cobdenite and Chartist views later in his life.[73] His principal contribution to Critical Social Theory was his *Facts and Fictions of Political Economists* (1842). He was influenced by earlier figures like William Thompson and was the conduit for Friedrich Engels' first acquaintance with Critical Social Theory.

Piercy Ravenstone (active 1821–1824) was a pseudonymous critical social theorist active in the early 1820s. His principal contribution to Critical Social Theory was his *A Few Doubts as to the Correctness of Some Opinions Generally Entertained on the Subjects of Population and Political Economy* (1821).[74] In it, he set himself against Malthus' population theory and the formulation of differential rent espoused by Malthus and Ricardo.[75] On evidence uncovered by Pierro Sraffa, Ravenstone has been tentatively identified as one Richard Puller the younger.[76] Puller was the son of a wealthy merchant banker, and the grandson of Christopher Puller, a Director of the Bank of England and the South Sea Company.

A final critical social theorist, about whom I have discovered little, is one T. Wayland of Lincoln's Inn. His name survives as the author of an 1832 pamphlet titled 'National Advancement and Happiness Considered in Reference to the Equalization of Property and the Formation of Communities'. The pamphlet marks itself as a work of Critical Social Theory through its critique of Robert Malthus and James Mill, and its vigorous defence of the doctrines of Robert Owen.

UTOPIANISM, RICARDIANISM, AND PROTO-MARXISM

We have now surveyed Critical Social Theory as a material process, tracing the people and social conditions that gave rise to it. By contrast, however, efforts to understand this body of work have been dominated by an idealist approach: they have tried to boil it down to supposedly unifying ideas like 'Ricardian socialism', 'utopian socialism', or 'proto-Marxism'. We can already see why this approach is wrong. Critical social theorists were unified by class sympathies, not by any 'ism'. They developed no doctrinal consensus because they focused on critiquing political economists, not ironing out internal disagreements. Their object of critique – political economy – was itself rife with debate and dissent.[77] As I will show, the search for 'core ideas' falsifies and obscures the depth and variety of Critical Social Theory. It also displaces the kind of careful reading that can illuminate its most brilliant moments and its genuine common themes.

Critical Social Theory is often incorrectly surmised as 'utopian socialism', especially by Marxists. I will address the charge of 'utopianism' here and return to that of 'socialism' later. Marx and Engels famously identified utopianism as: the advocacy of social change by 'appeal to the whole of society without distinction, even by preference to the ruling class'; the proposal of plans 'for the best possible society'; and the idealist view that 'anyone needs but to understand their system in order to recognise it as the best'.[78] By this definition, some critical social theorists certainly had utopian moments. But equally, others noticed these moments and critiqued them as harshly as Marx and Engels. James Napier Bailey, for example, decried what he called 'utopian visions'.[79] He explicitly attacked idealist accounts of historical change, arguing that 'mental powers alone' cannot transform society without a 'material subordinate agency'.[80] As I will show in Chapter 15, critical social theorists in fact overwhelmingly understood social change in materialist terms, as arising from social-property relations and class struggle. It is ironic that the term 'utopian' is misapplied to the very tradition that first critiqued utopianism.

Alongside 'Utopian Socialism', Critical Social Theory has also been mislabelled as 'Ricardian Socialism'. This term is likewise misappropriated from Marx. In 1847, Marx remarked that 'almost all the socialists in ... [England] have, at different periods, proposed the equalitarian application of the Ricardian theory'.[81] Here Marx was apparently referring to Ricardo's labour theory of exchange value. But it was not until 1899 that Herbert Foxwell formally applied the label 'Ricardian Socialism' to a specific clutch of critical social theorists. An anti-Ricardian and anti-socialist, Foxwell tried to bring Ricardo into disrepute by blaming him for both English socialism and the violent revolutions of the nineteenth century.[82] The label stuck.[83] Noel Thompson has used it more recently, defining it, along Marxian lines, as the 'attempt to construct a theory of labour exploitation on the basis of a labour theory of exchange value'.[84]

Unfortunately, these ideas poorly fit what critical social theorists actually wrote. Foxwell identified four so-called 'Ricardian Socialists': Hodgskin, Thompson, Edmonds, and John Francis Bray.[85] Noel Thompson identified a similar 'big four'.[86] Yet, examining their writings, Stafford has observed that '[u]nder no definition of the word can Ravenstone and Hodgskin be labelled socialist'.[87] In Chapter 14, I corroborate this, showing these theorists had a variety of social imaginaries. If they were not uniformly 'socialist', neither were they consistently 'Ricardian'. Hodgskin was arguably the most prominent of the so-called Ricardian Socialists, but there was nothing Ricardian about his theory of exploitation.[88] Ravenstone's historicism was likewise more Smithian than Ricardian.[89] Gray's Ricardianism is also hard to find. He thought in terms of utility, not exchange value.[90]

With the label of 'Ricardian Socialism' chafing, alternatives have proliferated. Noel Thompson, even while employing the term Ricardian Socialism, ruminates on whether it is better designated 'Smithian'.[91] Meek, heading in a different direction, has connected Hall and Ravenstone to the Physiocrats.[92] Thompson has been called a 'Smithian Benthamite', and Hodgskin a 'Lockean anarchist'.[93] From a materialist perspective, this proliferation of ill-fitting idea-based labels is unsurprising.[94] There are endless links between the ideas of Critical Social Theory and political economy, because the former was a *critique* of the latter. But the search for 'one idea to rule them all' is futile because Critical Social Theory was simply not a consensus-building enterprise.

More recent idealist efforts have tried to characterise Critical Social Theory by reference to the ideas of Marx and Marxism, adding irony and anachronism to earlier failures. Noel Thompson's definition of Ricardian Socialism, for example, turns largely on a contrast with Marxism – the former allegedly focused on exchange, the latter on production.[95] King, on the other hand, makes the inverse argument, seeing a fundamental *unity* of ideas between the Ricardian Socialists and Marx.[96] In these variants of idealist historiography, the 'unifying idea' of Critical Social Theory is not its Ricardianism but its proto-Marxism or its *failure* to be proto-Marxism. But Critical Social Theory has no unifying idea. Looking for one in Marxism is especially ironic, because he famously critiqued idealist approaches. It is also deeply anachronistic. Ricardo at least *could have* influenced early Critical Social Theory, whereas Marx's works appeared half a century *after* it.

There is, of course, a real material connection between Marx and Critical Social Theory. Marx was the heir of this proletarian tradition, and it is legitimate for scholars of Marx to ask how it may have influenced him, and perhaps his theories of rent.[97] But that is not the purpose of this book. And we cannot hope to understand what Marx drew from Critical Social Theory while its best insights are obscured by reductive, dismissive, idealist labelling. The tradition must first be reconstructed in its own material context, as this book seeks to do. Marxist terms like 'utopian socialism' or 'Ricardian socialism' are worse than useless for this task. The only useful 'ism' is the powerful *method* developed by Marx and others before and after him: historical materialism.

And while there is bad historiography to overcome, there has been good work to build on. In his *Machinery, Money and the Millennium* and his *Citizens and Saints*, Claeys has already deeply explored the thought of a group he calls the 'Owenite Socialists'.[98] He uses this label not reductively, but as a shorthand for the loose intellectual community that coalesced around Robert Owen. My exploration of Critical Social Theory encompasses the work of Claeys' Owenite Socialists, but focuses on how they used rent theory. Yet Claeys plumbs other depths I do not here: their theories of technological development, money, and exchange, their millenarian strains, and their political and anti-political moments.

McNally's *Against the Market* likewise provides an important materialist study of Critical Social Theory.[99] He defines Critical Social Theory not by its ideas but by its critical and proletarian orientation to political economy. He highlights how Critical Social Theory's critiques and imaginaries, despite their critical edge, often failed to transcend the horizon of capitalist social-property relations. He identifies its tendency to frame exploitation in terms of unequal exchange, which prompted abortive efforts to perfect or equalise market relations.[100] Much of Critical Social Theory, McNally carefully shows, was vulnerable to Marx's later critique of 'market socialism'. Without disputing McNally, the ensuing chapters of this book will show that the picture is more ambiguous. Critical Social Theory's focus on unequal exchange co-existed, often awkwardly, with richer theories of capitalist social-property relations. I will argue that these only become apparent with attention to neglected critical theories of rent. Even as Critical Social Theory contained moments of 'market socialism', it also contained the seeds of its critique.

And if Marx brilliantly *transcended* some of Critical Social Theory's ideas, the following chapters will show that some of his most characteristic ideas were in fact already formulated by critical social theorists. This elucidates Marx's contribution rather than diminishing it: whereas Critical Social Theory largely ignored its internal contradictions, Marx broke new ground, in part, by confronting them. This involved not only discarding, critiquing and transcending, but also adopting, developing and integrating. If the latter is surprising, it is only because Critical Social Theory has been so caricatured. Ideas, after all, do not spring fully formed from the heads of lone geniuses. They are always products of social processes and particular material conditions.

10
The critique of differential rent

In this chapter, I will outline political economy's paradigmatic theory of the capitalist rent relation – the differential theory of rent – and present Critical Social Theory's critique of it. I contend that the differential theory offered the British state a scientific framework for managing tensions between landed and manufacturing capital as Britain shifted from agrarian to industrial capitalism. Critical Social Theory's critique, articulated by Sismondi, systematically attacked the differential theory's premises. It demonstrated how these premises occluded the experience and condition of the British proletariat. Sismondi's critique, we will see, did not just refute the differential theory, but in doing so exposed how the capitalist rent relation enforced the proletarian condition, backstopping capitalist social-property relations.

In the early nineteenth century, Malthus and Ricardo each developed paradigmatic formulations of the differential theory of rent. The theory was stated implicitly in Malthus' *Observations on the Effects of the Corn Laws* (1814), and explicitly in his *Inquiry into the Nature and Progress of Rent* (1815). Ricardo adopted much of Malthus' presentation in his *Principles of Political Economy and Taxation* (1817), integrating it with his labour theory of value to build a broader theory of distribution.[1] The differential theory became part of Ricardo's impressively unified theory of rents, profits, wages and prices. Because of this, it is often referred to as 'Ricardian', yet neither Ricardo nor even Malthus discovered it.[2] James Anderson formulated a little-noticed version of it as early as 1777.[3] By 1814, however, the theory's time had come. In that year, it was advanced contemporaneously by Malthus, West, Rooke and perhaps even Torrens.[4]

The differential theory's sudden elevation, I contend, stems from the material conditions of early nineteenth-century Britain. It was a time of rising tension between the established interests of agrarian capital and the ascendant interests of urban manufacturing capital. For landlords and agrarian capitalists, profit and rent depended on food prices remaining high. Manufacturing capital, by contrast, saw the price of food as a key component of wages. Lower food prices meant cheaper manufacturing labour and greater profits. This perceived divergence of interests generated significant antagonism within Britain's propertied classes.

A view gained currency among manufacturing interests that landlords were pushing up food prices by charging high rents. Agrarian capitalists, they argued, were passing the cost of high rents to the consumer through high food prices, which were making it expensive for manufacturers to feed their labourers, depressing manufacturing profits. Malthus and other political economists turned to the differential theory at a time when 'hostility to landlords and to high rents was in the air'.[5]

Malthus and his followers saw the differential theory as a scientific way to diffuse the tensions of landed and manufacturing capital. The differential theory, he believed, demonstrated rents were not 'a value unnecessarily and injuriously transferred from one set of people to another; but ... most real and essential ... and placed by the laws of nature ... on the land'.[6] Despite the apparently divergent interests of manufacturing and landed capital, the differential theory proved that manufacturers would not be advantaged by curtailing landlords' rents. If rent was ordained by the 'laws of nature', trying to curtail it would cause a national disaster. The differential theory offered political economy a persuasively scientific solution to a key tension in British capitalism.

The differential theory rested on key assumptions. It assumed a stylised, abstract, purely capitalist class structure composed of landlords, agrarian capitalists, and wage labourers.[7] It thus modelled a purely capitalist rent relation. It assumed away the rump of British peasants who continued to pay tributary rents.[8] It was also largely inapplicable beyond Britain's shores, where peasant production still reigned. As Richard Jones observed in his 1831 essay 'Peasant Rents', the theory was applicable to only perhaps 1 per cent of the 'cultivated surface' of the planet.[9]

The theory also assumed competitive markets for land, labour, capital, and consumer goods. Competition was seen as an equilibrating force. Competition in commodity and labour markets would cause capitalists' profits and labourers' wages to converge on average rates over time. An agrarian capitalist, it was assumed, would not rent a piece of land unless he could earn at least the average rate of profit while paying the average rate of wages.[10]

The differential theory assumed that land varied in its productivity, that the best land was scarce, and that each plot yielded diminishing returns to capital.[11] High-fertility land was assumed to be in limited supply, but with an unlimited succession of progressively inferior plots available. Because only the best land was scarce, landlords were assumed to exercise only a 'partial monopoly'.[12] It was assumed, as Ricardo wrote, that capital could not 'be indefinitely employed without a diminished return' even on the best land.[13] As additional 'doses' of capital were applied to a plot of land, the overall yield would rise, but each additional dose would yield less as the land approached the limits of its productivity. Diminishing returns applied to labour too. '[W]ith every increase of the labour bestowed', wrote Senior, 'the aggregate return is increased, [though] the increase of the return is not in proportion to the increase of the Labour'.[14]

Finally, the differential theory assumed that demand for the produce of land was price inelastic. Food was understood as a 'necessary', rather than a luxury.[15] If the price of food rose, consumers would pay the higher price, rather than go hungry. Any rise in population would thus result in higher demand for food, while the supply of high-quality land remained fixed.

Together all these assumptions led to the differential theory. The theory posited capitalists would first apply their capital to the highest-grade land, where the crop yield per dose of capital – and hence the profit – was highest. But due to diminishing returns, they would receive a smaller additional yield for each dose of capital they applied to the best land. At some point, then, they would get better yields by applying additional doses of capital to virgin second-grade land, rather than lavishing more on the exhausted first-grade land. Rent, the theory concluded, was an inevitable result of needing to use different grades of land *simulta-*

neously to produce enough to feed the nation. When 'land of the second degree of fertility is taken into cultivation', Ricardo wrote, 'rent immediately commences on that of the first quality, and the amount of that rent will depend on the difference in the quality of these two portions'.[16] Rent was thus no more than a modest and essential price signal, efficiently allocating Britain's scarcest productive land.

The differential theory held that a landlord's rent was proportionate to the quality of his land. Competition for tenancies forced a capitalist bidding for high-grade land to offer any surplus profit it might yield to his landlord as a rent.[17] Once he paid his rent, the capitalist working high-grade land should finish with no more profit than the one farming the poorest or most 'marginal' land in Britain. A landlord's rent was thus a differential: the extra profit that could be made farming *his* land compared to the worst land being used anywhere.[18] This led to the surprising implication that a capitalist farming such 'marginal land' must be paying a rent of *zero*.[19]

The assertion that marginal land is free was not just a curiosity; it was the crux of an important theory of food prices. The differential theory posited that the price of corn was set by its cost of production on marginal land.[20] The best quality land was scarce and subject to diminishing returns – so it could not supply the whole nation's food. To induce capitalist farmers to supply enough food to feed the nation, consumers had to pay food prices high enough to ensure capitalists could resort to lower grades of land while still making a profit. Even the farmer using marginal land, the worst land resorted to anywhere, still had to make a profit. Food prices had to cover his costs. While this farmer paid zero rent, he was working with the poorest soil any capitalist had to suffer, and hence, even when producing efficiently, he faced the highest labour and capital costs per unit he produced. '[T]he price of produce …' Malthus concluded, 'must be just about equal to the cost of production on land of the poorest quality actually in use'.

As a theory of food prices, the differential theory of rent purported to prove a key claim: that 'rent is an effect of high price, not a cause thereof'.[21] As just outlined, the price of food, according to the differential theory, was set by the cost of production on marginal land. But this cost did *not* include rent because, according to the differential theory, marginal land is rented for free. '[R]ent', Ricardo surmised, 'is not a component part of the price of commodities'.[22] Indeed, according to the differential theory, causation ran in the opposite direction. Because consumers had to offer prices high enough to induce production on marginal land, capitalists on higher-grade land received a windfall price – well above their costs of production – resulting in above-average profits. Through competitive bidding for high-grade tenancies, capitalists gave up this surplus profit to landlords as rent. Thus, Ricardo concluded, 'the rent of land, is the effect, and never the cause of the high value of ... produce'.[23]

Political economy's differential theory of rent neatly and scientifically adjudicated antagonisms between landlords and other capitalist interests. It confirmed that landlords benefit from high food prices, while consumers and manufacturers suffer.[24] It confirmed that landlords had selfish interests in the Corn Laws, which restricted grain imports and drove up food prices.[25] But the theory also insisted rents were an *ineliminable* byproduct of capitalist agriculture when soil fertility varied. While landlords benefited from high food prices, their rents were not the cause. They could only demand high rents if agricultural prices were already high.[26] This seemingly proved that curtailing landlords' rent would not make food cheaper for workers or wages cheaper for manufacturers.[27] Antagonism resolved.

Critical social theorists typically accepted the differential theory.[28] Stafford argues Ravenstone rejected it, but this is questionable.[29] Of all the critical theorists I have surveyed, only Sismondi and his disciple Hopkins truly critiqued it. Sismondi developed his critique in his *New Principles*, taking Ricardo and Malthus as his principal foils.[30] He presented a laundry list of criticisms, attacking each of the theory's key assumptions. Hyse argues his intent was not 'to advance a new rent theory, but to make existing theory take account of actual practice'.[31] But this misses Sismondi's guiding principle. For Sismondi, the theory's key flaw was that its 'very abstract discussion had failed to deduce "any conclusion applicable to the man who cultivates" the land – that is, the agricultural labourer'.[32] His purpose in systematically attacking the theory's premises was to reveal the proletarian experience. As I will show, he did not merely negate the differential theory. He developed a striking alternative picture of the capitalist rent relation that centred the proletarianising character of rent and its role in capitalist social-property relations.

Sismondi argued that the differential theory's assumptions obscured the real conditions that capitalists and labourers faced. Capital and labour were not nearly as mobile as the differential theory assumed. A capitalist, Sismondi observed, may require 'twenty or thirty years to leave a trade in which fixed capital has been sunk'.[33] For workers, it was arduous to change trades, with each requiring 'a long apprenticeship'.[34] Capital mobility was unrealistic even *within* an industry.[35] '[F]armers from one district', he observed, 'find it difficult to migrate to another'.[36] These frictions and volatility, Sismondi argued, often compelled a worker or capitalist to accept 'an income below that of all others'.[37] These frictions meant the differential theory was wrong to suppose a 'stable equilibrium of profits in all industries'.[38] It was also wrong to suggest 'all farmers' profits are equalized' among different grades of land.[39] Sismondi was particularly scathing of the differential theory's assumption of an average rate of profit in *agriculture*. The industry was uniquely large and competitive. '[T]he number of farmers', he observed, 'is much larger than that of any men engaged in any trade'.[40] Brutal competition, market volatility, and immobile capital and labour meant agricultural profits and wages could fluctuate wildly compared to other industries, quite contrary to the tranquil vision of the differential theory.[41]

Sismondi further rejected the theory's assumption of perfect competition and the mechanical account of distribution that followed. He recounted how the differential theory assumed competition constrained both wages and profits to average rates, with landlords automatically receiving any differential 'surplus value' as rent.[42] This story was, in Sismondi's view, a misrepresentation.[43] He asserted that what he called 'surplus value' was in fact distributed by 'a double and even threefold battle' – a class struggle between landlords, capitalist farmers, and workers.[44] Each possessed different degrees of power 'according to [the] circumstances', the 'number of competitors' and the 'state of the market'.[45] This picture was a far cry from the orderly and automatic distribution posited by political economy, and it refuted the claim that rent was only ever an effect of high prices, never the cause. If conditions were favourable to landlords, Sismondi argued, they could dictate rents like a monopoly price.[46] These were the real conditions the proletariat faced, both as labourers and consumers.

Sismondi's most fundamental criticisms of the differential theory of rent, however, related to how it occluded the fundamental proletarian condition: landlessness. The theory, he noted, tried to 'abstract from space' by assuming unlimited, vacant, marginal land, and absurdly inferred that landlords rent such land for 'no compensation at all'.[47] Sismondi pointed out that all land was scarce, not just the best land, and so all land bore a 'monopoly price' or scarcity rent.[48] Were there such a thing as rent-free land, Sismondi argued, Britain's proletariat would not exist. Unemployed workers, he observed, could simply help themselves to 'new arable ground' for free.[49] While claiming to model a capitalist economy, the differential theory left workers' exclusion from the land – capitalism's fundamental precondition – glaringly unexplained. With a sleight of hand, it assumed capitalist farming was 'the sole means of taking advantage of agricultural wealth'.[50] It assumed away alternative uses of the land, especially subsistence farming.

Sismondi observed that subsistence and capitalist farming, in fact, operated on different rules of reproduction. Capitalist farmers rented land only if they could achieve a return covering wages, rent, and *profit*. Their product had to achieve a 'remunerative price' or profit, or they would not bother farming.[51] By contrast, wrote Sismondi, a subsistence farmer 'sows his own field in order to eat his corn'.[52] Subsistence farmers rent land if it will yield their subsistence plus the going rent. The subsistence farmer welcomed an additional 'profit' but, unlike the capitalist, did not require it. If a subsistence farmer sold his surplus, unlike the capitalist, he could afford to do so at any price, because his subsistence did not 'depend on the fluctuations of the market'.[53]

By assuming subsistence farming away, Sismondi argued, differential theory obscured the capitalist rent relation's proletarianising force and how rents were really set.[54] Even under purely capitalist social-property relations, Sismondi observed, capitalists always had to outbid would-be subsistence farmers to secure productive land.[55] This bidding war set a minimum beneath which a capitalist's rent could not fall, belying the existence of zero-rent land. With capitalists perpetually outbidding subsistence farmers, the rent relation repulsed the latter from the land and corralled them into wage labour.[56] If a former peasant 'would have liked to return to garden farming', wrote Sismondi, 'he will not anymore have the means'.[57] The rent relation thus generated and maintained the proletarian condition on which capitalism rested.[58]

Thomas Hopkins, an Anglophone Sismondian, was perhaps the only other critical social theorist to explicitly critique the differential theory. He built on Sismondi's critique of its key assumptions, arguing that capitalist farmers: did not apply their capital in neat marginal 'doses';[59] did not experience uniformly diminishing returns;[60] and did not rent land solely based on its yield per acre.[61]

Hopkins emphasised the monopoly or scarcity nature of rent, especially. Political economy, he argued, 'confounds the cause of … [differentials in rent] with the cause of the *existence* of rent itself'.[62] He compared a country with 'lands of twenty different qualities' to one with 'land of only one quality'.[63] The land in *both* countries, he argued, would be subject to rent, so long as it was monopolised by landlords.[64] If rent could exist without differentials, it could not be caused by them. Political economy had confounded 'the relative rents of lands … with the general average rate of rent'.[65] Once land was monopolised, Hopkins argued, even '[t]he poorest land that is occupied pays a rent'.[66] Marginal land was not 'rent-free'.[67] As even the worst land was subject to rent, Hopkins reasoned, he concluded, like Sismondi before him, that rent always added to the marginal cost of producing food, and hence to its price.[68]

In conclusion, this chapter has traced Critical Social Theory's reception and critique of the differential theory of rent. I began by showing how the theory came to prominence because it offered the state a seemingly scientific way to mediate tensions between landed and manufacturing capital. I then outlined Sismondi's critique, which was many-pronged but guided by the unifying principle of exposing rent's impact on the proletariat. His most fundamental criticism, I have argued, was that the differential theory obscured the proletarianising nature of the capitalist rent relation. As the next chapter will show, the characterisation of rent as a proletarianising relation was in fact ubiquitous in Critical Social Theory.

11

Capitalist rent as proletarianisation

If political economy converged on the differential theory of rent, then Critical Social Theory converged on a theory I call 'rent as proletarianization'. To guide their analysis of the capitalist rent relation, critical social theorists repeatedly posited two guiding norms, which I call the right to the earth and the right to the fruits of labour. Different critical theorists articulated these two norms differently, but they were ubiquitous and operated, I argue, as the normative lights guiding Critical Social Theory's scientific inquiry. They oriented the analysis towards proletarian interests.

Before explaining Critical Social Theory's norms, I must caution that while its *particular* norms were distinctive, 'normativity' did *not* itself make Critical Social Theory exceptional among scientific enterprises, let alone unscientific. Rising to prominence in the late nineteenth and twentieth centuries, I contend, scientistic and positivistic approaches to history and philosophy of science have led to prudishness about the role norms play in science. Critical social theorists were refreshingly overt about their norms. That this became unfashionable may partly explain why even critical historiography has rarely recognised Critical Social Theory's scientific status, nor what *unified* its heterogeneous elements into a single discourse. By comparison, the discourse of political economy – the celebrated scientific precursor to economics – equally had normative commitments. These included, at the very least, reproducing state power, upholding civil-social order, defending private property and promoting capital accumulation and national wealth.

Indeed, Critical Social Theory shares its normativity not only with political economy, but with *all* scientific enterprises. In material terms, every scientific enterprise is a goal-directed social activity conducted according to the norms of a discrete intellectual community. Such communities are always embedded in broader societies, and thus directed and constrained by broader social norms too. Critical Social Theory is not thus unscientific because it was guided by norms. Indeed, without norms, whether implicit or explicit, science and its products are unintelligible.

Critical social theorists often expressed the right to the earth and to the fruits of labour as natural rights. Bray provides a vivid example. 'Human rights are equal', he wrote, 'and the correct definers of man's authority over man'.[1] 'Every man has a right to do what he likes', he argued, '*provided the so doing interferes not with the EQUAL rights of his fellow man*'.[2] From this notion of equal liberty, he derived the right to the fruits of labour, asserting that 'all those who perform equal labour should receive an equal reward'.[3] Man had the right to appropriate, according to Bray, 'the various necessaries of life which he can, by his labour, compel the earth to yield to him'.[4] Bray derived from the right to the fruits of labour an implicit right to the earth. Man had the right 'to live upon that earth on which he has been placed by his Creator'.[5] '[T]he great field for all exertion', he wrote, 'and the raw material of all wealth – the earth – is the common property of all its inhabitants'.[6]

Other critical social theorists made utilitarian or consequentialist arguments. Sismondi, for instance, said the right to the fruits of labour was justified by the harms of violating it. '[E]very division of fruits', he argued, 'which separates ownership interest from interest in cultivation tends to destroy … the good effects which society had expected from the appropriation of land'.[7] Hopkins, influenced by Sismondi, argued that 'securing to each man of the fruits of his labour, more or less effectually, appears to be essentially necessary to the existence of any considerable community'.[8] In a similar vein, Thompson argued the right to the fruits of labour was justified by its tendency 'to increase the mass of human happiness'.[9]

Having elaborated twin rights to the fruits of labour and to the earth, rights which expressed fundamental proletarian interests, most critical social theorists conceptualised the capitalist rent relation precisely as a violation of these rights. Spence, writing in the late eighteenth century, was an early contributor to this tradition. For Spence, landlords were those who 'by slaughter and oppression, usurped the lordship and dominion of the earth … Or, at the best, [were] the purchasers of those ill-got domains'.[10] The mirror image of this class, in Spence's analysis, was a dispossessed proletariat who 'may not live in any part of this world ... but as strangers'.[11] Landlessness, Spence argued, forced the proletariat to sell its labour, and thus the full product of that labour, in return for mere subsistence. These 'indigent objects ...' wrote Spence, are excluded 'from a share in the soil, that want may compel them to sell their labour for daily bread'.[12] By this arrangement, Spence argued, 'the privileged orders ... deprive men of their labours for nothing'.[13] The rent relation proletarianised the worker, violating his right to the earth, forcing him into exploitative wage labour, in turn violating his right to his labour's fruits.

The real substance of rent, Spence concluded, was the surplus labour of a landless proletariat. He demonstrated his point by a thought experiment, writing that:

> You may suppose that after the emigration of all these beggarly people, everything would go on as well as before ... I tell you nay; for the farmer could neither proceed without labourers ... [nor find] purchasers for his corn and cattle ... [The landlord] could neither procure workmen to build, nor tenants to pay him rent.[14]

For Spence, then, violation of the right to the fruits of labour was constitutive of both rent and profit; the substance of both was proletarian labour expropriated through capitalist production. Spence saw the capitalist – chiefly the capitalist farmer – as the most proximate expropriator, passing a portion of his gains to the landlord as rent.[15] For Spence, market competition determined the level of rent as men 'bid over each other's head for ... the lucky spo[ts], [sic] thereby raising the rents till the landlord gets the whole fat of their labours'.[16]

Ogilvie, another early critical social theorist, argued that the capitalist rent relation originated from perversely privileging the right to the fruits of labour over the inalienable right to the earth.[17] Ogilvie affirmed, following Locke, that God had not intended land to remain in 'common and uncultivated', but to be used by the 'industrious and rational', and that 'labour was to be ... [their] title'.[18] But advanced nations, Ogilvie cautioned, in the name of the right to the fruits of labour, had allowed land to be appropriated 'in such a manner as that … cultivation and improvement should be stopped short, and the industry of millions … excluded from its proper field, and denied any parcel of the soil, on which it could be exercised, with security of reaping its full produce'.[19] Advanced societies had thus, according to Ogilvie, perversely deployed one natural right in violation of another, generating two *unnatural* classes: proletarian labourers and landholders.

In Ogilvie's view, the rent relation expressed the exploitation of landless by the landed. 'Whoever enjoys any revenue', he wrote, 'not proportioned to [his industry] … has found means to cheat or rob … the public, and more especially the indigent of that district in which he lives'. '[T]he hereditary revenue of a great landholder', he reasoned, 'is wholly independent of his industry … It increases also without any effort of his, and in proportion to the industry of those who cultivate the soil. In respect of their industry, therefore, it is a *taille* or progressive tax of the most pernicious nature'. The content of rent, then, was expropriated proletarian labour.

Gray's point of departure, like Spence's and Ogilvie's, was how British property relations aberrated from the rights to the fruits of labour and to the earth. Landlords, or their ancestors, he observed, had acquired the land 'by conquest, or taking exclusive possession'.[20] Neither act, he argued, could legitimate their title.[21] Invoking the right to the earth, Gray argued landlords lived 'upon property, of which the productive classes are the true proprietors, and of which they have … been deprived'.[22] With no means of production, the expropriated producers were vulnerable to exploitation. The unproductive classes, wrote Gray, could 'buy their labour from them at one price, and sell it at another'.[23] For Gray, then, wage labour was the mechanism of proletarian exploitation, but its cause was Britain's underlying social-property relations. Contrary to Gray's portrayal as a 'Ricardian socialist', his theory of exploitation was derived from the right to the fruits of labour and to the earth, not from Ricardo's labour theory of value.

Based on the above analysis, Gray elaborated a theory of the capitalist rent relation, writing that:

> the real income of the country, which consists in the quantity of wealth annually created by the labour of the people, is taken from its producers, chiefly, by the rent of land, by the rent of houses, by the interest of money.[24]

Gray thus saw rent as a distributive category. Of the total mass of proletarian labour expropriated by those classes which together monopolised the means of production, rent was the fraction appropriated by landlords.[25]

John Francis Bray likewise situated his account of rent within an analysis of capitalist social-property relations, described by reference to rights to the earth and the fruits of labour. Capitalism arose, he wrote, when an 'individual appropriate[s] to himself the field on which all labour is exerted ... contrary to the common equality of rights'.[26] Capitalism was thus constituted by the monopolisation of land in violation of the right to the earth. The monopolisation of land and capital, he elaborated, 'makes one class dependent upon another for the means of labour ... life and happiness'.[27] Without its own means of production, Bray reasoned, the proletariat was compelled to sell its labour to capitalists, and capitalists had the upper hand in the wage bargain. They could, Bray wrote, deny the labourer the opportunity to 'eat a meal until he has produced two'.[28] Bray drew a direct line from landed property and rent, violating the right to the earth, to capitalist exploitation and wage labour, violating the right to labour's fruits. '[W]herever one man possesses land', he wrote, 'and another has none, the latter must always be the slave of the former'.[29]

Bray further conceived rent as a share in capitalist profits. He divided society into two classes: landless labourers and propertied capitalists. Landlords, he argued, were a subspecies of the capitalist class.[30] Accordingly, he reasoned, rent represented a share in the surplus labour extracted from proletarians by capitalists. '[T]he proprietor of the land', he explained, 'demands from the cultivator of it, in the shape of rent, a large share of the produce'.[31] He observed that under capitalism, workers did not directly pay rent for productive land. Rather, it was paid by capitalist tenants to capitalist landlords. Nevertheless, he reasoned, rent's 'whole accumulated weight rests solely upon the working class'.[32] When capitalists paid rent they always recouped the cost 'by placing a certain profit upon the articles in which they deal. Thus, the charge is perpetually shifted … below'.[33] Capitalist rent thus always represented 'so much produce and so much labour' extracted from the labouring classes.[34]

John Francis Bray's namesake Charles Bray proceeded in similar terms. 'When the poor man comes into the world …' he observed, 'every part of it … is already appropriated. All the means by which labour is made available to production are private property'.[35] Deprived of his right to the earth, the landless worker is forced to strike a 'bargain', selling his labour to 'those who possess the means of setting him to work'.[36] In this bargain, the landless labourer parted with the full fruits of his labour, in exchange for only 'the means of subsistence'.[37] Thus, Bray concluded, although labourers 'produce everything, they receive but one-third of the produce'; the labourer was thus 'deprived of a large portion' of '*the fruits of his labour*'.[38] The wage bargain, founded on a violation of the right to the earth, led inexorably to the expropriation of labour's fruits.

Building on this analysis, Charles Bray defined rent and profit as shares of the surplus time the labourer worked beyond that required to produce his subsistence. 'Of every twelve hours' labour …' wrote Bray, 'two hours, is required for the expenses of Government, five hours for the landowner and capitalist, in the shape of rent and profits, and one hour for the retailers and distributors. The remaining four hours … scarcely provide the means of keeping life together'.[39]

For another theorist, Hopkins, rent's origins lay in a monopoly on land. This took the form of 'private property' exercised by a small group of landlords against the rest of the population.[40] 'The effect of the monopoly', he wrote, was that landlords could 'exact a rent or payment from others for permission to use the land'.[41] Under capitalism, he argued, this permission was purchased by capitalists. With both land and capital at their disposal, capitalists confronted landless labourers, offering them the opportunity to produce on condition of accepting a 'low rate of wages'.[42] Labourers accepted the bargain, giving up 'part of the gross produce of their labour in return for … the use of stock and of land'.[43] Capitalists, having extracted a surplus, divided it between themselves and the landlord – as profit and rent. The ultimate source of rent, Hopkins inferred, was the expropriated 'fruits' of proletarian labour.[44]

Thompson likewise defined capitalist rent as a violation of the right to the fruits of labour. Capitalist conditions, he observed, left the labourer:

> with no other possession than his capability of producing; for all the physical materials … [are] in the hands of others with interests opposed to his, and their consent being a necessary preliminary to any exertion.[45]

Thompson viewed landlords and capitalists as working in concert to deny workers access to the means of production, land and capital. He argued this denied workers 'property in the fruits of their labour'.[46] Under capitalist conditions, he explained, the labourer must 'always remain, at the mercy of these capitalists *for whatever portion of the fruits of his own labour they may think proper to leave at his disposal in compensation for his toils*'.[47] The worker's 'stimulus to labour' was thus reduced, from enjoying its full fruits, to 'maintaining existence alone'.[48]

With the worker deprived of labour's full fruits, the resulting surplus was appropriated by those who owned the means of production. In production, Thompson reasoned, 'the whole capital for which the labourer pays, rent and profit, [can] be regarded as one common instrument'.[49] But once production was completed, the capitalist and landlord would share the surplus product in proportion to the capital each had provided.[50] Rent was thus a distributive share in the expropriated fruits of proletarian labour.

Dove likewise theorised capitalist rent as expropriated proletarian labour. Rent, he argued, sprang from a 'system of diversity [i.e. inequality] of rights to the natural earth … being perpetuated from generation to generation'.[51] This violation of the right to the earth generated 'a few aristocrats endowed with vast wealth without labor, and a multitude of laborers reduced to poverty'.[52] 'Inasmuch as the land belongs to the [landlords] …' Dove argued, 'laborers cannot obtain their sustenance without laboring for them'.[53] Within this frame, rent was a 'vast revenue' *consisting* of labour which the landlord 'procured … *without* labor'.[54] Rent, Dove asserted, was the expropriated 'common produce of the whole labor of a community'.[55]

Hall was exceptional among critical social theorists in that he did not use rights to the earth or the fruits of labour to frame his theory of rent. Hall theorised rent instead, using Adam Smith's concepts of 'rent' and of 'labour commanded'. Before the rise of political economy's differential theory of rent, Smith's theorisation had prevailed: 'the landlords, like all other men', Smith had written, 'love to reap where they never sowed ... [The labourer] must give up to the landlord a portion of what his labour either collects or produces'.[56] Dove built on Smith's idea, tracing rent's origin to a monopoly on the means of production. '[A] small number of people', Dove wrote, 'have first got possession of the land, the stock on it and everything that it produces'.[57] By means of their monopoly, Dove continued, in distinctly Smithian terms, capitalists and landlords had 'obtained the command of the labour of the people'.[58]

Another theorist, Hodgskin, despite being mislabelled as a 'Ricardian socialist', built his theory of rent not on Ricardo's, but on a critique of the Cambridge moral philosopher William Paley (1743–1805). Hodgskin's published works feature repeated citations of Paley's *Principles of Moral and Political Philosophy* (1785).[59] In his *Principles*, Paley asserted a right to the fruits of labour: 'the full and entire advantage of every improvement', Paley wrote, should 'go to the benefit of the improver; that every man work for himself, and not for another; and that no one share in the profit who does not assist in the production'.[60] On this basis, Paley had argued that only improving landlords, not absentees, should be able to claim rents.[61] Yet, Paley himself never crossed the threshold into Critical Social Theory. Facing the awkward fact that even 'improving' landlords did not work the land themselves, Paley argued it was acceptable for profit to go 'not so much [to] the person who performs the work, as him who procures the labour and directs the management'.[62] Hodgskin cited Paley's work approvingly, but called the defence of improving landlords 'pitiable quibbling, in order to defend an injustice ... [Paley] dared not condemn'.[63]

Radicalising Paley's reasoning, Hodgskin argued rent was an indefensible violation of the right to the fruits of labour. As early as 1813, Hodgskin wrote of the 'unjust and injurious influence of property ... [which] absolutely ... takes from the daily labourer to give to the idle gentleman'.[64] 'The receivers of rent and profit', he wrote later, in 1827, 'subsist on the produce of other men's labour'.[65] Like earlier critical social theorists, Hodgskin saw rent as labour expropriated from proletarian wage labourers by monopolising the means of production. He thus defined landlords as mere 'owners of rent' who 'do nothing for other men', and who were 'not a part of the natural system of social order'.[66]

Watts, like earlier critical social theorists, connected landed property, rent, and proletarianisation. Invoking the right to the earth implicitly, he asserted it was unjust for one class to appropriate land at the expense of another.[67] He calls this 'the master curse of human nature'.[68] '[I]f we once acknowledge the Justice of rent', he wrote, 'we adopt permanent appropriation as right; and then ... all who are not landowners ... hold, not only their means of enjoyment, but even life itself, at the will of the wealth-made tyrants'.[69] The appropriation of land in violation of the right to the earth was thus not only the source of rent, but of the proletarian condition. Landless wage labourers were either 'not permitted by their tyrant fellows to produce, or ... not allowed to use the product of their own labours'.[70] Both profit and rent, Watt concluded, consisted in the appropriation of 'another's labour'.[71] Violating the right to the earth thus enabled violating the right to the fruits of labour. For Watts, then, capitalist exploitation originated in the rent relation.

Wayland likewise proceeded by characterising landed property as violating the right to the earth. '[H]e who created the earth', he wrote, 'neither sold nor gave it to any man in particular'.[72] Appropriating the earth had generated two classes, one propertied, the other a landless proletariat. Deprived of means of production, the proletariat's labour was 'exposed for sale as a merchantable article'.[73] Without alternative options, proletarians could be induced to work for wages so low that they lived perpetually in 'famine and the agonies of desperation'.[74] In usurping the land, the propertied class had also 'usurped the power of buying and selling

… labour'.[75] By violating the right to the earth, proprietors could expropriate the fruits of labour. Thus corralled into wage labour, capitalists could appropriate proletarians' surplus product, and the latter could 'never do more than subsist'.[76] Being guardians of the land monopoly at capitalism's base, Wayland saw landlords as a fraction of the greater capitalist class, and rents as landlords' share in the capitalist surplus. He compared rents to sinecures funded by taxes on labour.[77]

A final theorist, Ravenstone, proceeded from the right to labour's fruits. As soon as the means of production are monopolised as private property, he wrote, the propertyless man 'cannot exercise his faculties without paying for the permission so to do … without sharing the produce of his labour with those who contribute nothing'.[78] This violation of the right to the fruits of labour was 'the basis of property of every description', practised first by landlords, later by capitalists.[79] It converted the 'surplus produce of the labour of the industrious' into a 'fund for the maintenance of the idle'.[80] Thus, for Ravenstone, rent was the landlord's share in this 'surplus produce'.

In this chapter, I have shown how Critical Social Theory repeatedly converged on striking theorisations of rent as a proletarianising relation with exclusory and exploitative dimensions. It did so using an explicitly normative framework that articulated key proletarian claims: a right to the earth, and a right to the fruits of labour. The analyses these theorists repeatedly derived will be strikingly familiar to readers familiar with Marx. Yet they have been all but entirely overlooked by both mainstream and critical historiography. This may be, I have argued, a legacy of positivism and scientism, which falsely believe norms have no place in science. It may also be that both Marx and his historiographers have tended to dramatise his breaks with previous thinking – with Ricardianism, utopianism and with market socialism – rather than the continuities. Nevertheless, referring not to Marx but their own material conditions, these forgotten critics converged on a theory of rent: rent as proletarianisation. They reached the same fundamental conclusion this book seeks to recover: that rent is the mother of capital.

12
Rent and capitalist domination

In this and the remaining chapters I will show how Critical Social Theory's proletarian perspective opened a research programme that went well beyond 'rent as proletarianization'. While political economy had settled on a specialised, economistic and ahistorical theory of the rent relation, Critical Social Theory extended rent theory in directions that would clarify the proletariat's material conditions and interests. For Critical Social Theory, rent theory unlocked the nature of class domination in capitalist society, opening the way for theories of ideology, alternative social imaginaries, and theories of social change. In this chapter I will show how Critical Social Theory's theorisation of rent formed a platform for its broader critique of capitalist domination.

Critical social theorists knew that landlords controlled the British state. Britain's government, wrote Dove, was 'to all intents and purposes, a landlordocracy'.[1] Thompson observed that British politicians were either members of the propertied classes or their 'dependants, expectants, and men of business'.[2] Sismondi observed how landlords subdivided their properties to create 'a large number of poor freeholders who vote in accordance with their orders in the county elections'.[3] Hall concluded 'the vote of a poor man … [was] almost always directed by some kind of influence or other of the rich'.[4] Meanwhile, most of Britain's proletariat and remnant peasantry could not vote at all.

Critical social theorists went further, however, positing that 'landlordocracy' reflected an *inherent* connection between the capitalist rent relation and political power. '[I]ndividual possession of the soil', argued John Francis Bray, generated a 'deprivation of political power'.[5] '[L]aws', Bray wrote, 'are made by the proprietors in their character of rulers – they acquire this authority by means of their wealth – they obtain this wealth as rent'.[6] For Bray, then, the capitalist rent relation, notwithstanding its purely economic appearance, always cast a political shadow. Hall made a similar argument. Landlords, he wrote, had two fundamental objectives: to secure their 'great advantages over the rest of the people; and ... [to] put it out of the reach of those people to recover them'.[7] To achieve these objectives, Hall wrote, they assumed 'legislative power ... by means of their wealth'.[8] They then used the state to enact harsh laws to defend their property.[9] State power, Hall argued, was both 'the means of securing itself as well as the wealth which is the foundation of it'.[10] Political power reinforced economic power and vice versa.

Hodgskin argued that upholding the capitalist rent relation was the state's most essential function. '[T]he landed aristocracy and the government are one', he argued, 'the latter being nothing more than the organized means of preserving the power and privileges of the former'.[11] The law's function was thus to 'guarantee the possessions and the wealth of the land-owners'.[12] Law 'compels the payment of rent ... but it does not ensure to labour its produce'.[13]

Ravenstone saw the nexus between rent and state power in the enforcement of private property. He argued 'property alone confers power'.[14] Once property was established, it was inevitable that the man of property would assume judicial and executive power. '[T]his power', wrote Ravenstone, 'will ... enable him to make still farther encroachments, to exact a larger share of the earnings of his dependants'.[15] As lawmakers, he wrote, the landed class could 'sanction all their usurpations'.[16] Rent conferred state power, and state power enabled the extraction of still more rent.

Charles Bray saw a nexus of rent and state violence in the institution of private property. In his *Philosophy of Necessity*, he wrote 'rights of property were established and maintained by the strong arm of force alone ... Here then was the foundation of an aristocracy'.[17] To enforce private property, society generated a 'profession of arms ... with leaders whose interests were at variance with those of the people'.[18] As civil society and its property relations developed, the state, which enforced those relations, also developed. 'When trade and commerce flourished ...' Bray reasoned, 'the laws of property became necessarily more complicated; hence a class was called forth for the expounding of those laws, and their administrators rose in proportional importance'.[19] The modern military-bureaucratic state was, for Bray, the necessary counterpart of a society based on privately owned land and capital. The state was a corollary of profit and rent.

Thompson likewise argued that state power was integral to the reproduction of rents and profits, as well as the 'Idle' or propertied classes relying upon them. The Idle Classes, he wrote, enjoyed a 'factitious existence ... [depending] on the dread of violence, and ... reposing under its shelter'.[20] The 'unnatural distribution is forcibly maintained – for without force ...' he insisted, 'it could not be'.[21] The Idle exerted force with the state. The state was, for Thompson, an 'immense military force' deployed to 'control the actions and seize the products of the labour of the industrious'.[22] Behind the civil and economic relations of capitalist civil society, state violence lurked, defending the property of the privileged few and corralling the landless many into the 'system of competition' that exploited their labour.[23] State violence reproduced the Idle Classes. Laws of inheritance, primogeniture and entail, wrote Thompson, enabled landlords and capitalists to 'perpetuate forced inequality of wealth ... [and] perpetuity of property, without labour, in the descendants of particular individuals'.[24]

Beyond enforcing landed property, Critical Social Theory highlighted various other ways the landed class used state coercion. Ravenstone argued the landed class took every opportunity to apply state power to 'increase rent, taxes, and capital' and 'to take from the labourer everything ... possible'.[25] He argued landlords frequently made laws which conflated their own interests with 'the interests of the whole community'.[26] Thompson referred to 'monopolies, privileges ... [and] unequal law[s] favoring the rich'.[27] Others gave examples. Ogilvie noted landlords obstructed taxes they considered exorbitant.[28] Sismondi cited how the Poor Laws subsidised capitalist landlords while placing a disproportionate tax burden on peasant proprietors.[29] Several theorists noted how the Corn Laws boosted rents by restricting food imports.[30]

Having theorised the politics of capitalist rent, they turned to its role in civil society. Their conception of rent as a proletarianising force led them to reject political economy's vision of civil society as a realm of liberty. Sismondi argued, for example, that proletarianisation had granted capitalists and landlords together a dominion over workers that feudal lords could only dream of:

> by taking the direction of his labour out of the peasant's hands … [wage labourers who are] performing all the labours of agriculture, under the command of a rich farmer, are not only more dependent than metayers, but even than serfs … [The wage-labourer] lives each week on the wages of the last. Ever exposed to the want of work … he runs all the risks of ruin without … the chances of fortune.[31]

In this passage, Sismondi juxtaposes tributary and capitalist rent to illuminate what he sees as two historically unprecedented features of capitalist domination. First, despite having new civil-social freedoms – freedom of movement and freedom of contract – economically speaking, the capitalist wage labourer is not less but more exploited than his enserfed predecessor. When feudal lords exacted tribute, they confronted serfs who had significant bargaining power because they had physical possession of both farmland and, at least at first instance, their harvests. Stripped of both these advantages, the modern wage labourer faced unprecedented dependence and hence exploitation. Second, Sismondi highlighted how these conditions gave capitalists unprecedented control over the wage worker's labour process, corresponding to an unprecedented curtailment of workers' productive autonomy. Behind the new liberties of capitalist civil society lurked a form of economic domination that eclipsed serfdom. Sismondi derived his conclusions not from an abstract analysis of capitalism, but from a historical materialist analysis of the shift from a tributary to a capitalist rent relation.

Sismondi used this mode of analysis to derive further conclusions. He observed how the old class struggle between lord and peasant over the tributary surplus had been replaced by a new class struggle between capitalist and worker over wages and working conditions. Unlike tributary lords, capitalism's landlords, wrote Sismondi, 'take no part in the battle; it is only after its conclusion that their rent, less the profits of capital, will be handed over to them'.[32] Yet, despite this remoteness, Sismondi insisted, landlords were equal partners in the domination of proletarians, acting 'in concert' with capitalists.[33] If the capitalist employer held the whip, the rack renting, enclosing, and proletarianising landlord provided the corral. Together, Sismondi wrote, they had 'brought into being' the proletariat 'for their own use'.[34]

Ogilvie likewise used a historical comparison with the tributary rent relation to expose the uniquely impersonal form of capitalist economic domination. The rapacity and violence of feudal lords, Ogilvie argued, had been checked by two factors. First, lords 'depended on' the peasantry for 'assistance and military services, and would not, therefore, hazard the diminution of their attachment'.[35] Under capitalism, the landlord had no direct relation with the wage worker, so personal ties no longer acted as a 'natural check' on exploitation.[36] The modern landlord, wrote Ogilvie, had 'hardly any obvious interest but to squeeze … [the labourer's] industry as much as he can'.[37] Secondly, feudal tenants had 'means of concealment and evasion … by which … rapacity might be effectually eluded'.[38] They worked their own land and took first possession of its harvest. They could thus temper tributary rents through evasion or concealment. The wage labourer's work, by contrast, was always under the capitalist's eye. And the product could not be concealed or withheld, because the capitalist already possessed it. For Ogilvie, as for Sismondi, juxtaposing tributary and capitalist rent illuminated the brutally impersonal nature of capitalist economic domination.

Dove likewise juxtaposed tributary and capitalist rent to argue that capitalism represented not liberation but a shift from political exploitation to economic exploitation. He too contrasted the conditions of capitalism's free proletarian wage labourers with those of unfree feudal serfs. 'The villeins of England have attained to personal liberty …' he wrote, but 'they are compelled by natural causes, starvation, hunger, &c., to do the work for a bare subsistence … instead of individual aristocrats ruling individual serfs, a general court or assembly of aristocrats now rules the whole mass of labor'.[39] For Dove, aristocratic government and economic exploitation through rent and profit *co-existed* with the apparent civil freedom of post-feudal England.

DOMINANCE WITHIN THE RULING CLASS

We have now seen how critical social theorists used their analysis of rent to expose the nature of domination in both capitalist politics and civil society. And while they emphasised ruling-class collusion against the worker, their analysis led them to conclude the whole system was fractious. 'Our whole social fabric', wrote John Francis Bray, 'is one vast Babel of interests ... the interest of every class is opposed to the interest of every other class'.[40] An important question for Critical Social Theory, then, was how rent related to capital – how landlords and capitalists interacted as fractions of capitalism's ruling class. As I will show, the principal debate on this issue was between Hodgskin and Thompson. The former argued landlords were increasingly subordinate to capitalists; the latter, conversely, saw landlords as hegemonic.

In Hodgskin's view, under capitalism, landowners were 'neither the most important, nor the most opulent' class, and were 'far surpassed in numbers and in wealth by the capitalists'. [41] Capitalists marshalled the means of production, directed production and controlled its product. After paying rent, wages and taxes, Hodgskin argued, the capitalist retained 'a continually augmenting share of the annual produce of labour'.[42] Moreover, he observed, capitalists increasingly sunk their fortunes into land and thereby gradually dissolved the social division between them and landlords.[43] It was increasingly the case, Hodgskin wrote, that landed property 'is derived from, or represents, capital'.[44] As rent and profit mingled, they became indistinct. The landed class, moreover, was in relative decline. Through measures like the Corn Laws, it applied its political power in a rearguard action to defend its rents and class identity. But it was not possible, Hodgskin argued, to 'preserve by legislation ... [that] to which nature has decreed a termination'.[45] The landlord's rearguard efforts only succeeded in 'bringing on himself contempt and hatred, hastening his demise'.[46]

Thompson, by contrast, rejected the view that landlords had been reduced to 'comparative insignificance' and that the capitalist had 'inherited his power'.[47] Rather, argued Thompson, '[b]oth species of aristocracy, the capitalist and the feudal ... have formed a *coalition* against the Industrious Classes'.[48] Thompson argued landlords had deployed their political hegemony adroitly to coopt the rising capitalist class. Landlords used the process of capitalist competition, he argued, to identify 'men of merit, who emerge by their wits, by exchanges, or by chance, from the drudgery of their fellows'.[49] With control of the state, the landlord aristocracy could offer the most successful capitalists 'rewards and honors, colonial, church, army and navy, fiscal, legal, &c. crowned with the ultimate hope of hereditary law-making'.[50] Through the 'meritocratic' extension of privilege, argued Thompson, the upper echelons of the capitalist class were absorbed into the aristocracy. Through the aristocratic state, the nation's leading landlords exercised a ruling-class hegemony that subsumed lesser landlords, capitalists and all state-adjacent classes. In Thompson's words, the state was 'the aristocratical law-making committee of the Idle Classes'.[51]

Thompson argued that meritocracy was a powerful tool by which the landed class exercised hegemony over capitalists. The prospect of merit-based admission to the aristocracy encouraged successful capitalists to repudiate their humble origins and acquire a 'lordly antipathy' to the 'poverty, ignorance, and manners' of the working class.[52] Capitalists became 'bitter enemies ... of [those] whose hardships they so lately partook'.[53] This mitigated the potential for any capitalist-proletarian alliance against the landed class.[54] At the same time, it fostered in capitalists an aspirational identification with the landed class. Far from subordinating landlords to capitalists, class-mobility, rationed through meritocratic competition, was an essential tool of landlord hegemony.

THE ORIGINS OF CAPITALIST DOMINATION

Having shown how Critical Social Theory's analysis of rent led it to accounts of capitalist domination, I will conclude this chapter by showing how the same approach led it to accounts of capital's origins. While such accounts varied, most, I argue, traced both rent and capital to a common point of origin: the original appropriation of land. Some theorists, like Ravenstone, traced hereditary landed property to the ossification of patriarchal authority.[55] Others, like Hodgskin and Spence, traced it to historical acts of violence and domination.[56] My discussion will focus, however, on Sismondi and

Hopkins, who offered the most detailed accounts. As I will show, in striking concordance with this book's thesis, they both traced the origin of capitalism to rent's transformation into a proletarianising relation. Like this book, they took a materialist approach, focusing on the adaptive interplay between the rent relation's structure and the agents operating within it.

For Sismondi, capitalism was born as the rent relation evolved from a tributary logic, where rent was extracted from peasants, to a capitalist logic where rising rents forced peasants off the land into capitalist wage labour. He emphasised that the rent relation's dynamics generated a class struggle and saw this as a major driver of the social transformation. In feudal Britain, Sismondi observed, rents were originally 'fixed by the will of the lord'.[57] But this feudal condition of lordly dominance eventually collapsed. The peasantry was for a time able to establish that rent would be fixed by 'customs of the manor, and that those were inalterable'.[58] Once rents became 'perpetual and unchangeable', Sismondi observed, the 'depreciation of the coinage [i.e. inflation] … made them almost everywhere light in relation to the value of the land'.[59] But peasants' inroads against the rent relation were fleeting. Scottish and Irish customary tenants never achieved freehold property rights, nor did they apply in England, wherever leasehold tenure pertained.[60] Where landlords could impose leasehold tenure, Sismondi wrote, they could 'at each renewal' impose 'new conditions or increase the dues of their tenants'.[61] Resurgent landlords thus eventually effected 'gradual expropriations of peasants in Britain's three kingdoms'.[62]

For Sismondi, the Scottish Highland clearances were the paradigm case of how the rent relation enabled expropriation.[63] Through 'a cruel abuse of legal forms' – acquiesced in by the Crown – Scottish landlords had established their tenants had no legal right 'to the land which they … [had] occupied for centuries'.[64] Exploiting their power within the rent relation, Sismondi observed, Scotland's lords converted previously nominal rights into 'unlimited proprietorship'.[65] Customary tenure was substituted for leasehold and rack rents. Customary tenants were forced off the land.

On Sismondi's account, as landlords exploited this newly competitive rent relation, they generated an entirely new class. 'The fundamental change …', argued Sismondi, 'is the introduction of the proletary … the name of whom, borrowed from the Romans, is ancient, but whose existence is quite new'.[66] The proletariat was born as landlords exercised their new 'power of monopoly' to price peasants off the land.[67] Corralled into the labour market, they were forced to 'outbid each other, and to finally offer to work for the most pitiable wages'.[68]

For Sismondi, England's unique system of competitive rents created not only a proletariat but also the capitalists who exploited them. In continental Europe, he observed, arbitrary tributary rents prevented capital accumulation and the reinvestment of profit. Profit, Sismondi wrote, was 'absorbed by the rent of land'.[69] Nor did Europe have a substantial proletariat for capitalists to employ. Workers with land of their own were unwilling to work for subsistence wages. But in England richer peasants could now lease land at competitive yet fixed rents, allowing them to retain and reinvest their profits. They also had access to ample proletarian labour. Thereby, Sismondi observed, they could 'raise great fortunes'.[70] From a new form of rent, a new class of capitalist farmers was born.

Like Sismondi, Hopkins' account of capitalism's birth was focused on the interplay of the rent relation's dynamics and how lords and peasants responded to them. Under the feudal system, Hopkins observed, tenants' obligations were defined 'according to the known wants of the chief, rather than in consequence of any previous definite contract'.[71] The chief aim of a feudal lord, he wrote, was to promote the number, loyalty, military ability and spirit of his partisans.[72] A lord's incentives were to 'cultivate popularity among the most numerous tenantry his lands would support' and to spend rents on 'hospitable entertainment'.[73] Lords were interested in accumulating political support, not wealth. Rents were thus kept low to stimulate population growth.[74] The 'spirit' of the rent relation, Hopkins observed, was 'family pride among the superior, and strong clanish feelings among the inferior classes'.[75]

However, from the end of the thirteenth century, Hopkins explained, the rent relation was transformed. The Crown gradually monopolised force and demilitarised the landed class.[76] As political accumulation was precluded, the landed class turned to economic accumulation, taking '[money] rents instead of feudal service'.[77] In the fourteenth and fifteenth centuries, adapting to its new constraints, the landed class began to adopt a 'commercial spirit'.[78] 'A passion for wealth and luxury … succeeded to feudal feelings … [in] the higher classes of society'.[79] Feudalism, Hopkins argued, was defunct by the early sixteenth century.[80]

Landlords' new commercial spirit, Hopkins argued, became a force of capitalist transformation. As money became the measure of accumulation, landlords began demanding higher rents. Yet the old system of labour-intensive peasant agriculture left little room for rent increases. So landlords achieved higher rents by the 'breaking up of small farms, and the conversion of arable into pasture land'.[81] '[I]t was not …' wrote Hopkins, 'until advancing rent had driven away or destroyed a great part of the population, that rents could be raised materially above the old rate'.[82] On Hopkins' account, landlords' pursuit of commercial rents thus drove depopulation and poverty, creating a proletariat. Capitalist pastoralists and farmers, drawn from the wealthier strata of the peasantry, were able to take advantage of the emergent proletariat. They did so, wrote Hopkins, by hiring 'land from an owner … [and] preventing labourers from cultivating it, unless they will submit to receive only the low rate of wages'.[83] Once landlords had enclosed and rack-rented the best arable, wrote Hopkins, they began enclosing the wastes and commons.[84] The unfolding of a new 'commercial' rent relation, Hopkins concluded, had extirpated the peasantry and corralled the emerging proletariat into a new capitalist mode of production.

In conclusion, I have shown in this chapter how critical social theorists used their distinctive conception of rent as a proletarianising relation to theorise capitalism as a system of social domination. They argued landlords safeguarded the political preconditions of both rent and capital through an aristocratic monopoly on the state. Complementing this critique of politics, they juxtaposed feudal and tributary rent to argue that capitalism's civil-social freedoms concealed an economic domination that eclipsed feudalism. They theorised domination not only between rulers and ruled but *within* the ruling classes, debating whether landlords or capitalists were hegemonic. Finally, we saw that some critical social theorists, in striking concordance with this book's thesis, located capitalism's origins in a mutation of the tributary rent relation.

13

The ideology of capitalist rent

Having theorised rent as a proletarianising relation and capitalism as social domination, it was natural for critical social theorists to then ask: why did so many proletarians accept the prevailing social order? I call this question the 'paradox of consent'. Critical social theorists posed it repeatedly. Sismondi, for example, remarked that 'the arrogant pretensions' of the English aristocracy were met by 'a deference which astonishes us'.[1] John Francis Bray wrote that proletarians 'cringe to their oppressors, and kiss the hand that smites them'.[2] Hall likewise observed that working men submitted to their deprivations in a 'regular orderly, silent manner'.[3] To advance proletarian interests scientifically, critical social theorists sought to resolve this paradox. They sought to explain why, as Marx later put it, the 'ruling ideas of an age were always but the ideas of the ruling class'.[4] In other words, as I will show in this chapter, they developed theories of ideology and, specifically, of the ideology of rent and capital.

Some critical social theorists explained the paradox of consent as a demoralised acquiescence to material conditions. Dove, for instance, argued ruling-class domination had instilled a state of 'hopelessness' and 'apathy' in the 'public mind'.[5] The public, he argued, harboured 'a very extensive suspicion that the present distribution of the land is the true and main cause of England's distress and Ireland's wretchedness'.[6] Yet that suspicion remained latent, because many people had been 'deterred … from openly attacking the question'.[7] The public, Dove wrote, were instilled with a 'fear of advocating' alternatives and were demoralised by the 'apparent hopelessness … of affecting any radical change'.[8] Thus cowed, people adopted a 'habitual credence, transformed into a rule of action … ere long realized as a palpable fact'.[9]

Writing in similar terms, John Francis Bray explained the paradox of consent as a habituation to tyranny. 'Wherever the body is enslaved', wrote Bray, 'the mind is still more tyrannized'.[10] The working man, he argued, was caught in 'conventional cobwebs which, spun by his own ignorance, and fastened upon him by his own hands, have for ages bound his body and his soul'.[11] Those 'conventional cobwebs', in Bray's view, entailed the habituation of all classes to their roles, both rulers and ruled. They ensnared 'the minds alike of the oppressed and the oppressor', giving both a 'warped and confined' perspective.[12]

Other theorists made comparable arguments. Spence attributed subaltern consent to a 'habit of thinking'.[13] Habituation, Spence argued, allowed the ruling class to remain 'unquestioned, or not called to an account for ... usurpations and unjust claims'.[14] Ogilvie wrote that 'the natural submission of dependents has been insensibly enforced' and that the labouring classes were not 'sufficiently aware to protect their own right'.[15] Habituation, according to Ogilvie, could blindly reproduce class domination without any 'premeditated and intended ... oppression'.[16]

But Critical Social Theory also converged on the view that proletarian acquiescence was not produced by coercion alone. '[L]aws', observed Ravenstone, 'are of little efficacy when not supported by the feelings of those who are to submit to them'.[17] The maintenance of the class system, wrote Hodgskin, required 'consenting submission in the party impoverished'.[18] Something beyond force – or habituation to it – was needed to fully account for the paradox of proletarian consent. The missing element, most critical social theorists believed, was the pervasiveness of practices and modes of thinking that obfuscated or mystified capitalist social-property relations, and thereby promoted proletarian consent to them. The critical social theorists were theorising what is termed ideology, though before the term existed.

Critical social theory developed accounts of ideology because the existence and persistence of rent and capitalist domination seemed inexplicable without one. Hodgskin exemplifies how confronting the paradox of consent led critical social theorists to develop theories of ideology. Hodgskin began with the paradox, observing that despite their exploitation, proletarians retained a 'veneration for the human lawgiver'.[19] To explain this he drew, as we have seen him do before, on the thought of William Paley, and in particular on Paley's concept of the 'folly of political obedience'.[20] Paley posited a species of 'opinion … founded upon prescription', whereby men 'obey from prejudice', their opinions 'determined by … their governors', not 'founded upon argument'.[21] For Paley, deference to opinions prescribed by authority was not due to incuriosity or ignorance, or even violence. It was rather a state cultivated by the 'whole course, and all the habits of civil life'.[22] On Paley's view, and thus on Hodgskin's, the ruling classes secured subaltern consent through the unceasing process of inculcation and indoctrination. For Hodgskin, ideology was an active process, whereby the ruling class produced ideas '[a]ddressed to the people, to assist in mystifying them, and to keep up the grand system of political humbug'.[23]

Hall and Dove conceptualised ideology similarly, as a ruling-class intellectual art form that mystified oppression and invited subaltern consent. Proletarians acquiesced to ruling-class oppression, Hall argued, because it was always executed 'under specious forms, with the external appearance of liberty, and even of charity'.[24] The class system was not a function of mere coercion, but a 'deliberate, systematic junction of art and force'.[25] Dove made the same point, arguing that the ruling classes, to perpetuate themselves, elaborated 'propositions on which to base so iniquitous a system'.[26] They found intellectual grounds for their domination 'in the study of external nature, or of man, or of revelation'.[27]

Thompson saw ideology as promulgated through the medium of public opinion. 'What is called *public* opinion', he wrote, was really 'the opinion of the influential classes', and that influence was attendant upon 'the possession of superior masses of wealth'.[28] Through public opinion the ruling classes exerted 'control … over the actions of their fellow creatures'. Control was indirect, exercised through 'opinions or conduct', by bestowing 'benefits or evils', and by instilling 'hope or terror' in the public. '[O]pinions & prejudices', wrote Thompson, were 'deferred to, or even encouraged by the influential classes' as a means of 'rendering subservient and managing the people'.

Thompson argued that the ruling class disseminated ideology through its civil-social organs. He identified the aristocracy, the legal profession, and the Church as 'institutions repressing all freedom of inquiry'.[29] These institutions, he wrote, produced the 'noble, the lawyer, the priest… drilling them … to the reverence for … dogmas, regulations, and establishments'.[30] These agents propagated ideology using civil-social pressure, operating on the principle 'that those who dispute their notions, ought, if possible, to be tormented till they cease disputing them'.[31]

Like Thompson, Charles Bray located the organs of ideology in capitalist civil society. Only in a classless society, Bray argued, could there be an 'enlightened public opinion'.[32] By contrast, in a class society composed of 'separate and frequently conflicting interests', the 'advantage' of those interests was frequently 'connected with error'.[33] Instead of speaking truth, questions were answered according to how they affected 'the interests of the Church, or of the Law, or of the Medical Profession, or of the Government, or of the Aristocracy [etc.]'.[34] '[U]pon most of the questions bearing upon the happiness of man', Bray wrote, a person's 'opinions … [were] borrowed generally from those of the class or caste in which they have been educated'.[35]

Alongside other civil-social institutions, Critical Social Theory often pointed to political economy as a key source of ideology. Sismondi, for example, attributed the persistence of England's class system partly to 'false economic guidance'.[36] Charles Bray criticised political economy for presenting 'the present form and constitution of society as one that must always exist'.[37] Watt argued political economy laboured 'to make the state of society … appear right … to defend the wrong doers by the defence that they have fairly acquired what they have; and, if … [opinion turns against it] to talk of it as a necessary evil'.[38]

Even as Critical Social Theory argued ideology was inherent to capitalist civil society, it also theorised that ideology was connected to state coercion. The pressure of public opinion, Thompson wrote, was often reinforced by 'the use of force and the means of annoyance', but a 'person [still] unconvinced could be physically *compelled* to submit'.[39] 'Force is never called in, in matters of government …', he wrote, 'but as a succedaneum for persuasion and voluntary acquiescence'.[40] Further, he argued, ideology functioned to *legitimate* the use of force. The ruling class had 'factitious methods … of converting … opinion into mandates of terror for the control of conduct and the suppression of truth'.[41] John Francis Bray thought in similar terms. The Church, Bray argued, while ostensibly operating in the civil-social sphere, really functioned to legitimate state violence. [T]he anathema of the priest', he wrote, 'is ever at the call of the despot'.[42]

Critical Social Theory sought to explain not just ideology and the paradox of consent, but how they could be overcome. Dove believed, for instance, that ideology would be overcome by the spread of reason. He argued that a 'great theoretic change' would achieve 'the abolition of the belief that one generation of men can be bound by the arrangements of past generations; and … the substitution of a belief that men in every age must be governed by reason'.[43] This change was crucial, he believed, to overcome the habitual obedience to unjust laws. The 'canon of law' had to be subordinated to the 'more valid and more stable … canon of reason'.[44]

John Francis Bray argued that intellectuals could assist the mass of society to overcome ideology. It was time, he wrote, for mankind to break free of 'conventional cobwebs'.[45] Intellectuals – 'individuals in mental advance of … the main body of a people' – were to have a key role in the process.[46] Bray saw intellectuals as 'pioneers to the march of mind'.[47] Yet they would not march on a royal road. If intellectuals 'make the road to knowledge', Bray argued, '… they do so only by paving it with their own bones'.[48] On the one side, they would be persecuted by 'despots, and all other upholders of usurped power and unjustly-acquired wealth'.[49] On the other hand, by being in 'mental advance' of the people, Bray argued, intellectuals would appear 'in opposition' to them.[50] So subalterns would attack them too. Intellectuals thus had to overcome both 'tyranny' and 'ignorance'.[51] Therefore, Bray concluded, 'knowledge of truth and liberty progresses slowly'.[52]

Hodgskin likewise emphasised the role of intellectuals in overcoming ideology, citing his own work as an example.[53] The intellectual's role, Hodgskin argued, was both to propagate wisdom and to 'stigmatise' what he called 'the grand system of political humbug'.[54]

Having proposed that intellectuals could play a counter-ideological role, Critical Social Theory set to work doing just that. They sought to deconstruct ideas that, they believed, mystified the capitalist rent relation. And by overcoming these, they hoped to pierce the rent relation's ideological armour and lay it bare as a relation of exploitation, exclusion, and social domination.

Dove, for example, took aim at ruling-class efforts to present rent as the fruit of landlords' labour, rather than expropriated proletarian labour. '[W]hen the privileged classes had monopolized the land', Dove wrote, 'they called it theirs *in the same sense* in which labor is supposed to belong to the labourer'.[55] This, he asserted, was a 'groundless superstition'.[56] It was particularly difficult to defend, Dove observed, where the landlord was an absentee.[57]

Spence pursued a similar critique. The landed class, he argued, tried to justify rent by comparing themselves to workers who 'take all they can get for the products of their hands'.[58] He sarcastically dubbed landlords 'the land-makers'.[59] Landlords, he scoffed, defended making nothing by the absurd claim that they had made everything. Landlords, wrote Spence, fancied that 'by granting the means of life, they granted the life itself; and of course, they thought they had a right to all the services and advantages that the life or death of the creatures they gave life to could yield'.[60]

Critical Social Theory also critiqued the idea that rent is derived from the land. Political economy, Sismondi observed, divided society into 'landed proprietors, capitalists, and day-labourers or proletaries'.[61] It then established an alleged reciprocity between classes' contributions and their incomes: '[t]he first give land, the second employment, and the third hand-labour; in return, the first receive rent, the second profit, and the third wages'.[62] On this basis, Sismondi said, it was 'usual to recognize three types of income … coming from the three different sources, the earth, accumulated capital, and labour'.[63] But this, he argued, was an illusion. 'On closer inspection', Sismondi discerned, 'one realizes that these three divisions are three different ways in which to share in the fruits of the work of man'.[64] Beneath its appearance as a relation of reciprocal, voluntary exchange, rent was non-reciprocal, coercive and expropriative. The landlord could not be *contributing* land in exchange for rent, because, Sismondi insisted, land was 'a productive force which does not in any way come from man'.[65] The landlord was rather *withholding* land, by means of his monopoly over it, to extort the labourer's surplus in the form of rent.

Thompson likewise attacked the notion that rent is derived from the land. '[T]he whole capital for which the labourer pays, rent and profit', wrote Thompson, could 'be regarded as one common instrument to *add* to the productive powers of his labour'.[66] On this view, he reasoned, the 'several owners of this [land and capital] share between them ... the *additional* value thus given to the labour of the ignorant producer'.[67] In reality, however, Thompson maintained, rent and profit were shares of the total surplus extracted from workers – divisions of the overall flow from the 'Industrious' to the 'Idle'.[68]

Another construct Critical Social Theory attacked was the defence of rent as tradition. Ogilvie wrote that the 'system of landed property, like systems of corrupted religion, is regarded with superstitious reverence in countries where it has long obtained'.[69] 'Nothing can be more absurd', wrote Dove, 'than to suppose that a past generation can make arrangements to deprive the present generation ... of its full right to dispose of the earth in the mode that is best for the present generation'.[70] Ravenstone likewise critiqued the ideology of tradition. 'The inconvenience of changes', he wrote, 'the force of habit, will continue to the son the prerogatives of the father; the rights which have been exercised by the one, will appear to devolve naturally to the other'.[71] According to this illusion, he wrote, to 'refuse to the son, what had been accorded to the father, would intimate a diminution of respect and attachment'.[72] Ideology, in other words, had equated paying rent with respect for patriarchal authority, the latter being sacrosanct not only as the basis of the British family but, presumably, of civilisation itself.

While some critiqued the grounding of rent in tradition, others focused on its ideological presentation as 'natural'. Political Economy's differential theory of rent, Hopkins argued, presented rent as the result of a 'natural inequality in the returns from equal quantities of labour' on different grades of land.[73] Political economy thus insisted rent existed due to 'the laws of nature' and that 'the arbitrary will or discretion of the proprietor has nothing at all to do with the matter'.[74] However, Hopkins argued, a simple example could prove this false: if landed property were distributed equally, he observed, no one would pay rent. Rent, he concluded, was thus the 'offspring of social institutions, and not a law of nature'.[75]

John Francis Bray likewise took aim at the naturalisation of the inequality of property. He noted the common-sense notion that inequality was caused not by exploitation, but by natural variations in individual character and aptitude. But this was a mystification, he argued; the real situation was precisely the inverse. The 'inequality of powers', he wrote, was 'induced, in a great degree, by the favourable or unfavourable circumstances in which individuals have been placed, in respect to position in society and means of development'.[76] Social conditions explained not only the uncultivatedness of the working class individual, but also the aristocrat's appearance as 'a wiser and a higher being'.[77] The aristocrat's superior abilities, Bray wrote, to the extent they existed, were due to the 'leisure and means' afforded by the 'toil and privation of the working man'.[78] Unequal aptitude was, for Bray, the *product* of an inequality of property, not the cause.

Dove's critique of the ideology of rent focused on how landlords justified their landed property. The landed class, he wrote, conflated the question of '[w]hat ought to be property, and whose property ought it to be', with the question of 'whether there ought to be any property at all'.[79] These questions, Dove argued, should be 'essentially distinguished'.[80] The abolition of slavery, he wrote, 'is a question of the destruction of property. Destroy the property, and the slave is a freeman. This circumstance shows that there is nothing so very alarming in the terrible phrase, "destruction of property"'.[81] Dove observed a further ideological tendency to reify landed property, mystifying its relational nature. 'Property', he wrote, 'is usually regarded as an object'.[82] This was, however, a 'superstition'. Property was in fact a 'political arrangement' between men, whereby '[a]ll persons in the nation are forbidden, under pains and penalties, to use a certain portion of land, with the exception of the grantee, or by his permission'. While rent appeared as a relation between man and nature, it was really a social relation, and a coercive one at that.

On Ravenstone's view, the very form of modern landed property mystified the nature of rent. All property, he wrote, was 'in reality but a rent charge on productive industry'.[83] He argued this was easy to see for feudal estates, where there was a direct relation between the exploiting lord and the exploited producer. But under the capitalist form of landed property the relation was indirect.[84] Under capitalism, rent appeared to derive from land not labour, and land was 'supposed to have a value independent of the labour exerted upon it'.[85] The capitalist form of landed property had thus, on Ravenstone's view, obscured rent's social and relational nature.

Dove argued that landed property was buttressed by an ideology of depoliticisation. '[T]he doctrine now prevalent' wrote Dove, was that 'lands, once alienated by the king's gift, could not be reassumed by the nation without a breach of equity – without ... "attacking the rights of property"'.[86] 'The laws with regard to crimes have been considered alterable', he observed, but not 'the laws with regard to property'.[87] Capitalist politics thus protected the rent relation by regarding landed property as beyond political choice. Dove insisted, however, that landed property was not in fact 'morally permanent'; it could, in fact, be 'revised, amended, or abolished'.[88]

Critical social theorists also analysed the ideological practices by which the landed class upheld its social authority, especially the way landlords presented their interests as universal. The landholder's interests, wrote Ogilvie, were often 'directly opposite to ... the great body of the community'.[89] And yet, he observed, they presented themselves precisely 'as the nation itself, or at least as being representatives of the nation, and having the same interest with the whole body of the people'.[90] Sismondi criticised political economy for making the same ideological move. Political economists, he argued, tended to judge systems of cultivation by the quantity of rent or profit they produced, treating the interests of proprietors as universal.[91] '[W]hat should engage the economist's undivided attention', he argued, was not the surplus but the *total* product, 'by which subsistence is provided for the whole nation, and the comfort of all classes is secured'.[92]

Another ruling-class ideological practice Critical Social Theory sought to expose was *noblesse oblige*. John Francis Bray noted that the capitalist ruling classes – 'livers upon rent and profit' – portrayed themselves as providing a 'stewardship' to the proletariat even while they exploited it.[93] This ethic of service, Bray argued, provided cover for 'rapacity' and 'idleness'.[94] Sismondi likewise observed that Britain's unparalleled inequality was accompanied by an unparalleled ruling-class commitment to charity. '[I]n no other country', he wrote, 'is pity more widespread, or the wealthy more eager to come to the aid of the distressed'.[95]

To conclude, I have shown in this chapter how Critical Social Theory repeatedly confronted the paradox that subalterns typically *consented* to capitalist domination. Theorists responded, as I have shown, by developing what can only be termed theories of ideology. Seeking to advance proletarian interests, critical social theorists argued the proletariat could free itself from ideology through reason and science, and that intellectuals, including the critical social theorists themselves, had a role to play in this process. They tried to fulfil this role by exposing and critiquing the ideologies of rent and capital in particular. They attacked the proposition that rent was derived from the productive activities of landlords, or from the productivity of the land itself. They attacked the defence of rent by appeals to tradition and naturality. Finally, they sought to expose how Britain's capitalist elites reproduced their social authority, whether by presenting their interests as universal or through the practice of *noblesse oblige*. Most critical social theorists, however, believed that overcoming ideology was just one step toward liberation. As we will see in the next two chapters, alongside its critiques, Critical Social Theory developed visions of alternative social systems, free from rent and capital, as well as theories about how such visions might be realised.

14
Proletarian imaginaries

Political economy and Critical Social Theory diverged widely on the question of alternative social systems. As a science of capitalist statecraft, political economy's research programme cleaved to the interests of the capitalist state. The state located its interests firmly in the reproduction and expansion of capital, so political economy spent little energy imagining alternative social systems. We have seen that Critical Social Theory's research programme, by contrast, was directed by proletarian interests, expressed as rights to the earth and to the fruits of labour. The capitalist rent relation was seen as a proletarianising relation that violated the former right by forcing workers off the land, and the latter by corralling them into exploitative wage labour. It was a logical extension of this analysis, then, to imagine alternative social arrangements that might uphold the right to the earth and the fruits of labour and emancipate workers from rent and capital. As we will see, along these lines, critical social theorists developed a spectrum of more or less radical proletarian imaginaries.

AMELIORATION

Of all the critical social theorists, Ravenstone had perhaps the most modest proletarian imaginary; he argued that proletarian interests demanded only the attenuation of rent and wage exploitation, not their outright abolition. Rent, taxes and capital, he wrote, were 'scourges when pushed to excess' but were nevertheless 'beneficial to society, when exerted with moderation'.[1] 'Some force on the industry of individuals', he argued, 'seems necessary to bring out all their powers'.[2] He warned against too strict an adherence to the right to the fruits of labour, writing that 'to leave every man in full possession of his own earnings would only destroy industry'.[3]

A class system, he argued, was ultimately necessary to ensure individuals reproduced their society. '[T]he love of distinction ...,' he wrote, 'alone is able to overcome the love of indolence.'[4] The 'pyramidal form of society is that which contributes most to its strength; is that which most assures its stability.'[5] The proletarian condition was, for Ravenstone, to be ameliorated but not abolished.

Spence envisioned, more boldly, the satisfaction of proletarian interests through state redistribution of rent. Land was to be owned by the state, through subsidiary levels of government. Each local community was to form a parochial corporation, which would hold all parish land and houses.[6] The parish could 'let, repair or alter' land and houses, but could not alienate them.[7] Parishioners were to pay rents to the parish, from which the parish would pay taxes to the national government. National and parish governments were to be democratic, spending rents on public purposes such as unemployment relief, public officials, infrastructure, defence.[8] Once public expenses were met, Spence envisioned that surplus rent would be distributed 'fairly and equally among all the living souls in the parish ... giving to the head of every family a full and equal share for every name under his roof'.[9] Upon the nationalisation of rent, he argued, there would be 'no private landed estate, no [private] tenants ... nor ... any privilege.'[10] Production was still to be undertaken on the basis of private capital, wage labour, and competition, but with rents shared equally 'a fair, salutary, and democratic competition,' he wrote, would 'pervade everything.'[11]

Dove likewise envisaged ameliorating the proletarian condition by recycling the rent surplus back to the proletariat. This was to be achieved by the 'abolition of private property in land, and the restitution of the soil to the state.'[12] The state as landlord would collect all rent, ensuring 'the division of its annual value' among the proletariat, after meeting the expenses of government.[13] To ensure the state was faithful to proletarian interests, it was to be constituted as 'a republic with universal suffrage.'[14] While Dove referred to this doctrine as 'communism,' he rejected any proposal to 'obliterate private property altogether.'[15] He advocated neither common nor state ownership of capital.

SMALL PROPERTY

A more radical group of critical social theorists proposed the outright abolition of the capitalist rent relation and wage labour, and by extension the proletariat itself. Several thinkers in this group, including Ogilvie, Sismondi, Hopkins, Hall, and Hodgskin, envisaged the transformation of proletarians into independent producers. Ogilvie referred to this transformation as the 'progressive Agrarian' principle.[16] By becoming peasants, proletarians could reclaim the right to the earth, escape wage labour, and attain a state of 'competent independence and rustic plenty'.[17]

Ogilvie could imagine the end of capitalism but thought the total dissolution of Britain's powerful landed class impracticable. So he proposed that the proletariat cum peasantry would still pay limited tributary rents. This compromise, he argued, would accommodate 'the principles of a progressive Agrarian to the supposed rights and legal possessions of the body of landholders'.[18] It would produce 'very beneficial effects', even if not 'the best'.[19] Ogilvie contemplated numerous measures to implement his 'progressive Agrarian'.[20] His principal proposal, however, was that every landless citizen, upon turning 21, be entitled to claim a tenancy of 40 acres of well-situated land in perpetuity.[21] The existing landlord would receive a 'reserved perpetual rent' determined by a state judge or arbitrator, and the existing tenant – for example, a capitalist farmer – would receive temporary compensation.[22] The proletariat would be progressively transformed into a tribute-paying peasantry, albeit under lighter, fixed rents and taxes.

Sismondi, like Ogilvie, placed peasant proprietorship at the core of his imaginary. His programme was self-consciously nostalgic, seeking 'the rebirth of this independent and proud class of countrymen, this yeomanry … [mourned] today as almost extinct'.[23] In practical terms, the state would buy up waste lands and rent them to the poor 'at a low fixed rent', later allowing them to purchase the land outright.[24] Laws supporting the preservation of 'great fortunes' would be abolished.[25] The right to the earth would be restored. '[A]ppropriation of land' would guarantee the worker 'fully the fruits of his labor'.[26] The peasant proprietor would neither pay 'rent to any one above him, nor wages to any one below him' –

although he would presumably pay taxes to the state.[27] He would be self-sufficient, prosperous, subject only to light taxes, and no longer to the whims of the market and 'revolutions of commerce'.[28]

As a disciple of Sismondi, Hopkins also imagined restoring the right to the earth through peasant proprietorship. He proposed that a million proletarian families be settled on the land, each receiving around 30 acres.[29] He argued for 'an equitable division'.[30] Land was to be allocated annually, in *quality-adjusted* portions.[31] Under these conditions, he argued, there would be no 'natural rent of land'.[32] In line with the right to the fruits of labour, 'all the wealth brought into existence by the new population' was to be 'enjoyed solely by the labouring class'.[33]

Hall too envisaged peasant proprietorship. He imagined a society where the producers' labour 'would be for ever free and under their own direction',[34] and in which they received 'the whole of the fruits' of their labour.[35] The biblical Jubilee would be reinstituted, with debts cancelled at regular intervals and the right to the earth secured by 'unalienable allotments'.[36] Large-scale manufacturing would revert to petty agrarianism, with a 'system of direct exchange between small farms'.[37] Equality, universal private land ownership, and petty production would eliminate both rent and wage labour. The state would continue to extract taxes, but with the new aim of enforcing an equality of conditions. The state would tax income progressively, abolish primogeniture, prohibit marriage between heirs and heiresses, and impose punitive taxes on luxuries.[38]

Hodgskin's post-rent vision was similarly one of liberation through small property, but in contrast to agrarian imaginaries, his vision was urban and artisanal. He foresaw the displacement of proletarian, landlord, and capitalist by a new 'middle class' of skilled industrial workers, 'at once labourers and capitalists'.[39] These workers, 'without being relieved from the necessity of labouring', would be 'placed far above, the condition of the great majority of slave-labourers [i.e. proletarians] and their descendants'.[40] They would own their own means of production – workshops, tools, etc. – and be 'at once labourers and capitalists'.[41] They would supersede both the low-skilled, propertyless, exploited proletariat, *and* the propertied classes who extracted 'the rent of land or the interest of money'.[42] Owning the urban land beneath their feet and the fruits of their skilful labour, this new middle class would produce for the market, flourishing under conditions of competition and free exchange.[43]

COLLECTIVE OWNERSHIP

A final group of thinkers shared the ambition of abolishing rent, capital, and the proletarian condition, but they rejected small property as the vehicle. The right to the earth and to the fruits of labour had to be reinterpreted in ways that grappled with modern, capital-intensive collaborative methods of production. It was 'impracticable', Thompson observed, 'or very difficult, so to arrange, that every *individual* laborer should have even a fair chance of possessing the materials and implements, neither more nor less than are necessary to render his isolated labor productive'.[44] As soon as 'improved machinery and complicated processes of industry' are considered, Thompson wrote, it becomes 'impossible ... to award to any *individual* laborer the whole products of his labor, inasmuch as ... it would be impracticable to ascertain what those products are'.[45]Under modern conditions, then, the right to the fruits of labour did not entitle the labourers to the *individual* things they produced, but to a share in the total *social* product in proportion to their effort.

Dove likewise argued that individual property could no longer guarantee the right to the earth, pointing out that there was no way to divide rare and large-scale resources like mines into parcels of individual property.[46] He argued further that even if property were initially divided equally, a proletariat would re-emerge. Inheritance would erode equality and gradually deny 'successive generations of men ... their fractional share of the actual soil'.[47]

Having rejected the model of small property, several critical social theorists, particularly those influenced by Robert Owen, developed imaginaries in which rights to the earth and the fruits of labour would be secured through collective ownership of all productive land and means of production, accompanied by cooperative (rather than competitive) relations of production.

Thompson, for example, argued right to the fruits of labour demanded a new 'mode of production by labour, with mutual cooperation'.[48] The means of production were to be made 'the equal property of all'.[49] Each would have 'an equal command of the means of production',[50] along with 'the means of acquiring knowledge and skill, and all the other conditions necessary to equal chance of happiness'.[51] Labourers, 'having no masters', would act as 'masters and employers to each other'.[52] Productive property would not be used individually but cooperatively. Its use would be 'regulated by the general voice, so as to produce the greatest sum of happiness to all'.[53]

Thompson envisaged a society built from the community upward.[54] He imagined that most problems of the social economy would be solved by cooperative production and consumption at the community level, rather than any national plan.[55] In his earlier work, he contemplated inter-communal trade and competition. Later, he doubted such competition was beneficial or compatible with free association.[56] While it is clear that Thompson believed in equality between cooperatives, he did not describe how this would be achieved.[57] Like many Owenites, he imagined cooperatives uniting in some sort of federation.[58] But as Kaswan observes, he never resolved 'the economic relationship among communities and with the society beyond'.[59]

John Francis Bray likewise envisioned a communitarian communism. Every type of 'reproducible wealth, except the personal property of individuals' was to be owned in common.[60] The right to the earth was to be secured thereby. Communities were to plan and coordinate production and consumption through 'general and local boards of trade'.[61] 'Universal labour' was to end 'the maintenance of one class at the expense of another'.[62] '[N]either individuals nor companies' would derive 'gain from the loss of others'.[63]

Charles Bray, a fellow Owenite, had a vision similar to his namesake. He likewise imagined a society of collective ownership, built up from 'communities of united interests'.[64] Communities would trade, but their competition would be regulated.[65] A 'Governor or Board of Directors … chosen by the members themselves' would 'provide that each should be employed in that occupation for which nature or education had best fitted him'.[66] '[D]ull, monotonous, soul destroying employment' was to be eliminated or 'so blended as to ensure the largest return of health and happiness'.[67] As equal proprietors, Bray wrote, all would 'share the labour required for everything produced'.[68]

Whereas Thompson and the two Brays' visions of collective ownership were communitarian, Gray's was constituted nationally. All land and other means of production, exchange, and distribution would be subsumed into a single 'national capital'.[69] The national capital would be owned by all and all would act as 'one body of commercial partners'.[70] '[T]he existing system of competition', wrote Gray, would be replaced by 'a system of Mutual Cooperation in the production of wealth'.[71] 'Competition in the employment of capital' would end.[72]

Gray envisaged a centrally planned social economy.[73] A Chamber of Commerce would be elected and invested with a 'supreme power' to 'control, direct, and regulate the affairs of the association'.[74] The Chamber would implement 'a thoroughly organized plan of producing, exchanging, and distributing the wealth of the country'.[75] It would appoint 'servants or managers, to be hired at fixed salaries' to undertake its tasks.[76] Individuals would be free to choose their occupations, but employment would be regulated to be 'consistent with, instead of being opposed to, the interests of other men'.[77] All would have equal access to education.[78]

Just as collective ownership sought to guarantee everyone's right to the earth, its distributive principles sought to guarantee them the fruits of their labour. Gray's central planning system was the exception that proved this rule. In his earlier *Lecture* he proposed a strict equality of distribution, but by his later *Social System* he returned to the right to the fruits of labour, arguing for 'equal reward for equal toil'.[79] Distribution was to reward 'greater industry with greater abundance'.[80] Gray reflected the right to the fruits of labour through several distributive principles: he proposed salary gradations based on the difficulty of work and skill;[81] he argued for the regulation of consumer prices to ensure a proportionate return to labour;[82] and he insisted 'NO ONE would be taxed either with rent, interest, or profit on his labour'.[83]

The Brays and Thompson likewise argued for distribution according to the right to the fruits of labour. For Charles Bray, this meant the union of universal labour and universal consumption – each would employ his talents 'for the good of all' and 'all would share alike the fruits of such labour'.[84] The right to labour's fruits would not be applied rigidly, though: the 'weak would be assisted by the strong – the sick by the healthy – the old by the young'.[85] John Francis Bray's vision was similar. Under the 'joint-stock system', he wrote, 'every person would ultimately receive the whole fruits of his labour'.[86] Although 'a parsimonious man may become rich', Bray wrote, 'his wealth will be no more than the accumulated produce of his own labor'.[87] In risky fields like agriculture, men would be remunerated 'according to their labour, and not by the amount of crop', so that 'society at large would receive the benefit, or bear the loss' of the venture.[88] Thompson likewise foresaw distribution proportionate to effort. '[E]very individual equally exerting, or equally willing to exert, his or her faculties for the common good', he wrote, would receive 'equal means of physical, intellectual, and social enjoyments'.[89]

Some critical social theorists argued that communal ownership and cooperative production would not only abolish rent, capital and the proletarian condition, but also spark radical and liberating social transformations. These would span production, consumption, human development, relations between individuals and society, gender and the family, and the nature of the state.

Thompson and Charles Bray, for example, both argued that cooperative social-property relations would unleash the forces of production. With the burden of the most unpleasant labour shared by all, Bray argued, 'master minds would be turned towards inventions and expedients for shortening such labour'.[90] Thompson argued that if workers felt the 'full benefit' of machinery in the fruits of their labour, they would embrace it.[91] If workers became 'directors of the use of scientific power, instead of ... its victims', they would rapidly adopt new technology.[92] Cooperative production would give free play to the individual drive to discover 'new sources and combinations of happiness, and to render always more productive those already known'.[93] Bray and Thompson both argued that whereas competition incentivised the hoarding of knowledge, cooperation encouraged its speedy and maximal diffusion.[94]

Charles Bray and Thompson argued further that in a society of common ownership, the right to the fruits of labour would transform consumption. In capitalist society, Bray observed, the propertied classes cultivated 'artificial wants' – lavish desires only satiable by expropriating proletarian labour. But if man was restricted to the fruits of his *own* labour, such wants would be discarded, because they 'cost more labour than society will be willing to bestow in exchange for them'.[95] Thus, wrote Bray, under common ownership, the 'standard of utility would supplant that of caprice and fashion … All artificial wants would give place to real ones, and those the most essential and the least costly would be first attended to'.[96] Thompson wrote, in similar terms, that products would be valued for 'the real pleasures they are capable of affording', rather than 'the mere sake of distinction'.[97]

Thompson and both Brays argued that under cooperative production, capitalist dynamics of competitive consumption and accumulation would be subordinated to the human drive for self-development. Material wealth, wrote Thompson, 'will serve but as a theatre on which the new course of human existence, the development of the physical and intellectual powers of the human race, will proceed unrestrained'.[98] All persons, wrote John Francis Bray, would 'acquire a degree of physical, moral, and intellectual excellence to which, under the present system, they can never attain'.[99] Charles Bray wrote, in similar terms, that 'each mind would take a peculiar bent from its own peculiar combination of intellectual powers and the different pursuits to which this would lead'.[100]

Thompson, Charles Bray and Bailey all argued that cooperative social-property relations could reconcile the competitive and conflicting interests generated by earlier relations. Thompson wrote that under cooperative conditions, man would apprehend the 'necessary connexion between his happiness and that of all those with whom he associates'.[101] Individuals would pursue happiness 'with others, for mutual enjoyment, through mutual cooperation'.[102] Charles Bray wrote that 'the happiness of the individual would result from well-directed efforts for the general good'.[103] Bailey wrote that socialism would 'give self-love a proper direction. Being convinced that the happiness of each individual is bound up with the happiness of the whole population; and that the item [i.e. individual] takes the most effective method of promoting his own happiness, when he labours to promote the happiness of the aggregate.'[104]

Both Brays highlighted that common ownership would transform gender and family relations. Community of ownership, wrote John Francis Bray, entailed arrangements 'for the support of women and children, without the former being dependent on their husbands, or the latter on their parents.'[105] Women would enjoy 'most perfect equality' with men.[106] Every child would 'be regarded and protected as the child of society' and society would 'be as a helping child to every aged parent.'[107] Parents would have 'no offices to perform but the caressings of parental love.'[108] Charles Bray wrote that in a cooperative society marriages would be based on 'mutual affection' rather than 'worldly circumstances.'[109] Children would learn 'they were all of one family, and that the duty of love is to all, not merely to those who are parents, or brothers and sisters.'[110]

Thompson foresaw a similarly radical transformation of family and gender relations. Cooperative social-property relations implied a 'real and equal personal independence of both sexes.'[111] Women would be empowered to 'contribute their half, by useful productive labour, to human enjoyment.'[112] They would be liberated from the 'despotism of the marriage laws.'[113] Women's reproductive labour was to be 'as much as possible abridged.'[114] The 'family despotism' in which a father was considered 'uncontrollable within the precincts of his little domain' would end.[115] Children would be liberated from the 'tremendously despotic power' of financial dependence on their parents.[116]

Several critical social theorists argued that common ownership would obviate the need for a coercive state apparatus. Gray argued the state – composed of officials, soldiers, judges, lawyers – was a reflection of a class-divided society and would be obsolete in a classless society of material abundance.[117] John Francis Bray likewise argued that the coercive state 'would be superseded by administration for the common good.'[118] His namesake Charles Bray likewise argued the coercive state would no longer be required to defend property rights as 'offences against property must cease when all were joint proprietors.'[119] For Thompson, similarly, cooperative society implied that 'political institutions ... be supported without standing armies, without force of any sort' and that all taxes be 'voluntarily paid'.[120] Police powers would be abolished in favour of 'a government purely civil, of persuasion alone'.[121] Laws – if rules unbacked by force can be called that – would be 'made by those whose interests they affect', and those affected would 'permit none but equal laws to be made'.[122]

In this chapter, I surveyed how the rights-based framework that Critical Social Theory used to critique rent and capital led to a spectrum of alternative imaginaries. Some envisioned *ameliorating* the proletarian condition, others abolishing it. The abolitionists were likewise divided. Some proposed converting the proletariat into independent producers with their own means of production. The most ambitious, however, contemplated entirely new social-property relations based on common ownership and cooperative production. For some, the horizon of proletarian emancipation stretched further still to a comprehensive social transformation: technological advancement; the subordination of production and consumption to human self-development; the reconciliation of individual and social interests; liberation from oppressive familial and gender relations; and finally, the dismantlement of the coercive machinery of state. Having explored Critical Social Theory's visions of proletarian emancipation, the next chapter will canvas how it thought such transformations might be achieved.

15
Deproletarianisation

In contrast to political economy, eighteenth- and early nineteenth-century critical social theorists defined the proletarian condition as one in which the rent relation had deprived workers of their right to the earth and enabled the fruits of their labour to be expropriated through capitalist wage exploitation. In the last chapter, we saw how this analysis also led them to visions of a post-proletarian society that made good on the right to the earth and the fruits of labour. In this chapter, we will see how Critical Social Theory took this framework further, theorising how a post-proletarian society might be realised. With its loose sociological structure, Critical Social Theory settled on no single theory. As I will show, however, its proletarian orientation led to a convergence on two key themes: self-emancipation and endogenous transformation. Put simply, proletarians would emancipate themselves, and capitalism itself would make this possible.

SELF-EMANCIPATION

Most critical social theorists believed deproletarianisation would be accomplished through workers' own agency. Dove, for example, wrote that if the labouring classes were to 'seriously take up' the question of their condition 'they would resolve never to rest satisfied till they had abolished the landed aristocracy of England, and emancipated their own labor from the burdens that have been imposed upon them from the allocation of the land to the aristocracy, and of … taxation'.[1] The industrious world', wrote Thompson, 'is indeed like a mighty giant … But would he really open his eyes … he would break his tiny fetters with contempt, and, with a smile, bid his Lilliputian leader goodbye'.[2] The two Brays wrote in similar terms. Charles Bray described the working class as 'a new power in the world' which could assert its interests through collective action.[3] John Francis Bray wrote that 'even partially united … devoting their now divided energies to one purpose, [workers] could … overturn, by one movement, the whole social fabric'.[4] A third of the population, 'more or less bonded together, and organised, and containing intelligence as well as numbers', would be 'material amply sufficient to accomplish any change, whether social or governmental'.[5]

As I argued in Chapter 13, Critical Social Theory understood capital's domination as a matter not just of force but of ideology; critical social theorists therefore placed a strong emphasis on the maturation of class consciousness and self-organisation as preconditions for proletarian self-emancipation. Thompson, for instance, argued that liberation required the 'progress and diffusion of knowledge' and the 'gradual perception of their real interests by all'.[6] The capitalist order, he argued, could not reproduce itself, even by force, once the proletariat attained a consciousness sufficient to withdraw its consent. '[W]here there is public opinion founded on knowledge', he wrote, 'a minority can never long resist it; 'tis only where there is no knowledge, no public opinion, that a minority can rule by force'.[7]

The Brays made similar arguments. Charles Bray argued the working class had to be 'sufficiently enlightened to know their own interest' before they would be 'qualified to act together in such a co-operation of interests'.[8] '[A]ny great alteration of feeling and opinion', he wrote, would be a 'gradual process'.[9] But nevertheless, he argued, 'the people will ultimately become wise enough to take their own concerns into their own keeping, to govern and protect themselves; they will then withdraw the power which they formerly delegated, from those who have shown themselves unworthy of the trust'.[10] John Francis Bray likewise wrote that at such time as the 'unimprovable nature of the present system is perceived … and the utter futility of all mere governmental changes … the whole working class will unite as one man to demand a social change'.[11]

Contrary to their reputation as 'utopians', critical social theorists not only centred class struggle, but carefully considered the strategic and structural opportunities and constraints proletarians faced in their struggle for liberation.

While most critical social theorists argued against violence as a tool of proletarian self-emancipation, Spence argued it might be necessary. For Spence, self-emancipation consisted in reclaiming the right to the earth over and against landlords' wishes. To overthrow a system which landlords upheld by violence, Spence argued, the proletariat had to be prepared to use force. To minimise violence and prevent a protracted struggle, Spence argued landlords should be expropriated 'instantaneously, as by an elective shock'.[12] '[T]he people's oppressors', he wrote, 'must either submit to become undistinguishable in the general mass of citizens or fly the country'.[13] He bade landlords 'prepare yourselves peaceably to acquiesce to the new system' or 'let your blood be upon your own heads'.[14]

Other theorists, however, warned that violence risked reproducing what it sought to overthrow. For Thompson, as for Spence, there was no simple dichotomy between violent and non-violent means of changing capitalist society. The system was *already* constituted by violence. Thompson thus scorned ruling-class 'political mountebanks, surrounded with cannons and bayonets ... preaching to the Industrious Classes on the evils of violence'.[15] Nevertheless, he argued, violence could be a Pyrrhic path to proletarian self-liberation. 'If force, instead of persuasion, were used in the formation of the new arrangements of society', Thompson asked, 'what guarantee could be given that force would not be used by every succeeding majority?'[16] Force tended to perpetuate force. Wayland, another Owenite, hinted at the same paradox. Just because 'injustice ... is upheld by force', he wrote, the poor should not be 'too easily induced ... to attempt its correction' by force.[17]

Ogilvie, writing in the late eighteenth century, emphasised that violent revolution was particularly likely to be ineffective if it outran proletarian class consciousness and self-organisation. 'Internal convulsions have arisen in many countries', he wrote, 'by which the decisive power of the State has been thrown, for a short while at least, into the hands of the collective body of the people'.[18] And yet the dispossessed could not press the advantage, he observed, because they lacked leadership and did not understand their natural rights.[19] The working classes of the eighteenth century, he argued, were 'not much accustomed to reflection; they submit in most countries to their hard fate, as to the laws of nature, nor are they skilled … in making known their feelings'.[20]

Thompson and Hopkins made the inverse argument against violence: that the use of force, particularly state violence, might impede the development of precisely that consciousness and organisation requisite to *true* proletarian self-liberation. 'Reason', Thompson insisted, 'is the only agent worthy of effecting such a change. The puny and suspicious aid of self-constituted political power, would but mar the mighty work'.[21] Likewise, Hopkins wrote that '[p]ersuasion, and not force, is the legitimate instrument for influencing the human mind: and I shall never be justified in having recourse to the latter, while there is any rational hope of succeeding by the former'.[22]

Hopkins further argued that violent struggles were often circumscribed by capitalist dynamics, rather than offering a means to overthrow them. '[V]iolence', he asserted, 'does not lower … high rent'.[23] Despite violent resistance in Ireland, he observed, rents had 'risen more rapidly, and to a much higher rate, than … in peaceable England'.[24]

Other theorists pointed out that economic struggles – especially trade union struggles – were likewise constrained by the logic of capital. Charles Bray argued that struggles against capitalists 'for a more just share of the joint produce have failed, and always must fail, the workman being compelled to take what the capitalist chooses to give, or starve'.[25] Thompson reasoned that, in any case, a capitalist firm that yielded to union demands 'could not long, without ruin, continue his trade in competition' with other capitalists.[26] At best, a trade union struggle could only 'prevent wages from falling … much beneath that remuneration which capitalists elsewhere give'.[27] John Francis Bray likewise argued that trade union struggles were largely futile.[28]

Some critical social theorists proposed class compromise as an alternative to violence. Revolutions, wrote Sismondi, were 'frightful; the whole order of society is subverted; power passes into the hands of the multitude which … having suffered much, kept in ignorance by need, is hostile to all types of law, all degrees of distinction, all kinds of property'.[29] Yet the spectre of revolution, he believed, might prompt the rich to begin to 'think of the poor, from a regard for themselves, and care for their own safety'.[30] Ogilvie similarly suggested that, under the shadow of violence, the landless and landed, with their 'opposite interests', might 'compromise on a plan the least unjust to the former, and the least incommodious to the latter'.[31]

Spence, by contrast, argued that class compromise would necessarily fail to abolish the proletarian condition. When Thomas Paine famously proposed that landlords compensate England's landless workers with a universal inheritance, Spence called the plan 'an execrable fabric of compromissory expediency'.[32] 'After admitting that the earth belongs to the people', Spence complained, Paine had conceded that 'the people must nevertheless compromise the matter with their conquerors and oppressors, and still suffer them to remain as a distinct and separate body'.[33]

Several critical social theorists argued that through political reform, the proletariat could use the state as a vehicle for self-liberation. Heighton, for example, was optimistic that the state would serve the working class if workers could establish a 'UNITY OF INTERESTS ... between them and their [political] representatives'.[34] He called for politicians to be 'men of our own nominating, men whose interests are in unison with ours' and for 'a public opinion of our own, by which, in some measure, to direct and regulate [political] proceedings'.[35] '[W]hat individual', he asked, 'thus elected from the bosom of his associates and equals ... could ever be corrupted?'[36]

While less confident than Heighton, Thompson too mooted how a democratic, worker-controlled state could advance proletarian interests. He suggested to workers that they might attain '[s]imple representative institutions';[37] these would include 'representatives, removable at your pleasure' and 'the making of all laws by none others but your men-of-business'.[38] A worker-controlled state, Thompson argued, might assist a cooperative movement (which I will discuss further below) and protect 'all future products of labour' from expropriation.[39]

Several other critical social theorists likewise argued that proletarian interests could be advanced via the state. Ogilvie called for the state to implement 'gradual progressive innovation' to avert violent class struggle.[40] Sismondi likewise argued that the overriding public interest in stability 'ought to lead the legislator … to induce landowners and farmers to give up cultivation by day-labourers'.[41] In his later work, noting limited public support for more radical measures, Gray too argued for a social transformation through gradual state reforms, particularly to the currency.[42]

There was, however, a countervailing tide in Critical Social Theory, militating against politics and the state as vehicles for proletarian emancipation. After observing poverty in America, John Francis Bray lost faith in republican political reform.[43] Political leaders, he wrote, 'connected as they are with rich men, and living as they do upon rents and profits', were either 'blind' or 'hostile' to the workers' interests.[44] And there was a more fundamental problem too: 'misgovernment' he argued, 'is not a cause, but a consequence … of the inequality of possessions'.[45] The state and politics were just reflections of a class society, and thus could not upend it. Politics, in Bray's view, offered only a means of 'removing one rich tyrant and setting up another'.[46] Workers could not delegate the task of 'considering their own wrongs, and devising and adopting proper remedies' to representatives.[47] Liberation could only be achieved directly by the working class itself.

Thompson, likewise, was sceptical of what a democratised state could deliver. His earlier work championed democracy but noted the possibility that representation might be achieved even as 'the expedients of insecurity … [were] permitted to remain in existence'.[48] While a worthy aim, democracy might only deliver workers the power of 'changing … masters'.[49] In his later work he went further, concluding that social transformation could 'proceed without political reform'.[50] Indeed, many of Thompson's 'political' proposals called for using democratic power to *dismantle* the state and the various 'restraints of insecurity' it upheld.[51] Thompson thus proposed to abolish: wage regulations; restrictions on freedom of labour; prohibitions on unions; laws compelling unpaid labour; supports for capitalist associations; monopolies, including on trades and knowledge; bounties; game laws; privilege laws; hereditary political power; licences; and restrictions on land transfers.[52] More radically still, Thompson proposed the abolition of compulsory taxation, hereditary property and the state's coercive machinery itself. He called for the state to 'gradually disband all its legions of human butchers, till nothing but a mere nucleus remains to organize the industrious against foreign aggression.'[53] 'It is under free governments only ...', he insisted, 'that mutual co-operating communities can flourish.'[54] Thompson saw the proletariat substituting politics and the coercive state for a free association of producers.

As an alternative or complement to political reform, theorists influenced by Owen typically proposed cooperativism as a kind of civil-social pathway to proletarian self-liberation. 'In the system of mutual co-operation', Thompson wrote, 'no aid is demanded of the legislator ... the exactions of capitalists and the plunder of political power, and all the expedients or institutions of insecurity are passed by; no change is sought to be made in them.'[55] Cooperativism, he argued, required 'no immediate change in any political institution';[56] it could be pursued 'peaceably, at once';[57] and it proposed 'to take nothing of acquired property from any one.'[58] John Francis Bray described cooperativism as 'a mode of subverting the present system.'[59] It was subversive precisely because it proposed to undermine and supersede capitalism without either violating its civil-social norms of property or overthrowing its political order.

Owenite cooperativism proposed that workers form cooperative communities. Each community, Thompson explained, was to be a 'voluntary union of the industrious or productive classes, in such numbers as to afford *a market to each other*, by working together *for each other*, for the mutual supply, directly by themselves, of all their most indespensible wants.'[60] Communities were to be small, from a few hundred to a few thousand members.[61] Members would hold all capital in 'joint possession.'[62] Producing at cost, without wage labour, profit, or rent, the workers would mutually guarantee 'the command and the enjoyment of the whole products of their labor.'[63]

As a strategy for self-emancipation, cooperativism faced a fundamental problem. Owenites believed that to be proletarian was to lack land and capital. Cooperativism was to liberate proletarians by providing these things. And yet, no cooperative community could commence production unless its members *already* possessed land and capital. Despite confident declarations that 'capital would not be wanting', cooperativism was haunted by the question of how it might pull itself up by its own bootstraps.[64] Owenites spilt much ink in the search for persuasive solutions. Several suggested that while workers lacked sufficient capital on their own, they might have enough if they pooled their meagre savings.[65] Thompson argued, along these lines, that workers form a central union to buy land.[66] Recalling the example of Robert Owen, Charles Bray hypothesised another solution. The capital might be donated, he suggested, by 'philanthropists', or by 'wealthy capitalists willing to assist in the glorious work of human emancipation'.[67]

Another common answer to the bootstrapping problem was borrowing. Thompson, for instance, suggested cooperatives without sufficient starting capital could rent land, and borrow money at interest, to acquire buildings and stock.[68] In a variation on this theme, he suggested issuing shares to 'individuals inclined to advance small sums on interest, or without interest as sharers in the profit or loss' of the cooperative.[69] Gray suggested capitalists and landlords might offer land and capital in return for a 'fixed annual remuneration for the use thereof'.[70] All these methods, however, would encumber cooperative workers with obligations to produce surpluses, paid to property owners, whether in the form of interest, profit, dividends or rent. Borrowing, in other words, admitted the very encumbrances cooperativism was supposed to circumvent.

Cooperativists answered this secondary problem by assuming, often implicitly, that cooperatives would be highly productive and competitive in a capitalist environment. Robert Owen asserted, for example, that workers could 'quickly ... repay the capital advanced'.[71] Thompson suggested borrowed capital could be fully or partly repaid with 'the extra labor of a few years'.[72] Gray wrote that a cooperative might 'pay off, as rapidly as possible, the borrowed or hired capital with which it must commence, and ... provide itself with sufficient land and capital of its own'.[73] Mudie believed self-owned cooperatives could compete in the market briefly and successfully before retiring from it altogether.[74] Cooperatives would be so successful, Thomspon conjectured, that they might absorb ever more members, and provide an ever-wider array of goods and services on a cost basis, becoming increasingly independent of the capitalist economy.[75] Cooperativism, he wrote, would 'at every step … exclude the principle of competition and substitute the principle of co-operation'.[76] It would 'gradually supersede' capitalism.[77] The assumption of high productivity explains, at least in part, the enthusiasm of cooperativists like Owen and Thompson for 'experimental' communities.[78] If cooperatives were engines for self-sustaining or even exponential accumulation, one needed only to plant the seed.

Cooperativists were not, however, uncritical of their own assumptions, especially after the infamous failure of the Owenite cooperative experiments (see Chapter 8). Some of these internal critiques went to the heart of the cooperativist strategy. John Francis Bray, for example, noted that the strategy of small savings was based 'on the self-denial of masses of people' who were already 'living almost from hand to mouth'.[79] Even such a denial, he argued, would not be enough. Bray estimated the working classes received only two-fifths of the United Kingdom's annual product – around £200 million out of £500 million.[80] Working-class income, which barely covered subsistence, would never be sufficient to purchase the United Kingdom's capital stock, which he estimated at £5 billion.[81] The 'position, and the enormous burthens' of the working class, wrote Bray, 'will ever prevent them from being accumulators to any considerable degree under the present system'.[82]

Bray also critiqued the assumption that isolated experimental communities could thrive in the market on borrowed capital. Any such community, he argued, would be 'surrounded … by hostile interests of every description'.[83] It would 'stand somewhat in the character of a small farming and manufacturing establishment; and it is well known that the majority of small farmers and manufacturers can barely make ends meet, even when they are proprietors'.[84] Change, Bray concluded, could not be established by the '[d]esultory and isolated endeavours of mere fractions of society … only a general movement of the community at large can effect … deliverance'.[85]

With cooperativism stymied and with objections to violence, some critical social theorists tried to plot an intermediate path to social revolution: passive resistance. Thompson proposed that, rather than taking their birthright by force, by seizing land and capital, workers might simply withhold their labour and its fruits from the capitalist class. Most 'accumulated wealth', he wrote, was 'only nominal, consisting not of any real things … but of mere demands on the future annual productive powers of society'.[86] Proletarians did not need to expropriate capitalists. They only needed to prevent the use of capital 'as an engine for extorting … future products of labour from the producers'.[87] The proletariat could enforce its interests non-violently by permitting the owners of land and capital only to 'lend, or devote' it to productive workers (without interest or remuneration) or have it 'remain unproductive'.[88] The 'small minority' who owned 'real capital' would have to cooperate 'whether convinced … or not'.[89]

In a variation on this theme, John Francis Bray imagined the working class imposing a once-off compulsory acquisition of all capital.[90] Former capitalists and landowners would be expropriated but compensated by a 'voucher' redeemable 'to the full value of the things obtained'.[91] This 'voucher' was to be valid for *consumption* goods only. It would not be redeemable for land or capital, which were to be owned in common by all. It could not be invested for profit or rent. In this non-violent revolution, former capitalists and landlords would be pensioned off – left to enjoy a 'vast sum as they pleased, in the most perfect security'.[92]

ENDOGENOUS TRANSFORMATION

Critical Social Theory's interest in strategies of proletarian self-emancipation was an outgrowth of its proletarian orientation. This same orientation led it to theorise another source of social transformation. Having traced the origin of capital to the proletarianising dynamics of rent, it was natural for critical social theorists to suppose, in turn, that the conditions for proletarian liberation might emerge from the dynamics of capital. If capitalist dynamics brutally constrained proletarian agency, those same dynamics might also eventually unleash it. The idea of endogenous transformation – that societies are transformed by their own dynamics – was ubiquitous in Critical Social Theory.

Charles Bray expressed the idea of endogenous transformation with particular clarity. '[T]he different stages of man's progress', he wrote, 'were necessary towards his present position in civilization, to develop all his resources in the infancy of his higher faculties'.[93] '[T]he period of separation between Capital and Labour which commenced with the institution of the present Law of Property … appears to have been absolutely necessary to develop the resources of society in the non-age of man's highest faculties'.[94] Bray emphasised that capitalist dynamics themselves drove the development of proletarian agency. 'The necessity that so large a portion of the population is under to find employment', he wrote, 'even to live, fills up every channel for labour … developing every latent power, energy, and resource of man's nature'.[95]

But capitalist dynamics, Bray argued, were now inhibiting human development. 'Everything in the present system of society tends to keep the selfish and lower faculties predominant'.[96] '[E]very sound moral feeling is vitiated, every dissocial impulse called into habitual activity'.[97] Capitalism was, in Bray's view, 'a mere chaos of conflicting interests'.[98] '[I]t appears the right of each class of society to the distinction it claims was based upon utility; but the world is changed, and society pays homage to the shadows of things that were'.[99] The proletarian phase of man's social development had rendered itself obsolete, paving the way for new, higher social-property relations.

Hodgskin argued, along similar lines, that proletarian liberation lay in capital's propensity to stimulate technological development. Modern productive practices, he observed, had spurred a 'prodigious, comparative, multiplication … of men who labour a little, by, or in conjunction with … machinery'.[100] A new 'middle class' of skilled workers, he argued, had 'multiplied amazingly within the last fifty years' and 'must gradually extinguish' wage labourers, capitalists and landlords.[101] Whereas the unskilled labourers owned nothing, and the proprietor owned the labour of others, Hodgskin foresaw this emergent middle class as the successor to the capitalist system, owning valuable skills and being 'at once labourers and capitalists'.[102]

Even as capitalist social-property relations had gestated a new middle class, Hodgskin believed, those same relations would gradually inhibit production, prompting their own supersession. Hopkins argued that capitalist social-property relations, despite their productivity, were based on 'primitive aggression'.[103] Capitalist production was constantly 'tormented by open theft and secret fraud, which tended to destroy confidence, and making each man act as much as possible for himself, instead of all mutually exchanging their services'.[104] The conflictual nature of capitalist production '[checked the] division of labour far more even than restrictions on trade'.[105] Capitalist dynamics would ultimately be superseded not because they were immoral but because they stymied cooperation and hence production. Hopkins argued new social-property relations, which guaranteed an 'exclusive right to the produce', would ultimately prevail, not because they were more just, but because the right to the fruits of labour was 'the only incitement [to labour] which acts constantly and universally'.[106]

Sismondi saw a potential for endogenous transformation in how the same capitalist conditions which oppressed the proletariat also built its capacity for self-emancipation. The conditions of urban manufacturing, wrote Sismondi, exacted a heavy toll of 'spiritual degradation', but they also paradoxically tended to enhance the proletariat's agency and capabilities.[107] English 'factory workers', he observed,

> are superior in intelligence, in knowledge and morality, to farm workers ... Living continually together, less tired out by fatigue, and much more able to engage in conversation, ideas have spread much faster among them; since they have been awakened, emulation has put them soon well above the workers of any other country.[108]

They had lately 'acquired courage', wrote Sismondi, 'a powerful sentiment of honour, and a confidence in themselves'.[109]

Sismondi, Wayland and Ogilvie all posited that capitalism's proletarianised conditions tended to incite class struggle and revolution. '[T]he social order', Sismondi argued, 'is in danger when the greatest part of agricultural labour is performed by day-labourers'.[110] The French Revolution, he argued, had erupted 'at a time when the vast majority of the population was a stranger to ownership'.[111] In Sismondi's estimation, several features of proletarianised society portended revolution, including: the 'precarious and unhappy state of so large a proportion of the population, their secret hostility against the landowners, and the whole order of society, [and] their want of interest in the work they perform'.[112] Wayland warned, in similar terms, that proletarians, 'if not educated and befriended by the present proprietors, may exact terms of fiery vengeance and retribution'.[113] Ogilvie likewise warned, by analogy to antiquity, that 'political revolutions of government have frequently stripped the ancient proprietors of large tracts of land'.[114]

Critical social theorists did not blithely or uniformly see capitalist dynamics as leading to proletarian liberation, however. Ravenstone, for instance, identified endogenous dynamics he believed could lead to social collapse. Under capitalism, he observed, the labourer received 'no improvement from the more skilful employment of his industry'; any such improvement 'only adds to the income of the idle'.[115] Given this tendency, he argued, the idle surplus-taking classes would tend to proliferate as productivity improved, and would eventually constitute 'the larger proportion of the society, and by far the more powerful'.[116] Whereas other critical theorists linked the unfolding of capital to growing proletarian power and resistance, Ravenstone argued, inversely, that it might lead to an ever-swelling and smotheringly powerful unproductive class.

Such dynamics, Ravenstone argued, contained the seeds of crisis. Where the idle inexorably squeezed the industrious, he argued, 'the state is feeble'.[117] Such a society was 'incapable of any extraordinary efforts' and so was defenceless against external threats.[118] Ravenstone further posited an inversion of Malthus' population hypothesis: an immiserating proliferation not of the poor, but of the rich. 'When the rich become too numerous', he argued, 'all their means are scarcely adequate to their own subsistence'.[119] The 'weight' of the swelling idle classes, Ravenstone projected, could prove 'more than it is possible for industry to support'.[120] Capital might thus die a parasite's death, killing itself by killing its host.

Like Ravenstone, Hopkins also saw a potential for collapse in the dynamics of capital. As I outlined in Chapter 10, Hopkins saw capitalist rent as a monopoly impost. While markets regulated relative rents, he believed, the overall rent burden was ultimately arbitrary, limited only by landlords' greed and the available surplus. It was possible then, Hopkins reasoned, for rent to smother capitalist accumulation. The 'great body of the landowners', he wrote, 'are not disposed to relax in their demands, sufficiently to enable the tenants to recover their capital'.[121] If landlords sapped society's capital and productive capacity, the population would decline, until finally 'the landlords themselves' would be 'reduced to poverty'.[122] Hopkins suggested this tendency might tend to accelerate. As rent-takings fell, a landlord might raise rents even further, to 'compensate himself for the falling off in his income'.[123] In this way, Hopkins wrote, the landlord's reaction to crisis 'only accelerates the ruin of the productive classes, and the impoverishment of himself'.[124] Capitalist rent might thereby extinguish capitalism itself.

Ogilvie, like Hopkins, also suggested capitalist rent might eventually destroy capitalist society. If the burden of rent increased, he argued, 'the fortune of the community must fall into continual and accelerated decline, and the privileges of every rank become insecure'.[125]

Yet, even where critical social theorists saw potential disaster in capital's endogenous dynamics, they still saw room for agency. Hopkins, for instance, argued that labourers could resist landlords' tendency to monopolise the social product. Workers could achieve higher wages, he argued, by restricting the labour supply through 'voluntary late marriages and a system of emigration'.[126] The ruling classes too, Hopkins argued, could temper rents to avert catastrophe.[127] It was 'not the real interest of either governments or land-proprietors', he argued, to reduce workers to 'a state of wretchedness that will weaken their productive power'.[128] Ogilvie, like Hopkins, argued endogenous crisis could be averted through class compromise: the 'impending gloom', he argued, might awe the 'privileged classes ... into wisdom and humanity'.[129]

In summary, Critical Social Theory's proletarian orientation led it to theorise capital's endogenous dynamics while paying close attention to opportunities for proletarian agency. It thus largely avoided both voluntarism and structural determinism in its theorisation of social change. Whether capital's endogenous logic portended liberation or disaster, the future remained open.

In this chapter, then, I have shown how Critical Social Theory's proletarian orientation, which led it to theorise rent as a proletarianising relation, also led it to theorise how society might be deproletarianised. I have argued that Critical Social Theory developed a variety of theoretical positions on deproletarianisation, falling under two major themes: proletarian self-emancipation, and endogenous social transformation.

Examining what theorists actually wrote, instead of using lazy and reductive labels like 'utopianism', we have discovered a surprising range and sophistication of thought. Critical Social Theory's thought on self-emancipation covered proletarian agency; class consciousness; the uses and dangers of force; the limits of trade unionism; the possibilities and problems of class compromise; the potentialities and limits of political reform; cooperativism's merits and failings; and finally, passive resistance and non-violent social revolution.

We also saw that Critical Social Theory developed various theories of endogenous social change – theories that traced the potential for deproletarianisation to the dynamics of capital itself. Here, Critical Social Theory posited that capital both developed and inhibited humanity's productive and human potential, and that it tended to build proletarian organisational capacities even as it fomented the conditions for revolution. Critical Social Theory was not, however, utopian in its projections of capital's endogenous logic. Even as some critical social theorists saw in capital an emancipatory potential, others argued its dynamics might easily end in a collapse. Whether gloomy or optimistic, critical social theorists were not determinists. They studied capital's unstable dynamics not mechanistically, but to understand the opportunities and constraints that confronted proletarians in their quest for emancipation.

Conclusion: Capital, mother of what?

In this book, I have drawn on scholarship in the social-property relations tradition to make a general argument about 'the engine of history'. Long-term social and historical change is best explained, I claim, as the endogenous transformation of social-property relations – the relations that organise how society produces what it needs. I used this approach to present a new account of capitalism's birth: capital emerged, I argued, from the tributary dynamics of rent. In contrast with endogenous transformation, I examined and critiqued three alternative models of historical explanation, which I call 'non-transformation', 'exogenous transformation', and 'agent–structure dualism'. These three flawed models encompass not only all mainstream accounts of the rise of capitalism, but many Marxist accounts too, including most contemporary contributions to the social-property relations tradition itself.

The endogenous transformation model, in contrast, posits that social-property relations are transformed as they are reproduced. The process happens dialectically, through the interplay of two interconnected elements. On the one hand, there is 'structured agency': the strategies or rules of reproduction agents adopt in the face of prevailing social-property relations. On the other hand, there are 'agent-generated structures': the prevailing social-property relations that emerge when individuals adopt certain rules of reproduction *en masse*. Over time, the interplay of these two poles generates 'laws of motion' or societal tendencies. In the long run, the development and interaction of these tendencies generates societal change and/or crises. Change confronts agents with new conditions, incentives and choices, and they adapt by adopting new strategies or rules. This can cause entirely new social-property relations to emerge, with their own novel tendencies or laws of motion. On it goes.

The social-property relations approach, properly understood, zeroes in on this dialectic to offer a causal *explanation* of social and historical change. History's most famous materialist, Marx, placed capitalist social-property relations, then spreading rapidly across the world, at the centre of his work. He vivisected capitalism with an unrivalled focus and systematicity, with the ambition of laying bare its rules of reproduction; its laws of motion; its propensities for crisis; the dialectical interplay between its laws of motion and proletarian agency; and finally, what kind of society capital might give birth to. Over a century later, it is not hard to find things he got wrong, especially at his most speculative. But was his method of inquiry in error? One way we validate our methods of understanding the present and future is to apply them to the past and see if the results are persuasive. That is this book's ambition.

Instead of centring capital, as Marx did, I have centred rent. And yes, I claim, the method is sound. The old society indeed gave birth to the new. I am persuaded, and I hope the reader is too, that tributary rent transformed endogenously into what we now call capitalism. The tributary rent relation was a localised variety of tributary social-property relations. It organised medieval societies into peasants who possessed the means to produce subsistence, and a class of coercive, tribute-taking local lords. Its unfolding tributary dynamics generated commercialisation, population growth and immiseration. These tendencies, I have argued, together precipitated an endemic endogenous crisis in the mid-fourteenth century, culminating in the Black Death. I argued further that England's uniquely federalised variant of the tributary rent relation, which hybridised local and central tributary power, left England's lords in a unique position during this endemic crisis. English lords lost control of peasants' bodies, but unlike continental lords, with a strong Crown's backing, England's lords retained control of the land to a unique degree.

The peculiar structuring conditions England's lords faced during this endogenous crisis enabled them to adopt a new and peculiar rule of reproduction: granting tenures on competitive terms. Accordingly, the English tributary rent relation mutated into a *competitive* relation. This competitive social mutation gradually generated new macro-dynamics. Commercial rents not only generated new capitalist relations of production in the English countryside but also a tendency for English lords to use their tributary power in a new and transformative way. By racking rents and enclosing, they began to proletarianise the English peasantry, progressively but entirely uprooting the old tributary relations between lord and peasant. England's altered, competitive rent relation manifested itself as a *capitalist* relation. Its proletarianising tendency became constitutive of capitalism: high rents permanently barred any retreat to tributary-subsistence agriculture; they kept landless workers available as wage labourers and market-dependent consumers; and they guaranteed capitalists' permanent access to land and labour.

As this newly transmogrified *capitalist* rent relation unfolded, it drove a series of further transformations in English society. I have shown that beyond proletarianising the peasantry and entrenching capitalism, the rent relation generated England's capitalist state, its Protestant Reformation and the English Revolution too. The logic of capitalist rent, I argued, also spurred England's landed class into a Janus-faced role, spearheading England-cum-Britain's capitalist development. Dependence on capitalist rent impelled landed men to act as improving landlords in civil society, and aristocrats in politics. In summary, tributary rent gave birth to capitalism, the mode of production that now dominates the globe.

In parallel to this social historical thesis, I have equally defended a thesis about *intellectual* history. I have argued that pre-Marxian critiques of rent are not an intellectual blind alley, as both mainstream and Marxist scholars have assumed. These thinkers cannot be reduced to moralists, millenarians, or utopians. On the contrary, their work is a transcript of subaltern efforts to decipher the core relations that drove and generated their society. Applying materialist methods, I have presented their critiques as products of the social conditions and resistance movements they emerged from. I have treated critical theories of rent, regardless of their vintage and language, as serious contributions to the social-property relations tradition. I have recast forgotten critiques of rent in light of rent's neglected world-historical role.

A close examination of these critiques reveals they were directed by a close attention to the material conditions and interests of subalterns. Medieval critics were grounded in the struggles of the tributary peasantry; critics of early English capitalism, like the Diggers, reflected an emerging proletariat; and the critical social theorists, writing in Britain's classical capitalist epoch, reflected an increasingly assertive working class. In highlighting the proletarian basis of Critical Social Theory, I have exposed the key material distinction between critical theories of rent and those from the state-oriented tradition of political economy, and its successor, economics.

Guided by proletarian interests, expressed as rights to the earth and to labour's fruits, Critical Social Theory conceived rent as a *proletarianising* relation. It centred proletarianisation as the key transformative process that generated capitalism, and traced proletarianisation to the dynamics of rent. High rents, Critical Social Theory argued, drove workers off the land, violating their right to the earth, and compelled them to sell their labour for subsistence wages, violating their right to their labour's full fruits. For Critical Social Theory, 'rent as proletarianization' was the conceptual master key to capitalist social-property relations; it lifted capital's ideological veil and exposed its basis in political coercion and economic domination. And 'rent as proletarianization' ultimately pointed Critical Social Theory beyond both rent and capital: to the endogenous transformation of capitalist social-property relations; to proletarian self-emancipation; and, most radically, to a classless, stateless, deproletarianised society of common ownership and cooperative production. Thus, while I have needed to sketch and defend the endogenous transformation approach in this book – chiefly to distinguish it from its flawed competitors – it is not my invention, nor even that of Marx, Engels, or more lately, Robert Brenner. It is part of a diverse centuries-old tradition of subaltern-oriented social science.

The tradition this book unearths is alien to contemporary economic theory. As I observed at this book's outset, contemporary rent theory comprises a diverse set of intellectual tools that economists use to help states manage capitalist development. It primes them to identify rents – myriad forms of inefficient, unproductive or inequitable sources of income – and to fashion policies to eliminate them. Progressive and conservative economists differ mainly in that the former prioritise rents that exacerbate inequality, and the latter those that cause inefficiency.[1] Yet all are motivated by the same basic imaginary: a more perfect, rent-free capitalism. And this underlying goal, recognised or not, explains the paradox that economists see rents everywhere in contemporary capitalism but treat rent as something alien to capitalism, not intrinsic.

The exceptions to this rule tend only to prove it. Some economic theories do present rent as intrinsic to capitalism – like the Ricardian or differential theory, the neoclassical marginal productivity theory, or Schumpeter's theory of entrepreneurial rents.[2] But in these cases, the rents in question are always supposed to play a progressive role, advancing capitalism in some way, such as by promoting efficiency or innovation. These economic theories celebrate rent rather than condemn it, but their policy purpose remains the same: to perfect, preserve, and advance capitalism.

The contrast with Critical Social Theory is stark. Critical Social Theory proceeds not from the state perspective of political economy (or economics) but from a proletarian one. It analyses rent not as a blight on capital, but as the proletarianising relation that gave birth to it, and as part of its constitution. Critical Social Theory's critique of rent cuts to the basic relations of capitalist society: social-property relations. Critical Social Theory understands rent as intrinsic, not extraneous. It sees the myriad forms of unearned income that economic theory calls rent, not as deviations from some true and ideal form of capitalism, but as outgrowths of capitalism, as it really is. Critical Social Theory's interest is not in the perfection of capitalist social-property relations but, ultimately, what may lie beyond them. Critical theories of rent represent a fundamental break from economic theories, however progressive or conservative.

And as I argued at this book's outset, the tradition of Critical Social Theory extends far beyond those contributions I have excavated. It is not the sole preserve of its most famous figure, Marx. It encompasses all social theorists, past and present, whose proletarian orientation to social science leads them beyond the horizons of political economy or economics. Critical Social Theory is a centuries-old tradition. It is as old as 'social science', a term it coined. And Critical Social Theory, I have shown, is itself part of a far longer tradition. The tradition of analysing social-property relations from a subaltern perspective began long before the advent of social science. I have traced the tradition's analysis of rent to the eleventh century, and it is certainly much older. Subaltern critiques of social-property relations are as old as class society itself.

But what do arguments about the history of society have to tell us about its present and future? Throughout this book I have claimed that because the rent relation gave birth to capital, the history of rent and its critique has a neglected world-historical significance. I have also surmised that capital's birth in England triggered the global transition to capitalism. It is beyond the scope of this book to provide a detailed account of that transition. But I will at least explain why the birth of English and global capitalism were one and the same, and hence why long-forgotten Anglophone critiques of rent have world-historical significance.

I do not suggest England's capitalist rent relation is proletarianising the globe in a simple extension of how it proletarianised England. That would be a 'non-transformative' explanation of the kind I critiqued in Chapter 1. Rather, I claim, historical change results from endogenous transformation. Change happens because social-property relations mutate to adapt to conditions they themselves generate. On this model, the appearance of capital outside England, just like its birth within, was not a matter of extension but of transformation.

Following Ellen Meiksins Wood, Charles Post, Xavier Lafrance, and some other social-property relations theorists, I propose that a key endogenous mechanism by which English capital sparked a global transformation was geopolitical competition.[3] As I have already shown, both capitalist and tributary social-property relations require and generate states. States, whether tributary or capitalist, are impelled to defend and advance the social-property relations they rely on against both domestic and geopolitical threats. Anarchic geopolitical competition between capitalist and tributary states is a major way capitalist and non-capitalist social-property relations interact. It is a way they exert adaptive pressure on each other, and hence a source of endogenous transformation on a global scale.

Where a tributary state conquers a capitalist one, its demands for tribute can smother circuits of capital and prompt a reversion to tributary social-property relations. As I argued in Chapter 5, England's capitalist social-property relations were seriously threatened by the presence of tributary-absolutist France before Great Britain formed and consolidated a secure geopolitical position. In the same vein, Davidson has identified several potential historical instances where capitalist social-property relations might have emerged and flourished had they not been caged or stifled by greater tributary powers.[4] As it was, Great Britain was the first capitalist state to escape the tributary corral, and with that capital became a global force. Had this not happened, however, it remains plausible that some other nascent capitalism, born elsewhere – whether from rent or other tributary relations – would have escaped eventually.

Presuming a capitalist state survives infancy, a new geopolitical possibility emerges: capitalist states overwhelming tributary ones. This outcome is made ever more likely by the startling productivity of capitalist social-property relations, which supports the military expansion of capitalist states. This scenario portends different transformations of social-property relations. A common outcome was imperialism. A capitalist state would utilise or modify the tributary social-property relations of the conquered society in ways that supported capitalist development in the metropole. A capitalist state could demand and use imperial tribute, for instance, to lessen the burden of taxation at home, or to source 'cheap' inputs into domestic circuits of capital.[5] This model of capitalist imperialism was first applied by England in Ireland, through the imperial-tributary relations of cottier tenancy, plantation labour obligations, and absentee landlordism.[6] Imperial-tributary relations were later established in other British colonies, and most expansively in India.

Geopolitical competition between capitalist and tributary states may produce another transformative outcome, which I call 'tributary metamorphosis'. In this scenario, tributary political elites recognise that to survive geopolitical competition against capitalist states, they must reground themselves in social-property relations of comparable productivity. They therefore adopt radically new rules of reproduction, repurposing their coercive powers not to extract tribute, but to *uproot* tributary social-property relations.

They proletarianise peasantries and reorganise production on industrial lines. Peasants have incentives to resist, but also to acquiesce. Local elites are generally preferable to imperial ones, and proletarian life may offer a package of risks, comforts and opportunities more attractive than those of subsistence farming, at least in the long run. Nineteenth and twentieth-century political ideologies, like liberalism, nationalism, and communism, often expressed precisely these elite and popular imperatives, serving as ideologies of tributary metamorphosis.

On a global scale, tributary social-property relations have shown a great propensity to transform into capitalist ones. They are highly receptive to the metamorphic pressure capitalism exerts through geopolitical competition. This transformative tendency is self-perpetuating and tends to intensify. Each tributary state that metamorphoses into a capitalist one increases the geopolitical pressure on those remaining to follow suit. This process is endogenous neither to tributary nor to capitalist social-property relations alone, but to their *interaction*. And because both tributary social-property relations and capitalist geopolitical pressure express themselves differently in each locality, every tributary metamorphosis takes a different form. Capitalism has 'never emerged in the same way' in two localities.[7]

The first historical case of tributary metamorphosis, with its own peculiarities, was that of Scotland.[8] Around the late seventeenth century, Scotland's feudal-tributary elite faced a series of crises and humiliations spanning trade, war, famine, and colonial misadventure.[9] Weakness dictated a submissive approach to geopolitical competition with England, Scotland's thriving capitalist neighbour. In Davidson's summation, Scottish lords 'opted to abandon sovereignty altogether for incorporation into a greater power that would protect what they had'.[10] They acceded to a political union with England, forming the United Kingdom of Great Britain, and it was within this union that Scottish tributary relations metamorphosed. A vanguard of enclosing Scottish lords spearheaded Scottish capitalist development, emulating their English counterparts. At first, recalcitrant Scottish lords clung to feudal-tributary social-property relations, but once the unitary British state crushed their Jacobite political movement in 1745, they too pursued the proletarianising path of enclosure.[11] The metamorphosis was so rapid that by 1815, Scotland and England were equal partners in Britain's Industrial Revolution.[12]

Studies by social-property relations theorists show tributary metamorphosis as a key mechanism by which British social-property relations precipitated a global transition to capitalism.[13] 'Once industrial capitalism was consolidated in Britain over the second third of the nineteenth century', write Lafrance and Post, 'it became increasingly evident for continental ruling classes, which had clung to states as means of extra-economic appropriation and reproduction, that their survival depended on a capitalist restructuring.'[14] 'The international state system, fueled by geopolitical competition … acted as the conveyer belt of the first wave of the global propagation of capitalism to continental Europe and Japan.'[15]

In its barest outlines, this is the world-historical significance of rent: England's federalised tributary rent relation generated the capital relation in England; the productivity of English capital fuelled the geopolitical expansion of the English-cum-Great-British capitalist state; Britain's geopolitical advance and imperialism applied metamorphic pressure to surrounding tributary states; sparking a self-reinforcing process of tributary metamorphosis, precipitating the global transition. While this delineates the world-historical significance of rent, it offers only the scantiest account of capital's spread. A fuller account would cover various other endogenous dynamics. As British capitalism expanded geopolitically, it encountered the kin-ordered or tributary social-property relations of various indigenous societies.[16] The result could be disastrous for the latter, as in the settler colonialisms of North America and Australia.[17] Geopolitical competition *between* capitalist states was another crucial endogenous dynamic – playing out in capitalist-imperialist rivalry, two world wars, and post-war decolonisations.

And, of course, geopolitical competition is just one important interface between different forms of social-property relations. A fuller historical account would explore other channels for the transmission of metamorphic pressure, like migration, trade, communicable diseases, international investment, and technological diffusion, to name a few. Here, there are vast existing literatures to be mined – history, international relations, international political economy, anthropology, and development economics, to name a few.

Metamorphic encounters between capitalist and non-capitalist social-property relations can be contrasted with other ways of framing global proletarianisation. One is Harvey's concept of 'accumulation by dispossession.'[18] Harvey builds on Marx's account of the 'primitive accumulation' of capital, which Marx defined as the 'expropriation of the agricultural producer, of the peasant, from the soil.'[19] Harvey's rubric gives coercion and exclusion a central role in capitalism's global expansion.[20] But in doing so, it risks reducing a complex interplay of metamorphic forces to just one. It also tends to cast non-capitalist social formations passively, as objects capital can 'make use of.'[21] Non-capitalist agents are either 'violently repressed' or 'coopted.'[22] Non-capitalist societies become Southern or Eastern spatial voids into which Western and Northern capital expands. China, for instance, becomes 'a new *terrain* of accumulation.'[23] This recalls the structuralist and non-transformative models' of change I critiqued in Chapter 1.

Harvey does attempt to carve out space for non-capitalist agents. He acknowledges, for instance: that a non-capitalist social formation will sometimes deliberately 'insert itself into the logic of capitalist development';[24] that accumulation by dispossession is often orchestrated not by capitalist imperial powers but by the 'developmental states' of the Global South;[25] and that accumulation by dispossession has 'provoked political and social struggles and vast swaths of resistance.'[26] What is missing, however, is a deeper engagement with how *non-capitalist* social-property relations work. Agents in the Global South have responded to capitalist metamorphic pressures from within various *non-capitalist* relations, which entail their own specific opportunities, constraints, oppressions, freedoms, macro-dynamics, tendencies, contradictions and crises. Without a specific account of these, Southern agency is reduced to its posture towards capitalism – to resistance or acquiescence.[27] Without an account of what structures Southern agency, other than capitalism's advance, it can appear voluntaristic, futile, inevitable, or simply opaque.

The canon of Critical Social Theory gained much when Marx abstracted from rent to develop his account of profit in *Das Kapital* Volume 1.[28] But it lost something too. In narrating capital's exploitative economic logic 'from the inside', Marx exteriorised its political preconditions. These reappear at the end of Volume 1 as a creation story – the violent cataclysm of 'primitive accumulation'. The limits of this approach haunt Critical Social Theory. As Morozov observes, critical theorists still debate how to 'bridge' Marxian accounts of economic exploitation and political expropriation in a single theory of capitalism.[29] Pre-Marxian Critical Social Theory interiorised the relationship through an account of endogenously transforming social-property relations. A pre-existing coercive tributary rent relation transformed into a proletarianising capitalist relation. Rent established the political preconditions of capital's economic logic and became a constituent part of capital. As a transitional figure, Marx had access to *both* paradigms, each with its strengths. But it seems he reorganised Critical Social Theory so thoroughly that the earlier paradigm became unintelligible to his successors. Brenner's pathbreaking work made a recoupment possible by recentring social-property relations. Building on his work, this book reconstructs the lost history of rent and its critique.

And that history has consequences that go far beyond how we narrate the past. It demands a re-evaluation of the present and future.

If commercialisation is the indicium of capitalist transition, as both mainstream and Marxist theorists often assume, then the globalisation of commerce means that 'late capitalism' must have arrived. The equation of universal commerce with universal capitalism has also led theorists to conclude that tributary social-property relations, and therefore peasantries, no longer exist. Bernstein, for instance, argues that 'by the end of the colonial era', the bulk of the global peasantry, even in Asia and Africa, had become 'petty commodity producers' – in other words, creatures of capitalism.[30] Contemporary peasants, on this view, are not what they appear, because they now engage in wage labour and commodity production.[31]

Yet, as I have shown in this book, commercialisation, commodity production, and even wage labour are all endogenous to tributary social-property relations. Their presence does not necessarily signify capitalism. Their universality does not mean capitalism is universal, nor that the global peasantry is extinct. By contrast, the history of rent and its critique centres on *proletarianisation* as the key process and indicium of capitalist transition. If this criterion is applied, a strikingly different picture of contemporary global society emerges. We can acknowledge that global proletarianisation is incomplete, and a large land-possessing peasantry endures today, in the world's developing nations, most saliently in Asia and Africa.[32]

The size of the global peasantry and the prevalence of tributary relations is difficult to estimate. Statistical categories conflate tributary and capitalist market activity, and global statistics on non-market activity are patchy.[33] Even so, the very fact that the world remains so *agrarian* suggests that tributary metamorphosis has a way to run yet. In 2019, around 1.23 billion people were still employed or engaged in agrifood systems.[34] And this is only the statistically visible fraction of agrarian society. It encompasses billions more people, many engaged in domestic and reproductive labour, mostly women, as well as other people and classes supported by agrarian production, like children, elderly dependents, trades, domestic servants, scholars, clerics, state officials and so on. In 2021, there were still 608 million farms in the world.[35] Family farms produced roughly 80 per cent of the world's food in value terms, using 70 to 80 per cent of global farmland.[36] Farms smaller than two hectares alone produced roughly 35 per cent of the world's food using 12 per cent of all agricultural land.[37] A 2025 study suggests common techniques may underestimate the world's rural population by half or more, suggesting agrarian society remains more prevalent than realised.[38] These figures do not precisely distinguish tributary from capitalist relations, but neither is such precision possible amidst a global transition.

Capitalism, to use Marx's phrase, carries along with it 'partly still unconquered remnants' of non-capitalist social formations.[39] From the perspective of social-property relations, capital is globally dominant, but that dominance is not expressed in universalised capitalist social-property relations, but rather the incredible *metamorphic pressure* capitalism applies to remnant tributary and kin-ordered relations, through geopolitical competition, trade and other forms of social intercourse. This pressure is such that even when local elites or movements have tried to transform tributary societies in ostensibly *non*-capitalist directions – as in twentieth-century Soviet communism – those transformations ultimately took capitalist or peri-capitalist forms.[40]

The lens of tributary metamorphosis casts the contemporary global economy in a different light. Today, an increasing proportion of global economic growth is supplied by developing nations. Since 2010, China and other emerging and developing economies have accounted for over 60 per cent of annual global economic growth.[41] That growth is not endogenous to an already-universal capitalism. It represents the transformative *interaction* of capitalist and tributary social-property relations, and the marker of transformation is proletarianisation. It is no coincidence, for example, that China's extraordinary state-led development since 1978 has coincided with the rapid proletarianisation of its peasantry.[42] From the perspective of social-property relations, global economic vitality today stems not from capital per se, but largely from the temporary incandescence of a capitalist *transition* across the developing world.

And what does the ongoing multi-century rise of global capitalism suggest about its future? In the 'unipolar moment' of the early twenty-first century, capitalism was supposed to be eternal. The end of the Cold War heralded declarations that liberal-democratic capitalism represented the 'End of History' and that 'there is no alternative'.[43] History has since bluntly reasserted itself – with China's economic and geopolitical rise, the Global Financial Crisis, Climate Change, Big Tech and Artificial Intelligence, several international and civil wars, and a global pandemic – to name a few. Events like these insist that society is still transforming rapidly, but give us little confidence about where it is headed.

The social-property relations approach suggests that if we want a sense of history's direction, we ought to start with its social-property relations and trace their endogenous development. If it is at all possible to build a vantage point from which to glimpse our future, or even from which to posit plausible scenarios, we have no better method.

When thinking about how social-property relations might change, part of the difficulty is timescale. Individuals mark historical change in decades at most. But as this book has shown, social-property relations transform over centuries and millennia. Rent gave birth to capital in the mid-fifteenth century, and yet, nearly six centuries later, the epoch of capitalist transition continues. Still, transitions are ultimately transient.

From the perspective of social-property relations, the key question for global capitalist development may not be what happens when the world runs out of natural resources but what happens when it runs out of peasants. The fuel of proletarianisation can be burned only once. As developing nations become developed, their growth slows. China's annual economic growth hit a reform-era peak of 15 per cent in 1984 but had slowed to 5 per cent four decades later.[44]

Another feature of recent global history – rapid and sustained population growth – likewise appears to be neither capitalist nor tributary, but a product of interaction. Developed capitalist nations have the productivity growth to support growing populations but declining patterns of fertility, whereas tributary societies have historically had high birthrates that can outstrip their productivity. The epoch of rapid global population growth appears to have been a unique and transient interaction between capitalist productivity and tributary fertility patterns. As capital has expanded globally, it has become ever more reliant on this interaction for population and economic growth. For more than a quarter century, global population growth has come entirely from developing economies – those undergoing tributary metamorphosis – mainly in Asia, Oceania, and Africa.[45] As of 2025, 84 per cent of the world's population lived in developing countries, up from 66 per cent in 1950.[46] This is despite substantial migration from developing to developed nations. Half of the projected increase in world population by 2050 is expected to occur in just a few countries in Africa and Asia.[47] Even these islands of fertility are shrinking. Projections suggest that by 2100, sub-Saharan Africa will nurse half of the world's babies alone.[48]

As tributary relations recede, so does tributary fertility. Proletarians have far fewer children than peasants, and even peasants' fertility is declining globally – suggesting metamorphic pressures are at play. Across so-called 'least developed economies', total fertility declined from 6.1 births per woman in the period 1950 to 1955, to just 2.6 in the period 2015 to 2020.[49] By 2100, only 3 per cent of nations are expected to have total fertility rates above the accepted replacement level of 2.1 births per woman. The epoch of universal capitalism, it seems, will also be one of global depopulation, and theorists are only beginning to grapple with the implications.[50]

What role will popular agency play in the transformations ahead? History is not, I have argued, a process of 'exogenous transformation' where agents or classes can transform their social-property relations 'from the outside'. Changing the world is not just a matter of willpower. The options agents have, be they individuals, classes, states, or political movements, are always structured, constrained, and enabled by the prevailing social-property relations. As I argued at the outset of this book, people can only adopt new strategies if and when the dynamics of the prevailing social-property relations put these within reach. As social-property relations unfold, they can block old strategies, while opening startling new ones.

The social-property relations approach suggests that history's most radical acts – one of which turned out to be England's lords adopting competitive leasing – need not be done with radical intentions. Social revolutions can emerge from *ad hoc* adaptations to conditions generated by social-property relations themselves. As Brenner put it, capitalism was 'the unintended consequence of feudal actors pursuing feudal goals in feudal ways'.[51] Different unintended transformations could be underway today. In the early nineteenth century, Sismondi dubbed capitalism's landless working class the proletariat – reviving a classical Roman term meaning 'the class that reproduces'. In the twenty-first century, the global proletariat's most radical act may be its increasing *refusal* to reproduce. The significance of the coming global depopulation will depend on how far it goes and its interactions with capital's other secular tendencies – like technological development, capital deepening, productivity growth, services employment, wealth inequality, economic instability, international security competition, politics and anti-politics, and so on. The development and interaction of these tendencies is complex and unpredictable. Importantly, though, these are not the tendencies of so-called 'late capitalism', let alone *perpetual* 'late capitalism'. Global proletarianisation proceeds apace, so capitalism remains, in a definite sense, immature.

And if some have prematurely declared capitalism to be universal and eternal, others are perhaps prematurely carving its tombstone. From conservatives like Joel Kotkin to critical theorists like Varoufakis, Durand, and Dean, many now reference an emerging neo- or techno-feudalism – terms I use interchangeably.[52] Exponents use feudalism as a metaphor for what they see as regressive capitalist tendencies:[53] profit-seeking displaced by rent-seeking; social mobility ossifying into economic castes; workers morphing from 'producers' to 'servants' or 'vassals', as industry gives way to services; homeownership displaced by landlordism and precarious tenancy; a growing gulf between economic centres and neglected hinterlands; steady employment giving way to precarious 'gig' work; finance that extracts from the productive economy rather than enabling it; regulatory and policy capture by rent-seeking elites; public power and legal equality fragmenting ('parcellating') into realms of private governance; open markets giving way to private digital fiefdoms; law enforcement replaced by private surveillance, security, and arbitration; democratic decisions replaced by algorithms; tech giants ('new lords') monopolising data, algorithms, supply chains, networks, platforms, and attention, and using these tools to control, manipulate, surveil, and extract rents from businesses and consumers ('new serfs').

Techno-feudal theorists suggest it represents capitalism's endogenous transformation into a new system. '[C]apitalism is now dead', Varoufakis writes.[54] '[P]rofit, the engine of capitalism has been replaced with its feudal predecessor: rent'.[55] '[C]apitalist relations and forces of production', Dean writes, 'are undergoing systemic transformation and transitioning into a different mode of production'.[56] '[P]rofit, improvement and competitive advantage' are giving way to 'rents, destruction and hoarding ... extra-economic coercion ... privilege and dependency'.[57] Durand, in similar terms, calls techno-feudalism a 'positive reiteration of the politically or coercively enforced relations of appropriation that characterized feudalism in its time'.[58] For him, the death of capitalism 'depends ultimately on a question of threshold. When appropriation exceeds capitalist exploitation, the system will have mutated'.[59]

This new 'techno-feudal reason', like mainstream economic thinking, sees rent everywhere in capitalism, but paradoxically insists rent is not capitalist. It regards capitalism as exploitative but lacks a 'broader account of capitalist accumulation' that incorporates both 'redistribution and exploitation', both rent *and* profit.[60] It draws no distinction between tributary and capitalist rent, each grounded in different social-property relations. Lacking this, it equates profits with capitalism and rents with feudalism. The mode of production seesaws depending on the balance.

By contrast, Critical Social Theory conceived rent and profit as internally related elements of capitalist social-property relations. It saw economic exploitation and extra-economic coercion not as competing systems, but as symbiotic and internally related. It understood tributary 'extra-economic' power as enduring under capitalism, centralised in the capitalist state. It saw a state using this power to uphold exclusive property in land and capital, the politico-legal basis for proletarianised (capitalist) production, and wages, profit, and rent. Critical Social Theory saw the state (in reproducing itself and upholding capitalist social-property relations) as deploying 'extra-economic' power in myriad other ways too – from imposing taxes to granting all manner of private privileges, rights and monopolies.[61] For Critical Social Theory, state power upheld not only land rent but all other 'rents'. These represented distributive shares in the capitalist surplus, not 'feudal' exactions. This older perspective offers an escape from techno-feudal reason. It could allow rent to be theorised as part of 'techno-capitalism',[62] compared not to feudalism but *classical* capitalism: where rentiers drove capitalism forward to enlarge their share in its surplus.

If a resurgence of rent does not signify capitalism's end, what would? How would we know non-capitalism if we saw it? Centuries of Critical Social Theory identifies *proletarianisation* as structurally central to capitalism. In capitalism, the core relation of production is a class without means of production seeking employment from a class with these means. In non-capitalist societies, different principles are central. To imagine such societies, we can look to the kin-ordered and tributary societies of the past and present. We can also look to post-capitalist imaginaries, like those explored in the last chapter, or to the utopias and dystopias of science fiction.[63] In Frank Herbert's *Dune*, for example, we find a literal 'techno-feudalism' where workers are vassals indentured to and provided for by spacefaring guilds and warring Great Houses.[64] In Margaret Atwood's *The Handmaid's Tale*, we find a theocratic totalitarian society where the populace are state-owned slaves.[65] In Iain M. Banks' *Culture* novels, by contrast, there are no workers because benevolent artificial intelligences provide limitless abundance. Grim or hopeful, these are non-proletarian societies. We can debate edge-cases and transitional states, imaginary and historical. But the tradition of Critical Social Theory sets a higher bar than today's techno-feudal theories.

In 1843, Marx suggested that the more time passes, 'the more perfect will be the birth of the product that the present carries in its womb'.[66] I lack Marx's confidence about what will be born, how, or when. But history leaves me confident that like all previous social formations – whether over decades, centuries, or millennia – capitalism *is* endogenously transforming. Like every mode of production, it is fated to manifest its tendencies, contradictions, and crises. And like every mode of production, it must adapt to these. No system has been so adaptable. But neither has any changed its environment so radically or rapidly, placing so much transformative pressure on itself. If capital matured in the belly of rent, something surely stirs within capital too – unformed, unseen, but inevitable.

Notes

INTRODUCTION

1. See Ronald Bird and Vincent J Tarascio, 'Paretian Rent versus Pareto's Rent Theory: A Clarification and Correction' in *Vilfredo Pareto: Critical Assessments of Leading Economists* (Routledge, 1999) 473.
2. See, for example, EJ Mishan, 'Rent and Producer's Surplus: Reply' (1969) 59(4) *The American Economic Review* 635, 637.
3. See early texts such as Anne O Krueger, 'The Political Economy of the Rent-Seeking Society' (1974) 64(3) *The American Economic Review* 291; also, for example, James M Buchanan, Robert D Tollison and Gordon Tullock, *Toward a Theory of the Rent-Seeking Society* (Texas A & M University, 1980); Charles K Rowley, Robert D Tollison and Gordon Tullock (eds), *The Political Economy of Rent-Seeking* (Springer US, 1988); Gordon Tullock, *The Economics of Special Privilege and Rent Seeking* (Springer Netherlands, 1989).
4. See, for example, Mason Gaffney, 'Land Rent, Taxation, and Public Policy: The Sources, Nature and Functions of Urban Land Rent' (1972) 31(3) *American Journal of Economics and Sociology* 241; Mason Gaffney, 'Land Rent, Taxation and Public Policy: Taxation and the Functions of Urban Land Rent' (1973) 32(1) *American Journal of Economics and Sociology* 17; Fred E Foldvary, 'Public Revenue from Land Rent' in Jürgen G Backhaus and Richard E Wagner (eds), *Handbook of Public Finance* (Springer Science + Business Media, Inc., 2005) 165; Terence Dwyer, 'Taxation: The Lost History' (2014) 73(4) *American Journal of Economics and Sociology* 664.
5. Nick Srnicek and Laurent De Sutter, *Platform Capitalism* (Polity, 2017).
6. For a recent example, see Brett Christophers, 'The Problem of Rent' (2019) 6(2) *Critical Historical Studies* 303.
7. Joel Kotkin, *The Coming of Neo-Feudalism: A Warning to the Global Middle Class* (Encounter Books, Reprint edition, 2023).
8. McKenzie Wark, *Capital Is Dead: Is This Something Worse?* (Verso, Paperback edition, 2021) ('*Capital Is Dead*').
9. See Evgeny Morozov, 'Critique of Techno-Feudal Reason' [2022] (133/134) *New Left Review* 89; Cédric Durand, 'Scouting Capital's Frontiers' [2022] (136) *New Left Review* 29.
10. Yanis Varoufakis, *Technofeudalism: What Killed Capitalism* (Melville House, 2024); On techno-feudalism more generally, see Morozov (n 9) 107.

11. Jodi Dean, *Capital's Grave: Neofeudalism and the New Class Struggle* (Verso, 2025) 15 ('*Capital's Grave*').
12. Alexander Anievas and Kerem Nişancıoğlu, 'The Poverty of Political Marxism' [2014] (94) *International Socialist Review* https://isreview.org/issue/94/poverty-political-marxism; I note that the charge of methodological internalism is only one of several laid by Anievas and Nişancıoğlu against the social-property relations approach, including in their *How the West Came to Rule: The Geopolitical Origins of Capitalism* (Pluto Press, 2015); while it is beyond the scope of this study to attempt a review or rebuttal of all Anievas and Nişancıoğlu's criticisms, others have taken up the gauntlet: see Spencer Dimmock, 'The Eastern Origins of Capitalism?', *Historical Materialism* www.historicalmaterialism.org/book-review/eastern-origins-capitalism; Eren Duzgun, 'Against Eurocentric Anti-Eurocentrism: International Relations, Historical Sociology and Political Marxism' [2018] *Journal of International Relations and Development* 10–23 https://doi.org/10.1057/s41268-018-0146-0; Maïa Pal, '"My Capitalism Is Bigger than Yours!": Against Combining "How the West Came to Rule" with "The Origins of Capitalism"' (2018) 26(3) *Historical Materialism* 99, 104–108; Tibor Rutar, 'The Transition Debate Today: A Review of The Origin of Capitalism in England, 1400–1600 by Spencer Dimmock' (2018) 26(3) *Historical Materialism* 197; for a less categorical rebuttal, see also Neil Davidson, 'The Frontiers of Uneven and Combined Development' (2018) 26(3) *Historical Materialism* 52.
13. Naeem Inayatullah and David L Blaney, 'The Costs of Weaponizing Emancipatory Politics: Constituting What Is Constitutive of Capitalism' 8(1) *Spectrum Journal of Global Studies* 46, 24–25.
14. See TH Aston and CHE Philpin (eds), *The Brenner Debate: Agrarian Class Structure and Economic Development in Pre-Industrial Europe* (Cambridge Univ. Press, 1995).
15. See, for example, Spencer Dimmock, *The Origin of Capitalism in England, 1400–1600* (Brill, 2014) ('*OCE*').
16. On Brenner's derivation of the social-property relations approach from Marx, see Robert P Brenner, 'Property and Progress: Where Adam Smith Went Wrong' in Chris Wickham (ed), *Marxist History-Writing for the Twenty-First Century* (Oxford University Press, for the British Academy, 2007) 49 ('PP').
17. See, for example, Keith Tribe, 'Donald Winch 1935–2017' (2018) 25(1) *The European Journal of the History of Economic Thought* 196.
18. Karl Marx and Frederick Engels, 'The German Ideology [Composed in 1846]' in *The German Ideology: Including Theses on Feuerbach and Introduction to The Critique of Political Economy* (Prometheus Books, 1998) 27, 68.
19. Ibid.

20. Neal Wood, *Foundations of Political Economy: Some Early Tudor Views on State and Society* (University of California Press, 1994) 8–9 ('*FPE*').
21. Ibid. 9.
22. Marx and Engles called this the 'self-determination of the concept': see Marx and Engels (n 18) 70.
23. A materialist approach does not, however, assume theorists are simple 'ideological spokespersons' for their social classes: see Geoff Kennedy, 'Review of Citizens to Lords: A Social History of Western Political Thought from Antiquity to the Middle Ages' (2011) 19(1) *Historical Materialism* 304, 305.

1 CAPITALISM AND THE ENGINE OF HISTORY

1. Maurice Dobb, *Studies in the Development of Capitalism* (Routledge & Kegan Paul, 1946); Paul M Sweezy, *The Theory of Capitalist Development: Principles of Marxian Political Economy.* (Monthly Review P., 1970); Immanuel Wallerstein, *The Modern World-System I: Capitalist Agriculture and the Origins of the European World-Economy in the Sixteenth Century* (University of California Press, 2011); Robert P Brenner, 'Agrarian Class Structure and Economic Development in Pre-Industrial Europe' [1976] (70) *Past & Present* 30 ('ACS').
2. Xavier Lafrance and Charles Post, 'Introduction' in Xavier Lafrance and Charles Post (eds), *Case Studies in the Origins of Capitalism* (Palgrave Macmillan, 2019) 1, 22; cf. Ellen Meiksins Wood, *Democracy against Capitalism: Renewing Historical Materialism* (Cambridge University Press, 1995) 26 ('*DAC*'); for a sympathetic overview of the origins, precepts, reception and key criticisms of the social-property relations approach, see generally Lafrance and Post.
3. Karl Marx and Frederick Engels, *Capital: A Critique of Political Economy [First Published 1894]*, tr David Fernbach, vol 3 (Penguin Books in association with New Left Review, 1981) 927–928.
4. Lafrance and Post (n 2) 22.
5. Robert P Brenner, 'Property and Progress: Where Adam Smith Went Wrong' in Chris Wickham (ed), *Marxist History-Writing for the Twenty-First Century* (Oxford University Press, for the British Academy, 2007) 49, 58 ('PP'); see also Spencer Dimmock, 'The Eastern Origins of Capitalism?', *Historical Materialism* § 8 www.historicalmaterialism.org/book-review/eastern-origins-capitalism.
6. See Dimmock (n 5) § 9; Lafrance and Post (n 2) 23.
7. See, for example, Alexander Anievas and Kerem Nişancıoğlu, 'The Poverty of Political Marxism' [2014] (94) *International Socialist Review* https://isreview.org/issue/94/poverty-political-marxism.
8. Adam Smith, *Lectures on Jurisprudence*, ed Ronald L Meek, DD Raphael and Peter Stein (Liberty Classics, 1978).

9. For example, Dimmock (n 5) §6.
10. Eric R Wolf, *Europe and the People without History* (University of California Press, 2010) 73–100 ('*EPWH*'). Brenner describes the essential features of tributary social-property relations in similar terms, although he uses the more generic designation 'pre-capitalist'. See Robert P Brenner, 'The Social Basis of Economic Development' in John E Roemer (ed), *Analytical Marxism* (Cambridge University Press, 1986) 23, 27.
11. Ellen Meiksins Wood, *The Pristine Culture of Capitalism: A Historical Essay on Old Regimes and Modern States* (Verso, 1991) 149 ('*PCC*').
12. Ibid. 10; see also Brenner, 'PP' (n 5) 60–62.
13. Ellen Meiksins Wood, *The Origin of Capitalism: A Longer View* (Verso, New Edition, 2002) 61 ('*OCLV*'); see also ibid. 80, 193.
14. Andreas Bieler and Adam David Morton, *Global Capitalism, Global War, Global Crisis* (Cambridge University Press, 1st ed, 2018) 6, 27–50. Bieler and Morton compare and contrast dialectical historical materialist approaches to other approaches, including, structuralism, intentionalism, structuration theory, the morphogenesis approach, the Transformational Model of Social Activity, post-structuralism, constructivism.
15. Ibid. 30.
16. On how (class) agency is structured by capitalist social-property relations, see ibid. 41–46.
17. Ibid. 30.
18. Ibid. 43; On the structuredness of agency see Alex Callinicos, *Making History: Agency, Structure, and Change in Social Theory* (Brill, 2nd rev. ed, 2004) 96–101.
19. Bieler and Morton (n 14) 31.
20. Ibid. 36, 46; Samuel Knafo, 'Critical Approaches and the Legacy of the Agent/Structure Debate in International Relations' (2010) 23(3) *Cambridge Review of International Affairs* 493, 507.
21. Bieler and Morton (n 14) 31.
22. On structures as constraints or limits, ruling out particular courses of action, see ibid. 29–30, 44.
23. Callinicos (n 18) xxiii; Martijn Konings, 'The Pragmatic Sources of Modern Power' (2010) 51(1) *European Journal of Sociology* 55, 58.
24. Bieler and Morton (n 14) 44.
25. Brenner, 'PP' (n 5) 59; see also Wood, *OCLV* (n 13) 193; cf. Charles Post, 'Capitalism, Laws of Motion and Social Relations of Production' (2013) 21(4) *Historical Materialism* 71, 79 ('CLM').
26. Brenner, 'PP' (n 5) 59.
27. Ibid.; Wood, *OCLV* (n 13) 193; cf. Post, 'CLM' (n 25) 79.
28. See, for example, Brenner, 'PP' (n 5) 59; Post, 'CLM' (n 25) 79.
29. Brenner, 'PP' (n 5) 59.
30. Cf. ibid. 96.

31. Konings (n 23) 59. Konings draws this observation from the philosophical tradition of American Pragmatism.
32. Wood, *OCLV* (n 13) 52.
33. On the obstetric metaphor in Marx and Marxism, see GA Cohen, *If You're an Egalitarian, How Come You're So Rich?* (Harvard University Press, 2000) Chapter 3–4; Alexander Gray, *The Socialist Tradition: Moses to Lenin* (Longmans, Green and Co. Ltd.; Longmans, Green and Co., 1st ed, 1946) 299, 299n https://mises.org/library/socialist-tradition-moses-lenin; David Leopold, 'The Structure of Marx and Engels' Considered Account of Utopian Socialism' (2005) 26(3) *History of Political Thought* 443, 465.
34. Karl Marx, *A Contribution to the Critique of Political Economy*, tr NI Stone (Charles H. Kerr & Company, 1904) 12 http://archive.org/details/cu31924011249889 ('*CCPE*').
35. Wood, *OCLV* (n 13) 31–32.
36. Ibid. 32. Social-property relations theorists often nominate Paul Sweezy, Andre Gunder Frank and Immanuel Wallerstein as treating pre-capitalist commerce as proto-capitalism: see, for example: Robert P Brenner, 'The Origins of Capitalist Development: A Critique of Neo-Smithian Marxism' [1977] (104) *New Left Review* 25 ('OCD'); Wood, *OCLV* (n 13) 40–41; Lafrance and Post (n 2) 17. Maurice Dobb and Rodney Hilton have been identified as treating pre-capitalist petty commodity production as proto-capitalism: see Wood, *OCLV* (n 13) 38–39, 41–42, 51–52; Wood, *PCC* (n 11) 10.
37. Alan Macfarlane, *The Culture of Capitalism* (Blackwell, 1987) 197; for a detailed critique of Macfarlane's thesis from a social-property relations perspective, see Wood, *PCC* (n 11) Chapter 8.
38. Wood, *PCC* (n 11) 10; see also Wood, *OCLV* (n 13) 31–32, 50.
39. Lafrance and Post (n 2) 17.
40. Charles Post, 'The Use and Misuse of Uneven and Combined Development: A Critique of Anievas and Nişancıoğlu' (2018) 26(3) *Historical Materialism* 79, 87.
41. Wood, *OCLV* (n 13) 50.
42. Social-property relations theorists often nominate Paul Sweezy, Andre Gunder Frank and Immanuel Wallerstein as treating pre-capitalist commerce as proto-capitalism: see, for example: Brenner, 'OCD' (n 36); Wood, *OCLV* (n 13) 40–41; Lafrance and Post (n 2) 17. Maurice Dobb and Rodney Hilton have been identified as treating pre-capitalist petty commodity production as proto-capitalism: see Wood, *OCLV* (n 13) 38–39, 41–42, 51–52; Wood, *PCC* (n 11) 10. A more recent example of the non-transformation approach can be seen in Larry Neal and Jeffrey Gale Williamson (eds), *The Cambridge History of Capitalism* (Cambridge University Press, 2015). As Yazdani and Menon note, Neal and Williamson define capitalism by reference to private property,

enforceable contracts, markets, and supportive governments, which have existed at least since ancient Babylonia. See Kaveh Yazdani and Dilip M Menon (eds), *Capitalisms: Towards a Global History* (Oxford University Press, 2020) 2.

43. Brenner, 'OCD' (n 36).
44. Lafrance and Post (n 2) 7.
45. I have taken some of these examples from the following: Wood, *OCLV* (n 13) 20, 167; Brenner, 'OCD' (n 36); Brenner, 'PP' (n 5); Lafrance and Post (n 2) 6–7, 16; Ricardo Duchesne, 'Robert Brenner on Political Accumulation and the Transition to Capitalism' (2001) 33 *Review of Radical Political Economics* 79, 82, 94. On 'primitive accumulation' see: Karl Marx, *Capital: A Critique of Political Economy [First Published 1867]*, tr David Fernbach, vol 1 (Penguin Books in association with New Left Review, 1976) 871–930.
46. SR Epstein (ed), *Freedom and Growth: The Rise of States and Markets in Europe, 1300–1750*. (2002) 54–55.
47. Jamie C Allinson and Alexander Anievas, 'Approaching "the International": Beyond Political Marxism' in Alexander Anievas (ed), *Marxism and World Politics: Contesting Global Capitalism* (Routledge, 2010) 197, 205; see also Alexander Anievas and Kerem Nişancıoğlu, 'Lineages of Capital' (2018) 26(3) *Historical Materialism* 167, 174 ('LC'); Justin Rosenberg, 'The "Philosophical Premises" of Uneven and Combined Development' (2013) 39(3) *Review of International Studies* 569.
48. Anievas and Nişancıoğlu (n 47) 171.
49. Wood, *OCLV* (n 13) 64, 151. See further my discussion of tributary commercialisation in Chapter 3.
50. Lafrance and Post make this point in relation to accounts that view population cycles and commercialisation as primary causes of historical change: see (n 2) 18.
51. Post makes this point in relation to UCD when it is conceived as a transhistorical force or universal law: see Post, 'The Use and Misuse of Uneven and Combined Development: A Critique of Anievas and Nişancıoğlu' (n 40) 87. See also Eren Duzgun, 'Against Eurocentric Anti-Eurocentrism: International Relations, Historical Sociology and Political Marxism' [2018] *Journal of International Relations and Development* 8 https://doi.org/10.1057/s41268-018-0146-0; Sébastien Rioux, 'Mind the (Theoretical) Gap: On the Poverty of International Relations Theorising of Uneven and Combined Development' (2015) 29(4) *Global Society* 481; Neil Smith, 'The Geography of Uneven Development' in Bill Dunn and HK Radice (eds), *100 Years of Permanent Revolution: Results and Prospects* (Pluto Press, 2006) 180, 182; Sam Ashman, 'Capitalism, Uneven and Combined Development and the Transhistoric' (2009) 22(1) *Cambridge Review of International Affairs* 29; Neil Davidson, 'Putting the Nation Back into "the International"'

(2009) 22(1) *Cambridge Review of International Affairs* 9, 17–18; Benno Teschke, 'IR Theory, Historical Materialism and the False Promise of International Historical Sociology' (2014) 6(1) *Spectrum Journal of Global Studies* 66, 31 ('IRT').

52. Sébastien Rioux, 'The Collapse of "The International Imagination": A Critique of the Transhistorical Approach to Uneven and Combined Development' in Radhika Desai (ed), *Research in Political Economy* (Emerald Group Publishing Limited, 2015) 85, 107; See also ibid. 85; Rioux (n 51) 483.
53. Teschke has likewise traced the interactions of medieval states to the dynamics of tributary social-property relations. See Benno Teschke, 'Geopolitical Relations in the European Middle Ages: History and Theory' (1998) 52(2) *International Organization* 325 ('GRE'); Benno Teschke, *The Myth of 1648: Class, Geopolitics, and the Making of Modern International Relations* (Verso, 2003) ('*M1648*'); Benno Teschke, 'Bourgeois Revolution, State Formation and the Absence of the International' (2005) 13(2) *Historical Materialism* 3 ('BRSF'); Teschke, 'IRT' (n 51).
54. Moore Jason W. (ed), *Anthropocene or Capitalocene?: Nature, History, and the Crisis of Capitalism* (PM Press, 2016).
55. Mike Davis, *The Monster Enters: COVID-19, Avian Flu and the Plagues of Capitalism* (OR Books, 2020).
56. Guy Bois, 'Against the Neo-Malthusian Orthodoxy' [1978] (79) *Past & Present* 60, 67.
57. Ibid. This critique of Brenner remains common: see, for example, Epstein (n 46) 54.
58. Bieler and Morton (n 14) 43.
59. See, for example, Samuel Knafo and Benno Teschke, 'The Rules of Reproduction of Capitalism: A Historicist Critique' in *Symposium on the Work of Ellen Meiksins Wood* (2015) www.versobooks.com/blogs/2315-samuel-knafo-and-benno-teschke-the-rules-of-reproduction-of-capitalism-a-historicist-critique.
60. Ibid.
61. Knafo (n 20) 513.
62. Ibid. 506.
63. Ibid. 505.
64. See Maïa Pal, 'Introduction to "Britain versus France: How Many Sonderwegs?"' (2016) 24(1) *Historical Materialism* 3, 7.
65. Knafo (n 20) 509.
66. Ibid. 508.
67. Knafo and Teschke (n 59).
68. Charles Post, 'The American Path of Bourgeois Development Revisited: A Response' (2014) 78(3) *Science & Society* 369, 370.
69. Knafo (n 20) 505.

70. Ibid. 510.
71. Knafo and Teschke (n 59).
72. Ibid.
73. Charlie Post and George Souvlis, 'Class, Race and Capital-Centric Marxism: An Interview with Charlie Post', *Salvage* (19 January 2018) https://salvage.zone/online-exclusive/class-race-and-capital-centric-marxism-an-interview-with-charlie-post.
74. Ibid.
75. Ibid.
76. Ibid.
77. Ibid.
78. Knafo and Teschke (n 59); Post and Souvlis (n 73).

2 THE TRIBUTARY RENT RELATION

1. Eric R Wolf, *Europe and the People without History* (University of California Press, 2010) 79–80 ('*EPWH*').
2. Ibid. 80.
3. Ibid. 81.
4. George C Comninel, 'English Feudalism and the Origins of Capitalism' (2000) 27(4) *The Journal of Peasant Studies* 1, 27.
5. Michael Andrew Žmolek, *Rethinking the Industrial Revolution: Five Centuries of Transition from Agrarian to Industrial Capitalism in England* (Brill, 2013) 819.
6. Spencer Dimmock, *The Origin of Capitalism in England, 1400–1600* (Brill, 2014) 196 ('*OCE*').
7. Brenner introduced the concept of 'political accumulation' in Robert P Brenner, 'The Agrarian Roots of European Capitalism' (1982) 97(1) *Past & Present* 16, 36–41 ('AREC'). See also Robert P Brenner, 'The Rises and Declines of Serfdom in Medieval and Early Modern Europe' in ML Bush (ed), *Serfdom and Slavery: Studies in Legal Bondage* (Longman, 1996) 247, 249–250 ('RDS'); Robert P Brenner, 'Property and Progress: Where Adam Smith Went Wrong' in Chris Wickham (ed), *Marxist History-Writing for the Twenty-First Century* (Oxford University Press, for the British Academy, 2007) 49, 71 ('PP').
8. Perry Anderson, *Lineages of the Absolutist State* (Verso, 2013) 31–32.
9. Brenner, 'AREC' (n 7) 39.
10. Ibid.
11. Ibid. 38.
12. Brenner, 'RDS' (n 7) 249. I will explain tributary dynamics of intra-lordly competition and lord-peasant struggle below and in Chapter 3.
13. Spencer Dimmock, 'Expropriation and the Political Origins of Agrarian Capitalism in England' in Xavier Lafrance and Charles Post (eds), *Case*

Studies in the Origins of Capitalism (Palgrave Macmillan, 2019) 39, 56; Brenner, 'RDS' (n 7) 251–253.

14. Brenner, 'RDS' (n 7) 249. On absolutism as a centralisation of localised (feudal) tributary relations, see: ibid. 257–258, 272–275; Ellen Meiksins Wood, *The Origin of Capitalism: A Longer View* (Verso, New Edition, 2002) 46, 169 ('*OCLV*').
15. Wolf (n 1) 82.
16. Brenner, 'AREC' (n 7) 53.
17. Brenner, 'RDS' (n 7) 251; see also ibid. 258, 266.
18. Brenner, 'RDS' (n 7) 259–261.
19. Spencer Dimmock, 'The Eastern Origins of Capitalism?', *Historical Materialism* §29–31 www.historicalmaterialism.org/book-review/eastern-origins-capitalism.
20. Ibid.; citing John Robert Maddicott, *The Origins of the English Parliament, 924–1327* (Oxford University Press, 2010) 2–3; Pauline Stafford, *Unification and Conquest: A Political and Social History of England in the Tenth and Eleventh Centuries* (E. Arnold; Distributed in the USA by Routledge, Chapman, and Hall, 1989). See also Dimmock, 'Expropriation and the Political Origins of Agrarian Capitalism in England' (n 13) 42.
21. Tibor Rutar, 'The Transition Debate Today: A Review of The Origin of Capitalism in England, 1400–1600 by Spencer Dimmock' (2018) 26(3) *Historical Materialism* 197, 203.
22. Dimmock, 'Expropriation and the Political Origins of Agrarian Capitalism in England' (n 13) 42; Maddicott (n 20) 2–3.
23. Brenner, 'RDS' (n 7) 259–260.
24. Comninel (n 4) 22.
25. See, for example, Brenner, 'AREC' (n 7) 53.
26. Geoff Kennedy, 'Radicalism and Revisionism in the English Revolution' in Michael Haynes and Jim Wolfreys (eds), *History and Revolution: Refuting Revisionism* (Verso, 2007) 25, 223 (note 59).
27. Brenner, 'AREC' (n 7) 53.
28. Susan Reynolds, *Fiefs and Vassals: The Medieval Evidence Reinterpreted* (Oxford University Press, 1994) 345.
29. Rodney H Hilton, *Class Conflict and the Crisis of Feudalism: Essays in Medieval Social History* (Hambledon Press, 1985) 232 ('*CC*').
30. Reynolds (n 28) 345–347.
31. Ibid. 358–359. Lords who held their lands directly 'of the King' ('*in capite*'), were classified as tenants-in-chief. Lords who were tenants of another lord were classified as mesne lords. If they had large estates, mesne lords might have yet further layers of lords beneath them.
32. Ibid. 354.
33. Hilton, *CC* (n 29) 234; On the broad governance and economic functions of the manorial court, see Lloyd Bonfield, 'What Did English

Villagers Mean by "Customary Law"?' in Zvi Razi and Richard Michael Smith (eds), *Medieval Society and the Manor Court* (Clarendon Press, 1996) 103, 105–106.

34. Comninel (n 4) 28–29; Stroud Francis Charles Milsom, *The Legal Framework of English Feudalism: The Maitland Lectures Given in 1972* (CUP Archive, 1976) 11–17.
35. Christopher Dyer, 'Memories of Freedom: Attitudes towards Serfdom in England, 1200–1350' in ML Bush (ed), *Serfdom and Slavery: Studies in Legal Bondage* (Longman, 1996) 277, 279.
36. Brenner, 'RDS' (n 7) 262–263, 271.
37. Mark Bailey, *The Decline of Serfdom in Late Medieval England: From Bondage to Freedom* (The Boydell Press, 2014) 51–52.
38. See, for example, Bruce Campbell, 'The Agrarian Problem in the Early Fourteenth Century' (2005) 188(1) *Past & present* 3, 7; Rodney H Hilton, 'Feudalism in Europe: Problems for Historical Materialists' [1984] (147) *New Left Review* 84, 87 ('FE'); Richard Britnell, 'Commerce and Capitalism in Late Medieval England: Problems of Description and Theory' (1993) 6(4) *Journal of Historical Sociology* 359, 364; John Hatcher, 'English Serfdom and Villeinage: Towards a Reassessment' [1981] (90) *Past & Present* 3, 254–256; EA Kosminsky, *Studies in the Agrarian History of England in the Thirteenth Century*, ed Rodney H Hilton, tr Ruth Kisch (Blackwell, 1st ed, 1956) 152–196; JA Raftis, *Peasant Economic Development within the English Manorial System* (Sutton; McGill-Queen's University Press, 1997) 62; Bailey (n 37) 49.
39. Brenner, 'AREC' (n 7) 34.
40. Hilton, 'FE' (n 38) 87.
41. See Dyer (n 35) 277.
42. Alan Macfarlane, *The Origins of English Individualism: The Family, Property, and Social Transition* (Cambridge University Press, 1979) 151.
43. On aids and tallage, see Bailey (n 37) 47–48.
44. On heriot, see ibid. 52–53.
45. Rodney H Hilton, *Bond Men Made Free: Medieval Peasant Movements and the English Rising of 1381* (Temple Smith, 1973) 147 ('*BMMF*'); Hilton, *CC* (n 29) 124.
46. William Blackstone, *An Analysis of the Laws of England. To Which Is Prefixed an Introductory Discourse on the Study of the Law by William Blackstone, Esq. D.C.L. Barrister at Law, Vinerian Professor of the Laws of England in the University of Oxford, and Solicitor Generalto Her Majesty* (Printed for Elizabeth Watts, in Skinner-Row, 5th ed, 1766) 32–33.
47. William Easterby, *The History of the Law of Tithes in England. Being the Yorke Prize Essay of the University of Cambridge for 1887* (Cambridge: University press, 1888) 12–14 http://archive.org/details/historyoflawoftiooeast; for a general overview of the history of tithes in England, see Easterby; and Eric J Evans, 'A History of the Tithe System

in England, 1690–1850 with Special Reference to Staffordshire' (PhD Dissertation, University of Warwick, 1970) 1–20 http://webcat.warwick.ac.uk/record=b1732979~S15.

48. RR Davies, 'The Sinews of Aristocratic Power' in Brendan Smith (ed), *Lords and Lordship in the British Isles in the Late Middle Ages* (Oxford University Press, 2009) 158, 168; Hilton, 'FE' (n 38) 87; On millsuit, see Bailey (n 37) 55–56.
49. SR Epstein, 'Rodney Hilton, Marxism and the Transition from Feudalism to Capitalism' [2007] *Past & Present* 248, 258.
50. Bailey (n 37) 46.
51. Ibid. 40–41; ibid.
52. Bailey (n 37) 42–46; HSA Fox, 'Exploitation of the Landless by Lords and Tenants in Early Medieval England' in Zvi Razi and Richard Michael Smith (eds), *Medieval Society and the Manor Court* (Clarendon Press, 1996) 518, 530–531.
53. Campbell (n 38) 52.
54. Ibid. 18–19.
55. For a list of feudal incidents, see Patrick Edward Dove, *The Theory of Human Progression, and Natural Probability of a Reign of Justice [First Published 1850]* (Sanborn & Carter, 1856) 394–395 http://archive.org/details/theoryhumanprog01dovgoog.
56. The rights of wardship and marriage appear to have become entrenched in the twelfth and thirteenth centuries. See Reynolds (n 28) 369.
57. Dove (n 55) 391.
58. Primer seisin involved the seizure of land by the Crown upon the death of a tenant, until the payment of a relief. From 1267, only the Crown had this right, whereas other heirs had an enforceable right to take possession before paying reliefs. See Reynolds (n 28) 368.
59. Helena M Chew, *The English Ecclesiastical Tenants-in-Chief and Knight Service: Especially in the Thirteenth and Fourteenth Centuries* (Humphrey Milford, Oxford University Press, 1932) 3.
60. Reynolds (n 28) 363.
61. See GL Harriss, 'Aids, Loans and Benevolences' (1963) 6(1) *The Historical Journal* 1.
62. For instance, around 1193, when Richard I was held to ransom, a series of heavy aids, carucages, scutages and tallages were raised. See Nick Barratt, 'The English Revenue of Richard I' [2001] *English Historical Review* 635, 641.
63. Harriss (n 61) 11–12.
64. Robert Bartlett, *England under the Norman and Angevin Kings, 1075–1225* (Clarendon Press; Oxford University Press, 2000) 160–161.
65. The Crown often lacked sufficient seigniorial machinery to efficiently collect rents from peasants of the royal demesne. It thus often sold the

right to collect rents to sheriffs for a fixed fee known as at county farm, or *firma burgi* in the case of town estates.

66. See JF Hadwin, 'The Last Royal Tallages' (1981) 96(379) *The English Historical Review* 344.
67. Rodney H Hilton, *The Decline of Serfdom in Medieval England* (Macmillan, 2nd ed, 1986) 32 ('*DSE*').
68. See Hatcher (n 38).
69. Hilton, *CC* (n 29) 237.
70. Ibid. 126.
71. Ricardo Duchesne, 'Rodney Hilton and the Peasant Road to "Capitalism" in England' (2003) 30(2) *Journal of Peasant Studies* 129, 134; Rodney H Hilton, *The English Peasantry in the Later Middle Ages: The Ford Lectures for 1973 and Related Studies* (Clarendon Press, 1975) 41 ('*EP*').
72. Christopher Dyer, 'A Redistribution of Incomes in Fifteenth-Century England?' [1968] (39) *Past & Present* 11, 13.
73. Dimmock, *OCE* (n 6) 179.
74. Hilton, *CC* (n 29) 218, 127–133; for a pan-European survey of popular uprisings in the fourteenth century, see Jr Cohn Samuel K, 'Popular Insurrection and the Black Death: A Comparative View'. [2007] *Past & Present* 188.
75. On lordly solidarity in England compared to continental Europe see Dimmock, *OCE* (n 6) 178–179.
76. Ibid. 190–191.
77. Comninel (n 4) 24.
78. Campbell (n 38) 36.
79. Hilton, *DSE* (n 66) 24.
80. See Miriam Müller, 'A Divided Class? Peasants and Peasant Communities in Later Medieval England' (2007) 195 (Supplement 2) *Past and Present* 115, 119–123.
81. Campbell (n 38) 36.
82. Hilton, *DSE* (n 66) 19–21; Campbell (n 38) 26–27, 33.
83. Peter Franklin, 'Politics in Manorial Court Rolls: The Tactics, Social Composition, and Aims of a Pre-1381 Peasant Movement' in Zvi Razi and Richard Michael Smith (eds), *Medieval Society and the Manor Court* (Clarendon Press, 1996) 162, 170.
84. Campbell (n 38) 11.

3 TRIBUTARY TENDENCIES AND CONTRADICTIONS

1. Paul Latimer, 'Money and the English Economy in the Twelfth and Thirteenth Centuries: Money and the English Economy' (2011) 9(4) *History Compass* 246, 250; RH Britnell, 'The Proliferation of Markets in England, 1200–1349' (1981) 34(2) *The Economic History Review* 209;

Richard Britnell, 'Commerce and Capitalism in Late Medieval England: Problems of Description and Theory' (1993) 6(4) *Journal of Historical Sociology* 359; John Langdon and James Masschaele, 'Commercial Activity and Population Growth in Medieval England' (2006) 190(1) *Past & present* 35, 42–52.

2. Eric R Wolf, *Europe and the People without History* (University of California Press, 2010) 86–87 ('*EPWH*'); see also Rodney H Hilton, 'Feudalism and the Origins of Capitalism' [1976] (1) *History Workshop* 9, 23 ('FOC').
3. Wolf (n 2) 82–84.
4. Rodney H Hilton, 'Feudalism in Europe: Problems for Historical Materialists' [1984] (147) *New Left Review* 84, 87 ('FE').
5. Mark Bailey, *The Decline of Serfdom in Late Medieval England: From Bondage to Freedom* (The Boydell Press, 2014) 53.
6. Rodney H Hilton, *The Decline of Serfdom in Medieval England* (Macmillan, 2nd ed, 1986) 25 ('*DSE*'); Bailey (n 5) 67; Howard L Gray, 'The Commutation of Villein Services in England before the Black Death' (1914) 29(116) *The English Historical Review* 625.
7. Bailey (n 5) 50.
8. James Campbell, 'Observations on English Government from the Tenth to the Twelfth Century' (1975) 25 *Transactions of the Royal Historical Society* 39, 52.
9. Sally Harvey, 'The Knight and the Knight's Fee in England' [1970] *Past and Present* 3, 33–36. Some churches were paying scutage during the reign of Henry I (reigning 1100–1135): Susan Reynolds, *Fiefs and Vassals: The Medieval Evidence Reinterpreted* (Oxford University Press, 1994) 362. Scutage was first applied as a general levy on military tenants in 1159, with tenants-in-chief passing the levy onto lesser tenants, and disappeared after 1322: see Stephen Dowell, *A History of Taxation and Taxes in England: From the Earliest Times to the Present Day*, vol 1 (Longmans, Green, 1884) 39–40, 53, 56 https://archive.org/details/cu31924092572498. For primary sources on scutage, see Paul Halsall, 'Medieval Sourcebook: England: The Collection of Scutage, 1159–1195', *Fordham University: The Jesuit University of New York* (1998) http://legacy.fordham.edu/halsall/source/scutage.asp.
10. Britnell, 'The Proliferation of Markets in England, 1200–1349' (n 1); Britnell, 'Commerce and Capitalism in Late Medieval England: Problems of Description and Theory' (n 1); Ricardo Duchesne, 'Rodney Hilton and the Peasant Road to "Capitalism" in England' (2003) 30(2) *Journal of Peasant Studies* 129, 138–139; Rodney H Hilton, 'Rent and Capital Formation in Feudal Society' in *The English Peasantry in the Later Middle Ages: The Ford Lectures for 1973 and Related Studies* (Clarendon Press, 1975) 174 ('RCF').
11. Latimer (n 1) 248.

12. James Davis, *Medieval Market Morality: Life, Law and Ethics in the English Marketplace, 1200–1500* (Cambridge University Press, 2011) 145–147.
13. Britnell, 'The Proliferation of Markets in England, 1200–1349' (n 1).
14. Peter Turchin and SA Nefedov, *Secular Cycles* (Princeton University Press, 2009) 54–55.
15. Rodney H Hilton, 'Towns in English Feudal Society' (1979) 3(1) *Review (Fernand Braudel Center)* 3, 20 ('TEFS').
16. Ibid. 10–12.
17. Ibid. 14.
18. Rodney H Hilton, *Bond Men Made Free: Medieval Peasant Movements and the English Rising of 1381* (Temple Smith, 1973) 146 ('*BMMF*').
19. See WM Ormrod, 'Royal Finance in Thirteenth-Century England' in Peter R Coss and Simon D Lloyd (eds), *Thirteenth Century England V: Proceedings of the Newcastle Upon Tyne Conference 1993* (Boydell & Brewer Ltd, 1995) 141.
20. For example, Magna Carta states 'No man shall be forced to perform more service for a knight's "fee", or other free holding of land, than is due from it'. See British Library Board, 'English Translation of Magna Carta', *The British Library* (2015) 16 www.bl.uk/magna-carta/articles/magna-carta-english-translation.
21. See Ibid. 9.
22. See C Hilary Jenkinson, 'The First Parliament of Edward I' (1910) 25(98) *The English Historical Review* 231.
23. Stuart Jenks, 'The Lay Subsidies and the State of the English Economy (1275–1334)' (1998) 85(1) *VSWG: Vierteljahrschrift für Sozial- und Wirtschaftsgeschichte* 1; JF Hadwin, 'The Last Royal Tallages' (1981) 96(379) *The English Historical Review* 344, 356.
24. Jenks (n 23) 5–7; see also Dowell (n 9) 194.
25. Hadwin (n 23) 356.
26. Michael Mann, *The Sources of Social Power* (Cambridge University Press, 2012) 428–430.
27. The statute, also known as *A Statute Concerning Tallage*, 1297 stated: 'No Tallage or Aid shall be taken or levied by Us or our Heirs in our Realm, without the good will and Assent of Archbishops, Bishops, Earls, Barons, Knights, Burgesses, and other Freemen of the Land'. The use of the word 'tallage' in the statute had the general meaning of 'tax'; it did not refer specifically to the tallage of the royal demesne (Hadwin [n 23] 345n).
28. Dowell (n 9) 135–137.
29. Hadwin (n 23) 356.
30. John E Martin, *Feudalism to Capitalism: Peasant and Landlord in English Agrarian Development* (Macmillan, 1983) 141; c.f. Robert P Brenner,

Merchants and Revolutions: Commercial Change, Political Conflict, and London's Overseas Traders, 1550–1653 (Verso, 2003) 673 ('*MR*').

31. Rodney H Hilton and H Fagan, *The English Rising of 1381* (Lawrence & Wishart, 1950) 68 ('*TER*').
32. For a modern English translation of the Twelve Conclusions, see LD Benson, 'The Twelve Conclusions of the Lollards', *The Geoffrey Chaucer Page* (Faculty of Arts and Sciences, Harvard University, 6 July 2006) http://sites.fas.harvard.edu/~chaucer/special/varia/lollards/lollconc.htm; Benson works from HS Cronin, 'The Twelve Conclusions of the Lollards' (1907) 22(86) *The English Historical Review* 292, which reproduces the Twelve Conclusions in Middle English, as quoted in Roger Dymok's (1396–1397) manuscript 'Against the XII Heresies of the Lollards'.
33. Hilton and Fagan (n 31) 73.
34. Ibid. 71.
35. Ibid. 72; Rodney H Hilton, *Class Conflict and the Crisis of Feudalism: Essays in Medieval Social History* (Hambledon Press, 1985) 222 ('*CC*'); RB Dobson, *The Peasants' Revolt of 1381* (Macmillan; St Martin's Press, 1970) 373.
36. Rendered in Modern English from John Wycliffe, 'XV. OF SERVANTS AND LORDS'. in Frederic D Matthew (ed), *The English Works of Wyclif Hitherto Unprinted*, (Pub. for the Early English text society, by Trübner & co., 1880) 226, 229–231 https://quod.lib.umich.edu/c/cme/AEH6713.0001.001/1:17?rgn=div1;view=fulltext; relying partly on the rendition in Hilton, *CC* (n 35) 223.
37. James M Dean and Anonymous, 'Friar Daw's Reply' in *Six EcclesiasticalSatires*(1991)http://d.lib.rochester.edu/teams/text/dean-six-ecclesiastical-satires-friar-daws-reply ('FDR').
38. ME Aston, 'Lollardy and Sedition 1381–1431' (1960) 17(1) *Past & Present* 1.
39. Frederick Engels, 'On the Peasant Risings of the Middle Ages, Extracted from His The Peasant War in Germany (Moscow, 1956, pp. 55–60) [First Published 1850]' in *The Peasants' Revolt of 1381* (Macmillan; St Martin's P, 1970) 399, 401; Christopher Hill, 'The Many-Headed Monster' in *Intellectual Origins of the English Revolution Revisited* (Clarendon Press; Oxford University Press, Revised Edition, 1997) 327, 329 ('MHM').
40. Robert P Brenner, 'The Rises and Declines of Serfdom in Medieval and Early Modern Europe' in ML Bush (ed), *Serfdom and Slavery: Studies in Legal Bondage* (Longman, 1996) 247, 254, 274 ('RDS').
41. Spencer Dimmock, *The Origin of Capitalism in England, 1400–1600* (Brill, 2014) 81 ('*OCE*'); Brenner, 'RDS' (n 40) 254.
42. Robert P Brenner, 'Property and Progress: Where Adam Smith Went Wrong' in Chris Wickham (ed), *Marxist History-Writing for the Twenty-*

First Century (Oxford University Press, for the British Academy, 2007) 49, 72 ('PP').

43. On customary alienation, see Alan Macfarlane, *The Origins of English Individualism: The Family, Property, and Social Transition* (Cambridge University Press, 1979) 106–107, 124.
44. Campbell (n 8) 9.
45. See Dimmock (n 41) 82–83; Bruce Campbell, 'The Agrarian Problem in the Early Fourteenth Century' (2005) 188(1) *Past & present* 3, 51.
46. Dimmock (n 41) 63.
47. Spencer Dimmock, 'The Eastern Origins of Capitalism?', *Historical Materialism* §24 www.historicalmaterialism.org/book-review/eastern-origins-capitalism; see also Brenner, 'RDS' (n 40) 68–69.
48. Brenner, 'PP' (n 42) 68–69.
49. Langdon and Masschaele (n 1) 54–68; Turchin and Nefedov (n 14) 35–38, esp. 36 (Figure 2.1).
50. Robert P Brenner, 'The Agrarian Roots of European Capitalism' (1982) 97(1) *Past & Present* 16, 36–41, 124–126 ('AREC'); Robert P Brenner, 'Dobb on the Transition from Feudalism to Capitalism' (1978) 2(2) *Cambridge Journal of Economics* 121 ('Dobb').
51. See Hilton, 'RCF' (n 10).
52. Dimmock (n 41) 58; Brenner, 'RDS' (n 40) 249; Brenner, 'PP' (n 42) 85.
53. Turchin and Nefedov (n 14) 50–58; see also Brenner, 'PP' (n 42) 78–79.
54. Turchin and Nefedov (n 14) 50–58.
55. Campbell (n 45) 3–4.
56. Turchin and Nefedov (n 14) 49–51.
57. Langdon and Masschaele (n 1); Campbell (n 45).
58. On the limits of feudal territorial expansion see also Alexander Anievas and Kerem Nişancıoğlu, *How the West came to rule: the geopolitical origins of capitalism* (Pluto Press, 2015) 185.
59. Dimmock (n 41) 84–85; Turchin and Nefedov (n 14) 57.
60. See Turchin and Nefedov (n 14) 50–58.
61. Hilton, 'FOC' (n 2) 21; On the role of interstate conflict in the fourteenth century crisis, see Anievas and Nişancıoğlu (n 58) 255–256.
62. Turchin and Nefedov (n 14) 55.
63. Ibid. 57.
64. Peter Franklin, 'Politics in Manorial Court Rolls: The Tactics, Social Composition, and Aims of a Pre-1381 Peasant Movement' in Zvi Razi and Richard Michael Smith (eds), *Medieval Society and the Manor Court* (Clarendon Press, 1996) 162, 170; HSA Fox, 'Exploitation of the Landless by Lords and Tenants in Early Medieval England' in Zvi Razi and Richard Michael Smith (eds), *Medieval Society and the Manor Court* (Clarendon Press, 1996) 518, 564–565.
65. Macfarlane (n 43) 154.

66. Christopher Dyer, *An Age of Transition? Economy and Society in England in the Later Middle Ages* (Oxford University Press, 2005) 42; On marketisation in the thirteenth century, see Britnell, 'Commerce and Capitalism in Late Medieval England: Problems of Description and Theory' (n 1).
67. Dimmock (n 41) 82–83, 311.
68. Brenner, 'AREC' (n 50) 40–41.
69. Bailey (n 5) 62.
70. Robert Steven Gottfried, *The Black Death: Natural and Human Disaster in Medieval Europe* (Free Press; Collier Macmillan, 1983).
71. Turchin and Nefedov (n 14) 35–36; Donald C Coleman, *The Economy of England: 1450–1750* (Oxford University Press, 1977) 41.
72. Anievas and Nişancıoğlu (n 58) 77–79.
73. Christopher Dyer, 'A Redistribution of Incomes in Fifteenth-Century England?' [1968] (39) *Past & Present* 11, 22–24, 30.
74. Bailey (n 5) 54–55.
75. The rights and obligations of copyhold tenure were recorded in the manorial roll, with the tenant possessing a copy – hence 'copyhold': see CGA Clay, *Economic Expansion and Social Change: England 1500–1700*, vol 1 (Cambridge University Press, 1984) 87–90; see also Michael Andrew Žmolek, *Rethinking the Industrial Revolution: Five Centuries of Transition from Agrarian to Industrial Capitalism in England* (Brill, 2013) 66–67; Robert C Allen, *Enclosure and the Yeoman* (Clarendon Press; Oxford University Press, 1992) 66–72.
76. Allen (n 75) 64–66; Hilton, *DSE* (n 6) 33–44.
77. See Bailey (n 5) 55, 61–83, 285–306, 313–326, 345–346; Hilton, *DSE* (n 6) 33–44, 47–58.
78. Brenner and Dimmock assert that English lords were able to mitigate their loss of power compared to their continental counterparts because they were, in Dimmock's words, 'precociously self-centralised'; however, I formulate the argument in terms of the 'federalised' structure of England's tributary rent relation: see Brenner, 'Dobb' (n 57) 129; Brenner, 'AREC' (n 33) 84; Dimmock (n 48) 71, 178–179, 363.
79. Dimmock (n 41) 71, 178–179, 363; Brenner, 'AREC' (n 50) 84; Brenner, 'Dobb' (n 50) 129.
80. Bailey (n 5) 317–318, 322–326; Dimmock (n 41) 363.
81. Walter Scheidel, *The Great Leveler: Violence and the History of Inequality from the Stone Age to the Twenty-First Century* (Princeton University Press, 2017) 306–306.
82. Dimmock (n 41) 183; Bailey (n 5) 319–322.
83. Bailey (n 5) 337.
84. Rodney H Hilton, 'Medieval Market Towns and Simple Commodity Production' [1985] (109) *Past & Present* 3, 10–11 ('MMT').
85. Dyer (n 66) 173–210.

86. On key milestones of state formation in this period see Dimmock (n 41) 59.
87. On the rise of continental absolutism, see Brenner, 'PP' (n 42) 90–95; Perry Anderson, *Lineages of the Absolutist State* (Verso, 2013).

4 TRIBUTARY IDEOLOGY, RESISTANCE, AND CRITIQUE

1. On these aspects of ideology, see HM Drucker, 'Marx's Concept of Ideology' (1972) 47(180) *Philosophy* 152, 155.
2. Rodney H Hilton and H Fagan, *The English Rising of 1381* (Lawrence & Wishart, 1950) 51 ('*TER*').
3. 'Kyng ȝyf þou me my rente'. See Joseph Hall (ed), 'MS. Gg. 4. 27. 2. University Library, Cambridge: Horn' in *King Horn: A Middle-English Romance* (Clarendon Press, 1901) 3, 52 http://quod.lib.umich.edu/c/cme/ACN1637.0001.001/1:5?rgn=div1;view=fulltext. See also Cathy H Leeton-Robinson, 'King Horn: A Middle English Romance, a Modern English Translation' (Tennessee State University, 1992) www.worldcat.org/oclc/29177025 ('King Horn').
4. 'Rent, n.1' in *Oxford English Dictionary Online* (Oxford University Press) www.oed.com.
5. William Langland, *The Vision of Piers the Plowman [Translated into Modern English; First Published 1377]*, tr Walter W (Walter William) Skeat (London: A. Moring, 1905) 98 http://archive.org/details/visionofpiersplooolanguoft.
6. Ibid. 99.
7. Rodney H Hilton, *Bond Men Made Free: Medieval Peasant Movements and the English Rising of 1381* (Temple Smith, 1973) 222 ('*BMMF*').
8. See ibid.
9. Bruce Campbell, 'The Agrarian Problem in the Early Fourteenth Century' (2005) 188(1) *Past & present* 3, 36.
10. Ibid. 18–19.
11. William Blackstone, *Commentaries on the Laws of England* (T. Cadell and J. Butterworth and Son, 16th ed, 1825) 384 http://archive.org/details/in.ernet.dli.2015.216408; Hilton and Fagan (n 2) 54.
12. Peter Turchin and SA Nefedov, *Secular Cycles* (Princeton University Press, 2009) 57.
13. On monastic almsgiving, see Barbara F Harvey, *Living and Dying in England, 1100-1540: The Monastic Experience* (Clarendon Press; Oxford University Press, 1993) 7–33.
14. Hilton and Fagan (n 2) 71; Christopher Hill, 'A Bourgeois Revolution?' in *The Collected Essays of Christopher Hill: People and Ideas in 17th Century England* (Harvester Press, 1986) 94, 114 ('ABR?').

15. Christopher Hill, 'The Many-Headed Monster' in *Change and Continuity in Seventeenth-Century England* (Weidenfeld and Nicolson, 1974) 181, 189 ('MHM').
16. See, respectively: Hilton, *BMMF* (n 7) 222; and Hilton and Fagan (n 2) 66.
17. Rodney H Hilton, 'Feudalism in Europe: Problems for Historical Materialists' [1984] (147) *New Left Review* 84, 92 ('FE').
18. Hilton, *BMMF* (n 7) 233.
19. Hilton and Fagan (n 2) 76–78.
20. See Rodney H Hilton, *Class Conflict and the Crisis of Feudalism: Essays in Medieval Social History* (Hambledon Press, 1985) 159 ('CC'); Hilton, *BMMF* (n 7); Hilton, 'FE' (n 17) 92.
21. Mark Bailey, *The Decline of Serfdom in Late Medieval England: From Bondage to Freedom* (The Boydell Press, 2014) 311.
22. Walter Scheidel, *The Great Leveler: Violence and the History of Inequality from the Stone Age to the Twenty-First Century* (Princeton University Press, 2017) 311.
23. Bailey (n 21) 311; Judith M Bennett, 'Compulsory Service in Late Medieval England' (2010) 209(1) *Past & Present* 7, 23; Hilton, *BMMF* (n 7) 230–232.
24. Hilton, *BMMF* (n 7) 177.
25. Ibid. 184–185.
26. Ibid. 185, 221.
27. Ibid. 224.
28. Ibid. 225.
29. Thomas Walsingham, 'John Ball According to Thomas Walsingam, Extracted from His Historia Anglicana, Volume 2 (Rolls Series, 1863–4, pp. 32–3)' in *The Peasants' Revolt of 1381* (Macmillan; St Martin's Press, 1970) 373, 375.
30. Hilton, *BMMF* (n 7) 225.
31. Eric R Wolf, *Europe and the People without History* (University of California Press, 2010) 81 ('*EPWH*').
32. Hilton and Fagan (n 2) 175–188.
33. Ibid. 69–71.
34. Hilton, *BMMF* (n 7) 227–228.
35. John Ball is exemplary in that he began preaching in 1366—halfway, chronologically, between the Black Death and the Peasants' Revolt. See RB Dobson, *The Peasants' Revolt of 1381* (Macmillan; St Martin's Press, 1970) 372; Hilton and Fagan (n 2) 75.
36. Walsingham (n 29) 375.
37. Jean Froissart, *The Chronicles of Froissart*, ed George C Macaulay, tr John Bourchier Berners (Macmillan and Co., Ltd., 1899) 251 http://archive.org/details/chroniclesoffroioofroiuoft.

38. Dobson (n 35) 373; Frederick Engels, 'On the Peasant Risings of the Middle Ages, Extracted from His The Peasant War in Germany (Moscow, 1956, pp. 55–60) [First Published 1850]' in *The Peasants' Revolt of 1381* (Macmillan; St Martin's P, 1970) 399, 401.
39. Froissart (n 37) 251.
40. Ibid.
41. Ibid.
42. William Carew Hazlitt (ed), 'The Life and Death of Jack Straw' in *A Select Collection of Old English Plays* (Reeves and Turner, 4th ed, 1874) 375, 383 http://archive.org/details/selectoldenglisho5dods.
43. Hilton, *BMMF* (n 7) 225.
44. Walsingham (n 29) 375.
45. Ibid.
46. Froissart (n 37) 251.
47. Hilton, *BMMF* (n 7) 229.
48. Ibid.
49. Ibid. 225.
50. Christopher Hill, 'The Norman Yoke' in John Saville (ed), *Democracy and the Labour Movement: Essays in Honour of Dona Torr* (Lawrence & Wishart, 1954) 11, 11 ('TNY-a'); c.f. Asa Briggs, *The Collected Essays of Asa Briggs: Images, Problems, Standpoints, Forecasts*, vol 2 (Harvester Press, 1985) 217; Christopher Hill, 'The Norman Yoke' in *Intellectual Origins of the English Revolution Revisited* (Clarendon Press; Oxford University Press, Revised Edition, 1997) 361, 361 ('TNY-b').
51. Hill, 'TNY-a' (n 50) 11.
52. Ibid. 60.
53. Hill calls the Norman Yoke a 'backward-looking ideology': Ibid. 58.
54. Ibid. 64.
55. Froissart (n 37) 251.
56. Hill, 'TNY-a' (n 50) 17.
57. On the invocation of the Norman Yoke theory by diverse groups, from the sixteenth to nineteenth century, see: Ibid. 28 (the Levellers), 61–62 (Paine, Ogilvie, Critics of the Old Corruption, Chartists); WHG Armytage, *Heavens below: Utopian Experiments in England, 1560-1960* (Routledge and K. Paul, 1961) 20 (Winstanley and the Diggers); ML Bush, *The English Aristocracy: A Comparative Synthesis* (Manchester University Press, 1984) 145 (the English Jacobins); Briggs (n 50) 218 (Middle class political reformers); Hill, 'TNY-b' (n 50) 318 (the English nobility); David Martin, 'Land Reform' in Patricia Hollis (ed), *Pressure from without in Early Victorian England* (Edward Arnold, 1974) 131, 141 and 141n (the English nobility).
58. Hill, 'TNY-a' (n 50) 62.

5 FROM TRIBUTARY TO CAPITALIST RENT

1. See Perry Anderson, *Lineages of the Absolutist State* (Verso, 2013).
2. This is not to deny that husbandmen engaged in a degree of market production: see Christopher Dyer, *An Age of Transition? Economy and Society in England in the Later Middle Ages* (Oxford University Press, 2005) 245.
3. Ibid.; Spencer Dimmock, *The Origin of Capitalism in England, 1400–1600* (Brill, 2014) 37, 108, 188, 279 ('*OCE*').
4. Dimmock, *OCE* (n 3) 147.
5. Ibid. 185; see also ibid. 147, 156, 363; Dyer (n 2) 245.
6. Dimmock, *OCE* (n 3) 108.
7. Ibid. 183.
8. Ibid. 112; Dyer (n 2) 195–197.
9. Robert P Brenner, 'Dobb on the Transition from Feudalism to Capitalism' (1978) 2(2) *Cambridge Journal of Economics* 121, 134 ('Dobb').
10. Dyer (n 2) 245.
11. Dimmock, *OCE* (n 3) 203.
12. Ibid. 111–112.
13. Ibid. 332.
14. Neal Wood, *Foundations of Political Economy: Some Early Tudor Views on State and Society* (University of California Press, 1994) 17–21 ('*FPE*').
15. Robert P Brenner, 'The Agrarian Roots of European Capitalism' (1982) 97(1) *Past & Present* 16, 91 ('AREC').
16. Dimmock, *OCE* (n 3) 229.
17. Ibid. 314–315.
18. Ibid. 311–313.
19. Ellen Meiksins Wood, 'Locke against Democracy: Consent, Representation and Suffrage in the Two Treatises' (1992) 13(4) *History of Political Thought* 657, 658n ('LAD').
20. Neal Wood, *John Locke and Agrarian Capitalism* (University of California Press, 1984) 18 ('*JLAC*').
21. Wordie defines 'enclosed land' as 'falling completely under the power of one owner to do with as he pleases, whether or not he chose to enclose his land in the literal sense ... such land was free of all common rights, except possibly for a right of way'. See JR Wordie, 'The Chronology of English Enclosure, 1500–1914' (1983) 36(4) *The Economic History Review* 483.
22. On the historiography of English enclosure, see George C Comninel, 'English Feudalism and the Origins of Capitalism' (2000) 27(4) *The Journal of Peasant Studies* 1, 31–38.
23. Dimmock, *OCE* (n 3) 93; citing Keith Wrightson, *Earthly Necessities: Economic Lives in Early Modern Britain* (Yale University Press, 2000) 184–190.

24. Dimmock, *OCE* (n 3) 203; Rodney H Hilton, *The Decline of Serfdom in Medieval England* (Macmillan, 2nd ed, 1986) 57, and, on the nature of leasehold tenure, 44–47 ('*DSE*').
25. Dimmock, *OCE* (n 3) 93; citing Wrightson (n 23) 184–190.
26. Richard Lachmann, *Capitalists in Spite of Themselves: Elite Conflict and Economic Transitions in Early Modern Europe* (Oxford University Press, 2000) 176.
27. Brenner, 'Dobb' (n 9) 133.
28. Michael Andrew Žmolek, *Rethinking the Industrial Revolution: Five Centuries of Transition from Agrarian to Industrial Capitalism in England* (Brill, 2013) 135.
29. Dimmock, *OCE* (n 3) 329–330.
30. Ibid. 187.
31. Ibid. 101–107; Spencer Dimmock, 'Expropriation and the Political Origins of Agrarian Capitalism in England' in Xavier Lafrance and Charles Post (eds), *Case Studies in the Origins of Capitalism* (Palgrave Macmillan, 2019) 39, 47–50.
32. Dimmock, *OCE* (n 3) 182.
33. Lachmann (n 26) 190; as lease-hungry yeomen often served as manor court officials, they were well-placed to assist in boycotts: Dimmock, *OCE* (n 3) 187, 364.
34. Dimmock, *OCE* (n 3) 59.
35. Lachmann (n 26) 175–176.
36. On strategies used by landlords to extinguish peasant landrights, see ibid. 173–176.
37. See Dimmock, *OCE* (n 3) 153–155.
38. Ibid. 292–294.
39. Ibid. 339.
40. Christopher Hill, 'The Poor and the People' in *The Collected Essays of Christopher Hill: People and Ideas in 17th Century England* (Harvester Press, 1986) 247, 257 ('PP').
41. Dimmock, *OCE* (n 3) 340.
42. Ibid. 187.
43. Dyer (n 2) 241.
44. Christopher Hill, 'The Many-Headed Monster' in *Change and Continuity in Seventeenth-Century England* (Weidenfeld and Nicolson, 1974) 181, 188 ('MHM').
45. On falling real wages in fifteenth and sixteenth century England, see P Malanima, 'When Did England Overtake Italy? Medieval and Early Modern Divergence in Prices and Wages' (2013) 17(1) *European Review of Economic History* 45, 60; E Anthony Wrigley, 'Urban Growth and Agricultural Change: England and the Continent in the Early Modern Period' (1985) 15(4) *Journal of Interdisciplinary History* 683, 689.
46. Dyer (n 2) 193–194; Dimmock, *OCE* (n 3) 59.

47. Dyer (n 2) 245; Dimmock, *OCE* (n 3) 201.
48. Dimmock, *OCE* (n 3) 27.
49. Spencer Dimmock, 'The Eastern Origins of Capitalism?', *Historical Materialism* §45 www.historicalmaterialism.org/book-review/eastern-origins-capitalism.
50. Alexander Anievas and Kerem Nişancıoğlu, *How the West came to rule: the geopolitical origins of capitalism* (Pluto Press, 2015) 150–151, 275; Wood, *FPE* (n 14) 17–21.
51. Dimmock, *OCE* (n 3) 201; On the role of towns during the transition, see Spencer Dimmock, 'English Small Towns and the Emergence of Capitalist Relations, c. 1450–1550' (2001) 28(01) *Urban History* 5.
52. Žmolek (n 28) 800.
53. On lordly demilitarisation in the fifteenth century, see Dimmock, 'The Eastern Origins of Capitalism?' (n 49) §37.
54. Wood, *FPE* (n 14) 10–12.
55. Ibid. 3, 10.
56. Ibid. 13–14, 31–32, 238.
57. Accordingly, the first literary use of the term 'civil society' appears in the Tudor period: Ibid. 238.
58. Dimmock, *OCE* (n 3) 331.
59. John E Martin, *Feudalism to Capitalism: Peasant and Landlord in English Agrarian Development* (Macmillan, 1983) 142–150.
60. Dimmock, 'Expropriation and the Political Origins of Agrarian Capitalism in England' (n 31) 50.
61. Dimmock, *OCE* (n 3) 315–316, 331; Dimmock's study of Lydd between from the 1530s to 1570s show the anti-enclosure statutes having little effect: see ibid. 346.
62. Lachmann (n 26) 175.
63. Ibid. 37.
64. Dimmock, 'Expropriation and the Political Origins of Agrarian Capitalism in England' (n 31) 57.
65. See Lachmann (n 26) 271.
66. Hill, 'PP' (n 40) 257.
67. Žmolek (n 28) 115.
68. Lachmann (n 26) 174–176; Žmolek (n 28) 115.
69. Christopher Hill, 'A Bourgeois Revolution?' in *The Collected Essays of Christopher Hill: People and Ideas in 17th Century England* (Harvester Press, 1986) 94, 98–101 ('ABR?').
70. Brenner has rightly questioned whether a Crown that increasingly presides over capitalist social-property relations can properly be described as 'feudal': see Brenner, 'Dobb' (n 9) 139.
71. Žmolek (n 28) 798–799.

72. Ellen Meiksins Wood, *Liberty and Property: A Social History of Western Political Throught from Renaissance to Enlightenment* (Verso, 2012) 220 ('*LP*').
73. Robert P Brenner, *Merchants and Revolutions: Commercial Change, Political Conflict, and London's Overseas Traders, 1550–1653* (Verso, 2003) 661–662 ('*MR*').
74. Ibid.
75. Žmolek (n 28) 119.
76. Richard Bonney (ed), *The Rise of the Fiscal State in Europe, c. 1200–1815* (Oxford University Press, 1999) 57.
77. CGA Clay, *Economic Expansion and Social Change: England 1500–1700*, vol 2 (Cambridge University Press, 1984) 261.
78. See RB Outhwaite, *Inflation in Tudor and Early Stuart England* (Macmillan, 2nd ed, 1982).
79. Clay (n 77) 262; Donald C Coleman, *The Economy of England: 1450–1750* (Oxford University Press, 1977) 24–25.
80. Lachmann (n 26) 105.
81. Clay (n 77) 263.
82. Ian Gentles, 'The Sales of Crown Lands during the English Revolution' (1973) 26(4) *The Economic History Review* 614, 621; citing RH Tawney, 'The Rise of the Gentry, 1558–1640' (1941) 11(1) *The Economic History Review* 1, 25.
83. On this period generally, see Roger Lockyer, *The Early Stuarts: A Political History of England, 1603–1642* (Longman, 2nd ed, 1999); my account of parliamentary events in the period 1604–1629, except as otherwise indicated, is drawn from the surveys in Andrew Thrush and JP Ferris (eds), *The History of Parliament: The House of Commons 1604–1629* (Cambridge University Press, 2010) www.historyofparliamentonline.org/research/surveys/surveys-1604-1629.
84. Lockyer (n 83) 38; GL Harriss, 'Aids, Loans and Benevolences' (1963) 6(1) *The Historical Journal* 1.
85. Lockyer (n 83) 35–37.
86. Eric Lindquist, 'The Failure of the Great Contract' (1985) 57(4) *The Journal of Modern History* 617, 625–626.
87. Ibid. 647.
88. Ibid. 632.
89. See John Raithby (ed), 'Charles I, 1627: The Peticion Exhibited to His Majestie by the Lords Spirituall and Temporall and Co[m]Mons in This p[Re]Sent Parliament Assembled Conc[Er]Ning Divers Rights and Liberties of the Subjects: With the Kings Majesties Royall Aunswere Thereunto in Full Parliament'. in *Statutes of the Realm: Volume 5: 1628–80* (Great Britain Record Commission, 1819) 23 www.british-history.ac.uk/statutes-realm/vol5/pp23-24.

90. Martial law was a by-product of the practice of billeting. Billeted soldiers who committed crimes often claimed to be immune to the common law. Hence, a martial jurisdiction was introduced. See Boynton 'Martial Law and the Petition of Right' [1964] *English Historical Review* 255.
91. See LJ Reeve, 'The Legal Status of the Petition of Right' (1986) 29(02) *The Historical Journal* 257; also Andrew Thrush, 'The Parliament of 1628–1629' in Andrew Thrush and JP Ferris (eds), *The History of Parliament: The House of Commons 1604–1629* (Cambridge University Press, 2010) www.historyofparliamentonline.org/volume/1604-1629/survey/parliament-1628-1629.
92. For a detailed account of this period see Sharpe *The Personal Rule of Charles I* (Yale University Press, 1996)., especially 105–131, regarding revenue and finance.
93. For a detailed account of the period see Scott *Politics and War in the Three Stuart Kingdoms, 1637–49* (Palgrave Macmillan, 2004).
94. Lockyer (n 83) 238. citing Russell 'Charles I's Financial Estimates for 1642' (2008) 58(137) *Historical Research* 109.
95. John Raithby (ed), 'Charles I, 1640: An Act for the Declaring Unlawfull and Void the Late Proceedings Touching Ship Money and for the Vacating of All Records and Processe Concerning the Same'. in *Statutes of the Realm: Volume 5: 1628–80* (Great Britain Record Commission, 1819) 116 www.british-history.ac.uk/statutes-realm/vol5/pp116-117; John Raithby (ed), 'Charles I, 1640: An Act for the Prevention of Vexatious Proceedings Touching the Order of Knighthood'. in *Statutes of the Realm: Volume 5: 1628–80* (Great Britain Record Commission, 1819) 131 www.british-history.ac.uk/statutes-realm/vol5/p131. This fine was known as 'distraint'. On the obligations of knighthood and 'distraint' see Francis Morgan Nichols, 'XII. – On Feudal and Obligatory Knighthood' (1863) 39(01) *Archaeologia* 189. On the decline of 'distraint' see HH Leonard, 'Distraint of Knighthood: The Last Phase, 1625–41'. (1978) 63(207) *History* 23.
96. House of Lords, 'House of Lords Journal Volume 4: 15 March 1642' in *Journal of the House of Lords: Volume 4, 1629–42* (His Majesty's Stationery Office, 1767) 645 www.british-history.ac.uk/lords-jrnl/vol4/pp645-646#h3-0013.
97. Hill, 'ABR?' (n 69) 98–101.
98. Clay (n 77) 258.
99. Keith Wrightson, '"Sorts of People" in Tudor and Stuart England' in Jonathan Barry and Christopher Brooks (eds), *The Middling Sort of People: Culture, Society and Politics in England, 1550–1800* (Macmillan Education UK, 1994) 28, 45.
100. Brenner, *MR* (n 73) 668.
101. Hill, 'ABR?' (n 69) 97.

102. CH Firth and RS Rait (eds), 'February 1645: An Ordinance for Raising and Maintaining of Forces for the Defence of the Kingdome, under the Command of Sir Thomas Fairfax, Knight'. in *Acts and Ordinances of the Interregnum, 1642–1660* (His Majesty's Stationery Office, 1911) 614 www.british-history.ac.uk/no-series/acts-ordinances-interregnum/pp614-626.
103. See Wrightson (n 99) 41–49.
104. Brenner, *MR* (n 73) 643.
105. See Scott (n 93) 5. on the rise of the New Model Army.
106. On Pride's Purge, see Underdown *Pride's Purge: Politics in the Puritan Revolution* (G. Allen & Unwin, 1st paperback edition, 1985).
107. Christopher Hill, 'Sin and Society' in *The Collected Essays of Christopher Hill: Religion and Politics in 17th Century England* (Harvester Press, 1986) 117, 136 ('SS').
108. See CH Firth and RS Rait (eds), 'February 1646: Ordinance for Removing the Court of Wards'. in *Acts and Ordinances of the Interregnum, 1642–1660* (His Majesty's Stationery Office, 1911) 833 www.british-history.ac.uk/no-series/acts-ordinances-interregnum/p833.
109. See HE Bell, *Introduction to History and Records of Courts of Wards and Liveries* (Cambridge University Press, 2011) 150.
110. Thomas Littleton, *Lyttleton, His Treatise of Tenures in French and English. A New Edition, Printed from the Most Ancient Copies, and Collated with the Various Readings of the Cambridge MSS. To Which Are Added the Ancient Treatise of The Olde Tenures, and The Customs of Kent.*, ed TE Tomlins (S. Sweet, 1841) 117–118 explains 'free and common': 'free, as discharged from all service, and common, as not holden in capite, or of the crown'.
111. For a timeseries of English state finances, in real and nominal terms, between 1502 and 1688, showing relative fiscal constraints on the Crown before and after the English Revolution, see Table 14.1 at Michael Mann, *The Sources of Social Power* (Cambridge University Press, 2012) 451.
112. Clay (n 77) 265.
113. Ibid.
114. Ibid. 264.
115. Ian Gentles, 'The Sales of Bishops' Lands in the English Revolution, 1646–1660' (1980) 95(376) *The English Historical Review* 573.
116. Hill, 'ABR?' (n 69) 100.
117. Hill, 'MHM' (n 44) 203–204.
118. Hill, 'ABR?' (n 69) 109.
119. Samuel R Gardiner (ed), '105.: The Declaration of Breda'. in *The Constitutional Documents of the Puritan Revolution, 1625–1660* (Clarendon Press, 3rd ed, 1906) 465, 466 http://oll.libertyfund.org/titles/1434.
120. Hill, 'ABR?' (n 69) 100.

121. 'Charles II, 1660: An Act Takeing Away the Court of Wards and Liveries and Tenures in Capite and by Knights Service and Purveyance, and for Setling a Revenue upon His Majesty in Lieu Thereof' in *Statutes of the Realm: Volume 5: 1628–80* (1819) 259 www.british-history.ac.uk/report.aspx?compid=47272; see also Hill, 'ABR?' (n 69) 101–102.
122. Lockyer (n 83) 238.
123. (n 82) 635n; citing William A Shaw, *Calendar of Treasury Books, Volume 7, 1681–1685*, vol 7 (His Majesty's Stationery Office, 1916) xix–xx www.british-history.ac.uk/cal-treasury-books/vol7.
124. New excises were placed on tea, coffee, sherbet and chocolate. Bonney observes that, by the 1670s, Charles II would dispose 'of 2.7 times as much revenue as his benighted father had managed to collect just a half century earlier': Bonney (n 76) 57.
125. Wood, *FPE* (n 14) 16.
126. Lachmann (n 26) 215; Wood, *FPE* (n 14) 16; Tawney (n 82).
127. In the Stuart era, the Crown backed the episcopal clergy in an attempt to reclaim rights to lands, tithes, benefices and advowsons sold off to the landed class, but these efforts failed: Lachmann (n 26).
128. William Easterby, *The History of the Law of Tithes in England. Being the Yorke Prize Essay of the University of Cambridge for 1887* (Cambridge: University press, 1888) 32 http://archive.org/details/historyoflawoftiooeast.
129. Tithes were eventually formally commuted into a rent charge by a series of acts of Parliament from 1836: see Charles J Jones, *On the Collection and Recovery of Rent-Charge: Under the Statutes for the Commutation of Tithes in England and Wales; with Forms of Proceedings by Distress and Entry* (Francis & John Rivington, 2nd ed, 1849) 3–6 http://archive.org/details/oncollectionandoojonegoog; also Easterby (n 128) 40–46.
130. Christopher Hill, 'Religion, Politics, and Economics' in *Intellectual Origins of the English Revolution Revisited* (Clarendon Press; Oxford University Press, Revised Edition, 1997) 293, 304 ('RPE').
131. Lachmann (n 26) 271; In the Stuart era, the Crown backed the clergy in an attempt to reclaim rights to lands, tithes, benefices and advowsons sold off to the landed class, but these efforts failed: ibid. 173.
132. Wood, *LP* (n 72) 221; c.f. William Letwin, *The Origins of Scientific Economics: English Economic Thought 1660–1776* (Methuen, 1963) 81–82.
133. Christopher Hill, *Economic Problems of the Church: From Archbishop Whitgift to the Long Parliament* (Clarendon Press, 1956) ('*EPC*'); Lachmann (n 26) 117, 174.
134. Hill, *EPC* (n 133).
135. Hill, 'SS' (n 107) 117.
136. On Protestantism and property, see ibid. 135.

6 RESISTANCE AND CRITIQUE IN TRANSITION

1. Spencer Dimmock, *The Origin of Capitalism in England, 1400–1600* (Brill, 2014) 366–367 ('*OCE*').
2. Ibid. 332–339, 342.
3. Ibid. 222–223; John E Martin, *Feudalism to Capitalism: Peasant and Landlord in English Agrarian Development* (Macmillan, 1983) 150–157; Richard Lachmann, *Capitalists in Spite of Themselves: Elite Conflict and Economic Transitions in Early Modern Europe* (Oxford University Press, 2000) 180–185; Geoff Kennedy, *Diggers, Levellers, and Agrarian Capitalism: Radical Political Thought in Seventeenth Century England* (Lexington Books, 2008) 99; B McDonagh, 'Making and Breaking Property: Negotiating Enclosure and Common Rights in Sixteenth-Century England' (2013) 76(1) *History Workshop Journal* 32.
4. Christopher Hill, 'A Bourgeois Revolution?' in *The Collected Essays of Christopher Hill: People and Ideas in 17th Century England* (Harvester Press, 1986) 94, 101 ('ABR?').
5. Dimmock (n 1) 331; Spencer Dimmock, 'Expropriation and the Political Origins of Agrarian Capitalism in England' in Xavier Lafrance and Charles Post (eds), *Case Studies in the Origins of Capitalism* (Palgrave Macmillan, 2019) 39, 57–58.
6. On the 'power vacuum' in this period, see Martin (n 3) 154.
7. See, for example, Lawrence Stone, 'Patriarchy and Paternalism in Tudor England: The Earl of Arundel and The Peasants Revolt of 1549' (1974) 13(2) *Journal of British Studies* 19.
8. Dimmock (n 1) 188; Kennedy (n 3) 99; Lachmann (n 3) 180–185.
9. Michael Andrew Žmolek, *Rethinking the Industrial Revolution: Five Centuries of Transition from Agrarian to Industrial Capitalism in England* (Brill, 2013) 123.
10. See Dimmock (n 1) 102.
11. Alexander Anievas and Kerem Nişancıoğlu, *How the West came to rule: the geopolitical origins of capitalism* (Pluto Press, 2015) 191.
12. Robert P Brenner, *Merchants and Revolutions: Commercial Change, Political Conflict, and London's Overseas Traders, 1550–1653* (Verso, 2003) 688, see also 688–690 ('*MR*').
13. Ibid. 353.
14. On the historiography of Leveller (and Digger) thought, see Geoff Kennedy, 'Radicalism and Revisionism in the English Revolution' in Michael Haynes and Jim Wolfreys (eds), *History and Revolution: Refuting Revisionism* (Verso, 2007) 25, 30–36; On the relation between Leveller thought and agrarian capitalism, see also Kennedy (n 3) 123–125.
15. Žmolek (n 9) 114.
16. Henry Noel Brailsford, *The Levellers and the English Revolution*, ed Christopher Hill (Cresset Press, 1961) 449–450.

17. Richard Overton, 'An Appeale from the Degenerate Representative Body the Commons of England Assembled at Westminster. [17 July 1647, Anonymous]'. in Don Marion Wolfe (ed), *Leveller Manifestoes of the Puritan Revolution* (T. Nelson and Sons, 1944) 154, 178 ('AA').
18. Brailsford (n 16) 440.
19. Anonymous, *A New Engagement, or, Manifesto: Wherein Is Declared the Sence and Resolution of Many Thousands of Well-Affected People in and about London, and Some Adjacent Counties (Viz. Kent, Hartford, Buckingham, and Berks, &c.) Who Seeing All Present Authorities to Be Perverted from Their Naturall End, the Peoples Safety, Are Necessitated to Invite All Faithfull Englishmen to Put Themselves into a Posture of Defending Their Own and Countries Liberties, and to Labour for a Speedy Establishment of a Just and Equall Government. Published at the Desire of Some Honest and Eminent Persons, for the Satisfaction of All That Seek Not the Advancement of Parties and Factions, but Desire the Peace and Prosperitie of the Nation* (s.n., 1648) ('*ANE*'); see also Brailsford (n 16) 448.
20. Brailsford (n 16) 441; see also Christopher Hill, 'Feudal Tenures' in *Intellectual Origins of the English Revolution Revisited* (Clarendon Press; Oxford University Press, Revised Edition, 1997) 318, 323 ('FT').
21. Brailsford (n 16) 436–440; Christopher Hill, 'The Norman Yoke' in John Saville (ed), *Democracy and the Labour Movement: Essays in Honour of Dona Torr* (Lawrence & Wishart, 1954) 11, 28 ('TNY-a').
22. Anonymous, *ANE* (n 19); See also Brailsford (n 16) 440.
23. Brailsford (n 16) 441.
24. Anonymous, *ANE* (n 19); See also Brailsford (n 16) 440, 449: only in the early 1650s, when the Levellers had been driven underground, did they adopt more radical proposals, such as the conversion of copyholds to rent-free freeholds without compensation for landlords.
25. Brailsford (n 16) 433.
26. Overton (n 17) 194.
27. Brailsford (n 16) 431–436.
28. Anonymous, *ANE* (n 19).
29. Perry Anderson, 'Origins of the Present Crisis' [1964] (23) *New Left Review* 26, 29.
30. Overton, for example, called on the Army 'to bind up the wounds of the almost murthered Lawes and Liberties of England'. See Overton (n 17) 180.
31. Brailsford (n 16) 451.
32. Oliver Cromwell, 'At the Opening of Parliament Under the Protectorate [1654]' in *The World's Famous Orations. Great Britain: I. (710–1777).* (1906) 8 www.bartleby.com/268/3/11.html.
33. Brailsford (n 16) 429.

34. Christopher Hill, 'From Lollards to Levellers' in *The Collected Essays of Christopher Hill: Religion and Politics in 17th Century England* (Harvester Press, 1986) 89, 95 ('FLL').
35. Brailsford (n 16) 447; Hill, 'FLL' (n 34) 92.
36. WHG Armytage, *Heavens below: Utopian Experiments in England, 1560–1960* (Routledge and K. Paul, 1961) 24.
37. ML Bush, *The English Aristocracy: A Comparative Synthesis* (Manchester University Press, 1984) 135.
38. I have relied on the account of Armytage (n 36) 19–25.
39. On the Diggers' theological idiom, see Christopher Hill, 'The Religion of Gerrard Winstanley' in *The Collected Essays of Christopher Hill: Religion and Politics in 17th Century England* (Harvester Press, 1986) 185, 236 ('RGW'); Christopher Hill, 'Foreword' in *Left-Wing Democracy in the English Civil War: Gerarrd Winstanley and the Digger Movement* (Alan Sutton Publishing Limited, 1995) vii, vii ('Foreword').
40. Here I follow Petegorsky's approach. See Hill, 'Foreword' (n 39) vii; Hill, 'RGW' (n 39).
41. Hill, 'RGW' (n 39) 195, see also 195–200.
42. Anonymous, 'More Light Shining in Buckingham-Shire [1649]' in George H Sabine (ed), *The Works of Gerrard Winstanley: With an Appendix of Documents Relating to the Digger Movement* (Cornell University Press, 1941) 627, 627 ('MLS').
43. Ibid.
44. Gerrard Winstanley, *An Appeale to All Englishmen, to Judge between Bondage and Freedome, Sent from Those That Began to Digge upon George Hill in Surrey; but Now Are Carrying on, That Publick Workupon the Little Heath in the Parish of Cobham, Neare unto George Hill, Wherein It Appeares, That the Work of Diggingupon the Commons, Is Not Onely Warranted by Scripture, Butby the Law of the Common-Wealth of England Likewise* (1650) ('AA').
45. Richard Smith et al. 'A Declaration of the Grounds and Reasons Why We the Poor Inhabitants of the Town of Wellinborrow, in the County of Northampton, Have Begun and Give Consent to Dig up, Manure and Sow Com upon the Common, and Waste Ground, Called Bareshanke, Belonging to the Inhabitants of Wellinborrow, by Those That Have Subscribed, and Hundreds More That Give Consent. [1650]' in George H Sabine (ed), *The Works of Gerrard Winstanley: With an Appendix of Documents Relating to the Digger Movement* (Cornell University Press, 1941) 649, 649.
46. Gerrard Winstanley, 'A Letter to the Lord Fairfax and His Councell of War, With Divers Questions to the Lawyers and Ministers [1649]' in Thomas N Corns, Ann Hughes and David Loewenstein (eds), *The Complete Works of Gerrard Winstanley* (Oxford University Press, 2009) 43, 46 ('LLF').

47. Anonymous, 'MLS' (n 42) 634.
48. Smith et al. (n 45) 649.
49. Gerrard Winstanley, 'A New-Yeers Gift for the Parliament and Armie [1650]' in Thomas N Corns, Ann Hughes and David Loewenstein (eds), *The Complete Works of Gerrard Winstanley* (Oxford University Press, 2009) 108, 128 ('NYG').
50. Anonymous, 'MLS' (n 42) 634.
51. Ibid 627.
52. Robert Coster, 'A Mite Cast into the Common Treasury: Or Queries Propounded (for All Men to Consider of) by Him Who Desireth to Advance the Work of Publick Community [1649]' in George H Sabine (ed), *The Works of Gerrard Winstanley: With an Appendix of Documents Relating to the Digger Movement* (Cornell University Press, 1941) 655, 656 ('AMCCT').
53. Gerrard Winstanley, 'FIRE IN THE BUSH. THE SPIRIT BURNING, NOT CONSuming, but Purging Mankinde. OR, The Great Battell of God Almighty, between Michaell the Seed of Life, and the Great Red Dragon, the Curse Fought within the Spirit of Man. With Severall Other Declarations, and Testimonies of the Power of Life. [1650]' in Thomas N Corns, Ann Hughes and David Loewenstein (eds), *The Complete Works of Gerrard Winstanley* (Oxford University Press, 2009) 176, 189 ('FITB').
54. Coster (n 52) 656.
55. Winstanley, *AA* (n 44) 1.
56. Ibid.
57. Gerrard Winstanley, 'True Levellers Standard Advanced, or A Declaration to the Powers of England and to All the Powers of the World, Shewing the Cause Why the Common People of England Have Begun, and Gives Consent to Dig up, Manure, and Sow Corne upon George-Hill in Surrey; by Those That Have Subscribed, and Thousands More That Gives Consent. [1649]' in Thomas N Corns, Ann Hughes and David Loewenstein (eds), *The Complete Works of Gerrard Winstanley* (Oxford University Press, 2009) 4, 11 ('TLSA').
58. Anonymous, 'MLS' (n 42) 631.
59. Winstanley, 'FITB' (n 53) 216.
60. Ibid. 216–217.
61. Winstanley, 'NYG' (n 49) 141; c.f. Winstanley, 'TLSA' (n 57) 11: 'Those that buy and sell Land…, and are Landlords, have got it either by Oppression, or Murther, or Theft.'
62. Anonymous, 'Light Shining in Buckinghamshire [1648]' in George H Sabine (ed), *The Works of Gerrard Winstanley: With an Appendix of Documents Relating to the Digger Movement* (Cornell University Press, 1941) 611, 614 ('LSIB').
63. Winstanley, 'NYG' (n 49) 142.

64. Anonymous, 'MLS' (n 42) 636.
65. Winstanley, 'NYG' (n 49) 112; on this quotation see David W Petegorsky, *Left-Wing Democracy in the English Civil War: Gerarrd Winstanley and the Digger Movement* (Alan Sutton Publishing Limited, 1995) 195–196.
66. Winstanley, 'NYG' (n 49) 127.
67. Winstanley, 'FITB' (n 53) 189.
68. Winstanley, 'NYG' (n 49) 127.
69. Ibid.
70. Anonymous, 'MLS' (n 42) 633–634.
71. Ibid. 628.
72. Winstanley, 'FITB' (n 53) 200.
73. Anonymous, 'MLS' (n 42) 365.
74. The Diggers at Cobham, 'The Diggers Mirth [1650]' in George H Sabine (ed), *The Works of Gerrard Winstanley: With an Appendix of Documents Relating to the Digger Movement* (Cornell University Press, 1941) 665, 669 ('TDM').
75. Anonymous, 'LSIB' (n 62) 200.
76. Coster (n 52) 657.
77. Gerrard Winstanley, 'The Law of Freedom in a Platform: Or, True Magistracy Restored [1651]' in Thomas N Corns, Ann Hughes and David Loewenstein (eds), *The Complete Works of Gerrard Winstanley* (Oxford University Press, 2009) 278, 284 ('LFIP').
78. Ibid. 297.
79. Ibid. 285.
80. Anonymous, 'MLS' (n 42) 627–628.
81. Winstanley, 'LFIP' (n 77) 284.
82. Winstanley, 'LLF' (n 46) 50.
83. Coster (n 52) 656–657.
84. Anonymous, 'LSIB' (n 62) 612.
85. Winstanley, *AA* (n 44) Emphasis added.
86. Anonymous, 'LSIB' (n 62) 611.
87. Ibid. 614.
88. Ibid. 611.
89. Winstanley, 'TLSA' (n 57) 10.
90. Winstanley, 'LFIP' (n 77) 359–360.
91. Winstanley, 'NYG' (n 49) 128.
92. Ibid. 138.
93. As documented by Petegorsky (n 65) 200–202, Winstanley sometimes claimed the Diggers were no threat to the existing order. Arguably, however, these were tactical claims intended for the authorities. See, for example, Gerrard Winstanley, 'To My Lord Generall and His Councell of War [1649]' in Thomas N Corns, Ann Hughes and David Loewenstein (eds), *The Complete Works of Gerrard Winstanley* (Oxford University Press, 2009) 413 ('LGCW') – presenting his case to Fairfax and the

Army, Winstanley promised 'if this freedome were granted to improve the common lands then…the murmurings of the people against you & the Parliament would cease'.

94. Winstanley, 'NYG' (n 49) 133.
95. Winstanley, 'TLSA' (n 57) 15–16.
96. Winstanley, 'LLF' (n 46) 43.
97. Winstanley, *AA* (n 44) 1.
98. Anonymous, 'MLS' (n 42) 638; c.f. Anonymous, 'A Declaration of the Well-Affected in the County of Buckinghamshire [1649]' in George H Sabine (ed), *The Works of Gerrard Winstanley: With an Appendix of Documents Relating to the Digger Movement* (Cornell University Press, 1941) 643, 464 ('DWA'); see also, Hill, 'RGW' (n 39) 207–208; Bush (n 37) 134.
99. Smith et al. (n 45) 651.

7 THE POLITICAL ECONOMY OF CAPITALIST RENT

1. Ellen Meiksins Wood, *Democracy against Capitalism: Renewing Historical Materialism* (Cambridge University Press, 1995) 30 ('*DAC*').
2. Ibid.
3. Ibid.
4. Nicos Poulantzas, 'Marxist Political Theory in Britain' [1967] (43) *New Left Review* 57, 65.
5. Alexander Anievas and Kerem Nişancıoğlu, *How the West came to rule: the geopolitical origins of capitalism* (Pluto Press, 2015) 196.
6. For an account of aristocratic support for the Revolution, see John P Kenyon, *The Nobility in the Revolution of 1688* (University of Hull Publications, 1963).
7. See Henry Noel Brailsford, *The Levellers and the English Revolution*, ed Christopher Hill (Cresset Press, 1961) 276; see also Robert P Brenner, *Merchants and Revolutions: Commercial Change, Political Conflict, and London's Overseas Traders, 1550–1653* (Verso, 2003) 713 ('*MR*').
8. JV Beckett, *The Aristocracy in England 1660–1914* (Basil Blackwell, 1986) 10.
9. Ibid. 10, 406, 420; William Stafford, *Socialism, Radicalism, and Nostalgia: Social Criticism in Britain, 1775–1830* (Cambridge University Press, 1987) 24.
10. FML Thompson, *English Landed Society in the Nineteenth Century* (Routledge and Kegan Paul, 1980) 8–9.
11. Beckett (n 8) 3.
12. Ibid. 198.
13. Neil Davidson, *Discovering the Scottish Revolution, 1692–1746* (Pluto, 2003) 76.

14. HJ Habakkuk, 'English Landownership, 1680–1740' (1940) 10(1) *The Economic History Review* 2, 9–11; WA Speck, 'Conflict in Society' in Geoffrey S Holmes (ed), *Britain after the Glorious Revolution, 1689–1714* (Macmillan, St. Martin's Press, 1969) 135, 141.
15. Beckett (n 8) 199.
16. Philip Harling, *The Waning of 'Old Corruption': The Politics of Economical Reform in Britain, 1779–1846* (Clarendon Press; Oxford University Press, 1996) 56–57.
17. Anievas and Nişancıoğlu (n 5) 196.
18. On the escalating expenditures of the British fiscal-military state between 1695 and 1820, see Michael Mann, *The Sources of Social Power* (Cambridge University Press, 2012) 483–486.
19. See Harling (n 16) 3n.
20. Michael Andrew Žmolek, *Rethinking the Industrial Revolution: Five Centuries of Transition from Agrarian to Industrial Capitalism in England* (Brill, 2013) 212.
21. Anievas and Nişancıoğlu (n 5) 272.
22. James Martin, 'Introduction' in James Martin (ed), *The Poulantzas Reader: Marxism, Law, and the State* (Verso, 2008) 1, 8.
23. Thompson, *English Landed Society in the Nineteenth Century* (n 10) 4–7.
24. Ibid. 5.
25. Beckett (n 8) 11–12.
26. RJ Olney, 'The Politics of Land' in GE Mingay (ed), *The Victorian Countryside* (Routledge & Kegan Paul, 1981) 58, 61–62.
27. Beckett (n 8) 441–448.
28. William D Rubinstein, 'The End of "Old Corruption" in Britain 1780–1860' [1983] (101) *Past & Present* 55, 55–56.
29. WD Rubinstein, 'New Men of Wealth and the Purchase of Land in Nineteenth-Century Britain' [1981] (92) *Past & Present* 125, 147.
30. Perry Anderson, 'Origins of the Present Crisis' [1964] (23) *New Left Review* 26, 31.
31. John Locke, 'Some Considerations of the Consequences of the Lowering of Interest and Raising the Value of Money. In a Letter Sent to a Member of Parliament, 1691' in *The Works of John Locke in Nine Volumes* (Rivington, 12th ed, 1824) 1, 71 http://oll.libertyfund.org/titles/763.
32. Angus McInnes, 'The Revolution and the People' in Geoffrey S Holmes (ed), *Britain after the Glorious Revolution, 1689–1714* (Macmillan, St. Martin's Press, 1969) 80, 85.
33. On working class political activity from the late eighteenth century, see EP Thompson, *The Making of the English Working Class* (Vintage, 1966).
34. Stafford (n 9) 106.
35. Ibid. 29–30.
36. Beckett (n 8) 449.

37. See Edmund Burke, *Reflections on the French Revolution [First Published 1790]* (J. M. Dent & Sons Ltd; E. P. Dutton & Co. Inc., 1951) 117, 156–158, 218–219 https://archive.org/details/reflectionsontheo05907mbp.
38. Anderson (n 30) 40.
39. Alice Mary Hadfield, *The Chartist Land Company* (David & Charles, 1970) 11.
40. Ibid.
41. Christopher Hill, 'A Bourgeois Revolution?' in *The Collected Essays of Christopher Hill: People and Ideas in 17th Century England* (Harvester Press, 1986) 94, 103 ('ABR?').
42. Anderson (n 30) 29.
43. Donald Winch and Patrick Karl O'Brien (eds), *The Political Economy of British Historical Experience, 1688–1914* (Published for The British Academy by Oxford University Press, 2002) 124.
44. Beckett (n 8) 185–186.
45. Ibid. 184–185; ME Turner, JV Beckett and B Afton, *Agricultural Rent in England, 1690–1914* (Cambridge University Press, 2004) 35.
46. E Anthony Wrigley, 'A Simple Model of London's Importance in Changing English Society and Economy 1650–1750' [1967] (37) *Past & Present* 44, 60 ('A Simple Model').
47. EA Wrigley, 'Introduction: What Was the Industrial Revolution?' in *People, Cities, and Wealth: The Transformation of Traditional Society* (Blackwell, 1987) 1, 11.
48. E Anthony Wrigley, 'Urban Growth and Agricultural Change: England and the Continent in the Early Modern Period' (1985) 15(4) *Journal of Interdisciplinary History* 683, 684.
49. Wrigley, 'A Simple Model' (n 46) 55; citing Alan Everitt, 'Social Mobility in Early Modern England' [1966] (33) *Past & Present* 56, 71.
50. Wrigley, 'Introduction: What Was the Industrial Revolution?' (n 47) 11.
51. WA Armstrong, *The Flight from the Land*, ed GE Mingay (Routledge & Kegan Paul, 1981) 118.
52. Robert P Brenner, 'The Agrarian Roots of European Capitalism' (1982) 97(1) *Past & Present* 16, 100 ('AREC').
53. Wrigley, 'Introduction: What Was the Industrial Revolution?' (n 47).
54. BA Holderness, 'Agriculture and Industrialization in the Victorian Economy' in GE Mingay (ed), *The Victorian Countryside* (Routledge & Kegan Paul, 1981) 179, 14.
55. Rubinstein (n 29) 140.
56. Beckett (n 8) 469.
57. Peter Roebuck, 'Absentee Landownership in the Late Seventeenth and Early Eighteenth Centuries: A Neglected Factor in English Agrarian History' (1973) 21(1) *The Agricultural History Review* 1, 11.
58. Ibid.
59. Ibid. 12.

60. Ibid. 12–14.
61. Beckett (n 8) 6.
62. Roebuck (n 57) 15–17.
63. Ibid.; Beckett (n 8) 136–141.
64. Beckett (n 8) 6.
65. Ibid. 136–142; Roebuck (n 57).
66. Beckett (n 8) 150.
67. An 1804 manual for landlords specifies the qualities of a good tenant as capital, skill, industry and character, noting the difficulty of finding tenants with all these attributes. See ibid. 190; citing William Marshall, *On the Landed Property of England: An Elementary and Practical Treatise: Containing the Purchase, the Improvement, and the Management of Landed Estates* (Printed for G. and W. Nichol … [et al.], 1804) 391.
68. Beckett (n 8) 185.
69. Ibid.
70. Turner, Beckett and Afton (n 45) 35, 199.
71. Brailsford (n 7) 451–452.
72. Robert J Thompson, 'An Inquiry into the Rent of Agricultural Land in England and Wales During the Nineteenth Century' (1907) 70(4) *Journal of the Royal Statistical Society* 587, 609; Beckett (n 8) 158; However, the division of responsibility for investment between landlord and tenant varied according to the customs of the region. See ibid. 193n.
73. Beckett (n 8) 205.
74. Ibid. 180; citing Thompson, 'An Inquiry into the Rent of Agricultural Land in England and Wales During the Nineteenth Century' (n 72).
75. Beckett (n 8) 205.
76. Ibid. 176–177.
77. Ibid. 468.
78. Ibid. 177.
79. Ibid. 189.
80. Ibid.
81. Žmolek (n 20) 136.
82. Beckett (n 8) 174.
83. Habakkuk (n 14) 15.
84. Kathryn Beresford, '"Witnesses for the Defence": The Yeomen of Old England and the Land Question, c. 1815–1837' in Matthew Cragoe and Paul Readman (eds), *The Land Question in Britain, 1750–1950* (Palgrave Macmillan, 2010) 37, 38; Harling (n 16) 19n.
85. Burke (n 37) 156.
86. Christopher Hill, 'Feudal Tenures' in *Intellectual Origins of the English Revolution Revisited* (Clarendon Press; Oxford University Press, Revised Edition, 1997) 318, 322 ('FT').
87. Hill (n 41) 101.

88. Ibid. 14.
89. Regarding laws which enabled borrowing against life estates for improvements under the supervision of the Inclosure Commissioners, see David Spring, *English Landed Estate in the Nineteenth Century, Its Administration* (The Johns Hopkins Press, 1963) 151–161, 175–176.
90. Beckett (n 8).
91. Ibid. 173.
92. Ibid.
93. Spencer Dimmock, *The Origin of Capitalism in England, 1400–1600* (Brill, 2014) 63–64 ('*OCE*').
94. Beckett (n 8) 170.
95. Stafford (n 9) 13.
96. Beckett (n 8) 170.
97. Ibid. 173.
98. Žmolek (n 20) 819–823.
99. Brenner (n 7) 715–716.
100. Beckett (n 8) 69–70.
101. Wrigley, 'A Simple Model' (n 46) 54n.
102. Stafford (n 9) 27.
103. Žmolek (n 20) 826–831; On the rise of a 'working class' and their resistance to capitalist hegemony, see Thompson, *The Making of the English Working Class* (n 33).
104. McInnes (n 32) 83–84.
105. Regarding debates on the use of criminal law and policing as class power, see Harling (n 16) 19n.
106. Anievas and Nişancıoğlu (n 5) 151–152.
107. Žmolek (n 20) 826–827, 835–836.

8 RESISTANCE TO RENT UNDER CAPITALISM

1. The classic discussion is Marx on the length of the working day: Karl Marx, *Capital: A Critique of Political Economy [First Published 1867]*, tr David Fernbach, vol 1 (Penguin Books in association with New Left Review, 1976) 340–416.
2. Donald Winch, 'Introduction' in Donald Winch and Patrick Karl O'Brien (eds), *The Political Economy of British Historical Experience, 1688–1914* (Published for The British Academy by Oxford University Press, 2002) 1, 9.
3. Michael Andrew Žmolek, *Rethinking the Industrial Revolution: Five Centuries of Transition from Agrarian to Industrial Capitalism in England* (Brill, 2013) 820.
4. ML Bush, *The English Aristocracy: A Comparative Synthesis* (Manchester University Press, 1984) 145.

5. Christopher Hill, 'The Norman Yoke' in John Saville (ed), *Democracy and the Labour Movement: Essays in Honour of Dona Torr* (Lawrence & Wishart, 1954) 11, 48 ('TNY-a').
6. Thomas Paine, 'Rights of Man, Part II [1792]' in Bruce Kuklick (ed), *Political Writings* (Cambridge University Press, Revised Student Edition, 2000) 155, 220.
7. Ibid. 218.
8. Thomas Paine, 'Agrarian Justice [1797]' in Bruce Kuklick (ed), *Political Writings* (Cambridge University Press, Revised Student Edition, 2000) 319, 326.
9. Ibid. 327.
10. Bush (n 4) 130.
11. Allan Davenport, 'Republican, 18 October 1822' in *Class and Conflict in Nineteenth-Century England, 1815–1850* (Routledge, 1973) 21; George Petrie, '"Agrarius", Man, 21 July 1833' in *Class and Conflict in Nineteenth-Century England, 1815–1850* (Routledge, 1973) 21.
12. Winch (n 2) 9.
13. Gregory Claeys, *Citizens and Saints: Politics and Anti-Politics in Early British Socialism* (Cambridge University Press, 1989) 288–290 ('*CAS*').
14. David Martin, 'Land Reform' in Patricia Hollis (ed), *Pressure from without in Early Victorian England* (Edward Arnold, 1974) 131, 137.
15. FML Thompson, 'Land and Politics in England in the Nineteenth Century' (1965) 15 *Transactions of the Royal Historical Society* 23, 35.
16. FML Thompson, *English Landed Society in the Nineteenth Century* (Routledge and Kegan Paul, 1980) 285.
17. Martin (n 14) 156.
18. Alice Mary Hadfield, *The Chartist Land Company* (David & Charles, 1970) 12.
19. Malcolm Chase, 'Chartism and the Land: "The Mighty People's Question"' in Matthew Cragoe and Paul Readman (eds), *The Land Question in Britain, 1750–1950* (Palgrave Macmillan, 2010) 57, 59.
20. Claeys (n 13) 245.
21. Hadfield (n 18) 16.
22. Ibid. 17.
23. Ibid. 16.
24. Feargus O'Connor, circa 1845, quoted in WHG Armytage, *Heavens below: Utopian Experiments in England, 1560–1960* (Routledge and K. Paul, 1961) 227.
25. Feargus O'Connor, 'Northern Star, 26 April 1845' in *Class and Conflict in Nineteenth-Century England, 1815–1850* (Routledge, 1973) 307, 307.
26. Ibid.
27. Ibid. 307–308.
28. Ibid.

29. Feargus O'Connor, 'Evidence of Feargus O'Connor, Select Committee on the National Land Company (1848)' in *Class and Conflict in Nineteenth-Century England, 1815–1850* (Routledge, 1973) 309; he took the Flemish system of intensive farming for his model: Armytage (n 24) 227.
30. Armytage (n 24) 227.
31. Patricia Hollis, *Class and Conflict in Nineteenth-Century England, 1815–1850* (Routledge, 1973) 309.
32. Hadfield (n 18) 20.
33. Hollis (n 31) 308.
34. Hadfield (n 18) 18, 63.
35. Malcolm Chase, '"Wholesome Object Lessons": The Chartist Land Plan in Retrospect' (2003) 118(475) *The English Historical Review* 59, 58–59.
36. Hadfield (n 18) 29.
37. Andrew Doyle, 'Mr Doyle's Report on "The National Land Company" and Small Holdings' in *Royal Commission on Agriculture. Reports of the Assistant Commissioners. Mr Doyle's Reports on Wales, &c., &c., &c. [C.3357.III]* (George E. B. Eyre and William Spottiswoode for Her Majesty's Stationery Office, 1882) 68, 70.
38. Chase (n 35) 60.
39. Claeys (n 13) 288.
40. Chase (n 19) 68.
41. James Bronterre O'Brien, 'Operative, 18 November 1838' in *Class and Conflict in Nineteenth-Century England, 1815–1850* (Routledge, 1973) 13.
42. James Bronterre O'Brien, 'National Reformer, 16 January 1847' in *Class and Conflict in Nineteenth-Century England, 1815–1850* (Routledge, 1973) 24.
43. Gregory Claeys, *Machinery, Money and the Millennium: From Moral Economy to Socialism, 1815–60* (Polity Press, 1987) 159 ('*MMM*').
44. Martin (n 14) 149; David E Martin, *John Stuart Mill and the Land Question* (University of Hull Publications, 1981) 31.
45. Eldon Barry E., *Nationalisation in British Politics: The Historical Background* (Cape, 1st ed, 1965) 39; Martin (n 14) 149–150; Claeys (n 13) 279.
46. Arthur Eugene Bestor, *Backwoods Utopias: The Sectarian Origins and the Owenite Phase of Communitarian Socialism in America, 1663–1829* (Pennsylvania University Press, 2nd ed, 1970) 62, 66.
47. Ibid. 72.
48. Claeys (n 43) 190.
49. Bestor (n 46) 87–88.
50. JFC Harrison, *Robert Owen and The Owenites in Britain and America: The Quest for the New Moral World* (Routledge and Kegan Paul Ltd, 1969) 195.

51. On the Owenite communitarian model, see Bestor (n 46) 72–77.
52. Ibid. 72.
53. Ibid. 78.
54. Ibid. 86.
55. Ibid. 73, 91–92.
56. For a detailed discussion of Owen's thought and legacy in relation to class conflict see Ben Maw, 'Robert Owen's Unintended Legacy: Class Conflict' in Noel Thompson and Chris Williams (eds), *Robert Owen and His Legacy* (University of Wales Press, 2011) 155.
57. Bestor (n 46) 87.
58. Ibid. 79, 91–92.
59. Ibid. 75.
60. Hollis (n 31) 30; Bestor (n 46) 81.
61. Bush (n 4) 145.
62. Hollis (n 31) xxvii.

9 THE CRITICAL SOCIAL THEORISTS

1. Neal Wood, *Foundations of Political Economy: Some Early Tudor Views on State and Society* (University of California Press, 1994) 39; see also 2–4, 250 ('*FPE*').
2. Ibid. 4, 39.
3. Ibid. 30.
4. See ibid. 3–4 Leading contributors included Edmund Dudley (1462–1510), Thomas More (1478–1535), Hugh Latimer (circa 1485–1555), Thomas Starkey (circa 1499–1538), Thomas Smith (1513–1577), Thomas Lever (1521–1577), Robert Crowley (circa 1518–1588) Henry Brinklow (died 1546), and Francis Bacon (1561–1626).
5. Ibid. 2, 250.
6. Ibid. 3.
7. Ibid. 242.
8. Ibid. 41–42, 242.
9. Ibid. 241.
10. William Letwin, *The Origins of Scientific Economics: English Economic Thought 1660–1776* (Methuen, 1963) 97.
11. Ibid. 143; On Bacon's inductive scientific method, which he called 'new learning' or 'natural philosophy', see ibid. 122–127.
12. Neal Wood, *John Locke and Agrarian Capitalism* (University of California Press, 1984) 52 ('*JLAC*').
13. Ibid. 34–36, 52; Wood (n 1) 237; Letwin (n 10) 98.
14. For a comprehensive treatment of early English PE in the context of agrarian capitalism, see David McNally, *Political Economy and the Rise of Capitalism: A Reinterpretation* (University of California Press, 1988).

15. Anthony Aspromourgos, *On the Origins of Classical Economics Distribution and Value from William Petty to Adam Smith* (Routledge, 1996) 166.
16. Phillip O'Hara (ed), *Encyclopedia of Political Economy* (Routledge, 2002) 264.
17. On the reception of Longfield, see Prendergast 'Mountifort Longfield' in Nigel FB Allington and Noel W Thompson (eds), *English, Irish and Subversives among the Dismal Scientists* (Emerald, 1st ed, 2010) 351.
18. William Petty, 'A Treatise of Taxes and Contributions [1662]' in Charles H Hull (ed), *The Economic Writings of Sir William Petty, Together with The Observations upon Bills of Mortality, More Probably by Captain John Graunt* (Cambridge University Press, 1899) 1, 22 http://oll.libertyfund.org/titles/1677.
19. Adam Smith, *An Inquiry into the Nature and Causes of the Wealth of Nations [First Published 1776]*, ed Edwin Cannan (Methuen & Co., 5th ed, 1904) IV.I.1 www.econlib.org/library/Smith/smWNCover.html. Emphasis added.
20. JR McCulloch, *The Principles of Political Economy: With a Sketch of the Rise and Progress of the Science* (William and Charles Tait, 1st ed, 1825) 1 http://oll.libertyfund.org/titles/mcculloch-the-principles-of-political-economy-1st-ed-1825.
21. See Noel W Thompson, *The People's Science: The Popular Political Economy of Exploitation and Crisis 1816–34* (Cambridge University Press, 2002) 110 ('*TPS*').
22. Ibid. 87, 110.
23. Thomas Hopkins, *Wages, or, Masters and Workmen* (A. Wilkinson, 1831) 14–15 ('*WMW*').
24. Gregory Claeys, *Citizens and Saints: Politics and Anti-Politics in Early British Socialism* (Cambridge University Press, 1989) 61 ('*CAS*'); see also Gregory Claeys, *Machinery, Money and the Millennium: From Moral Economy to Socialism, 1815–60* (Polity Press, 1987) 92 ('*MMM*').
25. James Napier Bailey, *Preliminary Discourse on the Objects, Pleasures, and Advantages of the Science of Society* (J. Hobson, 1840) 5.
26. Ibid.
27. Patrick Edward Dove, *The Theory of Human Progression, and Natural Probability of a Reign of Justice [First Published 1850]* (Sanborn & Carter, 1856) 249n–250n http://archive.org/details/theoryhumanprog01dovgoog.
28. Ibid. 238; Cf. Thompson on the material interests driving mainstream analysis of free trade: 'Edinburgh Reviewers … of the Whig branch of the oligarchy, … trade in the words of liberality and justice that they may supplant their Tory competitors in the pleasures of ruling and … public-plunder-prizes of competition'. William Thompson, *Labour Rewarded. The Claims of Labour and Capital Conciliated, or, How to*

Secure to Labour the Whole Products of Its Exertions (Printed for Hunt and Clarke by R. Taylor, 1827) 96–97 ('*LR*').

29. JCL Simonde de Sismondi, *New Principles of Political Economy: Of Wealth in Its Relation to Population*, tr Richard Hyse (Transaction Publishers, 1991) 569 ('*NPPE*'); Cf. Thomas Hopkins, *Great Britain, during the Last Forty Years: Being an Historical and Analytical Account Of Its Finances, Monetary System, Economy and General Condition during That Period* (J. Pigot, 2nd ed, 1840) ('*GBLFY*'): 'national success, and even what is frequently called national prosperity, is not always accompanied by improvement in the condition of the great body of the people'.
30. Dove (n 27) 249n–250n.
31. Thompson, *LR* (n 28) 95.
32. TR Edmonds, *Political, Moral and Social Economy: Founded upon Reason, Observation, and Science, and Combining 'the Greatest Happiness of the Greatest Number', in Opposition to the Anti-Social and Fallacious Theories of Modern Political Economists* (S. and R. Bentley for E. Wilson, 1831) 1.
33. Dove (n 27) 249n–250n.
34. Sismondi (n 29) 569.
35. Michel Prum, 'Capital Pre-Visited' (1993) 19(1) *History of Economics Review* 55, 56.
36. Other theorists, for instance, Granville Sharp, are arguably part of the tradition of Critical Social Theory too, but are not treated in this study because of their limited contribution to the theorisation of rent. On Sharp, see GM Ditchfield, 'Granville Sharp: A Neglected Economist?' in Nigel FB Allington and Noel W Thompson (eds), *English, Irish and Subversives among the Dismal Scientists* (Emerald, 1st ed, 2010) 73. Sharp is attributed authorship of *Sketches on Political Economy: Illustrative of the Interests of Great Britain, Intended as a Reply to Mr. Mill's Pamphlet Commerce Defended. With an Exposition of Some of the Leading Tenets of the Economists.* (London, 1809). See also Claeys, *MMM* (n 24) 130–165 for some further contributions to Critical Social Theory in the late nineteenth century (after the period examined in this study).
37. Claeys, *MMM* (n 24) xxix, 34–66.
38. William Stafford, *Socialism, Radicalism, and Nostalgia: Social Criticism in Britain, 1775–1830* (Cambridge University Press, 1987) 114.
39. Stafford, for instance, reads Ogilvie as radicalising Locke's property theory: see ibid. 108–109.
40. Ibid. 111.
41. Ibid. 155, 158.
42. Ibid. 104–106.
43. TM Parssinen, 'Thomas Spence and the Origins of English Land Nationalization' (1973) 34(1) *Journal of the History of Ideas* 135, 139.
44. Ibid. 135–136.

45. Ibid. 140–141.
46. Ibid.; see also David Martin, 'Land Reform' in Patricia Hollis (ed), *Pressure from without in Early Victorian England* (Edward Arnold, 1974) 131, 135.
47. Rogério Arthmar, 'A Economia Clássica Contra Os Fatos Ou Sismondi Entre Os Ricardianos [Automatic English Translation]' (2009) 18(2) *Economia e Sociedade* 261, 264.
48. Ibid. 264; Margaret G Sheldrick, 'The Life and the Economic Contribution of Simonde de Sismondi' (Boston University, 1934) 27 https://archive.org/stream/thelifeeconomiccooshel.
49. Thomas Sowell, 'Sismondi: A Neglected Pioneer' (1972) 4(1) *History of Political Economy* 62, 65.
50. Sismondi (n 29) 3–4 (translator's note).
51. Ibid. 11.
52. Ibid. 11–12.
53. Ibid. 8.
54. Ibid. 327, 619–620.
55. See, for example, ibid. 147, 196.
56. Sowell (n 49) 67.
57. Sismondi (n 29) 14.
58. See, for example, Thompson, *LR* (n 28) 95.
59. Sismondi (n 29) 4 (translator's note).
60. Sheldrick (n 48) 24–25; ML Tuan, *Simonde De Sismondi As En Economist* (Columbia University Press, 1927) 27–29.
61. Claeys, *MMM* (n 24) 71.
62. Thomas Hopkins, *On Rent of Land, and Its Influence on Subsistence and Population: With Observations on the Operating Causes of the Condition of the Labouring Classes in Various Countries* (Hunt and Clarke, 1828) 1 ('*ORL*').
63. Terry Eagleton, 'The Radicalism of William Thompson' [2000] (26) *The Irish Review (1986–)* 80, 87n.
64. Stafford (n 38) 228.
65. Claeys, *MMM* (n 24) 90.
66. Thomas Hodgskin, *Popular Political Economy: Four Lectures Delivered at the London Mechanics' Institution... [Book I]* (Printed for Charles Tait and William Tait, 1827) 102; Thomas Hodgskin, *The Natural and Artificial Right of Property Contrasted: A Series of Letters, Addressed without Permission, to H. Brougham* (B. Steil, 1832) 55 ('*NAR*'); see also Thompson, *TPS* (n 21) 86.
67. Patricia Hollis, *Class and Conflict in Nineteenth-Century England, 1815–1850* (Routledge, 1973) 26; Claeys, *MMM* (n 24) 68.
68. Claeys, *MMM* (n 24) 68.
69. On Gray's thought generally, see ibid. 110–129.

70. An appendix to Gray's *The Social System: A Treatise on the Principle of Exchange* (W. Tait, 1831) contained detailed critique of Owenism.
71. Karl Marx, 'The Poverty of Philosophy. Answer to the Philosophy of Poverty by M. Proudhon' in *Marx & Engels: Collected Works, Volume 6* (Lawrence & Wishart Electric Book, 1976) 105, 138–142.
72. James Moffat Scott, Elder Smith & Co., *Dictionary of National Biography, 1885–1900*, ed Leslie Stephen, vol 6 'Bray Charles' 247.
73. M Hewitt, OUP, *Oxford Dictionary of National Biography*, ed David Cannadine (online at 20 September 2018) 'Watts, John (1818–1887)'.
74. On Ravenstone's reception in MCPE and HCPE, see Noel W Thompson, 'Piercy Ravenstone: Tory Democrat and Physiocratic Anti-Capitalist' in Nigel FB Allington and Noel W Thompson (eds), *English, Irish and Subversives among the Dismal Scientists* (Emerald, 1. ed, 2010) 303 ('PR').
75. Stafford (n 38) 200.
76. Thompson, 'PR' (n 74) 304–307.
77. As Read admitted in 1829, 'the science is at present in a very unsettled and unsatisfactory state. There is indeed scarcely a single doctrine… upon which there is a perfect and uniform, or even a general agreement': Samuel Read, *Political Economy. An Inquiry into the Natural Grounds of Right to Vendible Property, or Wealth* (Printed for the author, 1829) http://archive.org/details/politicaleconomyooreadrich; See Marian Bowley, *Nassau Senior and Classical Economics* (George Allen & Unwin, 1937) 91 for an example of Longfield, Senior, and Lauderdale as respectable 'dissenters' against Ricardo's theories.
78. Karl Marx and Frederick Engels, 'Manifesto of the Communist Party [First Published 1848]' in Terrell Carver (ed), *Marx: Later Political Writings* (Cambridge University Press, 1996) 1, 27.
79. Bailey (n 25) 21–22; cf. Charles Bray, *The Philosophy of Necessity: Or, the Law of Consequences: As Applicable to Mental, Moral and Social Science*, vol 2 (Longman, Orme, Brown, Green, and Longman, 1841) 438 http://archive.org/details/ThePhilosophyOfNecessityV2.
80. Bailey (n 25) 21.
81. Marx (n 71) 138.
82. EK Hunt, 'Value Theory in the Writings of the Classical Economists, Thomas Hodgskin, and Karl Marx' (1977) 9(3) *History of Political Economy* 322, 323.
83. For example, John E King, 'Utopian or Scientific? A Reconsideration of the Ricardian Socialists' (1983) 15(3) *History of Political Economy* 345; EK Hunt, 'The Relation of the Ricardian Socialists to Ricardo and Marx' (1980) 44(2) *Science & Society* 177; Esther Lowenthal, *The Ricardian Socialists*, vol 46 (Columbia University, 1911).
84. Thompson, *TPS* (n 21) 90.
85. See, for example, Hunt (n 82) 323.
86. Thompson, *TPS* (n 21) 82.

87. (n 38) 271.
88. Ibid. 239; see also Hunt (n 82) 333–337; Hopkins, another important critical social theorist, explicitly rejects the labour theory of value. See Thomas Hopkins, *Economical Enquiries Relative to the Laws Which Regulate Rent, Profit, Wages, and the Value of Money* (Published by Messrs. J. Hatchard, 1822) 52–53 ('*EE*').
89. Piercy Ravenstone, *A Few Doubts as to the Correctness of Some Opinions Generally Entertained on the Subjects of Population and Political Economy* (Printed for John Andrews, 1821) 209–219.
90. Claeys, *MMM* (n 24) 84.
91. Thompson, *TPS* (n 21) 102.
92. Ronald L Meek, *The Economics of Physiocracy: Essays and Translations* (Harvard University Press, 1963) 355–356.
93. Prum (n 35) 55.
94. See Claeys, *MMM* (n 24) xxii–xxvi for a critique of the incoherence and procrustean quality of doctrinal designations including 'Lockean', 'Smithian', and 'Ricardian' socialism.
95. Thompson, *TPS* (n 21).
96. King (n 83). While King resorts to the term 'Ricardian Socialism', fortunately he applies it loosely and so makes a wider survey of CST than most.
97. For examples of this kind of scholarship, see Diego Guerrero, *Sismondi, precursor de Marx* (Maia, 2011); Hunt (n 83); Eagleton (n 63).
98. Claeys, *MMM* (n 24); Claeys, *CAS* (n 24).
99. David McNally, *Against the Market: Political Economy, Market Socialism and the Marxist Critique* (New York: Verso, 1993) 62–138.
100. Ibid. 104–138; cf. Claeys, *MMM* (n 24) 1–33.

10 THE CRITIQUE OF DIFFERENTIAL RENT

1. Ronald L Meek, *Studies in the Labor Theory of Value* (Monthly Review Press, 2nd ed, 1973) 93.
2. Conway L Lackman, 'The Classical Base of Modern Rent Theory' (1976) 35(3) *American Journal of Economics and Sociology* 287, 291.
3. *An Enquiry into the Nature of the Corn-Laws with a View to the New Corn-Bill Proposed for Scotland* (Mundell, 1777).
4. Nigel FB Allington, 'John Rooke: Rent, Distribution, Money, and Repeal of the Corn Laws' in Nigel FB Allington and Noel W Thompson (eds), *English, Irish and Subversives among the Dismal Scientists* (Emerald, 1st ed, 2010) 243, 246; Edward R Kittrell, 'Wakefield and Classical Rent Theory' (1966) 25(2) *American Journal of Economics and Sociology* 141, 146; John M Hartwick, 'On the Development of the Theory of Land Rent' (1989) 65(4) *Land Economics* 410, 411n.

5. Jacob H Hollander, 'Introduction' in Jacob H Hollander (ed), *The Nature and Progress of Rent [1815]* (London, 1903) 3, 4 http://archive.org/details/inquiryintonaturoomaltuoft.
6. Thomas Robert Malthus, *The Nature and Progress of Rent [1815]*, ed Jacob H Hollander (The Johns Hopkins Press, 1903) 23 http://archive.org/details/inquiryintonaturoomaltuoft.
7. Marian Bowley, *Nassau Senior and Classical Economics* (George Allen & Unwin, 1937) 75.
8. On the exclusion of tributary rents from the theory, see Mountifort Longfield, *Lectures on Political Economy: Delivered in Trinity and Michaelmas Terms, 1833* (Richard Milliken and Son, 1834) 142.
9. Richard Jones, *Peasant Rents: Being the First Half of an Essay on the Distribution of Wealth and on the Sources of Taxation [First Published 1831]* (Macmillan, 1914) 167 http://archive.org/details/peasantrentsbeinoojonerich.
10. See, for example, Longfield (n 8) 142.
11. See David Ricardo, *On the Principles of Political Economy, and Taxation [First Published 1817]* (John Murray, 3rd ed, 1821) 7 http://archive.org/details/onprinciplespolooricagoog.
12. Ibid. 332–333.
13. Ibid. 60.
14. Nassau W Senior, *Political Economy [First Published 1850]* (Richard Griffin and Co., 3rd ed, 1854) 3.1 www.econlib.org/library/Senior/snP.html.
15. Ricardo (n 11) 86.
16. Ibid. 57.
17. Ibid. 59.
18. Ibid. 60; John Stuart Mill, *Principles of Political Economy with Some of Their Applications to Social Philosophy [First Published 1848]*, ed William J Ashley (Longmans, Green and Co., 7th ed, 1909) II.XVI.11 www.econlib.org/library/Mill/mlP.html.
19. See, for example, Ricardo (n 11) 128: 'In all countries, and all times, profits depend on the quantity of labour requisite to provide necessaries for the labourers, on that land or with that capital which yields no rent'.
20. Ibid. 61.
21. George Ramsay, *An Essay on the Distribution of Wealth* (A. and C. Black, 1836) 262.
22. Ricardo (n 11) 67.
23. Ibid. 76.
24. See, for example, ibid. 399.
25. Ibid. 400.
26. See ibid. 332–333: 'I always consider … [rent] as the result of a partial monopoly, never really regulating price, but rather as the effect of it'.
27. Malthus (n 6) 43; Ricardo (n 11) 332–333.

28. See, for instance, TR Edmonds, *Political, Moral and Social Economy: Founded upon Reason, Observation, and Science, and Combining 'the Greatest Happiness of the Greatest Number', in Opposition to the Anti-Social and Fallacious Theories of Modern Political Economists* (S. and R. Bentley for E. Wilson, 1831) 117, 123; William Thompson, *An Inquiry into the Principles of the Distribution of Wealth Most Conducive to Human Happiness [First Published 1824]*, ed William Pare (W.S. Orr, New ed, 1850) 431 https://archive.org/details/inquiryintoprincoothomrich ('*IPD*'); Thomas Hodgskin, *Labour Defended against the Claims of Capital, or, The Unproductiveness of Capital Proved [First Published 1825]* (Steil, 2nd ed, 1831) 6, 24 ('*LDC*'); John Gray, *The Social System: A Treatise on the Principle of Exchange* (W. Tait, 1831) 294–296; John Watts, *The Facts and Fictions of Political Economists: Being a Review of the Principles of the Science, Separating the True from the False* (A. Heywood [etc., etc.], 1842) 9–16.
29. William Stafford, *Socialism, Radicalism, and Nostalgia: Social Criticism in Britain, 1775–1830* (Cambridge University Press, 1987) 200–201; Ravenstone argued population and labour productivity was more important than soil fertility in determining rent levels, but he never dismissed the latter outright, see Piercy Ravenstone, *A Few Doubts as to the Correctness of Some Opinions Generally Entertained on the Subjects of Population and Political Economy* (Printed for John Andrews, 1821) 232; Ravenstone also directly applied differential reasoning when he said '[a]s rent is that which remains after paying the expense of cultivation, where that [i.e. rent] is highest the expense must be least'. See Piercy Ravenstone, *Thoughts on the Funding System and Its Effects* (Printed for J. Andrews, 1824).
30. JCL Simonde de Sismondi, *New Principles of Political Economy: Of Wealth in Its Relation to Population*, tr Richard Hyse (Transaction Publishers, 1991) 233 ('*NPPE*').
31. Ibid. 233 (translator's note).
32. Ibid. 233 (translator's note); JCL Simonde de Sismondi, *Political Economy and the Philosophy of Government; A Series of Essays Selected from the Works of M. de Sismondi. With an Historical Notice of His Life and Writings by M. Mignet [First Published 1837]* (John Chapman, 1847) 160 http://oll.libertyfund.org/titles/1963 ('*PEPG*').
33. JCL Simonde de Sismondi, 'Analysis of a Refutation of New Principles of Political Economy Published in the Edinburgh Review by a Follower of Mr. Ricardo [First Published 1820]' in Richard Hyse (trans), *New Principles of Political Economy: Of Wealth in Its Relation to Population* (Transaction Publishers, 1991) 599, 612 ('ARNP').
34. Sismondi, *NPPE* (n 30) 467.
35. Ricardo admitted capital was not perfectly mobile, but argued, that general social progress required the destruction of some capital, and

that such destruction could be mitigated by policies such as tapered protective tariffs. See Ricardo (n 11) 313, 318.

36. Sismondi, *NPPE* (n 30) 228.
37. Ibid.
38. Ibid.
39. Ibid. 469n.
40. Ibid. 467.
41. Ibid.
42. Ibid. 231.
43. Richard Hyse, 'Translator's Introduction' in *New Principles of Political Economy: Of Wealth in Its Relation to Population* (Transaction Publishers, 1991) xvii, xlii.
44. Sismondi, *NPPE* (n 30) 231–232.
45. Ibid. 231–232; The capitalist, for instance, 'dictates rent to the landlord, or gets it dictated, according to' the scarcity of capital: Ibid. 229.
46. Sismondi, *NPPE* (n 30) 232: 'sometimes the landlord not only receives the entire rent, but exacts a monopoly price whose loss is unequally divided between the farmer and consumer'.
47. JCL Simonde de Sismondi, 'On the Balance of Consumption with Production' in Richard Hyse (trans), *New Principles of Political Economy: Of Wealth in Its Relation to Population* (Transaction Publishers, 1991) 617, 626 ('BCP'); Sismondi, *NPPE* (n 30) 469n; also ibid. 229: 'The ownership of land always means something … where he [Ricardo] put zero he should at least have put one'.
48. Sismondi, *NPPE* (n 30) 229.
49. Sismondi, 'BCP' (n 47) 626.
50. Sismondi, *NPPE* (n 30) 228.
51. Ibid. 203.
52. Ibid.
53. Ibid.
54. On rent and proletarianisation, see ibid. 180–185.
55. 'After having sold his crop at a favorable price, and paid less to his hands, the planter of a thousand acres will be surely in a position to pay to the owner a larger rent than the fifty smallholders he will have displaced'.: Sismondi, *NPPE* (n 30).
56. Ibid. 181–182.
57. Ibid. 184.
58. For Sismondi, the Scottish Highland Clearances exemplified how the drive to maximise rents uprooted peasants in favour of capitalist agriculture. See ibid. 140.
59. Thomas Hopkins, *On Rent of Land, and Its Influence on Subsistence and Population: With Observations on the Operating Causes of the Condition of the Labouring Classes in Various Countries* (Hunt and Clarke, 1828) 12 ('*ORL*').

60. Ibid. 12–14, see also 4, 22.
61. Thomas Hopkins, *Great Britain, during the Last Forty Years: Being an Historical and Analytical Account Ofits Finances, Monetary System, Economy and General Condition during That Period* (J. Pigot, 2nd ed, 1840) 10 ('*GBLFY*').
62. Thomas Hopkins, *Economical Enquiries Relative to the Laws Which Regulate Rent, Profit, Wages, and the Value of Money* (Published by Messrs. J. Hatchard, 1822) 107 ('*EE*'). Emphasis added.
63. Hopkins, *GBLFY* (n 61) 12.
64. Ibid. Hopkins' theory of rent, based on the monopolisation of land, will be discussed further in the next chapter.
65. Hopkins, *ORL* (n 59) 30.
66. Ibid. 26–27.
67. Hopkins, *GBLFY* (n 61) 18.
68. Hopkins, *ORL* (n 59) 60–61.

11 CAPITALIST RENT AS PROLETARIANISATION

1. John Francis Bray, *Labour's Wrongs and Labour's Remedy, or, The Age of Might and the Age of Right* (D. Green, 1839) 35. Bray insisted women enjoyed equal human rights (p. 167), and that such rights could not be abrogated by a democratic majority (p. 36).
2. Ibid. 32.
3. Ibid. 84.
4. Ibid. 33; Cf. Charles Hall, *The Effects of Civilisation on the People in European States* (C. Gilpin, 1850) 149–150, who proposed the inhabitants of a country are 'entitled to the use of the produce of it for their subsistence'.
5. Bray (n 1) 33; Cf. Hall (n 4) 149–150, who proposed the inhabitants of a country are 'entitled to the use of the produce of it for their subsistence'.
6. Bray (n 1) 28.
7. See also Richard Hyse, 'Translator's Introduction' in *New Principles of Political Economy: Of Wealth in Its Relation to Population* (Transaction Publishers, 1991) xvii, 31; Cf. Piercy Ravenstone, *A Few Doubts as to the Correctness of Some Opinions Generally Entertained on the Subjects of Population and Political Economy* (Printed for John Andrews, 1821) 73: 'property, which is created for the good of society, incurs forfeiture, whenever forgetting its tenure, it becomes injurious to its interests'.
8. Thomas Hopkins, *Great Britain, during the Last Forty Years: Being an Historical and Analytical Account Ofits Finances, Monetary System, Economy and General Condition during That Period* (J. Pigot, 2nd ed, 1840) 6 ('*GBLFY*').

9. William Thompson, *Labour Rewarded. The Claims of Labour and Capital Conciliated, or, How to Secure to Labour the Whole Products of Its Exertions* (Printed for Hunt and Clarke by R. Taylor, 1827) 13 ('*LR*').
10. Thomas Spence, *The Rights of Infants; or, the Imprescriptable Right of Mothers to Such a Share of the Elements as Is Sufficient to Enable Them to Suckle and Bring up Their Young in a Dialogue between the Aristocracy and a Mother of Children. To Which Are Added, by Way of Preface and Appendix, Strictures on Paine's Agrarian Justice. [1797]* (University of Michigan Library, 2011) 7 http://name.umdl.umich.edu/004843040.0001.000.
11. Thomas Spence, 'The Real Rights of Man [First Published 1775]' in *The Pioneers of Land Reform: Thomas Spence, William Ogilvie, Thomas Paine, with an Introduction by M. Beer* (G. Bell and sons, ltd., 1920) 1, 9 www.archive.org/details/pioneersoflandreOOIondiala.
12. Spence (n 10) 15–16.
13. Ibid. 6.
14. Spence (n 10).
15. See, for example, ibid. 6.
16. Ibid. 3–4.
17. William Ogilvie, 'An Essay on the Right of Property in Land with Respect to Its Foundation in the Law of Nature, and the Rights of the People! [First Published 1781]' in *Birthright in Land* (K. Paul, Trench, Trübner, 1891) 1, 12–13 http://archive.org/details/birthrightinlanoomacdgoog: 'Rude nations have adhered to the first of these maxims, neglecting the second. Nations advanced in industry and arts have adhered to the second, neglecting the first'; Also, ibid. 11: 'In every country where agriculture has made considerable progress … labour is suffered to eclipse … occupancy'.
18. Ogilvie (n 17) 9n.
19. Ibid.
20. John Gray, *A Lecture on Human Happiness: Being the First of a Series of Lectures on That Subject, in Which Will Be Comprehended a General Review of the Causes of the Existing Evils of Society, and a Development of Means by Which They May Be Permanently and Effectually Removed* (Sherwood, Jones, & Co., 1825) 35.
21. Ibid.
22. Ibid. 52.
23. Ibid. 70.
24. Ibid.
25. See John Gray, *The Social System: A Treatise on the Principle of Exchange* (W. Tait, 1831) 238: 'Why is rent, interest, and profit, necessary for the support of certain classes of society, but because the classes who, for the most part, live thereby, are non-producers?'; also, ibid. 25: 'They give no equivalent for that which they consume. They obtain their incomes

from rent, interest, and the employment of capital'.; Gray's analysis of the rent-relation was adopted wholesale by the Owenite Socialist William Heighton in his *An Address to the Members of Trade Societies, and to the Working Classes Generally: Being an Exposition of the Relative Situation, Condition, and Future Prospects of Working People in the United States of America: Together with a Suggestion and Outlines of a Plan, by Which They May Gradually and Indefinitely Improve Their Condition* (s.n., 1827) 20.

26. Bray (n 1) 33. For Bray, these rights included the 'natural equality of the right to subsistence', 'the equal right of every human being' to the soil, and everyone's right to 'the fruits of his labour': Ibid.
27. Bray (n 1) 106.
28. Ibid. 137.
29. Ibid. 34.
30. Ibid. 106.
31. Ibid. 182.
32. Ibid. 187.
33. Ibid.
34. Ibid.
35. Charles Bray, *The Philosophy of Necessity: Or, the Law of Consequences: As Applicable to Mental, Moral and Social Science*, vol 2 (Longman, Orme, Brown, Green, and Longman, 1841) 397 http://archive.org/details/ThePhilosophyOfNecessityV2.
36. Ibid. 396–397.
37. Ibid. 386–387.
38. Ibid. 389.
39. Ibid. 389–390.
40. Hopkins (n 8) 6; Thomas Hopkins, *Economical Enquiries Relative to the Laws Which Regulate Rent, Profit, Wages, and the Value of Money* (Published by Messrs. J. Hatchard, 1822) 109 ('*EE*').
41. Hopkins (n 8) 8.
42. Hopkins (n 40) 109.
43. Ibid. 18.
44. Hopkins (n 8) 6. Note that Hopkins did not extend his critique to capitalists. Rather, he adopted the mainstream view that capitalists were 'merely in the possession and use of the fruits of their own industry, or of the industry of their fore-fathers' (ibid. 7). Capital, he insisted, was 'to some extent, always within the reach of the industrious and economical' (ibid.).
45. William Thompson, *An Inquiry into the Principles of the Distribution of Wealth Most Conducive to Human Happiness [First Published 1824]*, ed William Pare (W.S. Orr, New ed, 1850) 125 https://archive.org/details/inquiryintoprincoothomrich ('*IPD*').
46. Ibid. 405.

47. Ibid. 125.
48. Ibid. 126.
49. Ibid. 131.
50. Ibid.
51. Patrick Edward Dove, *The Theory of Human Progression, and Natural Probability of a Reign of Justice [First Published 1850]* (Sanborn & Carter, 1856) 351 http://archive.org/details/theoryhumanprog01dovgoog.
52. Ibid.
53. Ibid.
54. Ibid. Emphasis added.
55. Ibid. 382; Dove was not fully consistent, however, in attributing rent to labour, writing at ibid. 51: 'the land produces ... more than the value of the labor expended on it, and on this account men are willing to pay a rent'.
56. On the Hall-Smith connection, see William Stafford, *Socialism, Radicalism, and Nostalgia: Social Criticism in Britain, 1775–1830* (Cambridge University Press, 1987) 159.
57. Hall (n 4) 167–168.
58. Ibid.
59. See Thomas Hodgskin, *An Essay on Naval Discipline, Shewing Part of Its Evil Effects on the Minds of the Officers, on the Minds of the Men, and on the Community; with an Amended System by Which Pressing May Be Immediately Abolished* (Printed for the author by C. Squire, Furnival's-Inn-Court, 1813) 29, 166 http://lf-oll.s3.amazonaws.com/titles/322/0074_Bk.pdf; Thomas Hodgskin, *Popular Political Economy: Four Lectures Delivered at the London Mechanics' Institution ... [Book I]* (Printed for Charles Tait and William Tait, 1827) 165, 172; Thomas Hodgskin, *The Natural and Artificial Right of Property Contrasted: A Series of Letters, Addressed without Permission, to H. Brougham* (B. Steil, 1832) 145 ('*NAR*').
60. William Paley, *The Principles of Moral and Political Philosophy* (Liberty Fund, 2002) 430 http://oll.libertyfund.org/titles/paley-the-principles-of-moral-and-political-philosophy.
61. Ibid. 476.
62. Ibid. 430.
63. Hodgskin, *NAR* (n 59) 146n–147n.
64. Hodgskin, *An Essay on Naval Discipline, Shewing Part of Its Evil Effects on the Minds of the Officers, on the Minds of the Men, and on the Community; with an Amended System by Which Pressing May Be Immediately Abolished* (n 59) 173. These words antedate the writings of both Ricardo and Malthus on rent, belying Hodgskin's classification as a 'Ricardian Socialist'.
65. Hodgskin, *Popular Political Economy: Four Lectures Delivered at the London Mechanics' Institution ... [Book I]* (n 59) 29.

66. Thomas Hodgskin, *A Lecture on Free Trade in Connexion with the Corn Laws: Delivered ... on January 31, 1843* (s.n., 1843) 16; Thomas Hodgskin, *'Peace, Law, and Order': A Lecture Delivered in the Hall of the National Association on September 29, 1842* (Printed and published by H. Hetherington, 1842) 14.
67. John Watts, *The Facts and Fictions of Political Economists: Being a Review of the Principles of the Science, Separating the True from the False* (A. Heywood [etc., etc.], 1842) 9.
68. Ibid. 7.
69. Ibid. 9–10.
70. Ibid. 7.
71. See ibid. 8, 11.
72. T Wayland, *National Advancement and Happiness Considered in Reference to the Equalization of Property and the Formation of Communities* (E. Wilson, 1832) 18.
73. Ibid. 21.
74. Ibid.
75. Ibid. 20.
76. Ibid.
77. Ibid. 16–17.
78. Ravenstone (n 7) 200.
79. Ibid. 199–200.
80. Ibid. 234.

12 RENT AND CAPITALIST DOMINATION

1. Patrick Edward Dove, *The Theory of Human Progression, and Natural Probability of a Reign of Justice [First Published 1850]* (Sanborn & Carter, 1856) 331 http://archive.org/details/theoryhumanprog01dovgoog.
2. William Thompson, *Labour Rewarded. The Claims of Labour and Capital Conciliated, or, How to Secure to Labour the Whole Products of Its Exertions* (Printed for Hunt and Clarke by R. Taylor, 1827) 8 ('*LR*').
3. JCL Simonde de Sismondi, *New Principles of Political Economy: Of Wealth in Its Relation to Population*, tr Richard Hyse (Transaction Publishers, 1991) 572 ('*NPPE*').
4. Charles Hall, *The Effects of Civilisation on the People in European States* (C. Gilpin, 1850) 60.
5. John Francis Bray, *Labour's Wrongs and Labour's Remedy, or, The Age of Might and the Age of Right* (D. Green, 1839) 32.
6. Ibid. 182.
7. Hall (n 4) 167.
8. Ibid. 168.
9. Ibid.
10. Ibid. 167–168.

11. Thomas Hodgskin, *The Natural and Artificial Right of Property Contrasted: A Series of Letters, Addressed without Permission, to H. Brougham* (B. Steil, 1832) 51 ('*NAR*').
12. Ibid.
13. Ibid. 56.
14. Piercy Ravenstone, *A Few Doubts as to the Correctness of Some Opinions Generally Entertained on the Subjects of Population and Political Economy* (Printed for John Andrews, 1821) 206.
15. Ibid. 214.
16. Ibid. 201.
17. Charles Bray, *The Philosophy of Necessity: Or, the Law of Consequences: As Applicable to Mental, Moral and Social Science*, vol 2 (Longman, Orme, Brown, Green, and Longman, 1841) 429 http://archive.org/details/ThePhilosophyOfNecessityV2.
18. Ibid. 430.
19. Ibid. 431.
20. Thompson (n 2) 42.
21. William Thompson, *An Inquiry into the Principles of the Distribution of Wealth Most Conducive to Human Happiness [First Published 1824]*, ed William Pare (W.S. Orr, New ed, 1850) 139 https://archive.org/details/inquiryintoprincoothomrich ('*IPD*').
22. Thompson (n 2) 8.
23. Ibid. 7–8.
24. Thompson (n 21) 251; see also Thompson (n 2) 7.
25. Ravenstone (n 14) 206.
26. Ibid. 201.
27. Thompson (n 2) 11–12.
28. William Ogilvie, *Birthright in Land*, ed DC Macdonald (K. Paul, Trench, Trübner, 1891) 3 http://archive.org/details/birthrightinlanoomacdgoog.
29. Sismondi (n 3) 578n; see also ibid 184, 579–580, 583.
30. See William Ogilvie, 'An Essay on the Right of Property in Land with Respect to Its Foundation in the Law of Nature, and the Rights of the People! [First Published 1781]' in *Birthright in Land* (K. Paul, Trench, Trübner, 1891) 1, 61 http://archive.org/details/birthrightinlanoomacdgoog; Dove (n 1) 143; Piercy Ravenstone, *Thoughts on the Funding System and Its Effects* (Printed for J. Andrews, 1824) 72; Bray (n 5) 182; JCL Simonde de Sismondi, *Political Economy and the Philosophy of Government; A Series of Essays Selected from the Works of M. de Sismondi. With an Historical Notice of His Life and Writings by M. Mignet [First Published 1837]* (John Chapman, 1847) 115 http://oll.libertyfund.org/titles/1963 ('*PEPG*'); Sismondi (n 3) 189; although Sismondi viewed the Corn Laws as a monopoly designed to boost rents, he also argued their repeal could create unemployment as domestic production was substituted for imports: see ibid. 200–202.

31. Sismondi (n 3) 181.
32. Ibid. 92–93.
33. Ibid. 578n.
34. Ibid. 578.
35. Ogilvie (n 30) 44n.
36. Ibid. 44.
37. Ibid.
38. Ibid. 44n.
39. Dove (n 1) 392n.
40. Bray (n 5) 28.
41. Hodgskin, *NAR* (n 11) 97.
42. Ibid. 98.
43. Ibid.
44. Ibid. 97.
45. Ibid. 127. Hodgskin's reference to 'nature' here is idiosyncratic, in Hodgskin's idiom 'natural laws' and 'moral principles' were not purely normative, but also referred to 'rewards' or 'incitements', which would now be called 'incentives': see ibid 144–145, 145n.
46. Thomas Hodgskin, *A Lecture on Free Trade in Connexion with the Corn Laws: Delivered ... on January 31, 1843* (s.n., 1843) 13; Hodgskin had a similar analysis of usury laws, by which heavily indebted landlords sought to suppress finance capital, see Hodgskin, *NAR* (n 11) 98–101.
47. Thompson (n 2) 7; Cf. Thomas Hodgskin, *Labour Defended against the Claims of Capital, or, The Unproductiveness of Capital Proved [First Published 1825]* (Steil, 2nd ed, 1831) 19n ('*LDC*'). This exchange provides a rare example of a debate internal to CST.
48. Thompson (n 2) 7.
49. Ibid. 9.
50. Ibid.
51. Ibid. 7–8.
52. Ibid. 8.
53. Ibid. 9.
54. Ibid. 7.
55. Ravenstone (n 14) 212–214.
56. Thomas Spence, 'The Real Rights of Man [First Published 1775]' in *The Pioneers of Land Reform: Thomas Spence, William Ogilvie, Thomas Paine, with an Introduction by M. Beer* (G. Bell and sons, ltd., 1920) 1, 8–9 www.archive.org/details/pioneersoflandreOOIondiala; Thomas Hodgskin, *'Peace, Law, and Order': A Lecture Delivered in the Hall of the National Association on September 29, 1842* (Printed and published by H. Hetherington, 1842) 14. Although Spence did not explicitly adopt the Norman Yoke theory, certain of his followers did. See Christopher Hill, 'The Norman Yoke' in John Saville (ed), *Democracy and the Labour*

Movement: Essays in Honour of Dona Torr (Lawrence & Wishart, 1954) 11, 52 ('TNY-a').

57. Sismondi (n 3) 171–172.
58. Ibid.
59. Sismondi (n 30) 171.
60. Sismondi (n 3) 172n.
61. Sismondi (n 30) 188.
62. Sismondi (n 3) 172n.
63. Richard Hyse, 'Translator's Introduction' in *New Principles of Political Economy: Of Wealth in Its Relation to Population* (Transaction Publishers, 1991) xvii, 140.
64. Sismondi (n 30) 188.
65. Ibid.
66. Ibid. 144.
67. Sismondi (n 3) 571.
68. Ibid.
69. Ibid. 314.
70. Ibid.
71. Thomas Hopkins, *On Rent of Land, and Its Influence on Subsistence and Population: With Observations on the Operating Causes of the Condition of the Labouring Classes in Various Countries* (Hunt and Clarke, 1828) 45 ('*ORL*').
72. Ibid. 45–46.
73. Ibid. 45.
74. Ibid. 48.
75. Ibid.
76. Ibid 49n.
77. Ibid.
78. Ibid. 49.
79. Ibid.
80. Ibid. 48.
81. Ibid.
82. Ibid. 63.
83. Thomas Hopkins, *Economical Enquiries Relative to the Laws Which Regulate Rent, Profit, Wages, and the Value of Money* (Published by Messrs. J. Hatchard, 1822) 109 ('*EE*').
84. Hopkins (n 71) 24.

13 THE IDEOLOGY OF CAPITALIST RENT

1. JCL Simonde de Sismondi, *New Principles of Political Economy: Of Wealth in Its Relation to Population*, tr Richard Hyse (Transaction Publishers, 1991) 10 ('*NPPE*').

2. John Francis Bray, *Labour's Wrongs and Labour's Remedy, or, The Age of Might and the Age of Right* (D. Green, 1839) 25–26.
3. Charles Hall, *The Effects of Civilisation on the People in European States* (C. Gilpin, 1850) 170–171.
4. Karl Marx and Frederick Engels, 'Manifesto of the Communist Party [First Published 1848]' in Terrell Carver (ed), *Marx: Later Political Writings* (Cambridge University Press, 1996) 1, 18.
5. Patrick Edward Dove, *The Theory of Human Progression, and Natural Probability of a Reign of Justice [First Published 1850]* (Sanborn & Carter, 1856) 332 http://archive.org/details/theoryhumanprog01dovgoog.
6. Ibid.
7. Ibid.
8. Ibid.
9. Ibid. 6.
10. Bray (n 2) 27.
11. Ibid. 27–28.
12. Ibid. 27.
13. Thomas Spence, 'The Real Rights of Man [First Published 1775]' in *The Pioneers of Land Reform: Thomas Spence, William Ogilvie, Thomas Paine, with an Introduction by M. Beer* (G. Bell and sons, ltd., 1920) 1, 7 www.archive.org/details/pioneersoflandreOOlondiala.
14. Ibid.
15. William Ogilvie, 'An Essay on the Right of Property in Land with Respect to Its Foundation in the Law of Nature, and the Rights of the People! [First Published 1781]' in *Birthright in Land* (K. Paul, Trench, Trübner, 1891) 1, 18 http://archive.org/details/birthrightinlanoomacdgoog.
16. Ibid.
17. Piercy Ravenstone, *A Few Doubts as to the Correctness of Some Opinions Generally Entertained on the Subjects of Population and Political Economy* (Printed for John Andrews, 1821) 216.
18. Thomas Hodgskin, *Popular Political Economy: Four Lectures Delivered at the London Mechanics' Institution ... [Book I]* (Printed for Charles Tait and William Tait, 1827) 109.
19. Thomas Hodgskin, *The Natural and Artificial Right of Property Contrasted: A Series of Letters, Addressed without Permission, to H. Brougham* (B. Steil, 1832) 162 ('*NAR*').
20. Ibid. 145; see William Paley, *The Principles of Moral and Political Philosophy* (Liberty Fund, 2002) 286–288 http://oll.libertyfund.org/titles/paley-the-principles-of-moral-and-political-philosophy.
21. Paley (n 20) 286–288.
22. Ibid.
23. Hodgskin (n 19) 163.
24. Hall (n 3) 170–171.
25. Ibid.

26. Dove (n 5) 226.
27. Ibid.
28. William Thompson, *Practical Directions for the Speedy and Economical Establishment of Communities: On the Principles of Mutual Co-Operation, United Possessions and Equality of Exertions and of the Means of Enjoyments* (Strange and E. Wilson, 1830) 251–252 ('*PD*'). Further quotations in this paragraph refer to the same.
29. William Thompson, *An Inquiry into the Principles of the Distribution of Wealth Most Conducive to Human Happiness [First Published 1824]*, ed William Pare (W.S. Orr, New ed, 1850) 225 https://archive.org/details/inquiryintoprincoothomrich ('*IPD*').
30. Ibid.
31. Ibid.
32. Charles Bray, *The Philosophy of Necessity: Or, the Law of Consequences: As Applicable to Mental, Moral and Social Science*, vol 2 (Longman, Orme, Brown, Green, and Longman, 1841) 462–463 http://archive.org/details/ThePhilosophyOfNecessityV2.
33. Ibid.
34. Ibid.
35. Ibid. 463.
36. Sismondi, *NPPE* (n 1) 10.
37. Bray (n 32) 386.
38. John Watts, *The Facts and Fictions of Political Economists: Being a Review of the Principles of the Science, Separating the True from the False* (A. Heywood [etc., etc.], 1842) 7.
39. Thompson, *PD* (n 28) 252.
40. William Thompson, *Labour Rewarded. The Claims of Labour and Capital Conciliated, or, How to Secure to Labour the Whole Products of Its Exertions* (Printed for Hunt and Clarke by R. Taylor, 1827) 42 ('*LR*').
41. Thompson, *PD* (n 28) 262.
42. Bray (n 2) 27.
43. Dove (n 5) 369.
44. Ibid. 334.
45. Bray (n 2) 5.
46. Ibid. 4.
47. Ibid.
48. Ibid.
49. Ibid.
50. Ibid. 26.
51. Ibid.
52. Ibid. 27.
53. Hodgskin (n 19) 162.
54. Ibid. 163.
55. Dove (n 5) 51. Emphasis added.

56. Ibid. 226.
57. Ibid.
58. Spence (n 13) 9.
59. Ibid. 9.
60. Ibid. 8.
61. JCL Simonde de Sismondi, *Political Economy and the Philosophy of Government; A Series of Essays Selected from the Works of M. de Sismondi. With an Historical Notice of His Life and Writings by M. Mignet [First Published 1837]* (John Chapman, 1847) 144–145 http://oll.libertyfund.org/titles/1963 ('*PEPG*').
62. Ibid.
63. Sismondi, *NPPE* (n 1) 80.
64. Ibid. 80.
65. Ibid. 91.
66. Thompson, *IPD* (n 29) 131. Emphasis added.
67. Ibid. Emphasis added.
68. Thompson, *LR* (n 40) 96.
69. Ogilvie (n 15) 57.
70. Dove (n 5) 370.
71. Ravenstone (n 17) 214.
72. Ibid. 216.
73. Thomas Hopkins, *Great Britain, during the Last Forty Years: Being an Historical and Analytical Account Ofits Finances, Monetary System, Economy and General Condition during That Period* (J. Pigot, 2nd ed, 1840) 10 ('*GBLFY*').
74. Thomas Hopkins, *On Rent of Land, and Its Influence on Subsistence and Population: With Observations on the Operating Causes of the Condition of the Labouring Classes in Various Countries* (Hunt and Clarke, 1828) 56–57 ('*ORL*').
75. Hopkins (n 73) 10.
76. Bray (n 2) 29.
77. Ibid.
78. Ibid.
79. Dove (n 5) 255.
80. Ibid.
81. Ibid. 257.
82. All quotations in this paragraph are from ibid. 332.
83. Piercy Ravenstone, *Thoughts on the Funding System and Its Effects* (Printed for J. Andrews, 1824) 14.
84. Ravenstone (n 17) 208.
85. Ibid. 214.
86. Dove (n 5) 331.
87. Ibid.
88. Ibid. 333.

89. Ogilvie (n 15) 22n.
90. Ibid.
91. JCL Simonde de Sismondi, *Political Economy* (1815) 3.3 http://socserv2.socsci.mcmaster.ca/~econ/ugcm/3ll3/sismondi ('*PE*'); Sismondi, *NPPE* (n 1) 563n.
92. Sismondi, *PE* (n 91), chapter 3, paragraph 3.
93. Bray (n 2) 86.
94. Ibid.
95. Sismondi, *NPPE* (n 1) 10.

14 PROLETARIAN IMAGINARIES

1. Piercy Ravenstone, *A Few Doubts as to the Correctness of Some Opinions Generally Entertained on the Subjects of Population and Political Economy* (Printed for John Andrews, 1821) 206.
2. Ibid. 228.
3. Ibid. 226.
4. Ibid.
5. Ibid. 228–229.
6. Thomas Spence, 'The Real Rights of Man [First Published 1775]' in *The Pioneers of Land Reform: Thomas Spence, William Ogilvie, Thomas Paine, with an Introduction by M. Beer* (G. Bell and sons, ltd., 1920) 1, 10 www.archive.org/details/pioneersoflandreOOIondiala.
7. Ibid. 10–11.
8. Ibid. 11–12.
9. Thomas Spence, *The Rights of Infants; or, the Imprescriptable Right of Mothers to Such a Share of the Elements as Is Sufficient to Enable Them to Suckle and Bring up Their Young in a Dialogue between the Aristocracy and a Mother of Children. To Which Are Added, by Way of Preface and Appendix, Strictures on Paine's Agrarian Justice. [1797]* (University of Michigan Library, 2011) 8–9 http://name.umdl.umich.edu/004843040.0001.000; Spence believed two-thirds of the total rent take would be available for redistribution, see TM Parssinen, 'Thomas Spence and the Origins of English Land Nationalization' (1973) 34(1) *Journal of the History of Ideas* 135, 137.
10. Spence (n 9) 5.
11. Ibid. 15.
12. Patrick Edward Dove, *The Theory of Human Progression, and Natural Probability of a Reign of Justice [First Published 1850]* (Sanborn & Carter, 1856) 251n http://archive.org/details/theoryhumanprog01dovgoog.
13. Ibid. 381, 387.
14. Ibid. 387.
15. Ibid. 251–252.

16. On precedents for Ogilvie's 'progressive agrarian' principle, see William Stafford, *Socialism, Radicalism, and Nostalgia: Social Criticism in Britain, 1775–1830* (Cambridge University Press, 1987) 112.
17. William Ogilvie, 'An Essay on the Right of Property in Land with Respect to Its Foundation in the Law of Nature, and the Rights of the People! [First Published 1781]' in *Birthright in Land* (K. Paul, Trench, Trübner, 1891) 1, 20, 27 http://archive.org/details/birthrightinlanoomacdgoog.
18. Ibid. 92.
19. Ibid. 51–52.
20. Ibid. 16, 28, 51–52, 57, 79, 86, 100n.
21. Ibid. 54.
22. Ibid.
23. JCL Simonde de Sismondi, 'On the Balance of Consumption with Production' in Richard Hyse (trans), *New Principles of Political Economy: Of Wealth in Its Relation to Population* (Transaction Publishers, 1991) 617, 582 ('BCP').
24. JCL Simonde de Sismondi, *Political Economy and the Philosophy of Government; A Series of Essays Selected from the Works of M. de Sismondi. With an Historical Notice of His Life and Writings by M. Mignet [First Published 1837]* (John Chapman, 1847) 71 http://oll.libertyfund.org/titles/1963 ('*PEPG*').
25. Sismondi, 'BCP' (n 23) 563.
26. JCL Simonde de Sismondi, *New Principles of Political Economy: Of Wealth in Its Relation to Population*, tr Richard Hyse (Transaction Publishers, 1991) 143 ('*NPPE*').
27. Sismondi, *PEPG* (n 24) 194.
28. Ibid.
29. Thomas Hopkins, *On Rent of Land, and Its Influence on Subsistence and Population: With Observations on the Operating Causes of the Condition of the Labouring Classes in Various Countries* (Hunt and Clarke, 1828) 125 ('*ORL*').
30. Thomas Hopkins, *Economical Enquiries Relative to the Laws Which Regulate Rent, Profit, Wages, and the Value of Money* (Published by Messrs. J. Hatchard, 1822) 109 ('*EE*').
31. Ibid.
32. Ibid.
33. Hopkins (n 29) 125.
34. Charles Hall, *The Effects of Civilisation on the People in European States* (C. Gilpin, 1850) 222.
35. Ibid.
36. Ibid.
37. Gregory Claeys, *Machinery, Money and the Millennium: From Moral Economy to Socialism, 1815–60* (Polity Press, 1987) 30 ('*MMM*').
38. Stafford (n 16) 150.

39. Thomas Hodgskin, *The Natural and Artificial Right of Property Contrasted: A Series of Letters, Addressed without Permission, to H. Brougham* (B. Steil, 1832) 180 ('*NAR*').
40. Ibid.
41. Ibid.
42. Ibid.
43. Steven Vincent, 'Visions of Stateless Society' in Gareth Stedman Jones and Gregory Claeys (eds), *The Cambridge History of Nineteenth-Century Political Thought* (Cambridge University Press, 2011) 433, 450–452 http://universitypublishingonline.org/ref/id/histories/CBO9780511973581.
44. William Thompson, *Labour Rewarded. The Claims of Labour and Capital Conciliated, or, How to Secure to Labour the Whole Products of Its Exertions* (Printed for Hunt and Clarke by R. Taylor, 1827) 122 ('*LR*').
45. Ibid. 115.
46. Dove (n 12) 381.
47. Ibid.
48. William Thompson, *An Inquiry into the Principles of the Distribution of Wealth Most Conducive to Human Happiness [First Published 1824]*, ed William Pare (W.S. Orr, New ed, 1850) 447 https://archive.org/details/inquiryintoprincoothomrich ('*IPD*'); For an alternative exposition of Thompson's System of Mutual Co-operation, see Mark J Kaswan, *Happiness, Democracy, and the Cooperative Movement: The Radical Utilitarianism of William Thompson* (State University of New York Press, 2014) 128–131.
49. Thompson, *LR* (n 44) 111.
50. Ibid. 11.
51. Ibid. 15.
52. Ibid. 110.
53. William Thompson, *Practical Directions for the Speedy and Economical Establishment of Communities: On the Principles of Mutual Co-Operation, United Possessions and Equality of Exertions and of the Means of Enjoyments* (Strange and E. Wilson, 1830) 6 ('*PD*').
54. Gregory Claeys, *Citizens and Saints: Politics and Anti-Politics in Early British Socialism* (Cambridge University Press, 1989) 162 ('*CAS*').
55. Claeys (n 37) xxx.
56. Ibid. 97–100.
57. Kaswan (n 48) 129–130.
58. Claeys (n 54) 99–100, 318, 337.
59. Kaswan (n 48) 129–130.
60. John Francis Bray, *Labour's Wrongs and Labour's Remedy, or, The Age of Might and the Age of Right* (D. Green, 1839) 170.
61. Ibid. 162.
62. Ibid. 110; see also ibid. 161.

63. Bray (n 60) 181.
64. Charles Bray, *The Philosophy of Necessity: Or, the Law of Consequences: As Applicable to Mental, Moral and Social Science*, vol 2 (Longman, Orme, Brown, Green, and Longman, 1841) 465 http://archive.org/details/ThePhilosophyOfNecessityV2.
65. Ibid.
66. Ibid. 408.
67. Ibid. 423.
68. Ibid. 418.
69. John Gray, *The Social System: A Treatise on the Principle of Exchange* (W. Tait, 1831) 108–109.
70. Ibid. 36; Claeys (n 37) 148.
71. John Gray, *A Lecture on Human Happiness: Being the First of a Series of Lectures on That Subject, in Which Will Be Comprehended a General Review of the Causes of the Existing Evils of Society, and a Development of Means by Which They May Be Permanently and Effectually Removed* (Sherwood, Jones, & Co., 1825) 4.
72. Claeys (n 37) 124.
73. Ibid.
74. Gray (n 69) 31.
75. Ibid. 341.
76. Ibid. 33.
77. Ibid. 233.
78. Claeys (n 37) 124.
79. Ibid. 119–120.
80. Ibid. 124.
81. Ibid. 122–123.
82. Gray (n 69) 63–64; See also Claeys (n 37) 122, 127.
83. Gray (n 71) 70; see also Gray (n 69) 192, 205–206, 320; Claeys (n 37) 117.
84. Bray (n 64) 485.
85. Ibid. 485–486.
86. Bray (n 60) 160.
87. Ibid. 109.
88. Ibid. 161.
89. Thompson, *PD* (n 53) 10; note, however, that for Thompson the RFL was to be supplemented by a 'scheme of universal mutual insurance', covering contingencies such as the destruction of buildings, disease, accident, death, orphanage and misadventure: see Thompson, *LR* (n 44).
90. Bray (n 64) 456.
91. Thompson, *LR* (n 44) 117.
92. Ibid. 109.
93. Ibid. 73.

94. Thompson, *IPD* (n 48) 455; Bray (n 64) 420–421.
95. Bray (n 64) 419.
96. Ibid. 418.
97. Thompson, *LR* (n 44) 101.
98. Ibid. 118.
99. Bray (n 60) 169.
100. Bray (n 64) 464–465.
101. Thompson, *IPD* (n 48) 326–327.
102. Ibid.
103. Bray (n 64) 486.
104. James Napier Bailey, *Preliminary Discourse on the Objects, Pleasures, and Advantages of the Science of Society* (J. Hobson, 1840) 12.
105. Bray (n 60) 165.
106. Ibid. 167.
107. Ibid. 166.
108. Ibid.
109. Bray (n 64) 427.
110. Ibid. 486.
111. Thompson, *PD* (n 53) 248.
112. Thompson, *IPD* (n 48) 289.
113. Thompson, *PD* (n 53) 245.
114. Thompson, *IPD* (n 48) 289.
115. Thompson, *PD* (n 53) 253.
116. Thompson, *IPD* (n 48) 266.
117. Gray (n 71) 22–24; Claeys (n 37) 113.
118. Claeys (n 54) 164.
119. Bray (n 64) 486.
120. Thompson, *LR* (n 44) 42.
121. Ibid.
122. Ibid. 15.

15 DEPROLETARIANISATION

1. Patrick Edward Dove, *The Theory of Human Progression, and Natural Probability of a Reign of Justice [First Published 1850]* (Sanborn & Carter, 1856) 386 http://archive.org/details/theoryhumanprog01dovgoog.
2. William Thompson, *The Age of Harmony, or, A New System of Social Economy: Eminently Calculated to Improve the Circumstances of the Oppressed, Enslaved, and Impoverished Portion of the People of Great Britain and Ireland, Addressed to the Industrious Classes* (Printed and published by W. & W. Miller, 2nd ed, 1834) 9 ('*AOH*').
3. Charles Bray, *The Philosophy of Necessity: Or, the Law of Consequences: As Applicable to Mental, Moral and Social Science*, vol 2 (Longman,

Orme, Brown, Green, and Longman, 1841) 432 http://archive.org/details/ThePhilosophyOfNecessityV2.

4. John Francis Bray, *Labour's Wrongs and Labour's Remedy, or, The Age of Might and the Age of Right* (D. Green, 1839) 175.
5. Ibid.
6. William Thompson, *An Inquiry into the Principles of the Distribution of Wealth Most Conducive to Human Happiness [First Published 1824]*, ed William Pare (W.S. Orr, New ed, 1850) 455 https://archive.org/details/inquiryintoprincoothomrich ('*IPD*').
7. Ibid. 454.
8. Bray (n 3) 450.
9. Ibid. 472.
10. Ibid. 433.
11. Bray (n 4) 175.
12. Thomas Spence, *The Rights of Infants; or, the Imprescriptable Right of Mothers to Such a Share of the Elements as Is Sufficient to Enable Them to Suckle and Bring up Their Young in a Dialogue between the Aristocracy and a Mother of Children. To Which Are Added, by Way of Preface and Appendix, Strictures on Paine's Agrarian Justice. [1797]* (University of Michigan Library, 2011) 9 http://name.umdl.umich.edu/004843040.0001.000.
13. Ibid. 5.
14. Ibid. 9–10.
15. William Thompson, *Labour Rewarded. The Claims of Labour and Capital Conciliated, or, How to Secure to Labour the Whole Products of Its Exertions* (Printed for Hunt and Clarke by R. Taylor, 1827) 42 ('*LR*').
16. Thompson, *IPD* (n 6) 454.
17. T Wayland, *National Advancement and Happiness Considered in Reference to the Equalization of Property and the Formation of Communities* (E. Wilson, 1832) 2.
18. William Ogilvie, 'An Essay on the Right of Property in Land with Respect to Its Foundation in the Law of Nature, and the Rights of the People! [First Published 1781]' in *Birthright in Land* (K. Paul, Trench, Trübner, 1891) 1, xii http://archive.org/details/birthrightinlanoomacdgoog.
19. Ibid.
20. Ibid. 40–41.
21. Thompson, *IPD* (n 6) 433.
22. Wayland (n 17) 23.
23. Thomas Hopkins, *Wages, or, Masters and Workmen* (A. Wilkinson, 1831) 14 ('*WMW*').
24. Ibid.
25. Bray (n 3) 391.
26. Thompson, *LR* (n 15) 78.
27. Ibid. 79.

28. Bray (n 4) 101.
29. JCL Simonde de Sismondi, *New Principles of Political Economy: Of Wealth in Its Relation to Population*, tr Richard Hyse (Transaction Publishers, 1991) 146 ('*NPPE*').
30. JCL Simonde de Sismondi, *Political Economy and the Philosophy of Government; A Series of Essays Selected from the Works of M. de Sismondi. With an Historical Notice of His Life and Writings by M. Mignet [First Published 1837]* (John Chapman, 1847) 198–199 http://oll.libertyfund.org/titles/1963 ('*PEPG*'); see also ibid. 203.
31. Ogilvie (n 18) 101.
32. Spence (n 12) 3.
33. Ibid. 15.
34. William Heighton, *An Address to the Members of Trade Societies, and to the Working Classes Generally: Being an Exposition of the Relative Situation, Condition, and Future Prospects of Working People in the United States of America: Together with a Suggestion and Outlines of a Plan, by Which They May Gradually and Indefinitely Improve Their Condition* (s.n., 1827) 29.
35. Ibid. 27.
36. Ibid. 28.
37. Thompson, *IPD* (n 6) 455; see also ibid. 253.
38. Thompson, *LR* (n 15) 119.
39. Ibid. 118–119; Thompson, *IPD* (n 6) 455.
40. William Stafford, *Socialism, Radicalism, and Nostalgia: Social Criticism in Britain, 1775–1830* (Cambridge University Press, 1987) 118.
41. Sismondi (n 30) 172.
42. Gregory Claeys, *Machinery, Money and the Millennium: From Moral Economy to Socialism, 1815–60* (Polity Press, 1987) 125–129 ('*MMM*').
43. Gregory Claeys, *Citizens and Saints: Politics and Anti-Politics in Early British Socialism* (Cambridge University Press, 1989) 154–155 ('*CAS*').
44. Bray (n 4) 99.
45. Ibid. 36–37.
46. Ibid.
47. Ibid. 99.
48. Thompson, *IPD* (n 6) 449.
49. Thompson, *LR* (n 15) 119.
50. Claeys (n 43) 160–161.
51. Thompson, *IPD* (n 6) 455.
52. Ibid. 455, 249–253; Thompson, *LR* (n 15) 119.
53. Thompson, *LR* (n 15) 42.
54. Thompson, *IPD* (n 6) 418.
55. Ibid. 316.
56. Thompson, *LR* (n 15) 114.
57. Ibid. 94.

58. Thompson, *IPD* (n 6) 426.
59. Bray (n 4) 155.
60. William Thompson, *Practical Directions for the Speedy and Economical Establishment of Communities: On the Principles of Mutual Co-Operation, United Possessions and Equality of Exertions and of the Means of Enjoyments* (Strange and E. Wilson, 1830) i ('*PD*').
61. Ibid. 20; Thompson, *LR* (n 15) 108, 113; Bray (n 3) 407–408; Thompson, *AOH* (n 2) 17.
62. Thompson, *IPD* (n 6) 379.
63. Thompson, *LR* (n 15) 91.
64. See Bray (n 3) 479.
65. Ibid. 407–408; Robert Owen, *A New View of Society and Other Writings* (J. M. Dent and Sons Ltd., 1927) 164–165 http://archive.org/details/in.ernet.dli.2015.191267; Bray (n 4) 153; Thompson, *LR* (n 15) 102; Claeys (n 43) 164.
66. Claeys (n 42) 102.
67. Bray (n 3) 128, 407–408, 479.
68. Thompson, *IPD* (n 6) 276; Thompson, *LR* (n 15) 116; Thompson, *PD* (n 60) 11.
69. Thompson, *PD* (n 60) 18.
70. John Gray, *The Social System: A Treatise on the Principle of Exchange* (W. Tait, 1831) 32.
71. Owen (n 65) 164; see also ibid. 176.
72. Thompson, *PD* (n 60) 9; see also ibid. 15, 250; Thompson, *LR* (n 15) 91, 106–109.
73. Gray (n 70) 36.
74. Claeys (n 42) 86.
75. Thompson, *LR* (n 15) 91, 123.
76. Ibid. 91.
77. Thompson, *IPD* (n 6) 426; cf. Bray's statement that co-operatives would 'undermine the present system in all directions, and bring it down in ruins': Bray (n 4) 128.
78. See, for example, Bray (n 3) 477.
79. Bray (n 4) 135.
80. Ibid. 171; Cf. recent similar estimates of United Kingdom nominal Gross Domestic Product, at Stephen Broadberry and Bas van Leeuwen, *British Economic Growth and the Business Cycle, 1700–1870: Annual Estimates* (Working Paper No 20, Department of Economics, University of Warwick, September 2010) 32 (Figure 8) http://wrap.warwick.ac.uk/57326/.
81. Bray (n 4) 171.
82. Ibid.
83. Ibid. 132.
84. Ibid.

85. Ibid. 136.
86. Thompson, *IPD* (n 6) 453.
87. Ibid. 455.
88. Ibid. 454–455.
89. Ibid. 454.
90. Bray (n 4) 174.
91. Ibid. 172–173.
92. Ibid. 172.
93. Bray (n 3) 452.
94. Ibid. 396–397.
95. Ibid. 455.
96. Ibid. 454.
97. Ibid. 434.
98. Ibid. 428.
99. Ibid. 432.
100. Thomas Hodgskin, *The Natural and Artificial Right of Property Contrasted: A Series of Letters, Addressed without Permission, to H. Brougham* (B. Steil, 1832) 180.
101. Ibid. 180–181.
102. Ibid.
103. Ibid. 161.
104. Ibid.
105. Ibid.
106. Ibid. 145.
107. Sismondi (n 29) 298.
108. Ibid.
109. Sismondi (n 30) 199.
110. Ibid. 171–172.
111. Sismondi (n 29) 146.
112. Sismondi (n 30) 172.
113. Wayland (n 17) 18.
114. Ogilvie (n 18) 64.
115. Piercy Ravenstone, *A Few Doubts as to the Correctness of Some Opinions Generally Entertained on the Subjects of Population and Political Economy* (Printed for John Andrews, 1821) 201.
116. Ibid.
117. Ibid. 202.
118. Ibid.
119. Ibid. 206.
120. Ibid. 234.
121. Thomas Hopkins, *On Rent of Land, and Its Influence on Subsistence and Population: With Observations on the Operating Causes of the Condition of the Labouring Classes in Various Countries* (Hunt and Clarke, 1828) 41.

122. Ibid. 42.
123. Ibid. 44.
124. Ibid.
125. Ogilvie (n 18) 71.
126. Hopkins (n 121) 139.
127. See ibid. 101.
128. Ibid. 139.
129. Ogilvie (n 18) 71.

CONCLUSION: CAPITAL, MOTHER OF WHAT?

1. For a progressive rent-theoretical analysis, see Michael Hudson, *Killing the Host: How Financial Parasites and Debt Destroy the Global Economy* (ISLET, 2015). For two key conservative contributions, see Anne O Krueger, 'The Political Economy of the Rent-Seeking Society' (1974) 64(3) *The American Economic Review* 291; James M Buchanan, Robert D Tollison and Gordon Tullock, *Toward a Theory of the Rent-Seeking Society* (Texas A & M University, 1980).
2. On entrepreneurial rents, for example, see Magnus Henrekson and Mikael Stenkula, 'The Entrepreneurial Rent: The Value of and Compensation for Entrepreneurship' (2017) 6(1) *Journal of Entrepreneurship and Public Policy* 11.
3. See for example Ellen Meiksins Wood, *The Pristine Culture of Capitalism: A Historical Essay on Old Regimes and Modern States* (Verso, 1991) 16 ('*PCC*').
4. Neil Davidson, *Discovering the Scottish Revolution, 1692–1746* (Pluto, 2003) 73–74.
5. See Jason Moore on 'Cheap Nature' in 'The Capitalocene Part II: Accumulation by Appropriation and the Centrality of Unpaid Work/Energy' (2018) 45(2) *The Journal of Peasant Studies* 237.
6. On the persistence of tributary relations in colonial Ireland, especially plantation farming and English absentee landlordism, see Dean M Braa, 'The Great Potato Famine and the Transformation of Irish Peasant Society' (1997) 61(2) *Science & Society* 193.
7. Xavier Lafrance and Charles Post, 'Introduction' in Xavier Lafrance and Charles Post (eds), *Case Studies in the Origins of Capitalism* (Palgrave Macmillan, 2019) 1, 25–26.
8. On the Scottish transition to capitalism generally, see Davidson (n 4).
9. Ibid. 73–103.
10. Ibid. 167.
11. Ibid. 214–227, 275–282.
12. Ibid. 275.
13. On the French case, for instance, see Xavier Lafrance, 'The Transition to Industrial Capitalism in Nineteenth-Century France' in Xavier

Lafrance and Charles Post (eds), *Case Studies in the Origins of Capitalism* (Palgrave Macmillan, 2019) 111, 124–131; Stephen Miller, 'Peasant Farming in Eighteenth and Nineteenth-Century France and the Transition to Capitalism Under Charles de Gaulle' in Xavier Lafrance and Charles Post (eds), *Case Studies in the Origins of Capitalism* (Palgrave Macmillan, 2019) 87, 100–102.

14. Xavier Lafrance and Charles Post, 'Conclusion' in Xavier Lafrance and Charles Post (eds), *Case Studies in the Origins of Capitalism* (Palgrave Macmillan, 2019) 343, 347.
15. Ibid.
16. On kin-ordered social property relations, see Eric R Wolf, *Europe and the People without History* (University of California Press, 2010) ('*EPWH*').
17. See, for example, Charles Post, *The American Road to Capitalism: Studies in Class-Structure, Economic Development, and Political Conflict, 1620–1877* (Brill, 2011) ('*The American Road*').
18. David Harvey, 'The "New" Imperialism: Accumulation by Dispossession' (2004) 40 *Socialist Register* 76 https://socialistregister.com/index.php/srv/article/view/5811.
19. Karl Marx, *Capital: A Critique of Political Economy [First Published 1867]*, tr David Fernbach, vol 1 (Penguin Books in association with New Left Review, 1976) 874–876. For a summary of processes of 'primitive accumulation', see Harvey (n 18) 74.
20. As Nichols has documented, there is a long subaltern tradition that links property to theft, especially in the settler-colonial context: *Theft Is Property! Dispossession & Critical Theory* (Duke University Press, 2020).
21. David Harvey, *The New Imperialism* (Oxford University Press, 2003) 141; Patel and Moore's account of capital's search for 'cheap labour' frames things similarly: *A History of the World in Seven Cheap Things: A Guide to Capitalism, Nature, and the Future of the Planet* (University of California Press, 2017).
22. Harvey (n 21) 146.
23. Ibid. 149. Emphasis added.
24. Ibid. 153.
25. Ibid. 29, 89.
26. Ibid. 162.
27. Harvey acknowledges, for instance, that hitherto non-capitalist states may orchestrate proletarianisation for 'predominantly internal' reasons, but does not specify what these reasons are. See ibid. 154–155.
28. Marx, *Capital: A Critique of Political Economy [First Published 1867]* (n 19).
29. Evgeny Morozov, 'Critique of Techno-Feudal Reason' [2022] (133/134) *New Left Review* 89.

30. Henry Bernstein, '"The Peasantry" in Global Capitalism: Who, Where and Why?' (2001) 37 *Socialist Register* 25, 29.
31. Ibid. 31–32.
32. On the persistence of contemporary peasantries, see Jan Douwe van der Ploeg, *The New Peasantries: Rural Development in Times of Globalization* (Routledge, Taylor & Francis Group, 2nd ed, 2018). On the persistence of peasant-tributary relations in India, see Krishna Bharadwaj, 'A View on Commercialisation in Indian Agriculture and the Development of Capitalism' (1985) 12(4) *The Journal of Peasant Studies* 7; Guruprasad Kar, 'The Enduring Prevalence of Semi-Feudal Agrarian Relations in India' (2018) 21(2) *Journal of Labor and Society* 193. On the Chinese case, see Jan Douwe van der Ploeg and Jingzhong Ye (eds), *China's Peasant Agriculture and Rural Society: Changing Paradigms of Farming* (Routledge, 1st ed, 2016).
33. National statistical definitions of employment increasingly exclude own-use or non-market agricultural production, making it difficult to measure. See Benjamin Davis et al. *Estimating Global and Country-Level Employment in Agrifood Systems* (No 23–34, FAO, 2023) 6–7 https://doi.org/10.4060/cc4337en. Further, from the perspective of social-property relations, market-oriented production by capitalists is distinct from subsistence farmers marketing their surpluses. Capitalist wage labour is likewise distinct from subsistence farmers employing or seeking seasonal wage labour. Labour and commodity market statistics do not generally capture these distinctions.
34. Ibid. 14. This includes people employed in agrifood production and associated trade and transport.
35. Sarah K Lowder, Marco V Sánchez and Raffaele Bertini, 'Which Farms Feed the World and Has Farmland Become More Concentrated?' (2021) 142 *World Development* 105455, 2.
36. Ibid.
37. Ibid.
38. Josias Láng-Ritter, Marko Keskinen and Henrikki Tenkanen, 'Global Gridded Population Datasets Systematically Underrepresent Rural Population' (2025) 16(1) *Nature Communications* 2170.
39. Karl Marx, *Grundrisse. Foundations of the Critique of Political Economy [Composed 1857–1858]* (Vintage Books, 1973) 105.
40. As Chattopadhyay has argued, the Soviet state was consciously and systematically driven by the goal of competing with developed capitalist states, and, in service of that goal, systematically expropriated (proletarianised) the Soviet peasantry. See Paresh Chattopadhyay, *The Marxian Concept of Capital and the Soviet Experience: Essay in the Critique of Political Economy* (Praeger, 1994) 61–63. Postone, as another example, characterises the 'actually existing socialism' of the twentieth century as a 'rigid, vulnerable, and oppressive form of state-interventionist capital-

ism': *Time, Labor, and Social Domination A Reinterpretation of Marx's Critical Theory* (Cambridge University Press, 1993) 14n.

41. World Bank, *Global Economic Prospects, June 2024* (World Bank, 2024) 5 https://openknowledge.worldbank.org/server/api/core/bitstreams/6feb9566-e973-4706-a4e1-b3b82a1a758d/content.
42. Sally Sargeson, 'The Demise of China's Peasantry as a Class' (2016) 14(13) *The Asia-Pacific Journal* 1.
43. See Slavoj Žižek, 'How to Begin from the Beginning' (2009) 57 *New Left Review* 43.
44. World Bank, 'GDP Growth (Annual %) – China', *World Bank Open Data* https://data.worldbank.org.
45. UN Trade and Development, 'Now 8 Billion and Counting: Where the World's Population Has Grown Most and Why That Matters', *UNCTAD* (15 November 2022) https://unctad.org/data-visualization/now-8-billion-and-counting-where-worlds-population-has-grown-most-and-why.
46. Ibid.
47. Ibid.
48. Natalia V Bhattacharjee et al. 'Global Fertility in 204 Countries and Territories, 1950–2021, with Forecasts to 2100: A Comprehensive Demographic Analysis for the Global Burden of Disease Study 2021' (2024) 403(10440) *The Lancet* 2057.
49. John Bongaarts and Dennis Hodgson, 'Fertility Trends in the Developing World, 1950–2020' in John Bongaarts and Dennis Hodgson (eds), *Fertility Transition in the Developing World* (Springer International Publishing, 2022) 1 https://doi.org/10.1007/978-3-031-11840-1_1.
50. See, for example: Shamil Ismail, *The Age of Decay: How Aging and Shrinking Populations Could Usher in the Decline of Civilization* (Shamil Ismail, 2023); Charles Goodhart and Manoj Pradhan, *The Great Demographic Reversal: Ageing Societies, Waning Inequality, and an Inflation Revival* (Palgrave Macmillan, 1st ed, 2020); Darrell Bricker and John Ibbitson, *Empty Planet: The Shock of Global Population Decline* (Crown, 1st ed, 2019); Eric Kaufmann, *Shall the Religious Inherit the Earth?: Demography and Politics in the Twenty-First Century* (Profile Books, 2010); Ben J Wattemberg, *Fewer: How the New Demography of Depopulation Will Shape Our Future* (Ivan R. Dee, 1st ed, 2004).
51. Chris Harman and Robert Brenner, 'The Origins of Capitalism' 111(Summer 2006) *International Socialism* www.marxists.org/archive/harman/2006/xx/wbrenner.htm.
52. Yanis Varoufakis, *Technofeudalism: What Killed Capitalism* (Melville House, 2024); Joel Kotkin, *The Coming of Neo-Feudalism: A Warning to the Global Middle Class* (Encounter Books, Reprint edition, 2023).
53. See, for example, Kotkin (n 52); Cédric Durand, 'Scouting Capital's Frontiers' [2022] (136) *New Left Review* 29; Jodi Dean, *Capital's Grave:*

Neofeudalism and the New Class Struggle (Verso, 2025); Varoufakis (n 52).

54. Varoufakis (n 52) 1.
55. Ibid. 1–2.
56. Dean (n 53) 15.
57. Ibid.
58. Durand (n 53) 33.
59. Ibid. 39.
60. (n 29) 125.
61. By contrast, Durand sees 'political intervention' to support profitability as a sign of a break from capitalism: (n 53) 32.
62. On 'techno-capitalism' see Morozov (n 29) 125–126; and Timothy Erik Ström, 'Capital and Cybernetics' [2022] (135) *New Left Review* 23.
63. Takēs Phōtopoulos, *Towards an Inclusive Democracy: The Crisis of the Growth Economy and the Need for a New Liberatory Project* (Cassell, 1997); Peter Frase, *Four Futures: Life after Capitalism: Visions of the World after Capitalism* (Verso, 2016).
64. Frank Herbert, *Dune* (Hodder & Stoughton, 50th anniversary edition, 2005).
65. Margaret Atwood, *The Handmaid's Tale* (Vintage, 2017).
66. Karl Marx, 'A Correspondence of 1843' in David McLellan (ed), *Early Texts* (Barnes & Noble, 1971) 74.

Index

absolutism 82–4
  see also tributary absolutism
agency, and social-property relations 16–18, 20–2
agent-structure dualism 28–33
agrarian capitalism 79, 82, 111–2, 151–2
agrarian economies 226
agriculture 75, 116–8, 155
  see also capitalist agriculture; subsistence farming
Alexander II, Pope 38
Anderson, James 137, 150
Anievas, Alexander 57, 111
anti-clericalism 67–8, 90
aristocracy 109–15, 121–4, 175, 179
artificial intelligence (AI) 227
artisans 122
Atwood, Margaret *The Handmaid's Tale* 232
Avian flu 27

Bacon, Francis 137
Bailey, James Napier 66, 146
Bailey, Samuel 137, 139
Ball, John 67–70
Banks, Iain M. *Culture* (novels) 232
Barons War
  1st (1215-17) 49
  2nd (1263-67) 50
Bastiat, Frédéric 138
Beckett, J.V. 110, 112
benevolences 43
Bentham, Jeremy 143
Bernstein, Henry 225
Bieler, Andreas 15–16
Big Tech 227
birth rate, fall in 228–9
Black Death 24, 26–7, 57–8, 60, 74, 216
Blaney, David 4
Bois, Guy 29
Bonney, Richard 84
Brailsford, Henry Noel 95–6
Bray, Charles 144, 164, 182, 170–1, 203, 207
  on collective ownership 194–8
  on self-emancipation 209–10
  on the working class 200–1, 208
  Philosophy of Necessity 144, 170
Bray, John Francis 146, 174, 203
  on the capitalist rent relations 169–70
  on class ideology 179–80, 183, 187–8
  on collective ownership 194–8
  on equal rights 160
  on inequality 186–8
  on political reform 205
  on the working class 201, 208
  Labour's Wrongs and Labour's Remedy 144
Brenner, Robert 56, 11, 23–4, 37, 39, 54, 55, 57–8, 95, 122, 218, 225, 229
  on the New Model Army 87–8
  on political accumulation 35–6
  on rules of reproduction 15, 17
  on social-property relations 12–13, 19–20, 29, 31–3
  on yeomanry 75
British capitalism 109–11, 133, 223
Buchanan, David 137
burgage 42
Burke, Edmund *Reflections on the French Revolution* 114, 121

Bush, M.L. 133

Callinicos, Alex 29
Cantillon, Richard 137
capitage (levy) 42
capital
  accumulation by dispossession 224
  primitive accumulation 24, 224–5
capitalism 1–2, 11, 14, 108
  landlord-led capitalism 118
  proto-capitalism 22–3
  see also agrarian capitalism; British capitalism
capitalist agriculture 77, 82, 112, 115–6, 154
capitalist dynamics, endogenous transformation of 209–12
capitalist pastoralism 75, 178
capitalist rent relations 79–83, 90–1, 94–5, 117, 119, 123–4, 162–8, 212–3, 217
  resistance to 125–34
Charles I, King 86–7
Charles II, King 89
Chartism 115, 126–32
chevage (levy) 42
childwite (fine) 42
China 224, 227–8
Church, the 45, 64–5, 90
  ideological role of 64–5
  relations with Crown 52–4
  and rents 52, 64
  see also anti-clericalism
Claeys, Gregory 131, 133, 143
  Citizens and Saints 148
  Machinery, Money and the Millenium 148
class 25, 26, 29
  as 'prime mover' 30, 32
  see also aristocracy; Idle Class; lords; middle class; ruling class; working class
class ideology 61–2, 64, 179–88, 201
Clay, C.G.A. 84, 88
climate change 27, 227
collective ownership 193–9
colonization 54, 223
Combination Act (1799) 122
commercialisation 23, 46–7, 178, 225–6
competition 152–3, 155, 194–5
competitive rent relation 74–8, 91–2, 107, 115–6, 177, 217
cooperative social-property relations 196–8
cooperativism 206–9
copyholds 58, 74, 77–8, 96, 116
Corn Laws 112–3, 154, 171, 174
Coster, Robert 100–4
  A Mite Cast into the Common Treasury 102
Court of Wards and Liveries 84, 86, 88
Covid-19 pandemic 27
craft workers 122
Critical Social Theory 13, 135–49, 159–60, 214, 218–20, 225, 231
Cromwell, Oliver 88–9, 97
Crown, the 37–45, 49–52
  and enclosures 81–2
  relations with Church 52–4
  relations with landlords 90–3
  relations with lords 37–41, 43, 51, 59–60, 83–5
  relations with Parliament 84–90, 109–10, 135–6
  transition into state 79–82
Crown rents 48, 83–4
currency and coinage 84–5

Danegelt 38
Davenport, Allen 126–7
Davidson, Neil 221–2
Davis, Mike 27
Dean, Jodi 3, 10, 230
developing countries 227–8
Diggers 13, 72, 97–106, 218

Dimmock, Spencer 58, 74–5, 81, 93
Dissolution of the Monasteries 90–1, 97
Dobb, Maurice 11
Domesday Book 40
Dove, Patrick Thomas Rowe 144, 169, 173, 193, 200
  on capitalist rent 165–6
  on class ideology 179, 181, 183–4, 186–7
  on political economy 140
  on the proletariat 190
  The Theory of Human Progression 144
Dudley, Edmund 137
Durand, Cédric 10, 230–1
Dyer, Christopher 41, 59, 78

East India Company 113
Economist 143
Edinburgh Review 142
Edmonds, Thomas Rowe 140, 144, 146
  An Enquiry into the Principles of Population 144
Edward I, King 50
Eliot, George 144
Elizabeth I, Queen 85
enclosures 76–9, 81–2, 107, 120–2
  resistance against 93
  violent enforcement of 78, 92
Engels, Friedrich 144
England
  Anglo-Saxon era 37–9
  rent relation in 37–9
  monarchy *see* Crown, the
English Civil War 84–5, 87, 97
English Revolution 87–8, 217
entry fines 42, 47, 54, 58, 77–8
Epstein, S.R. 24
European feudalism 34, 36–7

Fagan, H. 53
Feefarm 42
feudal incidents 43, 84
feudalism 2, 37, 178
  federalised feudalism 40–1
  techno-feudalism 2–3, 230–2
food prices 151–4
Foxwell, Herbert 146
freehold property rights 96, 121, 169, 176
French Revolution 113–4, 125–6, 211–2
Froissart, Jean *Chronicles* 69–70

George, Henry 1
Global Financial Crisis (2008) 227
Glorious Revolution (1688) 114, 118, 121
Gray, John 139, 143–4, 147, 162–3, 195, 198, 205, 207
  The Social System 195
Great Contract (1610) 86

Hales, Robert de 67
Hall, Charles 147, 166, 169, 170, 181, 192
  The Effects of Civilisation on the People in the European States 141
Harvey, David 224
hegemony 111–4
Heighton, William 204
Henry VIII, King 81, 84–5, 90
Herbert, Frank *Dune* 232
heriot (death duty) 42
Highland Clearances 176
Hill, Christopher 64–5, 70–2, 87, 91
Hilton, Rodney H. 44, 47–8, 53, 55, 64–5, 66, 69–70
historical change 24–8
historicism 31
Hodgskin, Thomas 139, 143, 146–7, 166–7, 170, 175, 180–1, 183, 192–3
  debate with Thompson 174–5
  on self-emancipation 210–1
  Labour Defended 143

Hopkins, Thomas 139–40, 142–3, 157, 160, 164, 185–6, 192, 212–3
 on the rent relations 177–8
 on violence 203
Hundred Years War 56
husbandmen 74, 76, 116
Hyse, Richard 154

Idle Class 171, 175
imperialism 221
Inayatullah, Naeem 4
Industrial Revolution 111, 117–8, 223
industrialisation 79
intellectuals 183–4

Jacobite Rebellion (1745) 222–3
James I, King of England 85, 86
John, King 49
Jones, Richard 137
 Peasant Rents 151
Justices of the Peace 60

Kaswan, Mark J. 194
Kett's Rebellion (1549) 93
King, John E. 147
King Horn (chivalric romance) 62–3
Knafo, Samuel 29–33
Konings, Martijn 20
Kotkin, Joel 230
 The Coming of Neo-Feudalism 2

labour
 forced labour 41
 unfree labour 41
 wage labour 57, 79, 172
Lachmann, Richard 85
Lafrance, Xavier 24, 220, 223
land 184–5
 common ownership of 197–9
 royal demesne 41, 43–5
 see also copyhold; freehold; leasehold
land improvements 119–20
land taxes 88–9
landlessness 156, 161–2, 164
landlord absenteeism 118–9
landlords 75–9, 169–70, 184–5
 relations with Crown 90–3
leasehold tenures 74, 115, 176
Levellers 72, 94–7, 98
Levellers' Agreement (1649) 95
leyrwite (fine) 42
Litster, Geoffrey 67
Locke, John 114, 137
Lollards 52–3
 and the Twelve Conclusions 52–3
Long Parliament 87
London 116–7
Longfield, Mountifort 137
lords and lordship 69–71
 hierarchies of 36
 ideology of 61–2
 junior and senior 42
 relations with Crown 37–41, 43, 51, 59–60, 83–5
 relations with peasants 34–6, 44–5, 61, 63
 see also landlords

Macfarlane, Alan 23
Magna Carta 49
Malthus, Thomas Robert 137, 141, 142, 145, 151, 153, 212
 Inquiry into the Nature and Progress of Rent 150
 Observations on the Effects of the Corn Laws 150
manorial courts 40–1, 78, 107
Martin, David 81, 127
Marx, Karl and Marxism 6–7, 11–13, 21–2, 34, 168, 179, 216, 224, 232
 on Critical Social Theory 147–9
 on Utopianism 145–6
 The German Ideology 7
 Das Kapital 7, 225

The Poverty of Philosophy 144
see also Political Marxists
McCulloch, John Ramsay 137, 138, 142
McNally David, *Against the Market* 148
Meek, Ronald L. 147
merchet (fine) 42
meritocracy 175
middle class 113–4, 127
Mill, James 137
Commerce Defended 143
Mill, John Stuart 143
Principles of Political Economy 137
Montfort, Simon de 50
Morozov, Evgeny 225
Morton, Adam 15–16
Mudie, George 141, 143, 207

Napoleonic Wars 113
neoliberalism 2
New Model Army 87–8
Newport Rising (1839) 128
Nişancioğlu, Kerem 57, 111
noblesse oblige 187–8
Norman Conquest (1066) 26–7, 38–41, 70–1
Norman Yoke 68, 70–2, 126, 128–9

O'Brien, Bronterre 128, 131
O'Connor, Feargus 128–30
Land Plan 129–30
Ogilvie, William 141, 161–2, 171, 173, 185, 187, 191, 204, 211–2, 213
on ideology 180, 187
on violent revolution 202–3
An Essay on the Right of Property in Land 141
Old Bourgeoisie 113
Old Corruption 113–4, 127, 131
Olney, R.J. 112
Ordinance for Removing the Court of Wards (1646) 88
Overton, Richard 96
Owen, Robert and Owenism 132–4, 141, 143–4, 148, 194, 206–8
Lectures on an Entire New State of Society 132

Paine, Thomas 204
Agrarian Justice 126
Rights of Man 126
Paley, William 166–7, 181
Principles of Moral and Political Philosophy 166
paradox of consent 179–81
Parliament 49–51
House of Commons 50
House of Lords 49–50
relations with Crown 84–90, 109–10, 135–6
peasants
proletarianisation of 76, 78–9, 177, 189–92, 218, 226
relations with lords 34–6, 44–5, 61, 63
resistance by 44, 65–7, 93–106
Peasants' Revolt (1381) 53, 59, 66–9
Petition of Right 86
Petrie, George 126–7
Petty, William 137, 138
Treatise of Taxes and Contributions 137
Physiocrats 147
Piers Ploughman (poem) 63–4
political accumulation 35–6, 54–6
Political Economy 135–40, 157
Political Marxists 13, 24–5, 29–33
Poor Laws 171
population growth 54–6, 228
Post, Charles 24, 30–3, 220, 223
Poulantzas, Nicos 108, 111
prerogatives 85–6, 87
Protestantism 84, 90–1
Prum, Michel 140
Puller, Christopher 145

Puller, Richard *see* Ravenstone, Piercy
purveyance 86

Quesnay, François 138

Ravenstone, Piercy 146–7, 154, 170–1, 175, 180, 185–7, 212
  on the proletariat 189–90
  on right to fruits of labour 168
  A Few Doubts as to the Correctness of Some Opinions Generally Entertained on the Subjects of Population and Political Economy 144–5
Read, Samuel 138
Reformation 81, 90, 217
rent 1–3, 6, 115–6, 219
  consumer rent 1
  differential rent 150–8, 185–6
  federalised rent relation 5
  ideology of 186
  money rents 41, 47–9
  paretian rent 1
  as reciprocity 62–4
  subaltern rent theory 6
  tradition of 185
  see also capitalist rent; competitive rent; tributary rent
Restoration, the (1660) 83, 89, 110
Ricardian socialism 145–8
Ricardo, David 137, 139, 141, 142, 145, 150, 152–4, 166
  Principles of Political Economy and Taxation 150
right to fruits of labour 99–100, 160–8
right to the earth 100–1, 106, 159–64, 167–8, 191, 194–5, 200, 202
Riot Act (1715) 122
Rioux, Sébastien 26
Roebuck, Peter 118–9
Rosehill Circle 144
rules of reproduction 15, 17–18, 21–2, 33
ruling class 179–84

Say, Jean-Baptiste 138, 142
Scheidel, Walter 66
Schumpeter, Joseph 219
Scotland 39, 176
  tributary metamorphosis of 222
  union with England (1603) 222–3
scutage (tax) 48
seigneurial charges 42
seigneurial courts 40–1, 42
self-emancipation 202, 204, 206–7, 209–11, 214
Senior, William Nassau 137–8, 152
serjeanty tenure 42
ship money 86, 87
Silk Road 27, 57
Sismondi, Jean Charles Léonard de 142, 160, 169, 182, 184–5, 187, 191–2, 204–5
  on differential rent theory 150, 154–7
  on political economy 140
  on proletarianisation 171–3, 229
  on the rent relations 176–7
  on revolution 203–4
  on self-emancipation 211–2
  De La Richesse Commerciale 142
  *Nouveaux principes d'économie politique*142, 154, 154
  'political economy' 142
slavery 186
Smith, Adam 11, 23, 137, 138–9, 141, 166
  Lectures on Jurisprudence 13
  On the Wealth of Nations 141
Smith, Richard 98
social change, non-transformation accounts of 22–4
social science 139–40, 219–20

social-property relations 3–4, 11–23, 228
  endogenous transformation of 4, 15, 19–21, 215–6
  see also tributary social-property relations
socialism *see* Ricardian socialism; utopian socialism
Sonship (relation with God as father) 99–100
Spence, Thomas 126, 131, 141, 160–1, 175, 180, 184
  rent and the proletariat 190, 204
  on self-emancipation 202
  The Real Rights of Man 141
Spencean Clubs 141–2
Sraffa, Pierro 145
Stafford, William 146, 154
state, the 80, 136, 170–1
  relations with the Church 183
state violence 170–1
Steuart, James 137
strikes 123
structuralism 29–30, 32
Stuart dynasty 84–5, 110
subinfeudation 40, 54
subsistence farming 48, 74–6, 116, 156–7
Sudbury, Simon, Archbishop of Canterbury 67
Sweezy, Paul 11

tallage (tax) 44
Tallagio non Concedendo (tax) 51
taxation 50, 88–9, 111
  subsidies 50–1, 59
tenants, competition for 58, 74–8, 119–20, 216–7
Tenures Abolition Act (1660) 89
Teschke, Benno 29–33
Thirty Years War 86
Thompson, Noel 146–7
Thompson, William 139, 143, 146–7, 169, 171, 185, 204
  on class ideology 181–3, 200–1
  on collective ownership 193–4
  on cooperativism 206–8
  debate with Hodgskin 174–5
  on democracy 205–6
  on Idle Class 171
  on passive resistance 208–9
  on right to fruits of labour 160, 165
  on violence 202–3
  Labour Rewarded 143
Thünen, Johann Heinrich von 138
tithes 42, 52, 91, 97
trade unions 203
tributary absolutism 83, 89, 90–1
tributary fertility 228–9
tributary metamorphosis 73, 221–4, 226–8, 222–3, 227
tributary proliferation 54–6
tributary rent relations 34–45, 73–9, 93–4, 107, 172–3, 177, 216–7
  federalised relations 37–8, 49, 74
  localised and centralised 34, 40, 74
  theological critique of 68–71
tributary social-property relations 14, 18, 26–7, 222
Tudor dynasty 80, 84, 136–7
Tyler, Wat 67

Uneven and Combined Development 4, 24, 26–7
unionism 123
urbanisation 48–9, 117
utopian socialism 145–6

Varoufakis, Yanis 3, 10, 230
villeins and villeinage 44–5
violence 200–4
voluntarism 29–31

Wakefield, Edward 137
Wallerstein, Immanuel 11
Walsingham, Thomas 69–70
Wars of the Roses 80

Watts, John 144, 167
Facts and Fictions of Political Economists 144
Wayland, T. 167, 202, 211–2
'National Advancement and Happiness Considered in Reference to the Equalisation of Property and the Formation of Communities' 145
William, Duke of Normandy, the Conqueror 38–40
see also Norman Conquest
William III, of Orange 110
Winch, Donald 127
Winstanley, Gerrard 97–106
Wolf, Eric 14, 34, 36, 47, 67
women and equality 198
Wood, Ellen Meiskins 13, 21, 23, 25, 34, 36, 82, 108, 220
Wood, Neal 7
Foundations of Political Economy 136
working class 114–5, 122–3, 134, 200–1
disciplining of 123
resistance by 125–7
submission of 179–81
Wrawe, John 67
Wrigley, E. Anthony 116, 117
Wycliffe, John 52–3

yeomanry 74–8

Žmolek, Michael 79–80, 95, 122